RAILROADS IN AMERICA

The American Heritage History of

RAILROADS IN AMERICA

by Oliver Jensen

Published by American Heritage Publishing Co., Inc., New York

Book Trade Distribution by McGraw-Hill Book Company

Author and Editor Oliver Jensen
Art Director Mervyn Edward Clay
Copy Editor Brenda Savard
Associate Editor Anne Longworth Garrels
Consultant Librarian Laura Lane Masters

Additional Text Richard Folger Snow

American Heritage Publishing Co., Inc.
President and Publisher Paul Gottlieb
General Manager, Book Division Kenneth W. Leish
Editorial Art Director Murray Belsky

Jacket/Slipcase Cover: "As The Centuries Pass In The Night," by William Harnden Foster, a famous New York Central poster; reproduced here from the original oil painting now owned and exhibited at the Edaville Railroad Museum at South Carver, Massachusetts. Permission to use it was kindly granted by the Penn Central Railroad. **Endpapers:** An extreme enlargement from a steel stock-certificate engraving, 2½ x 5½ inches in size, made by the American Bank Note Company, 1871, furnished by Culver Service. **Half-Title Page:** Group on the pilot of a Denver, Leadville & Gunnison locomotive, ca. 1890, by H. H. Buckwalter, courtesy Library of the State Historical Society of Colorado. **Title Page:** Handcar group by Charles R. Savage somewhere in the mountains of the West, nineteenth century, lent by Daniel W. Jones. **Below:** Constructing trestles for the Lane Cut-Off on the Union Pacific, just outside Omaha, sometime between 1905 and 1908, photographed by J. E. Stimson and provided by courtesy of the Union Pacific Railroad Museum, Omaha, Nebraska.

Library of Congress Cataloging in Publication Data: see page 320.

Contents

Foreword   7

1. *A New Breed of Horse*   10

2. *On to the Western Waters*   30

3. *The First Railroad War*   58

4. *The Race to Promontory*   82

5. *Building a New Nation*   102

6. *The Age of Bare Knuckles*   134

7. *The Romantic Image*   162

8. *Down Brakes!*   176

9. *Boomers, Hoggers, and Brass-Pounders*   190

10. *Turrets, Towers, and Rain Sheds*   204

11. *Great Days for the Passenger Element*   222

12. *They Went Everywhere*   242

13. *Days of the Dinosaur*   260

14. *The Long Haul*   270

15. *Days of Reckoning*   280

Epilogue: Two Railroads   304

Bibliography   314

Operating Railroad Museums   315

Permissions and Acknowledgments   315

Index   316

Foreword

The history of American railroads sometimes seems to the author of this book a paradigm of the history of the republic itself. Both were created through heroic struggles; both swelled to imperial influence and power; both, as is the way with empires, have fallen on difficult, uncertain times. Each, in a sense, created the other: free government and open country offered boundless opportunity to enterprising men, and they in turn made a nation. It is not too much to say that, in geographical and economic terms, railroads united the states, for they tied together the isolated cities of the East, opened the way to the straggling settlements of the Middle West, and created out of a wilderness that vast two-thirds of the republic which lies beyond the Mississippi. Behind the chuffing locomotives and little wooden cars followed the farmer, the miner, the merchant, the immigrant, and all that adventurous company who laid the rails, filled the empty lands, and made the desert, as the orator said, blossom like a garden.

The railroad was the biggest business of nineteenth-century America, and it made nearly all other businesses possible. Yet it is only in the United States, which had—indeed, still possesses in mere terms of length, with 206,000 route miles of line—the greatest system in the world, that the story ends in a decline and fall. In the countries of Western Europe, for example, the trains have never been abandoned; on the contrary they have been renewed and improved as parts of balanced systems of transportation. West Germany alone runs as many trains, twenty thousand a day, as did the United States in 1929 (only 247 are operated each weekday by Amtrak). And it has a great system of highways, as well, where driving is therefore what it ought to be, a pleasure. All over Western Europe today the trains are agreeable, infinitely faster, and reliable, and these countries are getting ready now for tomorrow by building a new express system of fast, straight, international lines, where speeds of 155 miles an hour will be possible, a project *The New York Times* compares, in scope and outlay, with America's costly system of interstates. Europe has, in a real sense, looked the energy crisis in the eye and made ready for it.

In the United States, on the other hand, the iron horse is a ragged, bony mendicant at the door. Taxed to death, overregulated by a bureaucracy which can and does take over ten years to make a ruling, the old thoroughbred is denied even a fair race. Although a few roads prosper, many must panhandle every few months merely to keep running rattletrap trains over weed-grown, broken rails, lest the business of America come to a halt. Most of the northeastern roads are in bankruptcy, thousands of miles of track are threatened with abandonment, the passenger service is a slow and plebeian shadow of its former self. Most empires and most republics suffer first from inner rot, or from forgetting their original high purposes; unconsciously they prepare the way for the enemy from without. In just such a way, the follies of the railroads themselves have only been compounded by heedless public policy. At the rails' expense we allowed the country to be laid waste by their competitors, especially the automobile and its mammoth mate, the truck, as though there would never be a day of reckoning or any danger to our land, our energy supplies, or the very air we breathe, let alone our ability to travel with any speed or comfort in the nightmare landscape of urban America.

Whether history and its sometimes seemingly inevitable processes can be altered by an act of will is an unanswered question, but if they can, if the giant highway and labor lobbies can be tamed, the time to save the railroads and achieve a really balanced system of transportation is now. This is the argument not only of environmentalists, but also of an increasing number of politicians and businessmen; it is the conclusion to which any writer on the subject is drawn. If we do not restore the railroads, as Lewis Mumford has said, they will have to be re-invented, and at infinite cost.

While this book often pauses to show in pictures various aspects of the great days of railroading, or to dip into romance and folklore, it is not intended as an exercise in nostalgia for its own sake. The purpose has been to bring back to life, as much as possible in a single volume, a century and a half of history. Consequently I have tried to concentrate on just enough men, events, achievements, and discoveries to give focus to a complex narrative, and to explore its meaning and consequences. A few feats of engineering, for example, must stand for many, a handful of notable manipulations for hundreds of others, the chronicles of a few railroads for thousands. Many topics, no doubt, have been slighted, especially the technical ones, and I urge the specialists whose enthusiasms are unsatisfied to turn to the bibliography, which, indeed, gives only a suggestion of the vast literature of railroading. I do include, however, a number of excerpts from the works or reminiscences of others, principally first-person experiences which recall, as nothing else can, what railroading was really like.

Since this is a rather personal and sometimes argumentative book, I should perhaps state my prejudices. I think our creative free enterprise system can

no more prosper in the face of a government-favored monopoly like the American automobile industry than it could under the equally dominating hand of socialism. Since few governmental organizations function very well, with such exceptions as the Park Service, the Library of Congress, the Smithsonian, and the United States Marines, I hope that any government take-over of railroad properties will stop with the tracks, and leave the operations to private companies, which is how the highways work. I tend to distrust monorails, "people movers," "hovercraft," and other space-age approaches to the already well-advanced technology of running trains on welded steel rail, and have to agree with Paul H. Reistrup, the able head of Amtrak, who has said that he is not interested in operating "airplanes with the wings sawed off."

I lost my heart to trains, I must add, at a very early age, thanks to my grandfather, Martin E. Jensen, who built me toy railroad cars big and sturdy enough for a boy to sit on and race down the garden walk into a pile of hay, and to my patient father, Gerard E. Jensen, who would take me on odd excursions just for the ride. They both shared with me and millions of others an affection for the great central display piece of railroading, the steam engine. It was a living thing, unlike any other piece of machinery, and it was a symbol that outlasted the device itself. It was the bride at the wedding.

I have had much generous help with this book, not only from our practiced staff at American Heritage but from many old friends, photographers, collectors of books and railroadiana, officers of museums and historical societies, and other authors and publishers who have permitted me to use quotations or illustrations. I am grateful to them all, as I am to my wife Alison, who has carefully read the manuscript. A full list of acknowledgments appears on page 315. Special mention should go here, however, to my friend Richard Folger Snow, an Associate Editor of AMERICAN HERITAGE magazine, who generously came to my aid during a battle with the deadline, writing additional text and captions in the latter part of the book, and to John H. White, Jr., Curator of Transportation at the Smithsonian Institution. He was kind enough to read the book in manuscript and rough layout form, and to offer useful comments and corrections in his fields of invaluable technical expertise, but he is not to be blamed for any errors into which I may have fallen in so broad a canvas.   — Oliver Jensen

Nos. 108, 990, *and* 152 *at the Pittsburgh Locomotive Works,* 1883

1. A New Breed of Horse

1. A New Breed of Horse

George Stephenson's birthplace stands at Wylam in the grimy collieries just west of Newcastle-upon-Tyne. His large family occupied just one room. In front is one of the old coal tramways.

PRECEDING PAGES: *"The Neigh of an Iron Horse," painted by A. Tapy, 1859, from the collection of Edgar William and Bernice Chrysler Garbisch.*

"Success has a thousand fathers," goes the old saw, "and failure is an orphan." And so, if we wish to find the birthplace of the railroad, we must look in a thousand places—to the anonymous Sumerian who invented the wheel some five thousand years ago, to the first maker of iron, to the first man to discover the irresistible power of steam. We can also fill an orphanage with inventors whose ideas failed to work, at least while important people were watching, or who were laughed at, or put away lest they harm honest folk, or who made the mistake of inventing something before the time was ripe.

In a practical sense, however, we can find the birthplace of the railway very easily. It stands in what was once the smoky colliery village of Wylam, on the north bank of the River Tyne, eight miles west of Newcastle in the north of England, a workman's house where, on June 9, 1781, George Stephenson was born. He was the second of six children in a family which inhabited one single room, with bare rafters and a clay floor. Since "Old Bob" Stephenson earned only twelve shillings a week, there was money for nothing but a hand-to-mouth existence, and not a penny for school, so that George, like almost all his fellows in the coal-workings, reached eighteen totally illiterate. But if it is easy to enumerate his disadvantages, it is more interesting to contemplate the other side of the ledger. The boy was courageous and strong, both in body and character. His father's job was as fireman of the old steam engine which the Wylam Colliery, like most others in the Newcastle area, used to pump out the water which gathers in coal mines. As a small boy he was soon sorting coal, then driving horses at the pithead. He early showed a native gift with machinery, becoming a fireman on another pumping engine, and then a "brakesman," or controller, on the engine that hauled men and coal up and down the shaft. It was a good place and time for a steady young man who relished mechanics: England at the onset of the Industrial Revolution.

The engines young George encountered were mostly based on the inventions of Thomas Newcomen and Thomas Savery: their power came from the atmosphere exerting its downward pressure on a piston beneath which a vacuum was created in a cylinder by condensing steam. On each laborious stroke, the piston was helped slowly up again by fresh steam. Curious by nature, Stephenson was forever taking the lumbering device apart, to clean it, indeed, but also to see how it worked. He was soon aware that there were other better machines, and newer ideas from such sources as James Watt, who improved on Newcomen by moving the steam-condensing process out of the piston cylinder into a separate chamber. Watt's low-pressure engines would pump better, and run machinery like looms. One could learn more about such matters from books, he realized, and so at eighteen, Stephenson hired a schoolmaster at threepence a week to introduce him to reading and writing, moving on as fast as he could into mathematics, working problems on a slate during spare moments and leaving off the slate for correction at night by his teacher. In his evenings he soled shoes and repaired clocks and watches to earn extra money.

As pits opened or closed, the Stephenson family moved about the Newcastle area, but George's direction was steadily upward. At the age of twenty-one he married a local girl; although she died very early, he was blessed with an only son, Robert, who would turn out to be even more inventive than he was. He acquired the reputation of an engine doctor, a man who could fix the unfixable, and throw in a few improvements. To avoid coal gas explosions in mines, he devised a primitive safety lamp popularly called the "Geordie" after his nickname; unfortunately for his fame, Sir Humphry Davy invented a very similar one at the same time, and described it to the Royal Society while miners were already using Stephenson's. At the Killingworth Colliery, just north of Newcastle, he built a gravity tramway on which loaded wagons descending to the dockside pulled up the empties by cable. Such a man was apt to attract the support and confidence of foremen and superintendents, not to mention the noblemen and other gentry who owned the mines. One of them, Sir Thomas Liddell, afterward Lord Ravensworth, principal partner at the Killingworth Colliery, was moved to appoint his shrewd and practical workman to the considerable post of enginewright in 1812. And thus Stephenson would enjoy loyal and enthusiastic backing in the project that by now consumed him, the creation of some better prime mover than a horse, or a lucky short run by gravity, for moving the Killingworth coal.

Neither the "locomotive engine," as it was called until the adjective took over alone for the noun, nor the railway itself was a new idea. Each had a long history, some of it known to Stephenson, some not, so that in the course of making his improvements he reinvented devices or processes that others had already toyed with. All the parts, one might say, were ready. That a wagon or cart will move with much less effort by man or beast if its wheels roll over a smooth surface, whether a hard Roman road or the wooden tramway at a mine, had been known in Europe for centuries; iron plates or rails, with flanges outside or inside to keep the wheels on the track, had become practical with the rise of iron foundries in England and America; the foundries could also make crude boilers and engine parts of cast iron or the more expensive wrought iron. The magic force generated by boiling water into steam in a confined space was discovered if not developed by the ancients; it was propelling steamboats like Fulton's in 1807, a year in which the young Stephenson, momentarily dejected by the bleakness of his life, contemplated emigration to America. But before Stephenson was born, a French engineer named Nicolas Cugnot had built in 1769 a self-propelled steam carriage which operated on the ordinary roads and streets. Its tiny boiler applied high-pressure steam to two small cylinders, whose pistons alternately pushed the single front wheel. It is said that he was trying to devise a better way of towing artillery than by horses, but Cugnot's car went no faster than two or three miles an hour and had to stop every ten or fifteen minutes to build a new fire under the boiler.

Even before the American Revolution, an eccentric genius from Delaware (they are all eccentric until they succeed, like Benjamin Franklin, and sometimes even after that, like Albert Einstein) named Oliver Evans had been reading Watt and experimenting with steam engines for gristmills, at which he was highly successful, and with steam carriages, at which everyone laughed. He redoubled the mirth by proposing a steam-powered railroad between Philadelphia and New York. It would have parallel rails of flat-topped logs with planks nailed to them, and the tongues of the carriages would be guided along a special rail in the center to keep the cars on the tracks. It would carry—fresh peals of laughter—both merchandise and passengers, who would eat and sleep

George Stephenson in his later years, from a formal engraving by T. L. Atkins; behind him is a train on the Liverpool & Manchester Railway.

Cugnot's road engine, 1769

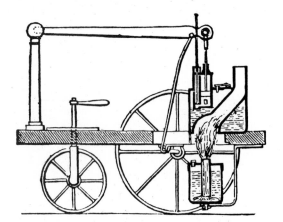

Section of Murdock's model engine, 1784

Evans' Oruktor Amphibolus, 1804

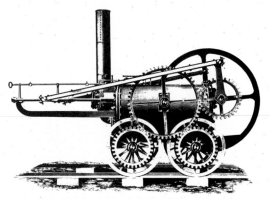

Trevithick: the first railway locomotive, 1804

aboard the cars. In 1801, for the Philadelphia Board of Health, he built a steam dredge which he named in classical fashion *Oruktor Amphibolus* because it would operate both on land and in water. The piston rod of this ponderous, twenty-one-ton affair was connected to the wheels and paddle by an arrangement of vertical and horizontal arms. It created a sensation on Market Street and worked well enough in the river, but nothing came of it. Evans died unhappily in 1819, but not before he had predicted that "I do verily believe that carriages propelled by steam will come into general use, and travel at the rate of 300 miles a day."

Back in England in 1784, an assistant of Watt, one William Murdock, built a successful model of a steam road carriage barely a foot high. It was three-wheeled like Cugnot's and carried its own fire in the form of a spirit lamp. No doubt to avoid possible failure and ridicule, Murdock ran his first experiment alone and at night on a straight walk leading to a church outside his home town of Redruth in Cornwall. The little engine took off smartly, flaming and hissing, with its inventor pursuing it on foot until the experiment was ended by a loud outcry of terror from the local minister who, according to Samuel Smiles, Stephenson's biographer, encountered what he thought was the Evil One himself, coming right at him. Murdock carried the idea no further, but he had made an impression on a fellow Cornishman, Richard Trevithick, a moody inventor who built several steam road carriages that worked and then adapted his ideas into what must be ranked as the very first true railway locomotive. This last ran successfully in 1804, pulling a ten-ton load in five wagons, plus some seventy passengers, making about five miles an hour over the cast-iron tramway of an ironworks at Pen-y-darran in South Wales. There was but one trip, since the hard-breathing and heavy dragon destroyed the fragile track, and the engine was set to work as a source of stationary power. Trevithick put people off and died so poor that friends had to buy his coffin, but he had contributed some important developments. He used his heat better by setting the furnace inside the boiler, and his single piston was pushed first forward and then back by applying steam alternately to each side. Its force was applied in a most indirect manner, however, with an elaboration of gears, and a huge flywheel was attached to the crankshaft to balance the action of the piston.

"There can be no doubt at all that if any one man is entitled to be called the inventor of the steam locomotive it is that great Cornishman Richard Trevithick." So says the careful modern biographer of the Stephensons, the late L.T.C. Rolt. Perhaps unconsciously denigrating all previous inventors in the process of building up his hero, George Stephenson, old Samuel Smiles, writing a century ago, sought to give him credit for the developments of others. While there is a tangle of claims, it seems clear that Trevithick, for example, had discovered the idea of a steam blast up the smoke stack. That is, by discharging his used steam into the stack, he improved the draft and made possible a hotter fire. Another battle was waged over the delusion that smooth locomotive wheels would spin on a smooth surface, and that it would be necessary therefore to rough them up, or else pull the engine along on cog rails of one sort or another. Despite Smiles' assertions, it seems clear that Trevithick's railway engines were smooth-wheeled, and that he realized that the weight of the engine was sufficient to maintain traction—provided that the track could support it.

Then in 1811, several years before Stephenson built his first locomotive, John Blenkinsop and Matthew Murray of Leeds began work on the first railway engine that would work regularly. Murray was a partner in an iron foundry who had invented a kind of slide-valve, and Blenkinsop was the agent, or manager, of the Middleton Colliery, which backed the new method of hauling coal, not from a desire to push technology forward but because the endless Napoleonic wars had driven the price of fodder for horses out of sight. The

Blenkinsop/Murray locomotive, first operated in June, 1812, rested its weight on four nondriving wheels while a cogged wheel on the left side (see picture at right) pulled it along a cogged track. It had two cylinders to Trevithick's one, although the latter had patented the idea of two and was paid £30 for the rights. Long connecting rods and spur gears linked the action of the vertical cylinders to the crankshaft. Eventually four Blenkinsop engines were at work at the colliery, and several were still in use into the 1830's. Stephenson is known to have seen Blenkinsop's and Murray's engines, and to have heard of or seen other early experiments. For example, at Wylam Colliery, William Hedley, the "viewer" of the colliery, conducted an experiment which proved that the weight of the locomotive was sufficient, without cogs or other devices, to pull a load. His 1813 engine, the famous *Puffing Billy*, made use of the principle.

Blenkinsop's locomotive, 1812

With this experience to profit from, George Stephenson set about designing his own first "travelling engine," patriotically named the *Blucher*, after the Duke of Wellington's then very popular Prussian comrade-in-arms. Though some called him a fool, Lord Ravensworth knew his man, and put up the money to build it. There were many obstacles, for neither the tools nor the facilities for constructing a locomotive had advanced beyond the most primitive state, and the workmen were inexperienced. The head mechanic was the colliery's blacksmith. In this first locomotive, Stephenson to some extent followed Blenkinsop's model, with a horizontal, cylindrical boiler some eight feet long and nearly a yard in diameter; a flue tube carried the hot gases from the fire through it. The two vertical pistons worked via an elaborate system of overhead rods and drove the wheels with gears. After a little experimenting on his own, and observing Hedley's engine, Stephenson cast away all ideas of cogs and rack rails and relied on simple adhesion. On July 25, 1814, the five-ton affair began operation, pulling eight wagons weighing thirty tons up a slight grade at about four miles per hour; thereafter it worked regularly.

Stephenson's Killingworth locomotive, 1815

The *Blucher* was nevertheless a clumsy affair, devoid of springs or grace. The gears rattled and jerked as the engine force was transmitted, unevenly, to the wheels. Stephenson experimented with piping his exhaust steam into the stack, but despite Smiles' claims, he found it made the fire burn far too hot, and abandoned it. In the next few years he constructed perhaps a dozen more little coal-hauling engines. Some of them had improvements, like a simple and direct communication between the pistons and the driving wheels, and the use of horizontal connecting rods—still visible on modern steam engines —which link front and rear wheels into a unit revolving at the same speed. Since ordinary leaf springs could not then be provided strong enough to support a locomotive, he devised a kind of steam spring to save the track from punishment. Nevertheless, the railway, and with it so much of the world's future, remained a curiosity of the coalyards. Man still travelled overland at the pace of his feet, or at best that of a horse or stagecoach, over the miserable roads of the time. From London to Liverpool by coach required thirty-seven jolting hours. In America in 1817, freight took fifty days to move from the new city of Cincinnati to New York, and thirty-nine hours (advertised if not met) was the travelling time by a special fast stage, for six persons only, between New York and Boston. Sea, rivers, and canals were, men thought, the answer.

Locomotion No. 1, *Stockton & Darlington, 1825*

By about 1820, George Stephenson had pushed his inventive powers, as far as the locomotive went, about as far as they would go, or as far as his very limited education would carry him. He still read with difficulty; nearly all his written words were dictated. He was brooding again over emigrating to the New World, where he thought of going into the steamboat business on the Great Lakes. It is interesting to speculate what might have happened to the history of railroads if he had gone.

The Stephensons' Rocket, 1829

The famous Rainhill Trials of steam locomotives were held in October, 1829, on part of the still-unfinished Liverpool & Manchester Railway, for a prize of £500. Many engineers and mechanics, including some from the United States, were in the crowd to see the Stephenson *Rocket* (at right in the drawing above) triumph again over the *Sans Pareil* of Timothy Hackworth (center) and the *Novelty* of Messrs. Braithwaite and Ericsson, the same John Ericsson who later developed the famous ironclad *Monitor.* On the final run of the trials, old George and young Robert opened up the throttle of the *Rocket* all the way and crossed the finish line at twenty-nine miles an hour, to the cheers of the crowd. Some months after the trials, George gave a ride on Robert's new locomotive *Northumbrian* to the beautiful young actress Fanny Kemble, shown in the likeness by Sir Thomas Lawrence above. Afterward she wrote that "The engine was set off at its utmost speed, thirty-five miles an hour, swifter than a bird flies. You cannot conceive what that sensation of cutting the air was; the motion as smooth as possible too. I stood up, and with my bonnet off drank the air before me." On she went, feeling no fear at all, this early rail enthusiast stated, adding that she had fallen "horribly in love" with both Mr. Stephenson and his locomotive.

Meanwhile, however, Stephenson was engaged in giving his son Robert all the advantages his rising fortunes could provide, the education he did not receive. Young Robert was sent to school at Newcastle, each night sharing the experience with his ever-curious father. At one point in studying mathematics together they were along far enough to build an accurate sundial at the door of their cottage. Then the father dug into his savings to send Robert to the University of Edinburgh, the only good one then in the reach of his modest means. Robert won a prize in mathematics, learned shorthand, took down all the scientific lectures, and came home to read them to his father. It was clearly one of the most rewarding father-and-son relationships in history, one that would last throughout their lives—the educated son who eventually built many great railways, the ruddy handsome old father who never lost his simplicity or his plain Northumbrian accent.

The first true railroad in the world was projected in 1821, when in the county of Durham a group of promoters headed by Edward Pease won a charter from Parliament to build a kind of public tramroad, open to anyone with cattle, horses, or carriages, between the port of Stockton, a short distance from the North Sea on the River Tees, and the coal areas inland at Darlington. Mr. Pease had no thought of locomotives until he received a memorable visit from a man who described himself simply as "only the enginewright at Killingworth," and said he wished to suggest that the new road use his steam locomotives. Pease remarked that he and his partners were looking to horse power, being satisfied that, as he put it, "a horse upon an iron road would draw ten tons for one ton on a common road." Stephenson, who had brought along a more polished friend to vouch for him and help with the talking, found himself instead eagerly stating that one of his locomotives would do the work of fifty horses.

"There was such an honest, sensible look about him, and he seemed so modest and unpretending," Pease recalled long afterward, that in very little time Stephenson was appointed engineer of the railway. The official letter to that effect nearly went astray, since it was addressed to "George Stephenson, Esquire, Engineer." The messenger could find no one of that description at Killingworth and was about to depart when one of the miners' wives wondered if, perhaps, he was looking for "Geordie the enginewright." Soon he was out in a dignified swallow-tailed coat and high boots resurveying the Stockton line for better grades, and incidentally saving three miles, while his son copied down the figures he read from the sights in a spirit level. Like an army, the crew lived off the country, dropping in on farms and cottagers, diverting the children and taking supper, or sometimes they would call at the house of Mr. Pease. There old George one day found the daughters struggling to do embroidery and volunteered to teach them.

"You will wonder how I learnt it," he said. "I will tell you. When I was a brakesman at Killingworth, I learnt the art of embroidery while working the pitmen's buttonholes by the engine fire at nights."

Wherever he went, the apostle of the railway instructed, entertained, and convinced all classes of society. In view of the poor state of the art, he told Mr. Pease, he proposed to build a little factory of his own in Newcastle. Here he and his son would employ their own skilled mechanics in erecting engines for the Stockton & Darlington. He would risk his own £1,000, the purse the coal operators had given him in gratitude for his safety lamp, but it would take another £1,000. Mr. Pease and a friend put it up, and a building, the beginning of a great industry in later years, went up late in 1823. There work was begun on the first engine, called the *Locomotion,* a lumbering, eight-ton affair intended to haul coal, for passengers were not dreamed of. Then there was the matter of the rails, once Stephenson had talked the directors out of wood. Iron it would be, but even though he had a small interest in a cast-iron rail factory, dating back to 1816, he urged them to use the much more expensive malleable rails. It would be £500 out of his pocket, Stephenson observed, but he told them that he had been able to compare durable Swedish malleable iron with the cast-iron variety at Killingworth. The former never gave way while the latter broke constantly. As to the matter of the gauge of the track, the distance between the inner edges of the two rails, it would be the same that Stephenson was used to, the same as the wagonways at Wylam and Killingworth, four feet, eight inches, with an extra half inch which Stephenson added to ease the clearances a little. Besides, the proprietors were buying some used coal cars in that gauge. As to how Wylam and other collieries had fallen into that width and whether it was indeed the gauge of Roman chariots and the ruts they left behind on their famous roads, there is much argument. But on the Stockton & Darlington Railway, George Stephenson began the process that eventually made four feet, eight and one-half inches, odd as it seems, the standard of most of the world's railroads, albeit not without many struggles in the years to come.

On September 27, 1825, the Stockton & Darlington opened. Following a horseman, whose task was to warn off the vast crowds that had assembled, including not a few canal and turnpike people who hoped to witness a failure, came the sturdy *Locomotion,* her tender, six cars laden with coal and flour bags, a box-like passenger coach for the directors (the first passenger car in history), twenty-one open freight wagons fitted with temporary seats, and six more coal cars. There were six hundred passengers when the world's first public railroad train reached Stockton, greeted by church bells, the thunder of cannon, and the crash of band music. And there was a grand banquet for George Stephenson.

For all its local success, however, the little twelve-mile line from Darlington to the sea still used horses a great deal of the time and did not convince very many people that railroads would rule the future. But that fact would be amply demonstrated five years later in the Stephensons' greatest triumph, the Liverpool & Manchester Railway, a much bigger and more ambitious project for which George built a line in the face of enormous manmade and natural difficulties. There was the bitter opposition of the turnpike companies, the horse-loving country gentry, and the powerful Duke of Bridgewater's canal, with its monopoly of freight haulage. At hearings before a committee of Parliament, the barristers for the opposition made great sport of Stephenson, with his country ways and speech and his absurd claims for steam locomotives. The main function of government sometimes seems to be the frustration of able men and new ideas, but a charter was eventually obtained, and George drove his majestic right-of-way across bridges, through deep cuts (English railways from the first were built for the ages), and across a dreaded and supposedly bottomless bog called Chat Moss.

The astonishing fact about the Stephensons is that the son, a kind of child prodigy, was an even greater inventor than his father. It was he, in his twenties, who ran the locomotive works and built the famous *Rocket* which won the great trials at Rainhill (see pages 16–17). The *Rocket,* with its simple, sensible design, its skillful use of the steam blast, its fine multi-tubular boiler, embodied the future, and helped spread railroads over the world. The prime minister himself, the Duke of Wellington, came to the grand opening. In the crush of the crowd and a moment of confusion William Huskisson, M.P. for Liverpool and a strong backer of the railway, fell in front of the *Rocket* and was rushed to medical help by George Stephenson himself in another locomotive making thirty-six miles an hour. That Mr. Huskisson died and became the first train casualty cast a pall over the proceedings, but nothing thereafter could dim the luster or impede the progress of railroads or of the remarkable father and son who had made it all succeed.

Robert Stephenson, born in 1803, the only son of George, was by far the greater engineer. At twenty he headed the locomotive works whence designs poured out in profusion beginning with the Rocket, *the* Northumbrian, *the* Planet, *and other types in which the early steam engine assumed modern shape. At thirty he became chief engineer in charge of building the 112-mile-long London & Birmingham Railway; he was one of the greatest railway builders of his age. His father had given railways and the Industrial Revolution a starting push and now Robert rode the whirlwind. His work took him all over the world; once he found and brought home the penniless, stranded Richard Trevithick. Robert built many notable bridges, was elected to Parliament, and was buried in Westminster Abbey in 1859. His able cousin, George Robert Stephenson, carried on as head of the great Stephenson Locomotive Works, which in 1955 was absorbed into English Electric.*

The grand opening of the Stockton & Darlington Railway in 1825, described in our preceding text, was precisely sketched at the time by John Dobbin.

showing the horseman ahead, Locomotion No. 1, *the single passenger car, the many goods wagons, and a fine Stephenson bridge across the River Tees.*

America Keeps Pace

The exciting events in England had not gone unnoticed in the United States. Curious American engineers had visited the Liverpool & Manchester and seen the Rainhill Trials. They had observed the methods, and overheard with awe how much the cost of shipping dropped when road haulage gave way to railways. The New World had its early gravity or horse-drawn tramways—among them one at Mauch Chunk, Pennsylvania, one at Quincy, Massachusetts, to carry granite to the waterside for the monument being built at Bunker Hill, and another which carried coal for the Delaware & Hudson Canal Company. For this last company its young engineer Horatio Allen had gone to England and ordered four locomotives. The Pennsylvania Society for Internal Improvements sent a young architect and engineer, William Strickland, abroad to see what he could learn about English railways, and for the first American common-carrier railroad, the ambitiously named Baltimore & Ohio Railroad, three young engineers had gone to look around.

These travellers came back fired up over steam locomotives, and Strickland reported to his employers that it "greatly changed the relative value of railways and canals." None of this, however, was news to America's least celebrated but perhaps most canny prophet of steam, a veteran of the Revolution named Colonel John Stevens, who had built a screw-propelled ferryboat for the Hudson and lived at a fine waterfront place—now the Stevens Institute—in Hoboken, New Jersey. When he was sixty years old, in 1812, he began to preach the superior advantages of steam railways. He spoke of "suits of carriages" weighing up to one hundred tons, carrying people and goods long distances. When in 1815 he applied to the legislature for a charter to build a railroad across New Jersey, it was granted, perhaps to humor a veteran; Pennsylvania did the same for him in 1823, for a line from Philadelphia to the Susquehanna. Charters are easy, but money, of course, could not be found. It was going into canals, like the Erie, finished with great éclat in 1825, but smarter money would have backed the Colonel. That very year, the year of the Stockton & Darlington, the doughty old gentleman, then seventy-six, built a small locomotive, operated by a cog-wheel and rack rail on a circular track in his yard, to prove the idea would work. It appears above on the opposite page, and beneath it the very sub-

stantial achievement of his sons (Stevens, like old George Stephenson, was also blessed in this department), Robert Livingston Stevens and Edwin A. Stevens.

In 1830 the two sons obtained another charter from New Jersey under which they built the famous Camden & Amboy Railroad, which was given a practical monopoly between New York and Philadelphia (with a water link at each end). Young Robert visited England and ordered a Stephenson-style locomotive, the *John Bull,* and devised the strong but economical T-shaped rail which is used to this day. At first it was mounted on stone sleepers, until it was discovered that spiking it to wooden crossties was easier and made a smoother ride. When the engine arrived in pieces, without much of a plan for assembling it, the puzzle was handed over to the line's master mechanic, Isaac Dripps, who had never seen a locomotive before. He was twenty-one, for early railroading was a

young man's world, and he put it together. Because English railroads were straight and sturdy, and American ones quite the opposite, the *John Bull* kept running off the track until Dripps loosened the front wheels and added a combined pilot and cowcatcher of either his own or of Robert Stevens' devising. It had sharp prongs and, the tale goes, a large bull was soon so firmly impaled that it took a block and tackle to separate engine and victim, whereupon the cowcatcher was depronged and gentled into the version now seen on every toy engine. Meanwhile the Camden & Amboy prospered, furnishing intercity service in seven hours for three dollars. For all the opposition from stagecoach lines and other vested interests, not to mention the timid (to whom the poster at right was intended to appeal), it soon made connections via other lines to Baltimore, Washington, and Pittsburgh. Eventually it was swallowed up in the Pennsylvania Railroad.

MOTHERS LOOK OUT FOR YOUR CHILDREN!

ARTISANS, MECHANICS, CITIZENS!

When you leave your family in health, must you be hurried home to mourn a

DREADFUL CASUALITY!

PHILADELPHIANS, your RIGHTS are being invaded! regardless of your interests, or the LIVES OF YOUR LITTLE ONES. THE CAMDEN AND AMBOY, with the assistance of other companies, without a Charter, and in VIOLATION OF LAW, as decreed by your Courts, are laying a

LOCOMOTIVE RAIL ROAD!

Through your most Beautiful Streets, to the RUIN of your TRADE, annihilation of your RIGHTS, and regardless of your PROSPERITY and COMFORT. Will you permit this? or do you consent to be a

SUBURB OF NEW YORK !!

Rails are now being laid on BROAD STREET to CONNECT the TRENTON RAIL ROAD with the WILMINGTON and BALTIMORE ROAD, under the pretence of constructing a City Passenger Railway from the Navy Yard to Fairmount !!! This is done under the auspices of the CAMDEN AND AMBOY MONOPOLY!

RALLY PEOPLE in the Majesty of your Strength and forbid THIS

OUTRAGE!

Colonel John Stevens built a kind of toy steam wagon (above) as a demonstration on his lawn at Hoboken, New Jersey, in 1825, when he was seventy-six. He had already run a successful screw-propelled steamboat in 1802; with his sons, especially Robert, he created the Camden & Amboy Railroad, shown below at the Camden ferry in E. L. Henry's painting (done long afterward and including a style of locomotive which was never used on that line). Some interests were extravagantly opposed to the new means of travel, as expressed by the poster shown to the right.

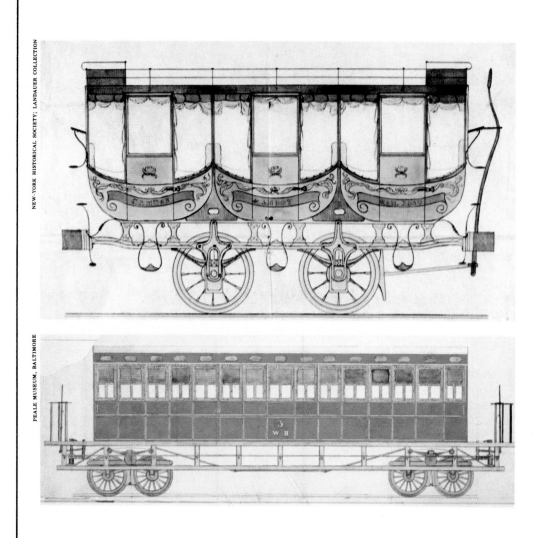

The swift evolution of the American railroad passenger car is evident from these two examples. The old one shown at left, really little more than a stagecoach with inside and outside seats, gave way in the 1830's to the center-aisle, all-inside plan employed in the car below, built in 1832 for the Washington branch of the B & O and ascribed to Ross Winans. The English lingered with many aspects of the old design, as shown at right by an American interior of 1852 and an English one below, from a genre engraving of 1857 by W. H. Simmons called "The Return." The young officer, the squire, and the shy, admiring daughter are travelling first class, where each compartment in the comfortable coach style has its own door.

Farewell to the Stagecoach

Since the business of carrying passengers was almost an afterthought in the invention of railroads (as it often seems, indeed, in America of the 1970's), the first cars were little more than adaptations of stagecoaches on different wheels. One paid a little more to sit inside, away from the hotter sparks and bigger cinders. The carriage design lingered longer abroad, with cars divided into compartments, of which an elegant example appears at the bottom of the opposite page. Democratic America, less concerned with privacy, soon created the much longer single-compartment car, an aisle down the middle, and set on swivelling four-wheel "bogie trucks" employed by the former horse dealer Ross Winans, who came to the Baltimore & Ohio to sell horse-flesh but remained to design cars and engines.

The amenities were few—stiff-backed seats and a stove at each end, so that in winter those near the stoves roasted and those in the middle of the car froze. Since modern couplings were unknown, the train started and stopped with a series of jerks. From time to time urchins passed through the cars peddling hot bricks for one's feet, water from a tin cup, and occasionally something to eat. Here and there railroads provided cars with shelves for beds, and as early as 1840 the Norwich & Worcester had parlor cars of a sort, with "apartments" for ladies, plus sofas, dressing table, and even a washstand.

Perhaps some of the flavor of it will come through from the travel journal of young Samuel J. Parker, riding by stage, railroad, and steamer from Ithaca, New York, to New York City in 1837. He got on the cars at Utica, only to be stalled at the first curve and ordered out with all the other male passengers to give things a push. Jumping back on as the train started, Parker made Herkimer and Little Falls without incident. But then:

"At Little Falls, while before the depot eating house, we were told that the bridge a little way off had been bored and plugged with powder to blow the bridge and cars up, by . . .

the Erie Canal men, who fought the cars because they damaged the canal interests. . . . So the locomotive was detached, and the bridge, a small one just beyond the depot, inspected, and the engine run over it; and backed up and we taken over it, without an accident. . . .

"Having been nearly without sleep the night before and wearied by the stagecoach ride to Utica, the time after midnight was excessively wearisome, as we 'enjoyed' the English style of cars, with eight on a seat riding backward and eight more facing these backward riders, with feet interlocked and one lantern as a lamp to two such satanic English style compartments, and the glass sliding rack, rattling as the springless cars rattled and thumped over the strap-iron rails spiked to the long sleeper logs that made the track. Yet to me and to most of us this first night and ride in the cars was sublime, as an excitement and a novelty, even if . . . the sparks of the locomotive flew over us in a perpetual shower, often burning holes in exposed clothes. . . ."

Illustrated London News, APRIL 10, 1852

The First Trip, Mohawk & Hudson

Two versions of the first train on the Mohawk & Hudson Railroad, on August 9, 1831, appear on this page. At top is a silhouette, its original six feet long, cut out from a sketch on the spot by William H. Brown, part of whose story is told in the adjoining text. The likenesses, he said, are of real people. In the engine, David Matthew; in the first car, Erastus Corning, a Mr. Lansing, ex-Governor Yates, J. J. Boyd, Thurlow Weed, John Miller, a Mr. Van Zant, and the penny-post carrier. Let the rest go and look to the painting below by Edward Lamson

Henry, done in 1892 but based, said that noted genre painter, on painstaking research. Henry's work appears at several other points in this book. We show only a detail of a canvas 110 inches long. It is the time of departure as the conductor runs up and down, trumpet in hand, making final arrangements, while the engineer stokes his fire. The usual detritus of railroading—stone ties, strap iron—lies about in the foreground. The train made the trip out, seventeen miles, in 105 minutes, but raced back in thirty-eight, to the delight of the promoters.

The railroad on which young Samuel Parker finished his trip to Albany was the Mohawk & Hudson, the third public carrier to operate under steam in America. We tell its story a little out of historical order to show the real difficulties, physical and political, faced by the little band of early railroad builders. The line was constructed in 1830 and 1831 by the celebrated engineer John B. Jervis, who was also the inventor of the swivelling truck which, placed at the front of nearly all American road locomotives as time went on, helped keep them on the often winding, weaving, and sharply curved tracks. Running directly over the high land between Albany and Schenectady, with an inclined plane handled by a stationary engine at each end, the Mohawk & Hudson reduced an all-day, forty-mile trip through many locks of the Erie Canal to a fast seventeen miles. Why was its first engine, shown at left below poised for the opening steam trip on August 9, 1831, named for the father of the Canal, DeWitt Clinton? One assumes the Mohawk & Hudson was thumbing its nose at a rival.

It had good reason. When the Erie Canal was projected years before, farseeing old Colonel John Stevens, he of the circular railroad mentioned earlier, had suggested to the powers in Albany that they would do better with a steam railroad. He was ignored by all except the noted Chancellor Livingston, who patiently wrote him about the dangers and difficulties of this new mode of haulage. But it was less lofty reasons that brought New York late into railroading. The Canal was a vested interest and so, especially when the Hudson and the Canal were frozen over, were the stages and wagoners. Their allies were the taverns, innkeepers, and businessmen of all the towns where stage and canal travellers had to make their involuntary stops. These interests wanted matters left as they were, which some modern chambers of commerce may understand. Attempt after attempt to finance a railroad failed; laws or local ordinances ensured stopovers profitable to various towns by forbidding steam-driven vehicles to enter them. There would have to be a string (as eventually there was) of short, disconnected lines. Freight could be carried only when the Canal was frozen closed. Passengers had to pay the same fare as the high one charged by the stages, and other railroad charters stipulated that any profit over 10 percent must be rebated to the Canal Company. The canny Dutchmen of Albany rubbed their hands; they had corked the bottle, and as many as one hundred charters were granted but failed of financing.

It was the capitalists of New York and the towns to the west, fearing the loss of trade, who finally pulled the cork. And so in time there was a Utica & Schenectady, a Rochester & Utica, and so on, but their financial condition remained perilous until about 1850, when it became evident that both New York and the upstate cities might lose out to other areas in trade, and the restrictive laws disappeared. Eventually, Erastus Corning, the mayor of Albany, and, much later, an old man named Cornelius Vanderbilt would emerge on the scene and put New York's railroads together. Vanderbilt had, by odd coincidence, been hurt in an early wreck on the Camden & Amboy, and for years avoided railroads.

All was joy and excitement, however, that August day in 1831 when the *DeWitt Clinton* prepared to set out on her maiden trip. Built at the West Point Foundry in New York City, she was a tiny affair of three and one-half tons (without water in her boiler). She had boiler fire tubes and two inclined cylinders to drive the four iron driving wheels, the latter linked together by outside connecting rods. (A working replica of the engine and her little stagecoach cars stood for years in Grand Central Station; the replica is housed now at the Henry Ford Museum at Dearborn, Michigan.) What the *DeWitt Clinton* did not have was bell or whistle, or pilot wheels, or headlight, or brakes, or even a cab, which left her engineer of the day, David Matthew, out in the weather. He may be seen in E.L. Henry's scene, opposite below, stoking the fire between the locomotive and the tender full of wood. Henry, of course, painted his scene, however painstakingly, years after the event, but there was an artist on hand, William H. Brown, author forty years later of "The First Locomotives in America," who made a sketch on the spot, and later turned it into the silhouette at left above. But let him tell it in his orotund way:

"This locomotive, the *DeWitt Clinton*, stood upon a track already fired up, and with a train of some five or six passenger-coaches attached to it (two only were represented in our sketch, for want of room). . . . On arriving at the top of the [inclined] plane at Albany on this memorable occasion . . . the peculiar appearance of the machine and train (the first ever seen by the author) arrested his attention, and he at once resolved to make a sketch. Drawing from his pocket a letter just received . . . and substituting his hat for a desk, he commenced. . . . The author had taken a hasty, rough drawing of the machine, the tender, the individual standing on the platform of the machine as its engineer, and the shape of the first passenger-coach, when a tin horn was sounded and the word was given, 'All aboard,' by Mr. John T. Clark, the master of transportation, who acted as conductor on that memorable occasion. . . .

"As there were no coverings or awnings to protect the deck-passengers upon the tops of the cars from the sun, the smoke, and the sparks, and as it was the hot season of the year, the combustible nature of their garments, summer coats, straw hats, and umbrellas, soon became apparent, and a ludicrous scene was enacted. . . .

"How shall we describe that start, my readers? It was not that quiet, imperceptible motion . . . of the present day. Not so. There came a sudden jerk, that bounded the sitters from their places, to the great detriment of their high-top fashionable beavers, from the close proximity to the roofs of the cars. This first jerk being over, the engine proceeded with considerable velocity for those times, when compared with stage coaches, until it arrived at a water-station, when it suddenly brought up with jerk No. 2, to the further amusement of some of the excursionists. [The jerking was lessened by wedging fence-posts between the cars, otherwise only loosely chained together]. . . .

"In a short time the engine (after frightening the horses attached to all sorts of vehicles filled with the people from the surrounding country, congregated all along at every available position near the road . . . [and] after causing thus innumerable capsizes and smash-ups of the vehicles and the tumbling of the spectators in every direction) arrived at the head of the inclined plane at Schenectady, amid the cheers and welcomes of thousands."

It was an earnest age, full of flowery sentiment, and the steam cars received a pious welcome. "We must not forget," wrote the *New Englander* magazine, "that the railroad is but one step in the ascending staircase on which the races are mounting, guided and cheered by heavenly voices. . . . We only mark the beginning."

Friends of the *Best Friend*

While northern cities boomed and tinkered with canals and railroads, the merchants of Charleston, South Carolina, sensed themselves in a decline, and resolved to build a railroad, from Charleston to Hamburg, to draw trade from the interior. Hamburg stood across the Savannah River from Augusta, Georgia. The new company's directors needed a chief engineer to lay out and build their line, and could have made no better choice than young Horatio Allen, six years out of Columbia College, where he had graduated with honors in 1823. He came highly recommended by his last employer, John B. Jervis, who was then chief engineer for the Delaware & Hudson Canal Company. Young Allen had several years of canal engineering behind him when Jervis sent him in 1828 to learn about railroads and buy some engines in England for the Canal Company, which was building a short rail line to link certain coal mines to its western terminus at Honesdale, Pennsylvania.

In England, Allen visited nearly everything, including George Stephenson's workings, and was received and instructed in that gentleman's characteristically hospitable way. Allen bought several locomotives in England, most notably the *Stourbridge Lion*, which turned out on its arrival to be much heavier than anticipated, especially for the rickety bridges. Nevertheless, quite alone, he mounted the monster on August 8, 1829, and took it up the new canal railroad. "Thus," as he wrote later, "on this first movement by steam on railroad in this continent, I was engineer, fireman, brakeman, conductor, and passenger."

As he recalled on other occasions, "I had never run a locomotive nor any other engine before. I have never run one since, but on August 8, 1829, I ran that locomotive three miles and back. . . . When the cheers of the onlookers died out as I left them on the memorable trip, the only sound to greet my ears until my safe return, in addition to that of the exhaust steam, was that of the creaking of the timber structure." The *Lion* was laid aside, as impractical, but Allen's next experience was all practicality.

His new employers, Allen discovered in South Carolina, were thinking of using horsepower. Allen went to work on them and made a ringing statement which is still remembered. "There is no reason to expect any material improvement in the breed of horses

Horatio Allen

in the future," he argued, "while, in my judgement, the man is not living who knows what the breed of locomotives is to place at command." Persuaded, although they did try horses for a time, and even sails, the directors commissioned Allen to order a steam locomotive, its first, from the West Point Foundry in New York City, which he called the *Best Friend of Charleston*. With a cannon firing salutes on the first car, and local dignitaries among the 141 passengers, Allen's little train set out on the short completed section of the new railroad line to score two firsts on Christmas Day, 1830: Here was the first locomotive ever built for sale in this country (that is, excluding the experiments of Evans, Stevens, and Peter Cooper), and also

the first scheduled steam railroad train to be operated in America. When the line was completed to Hamburg in 1833, it was, briefly, the longest single railway in the world, stretching 136 miles. Although Allen did many other notable things in a long life (1802–90), including serving as president of the Erie Railroad in 1843 and helping to build the great Brooklyn Bridge, not his least achievement was keeping the costs of construction within his estimates.

Preposterous as it may look, its vertical boiler standing up like a beer bottle on a platform, two cylinders busily turning the four driving wheels by means of cranks on the axles inside the frame, the *Best Friend* made a hit with Charleston, especially the sporting element which was astounded with her speed —alone, with no cars—of as much as thirty-six miles per hour. She appears immediately below, with accompanying artillery, on her first formal trip. The *Flying Dutchman* horse locomotive, which could do a smart twelve miles per hour while its four-footed prime mover agitated an endless chain, was retired. So was the sail car shown here; it was never thought more than an experiment, but the *Charleston Courier*'s jocular sports writer described the new locomotive as "out of a horse bred by Messrs. Watt and Boulton, and of the same breed as the *Novelty* and *Rocket*,

which contended for the purse of £500, at the late Liverpool and Manchester races. By crossing the breed with a Columbian sire, he has 'eclipsed' his progenitors upon the European, and stands unrivalled upon the American turf.''

Almost immediately, Allen ordered a second locomotive from the same foundry, a similar affair except that its boiler was horizontal, in the modern fashion, which made it much easier to communicate the power of the pistons to the wheels. It was called simply the *West Point,* after the foundry, not the celebrated military school, and Allen was fortunate in having it at hand because on June 17, 1831, disaster smote the *Best Friend* while her engineer had dismounted to attend to hitching up some cars. The fireman, annoyed by the steady hissing of steam from the safety valve, and apparently ignorant of its purpose, fastened it down while he waited. With a roar the boiler burst and was thrown twenty-five feet. The fireman later died of his injuries, and the engineer and another man were scalded badly, while the travelling public, such as it was, grew fearful.

Rising to the occasion, Allen reopened service with the *West Point* and certain well-publicized improvements. The safety valve was placed where only the engineer could reach it, and a special "barrier car," laden

AUTHOR'S COLLECTION; BROWN

with great bales of cotton to absorb any flying objects, was placed right behind the engine. This new arrangement, with a band merrily playing away behind the safety barrier, appears in the illustration at the bottom of the page. Nothing was done for the engineer and fireman.

Allen and his staff kept on inventing. When night operation was desired, they rigged up a small flatcar with a bed of sand in which they built a bright fire of pine logs, to be pushed in front of the engine. The *Best Friend* was re-

built as the *Phoenix,* with straight axles and outside connecting rods like a modern locomotive, and new and better engines added. On the South Carolina Canal and Rail-Road Company, as the line was called, one presently could go from Augusta to Atlanta, whence the Western & Atlantic crept north to Chattanooga. Thence railroads were built west (the Memphis & Charleston) and north (the Louisville & Nashville). Eventually, long after the Civil War, Allen's line became part of the huge Southern Railway, which from time to time still operates a replica of the original *Best Friend.*

Above: The Best Friend of Charleston, *1830. Below: The* West Point *and barrier car, 1831.*

AUTHOR'S COLLECTION; BROWN

AUTHOR'S COLLECTION; BROWN

27

"From Baltimore, bound to the Ohio"

The Carrollton Viaduct at Relay, Maryland, shown here in 1838, is still in use.

Of all the pioneer railroads built in the excitement of the late 1820's and early 1830's, by far the most significant was the Baltimore & Ohio, whose very name proclaimed its vast ambitions. America's third largest city at the time, yet two hundred miles nearer to the western waters than New York and one hundred nearer than Philadelphia, Baltimore was fearful of the competition of New York and her new Erie Canal. Although the city was the starting point for the colorful traffic over the famous National Road, crowded with Concord coaches and Conestoga wagons, farseeing men like Philip Thomas and his brother Evan, who had seen England's new coal-carrying railways, decided that only rails, albeit with only horse-drawn power, could preserve their competitive position.

The Baltimore & Ohio was chartered with Philip Thomas as president in 1827, and its cornerstone laid amid great parades and rejoicings on July 4, 1828. The first spadeful of earth was turned over by the venerable Charles Carroll of Carrollton, then over ninety and the last surviving signer of the Declaration of Independence. As the tradesmen marched smartly by, the floats glided through the streets, and the bands blared, old

Mr. Carroll quietly remarked to his friends, "I consider this among the most important acts of my life, second only to my signing the Declaration of Independence, if even it be second to that." Just about that time, the most impressive float of all, a miniature brig named the *Union*, manned entirely by Baltimore shipmasters in natty uniforms, paused before Mr. Carroll.

"Ship ahoy!" cried Carroll's aide. "What is the name of that ship and by whom commanded?"

"The *Union*; Captain Gardner," was the reply.

"From whence came you, and where bound?"

"From Baltimore, bound to the Ohio."

"How will you get over the mountains?"

"We've engaged a passage by the railroad."

Much cheering, no doubt, although it would take twenty-four years to get to the Ohio. But there was much to cheer about, for the Baltimore & Ohio would grow, and last, reaching into thirteen states and most of the largest cities in America, albeit one must, in recent years, drop one's voice and admit that it is now a subsidiary of another railroad, the Chesapeake & Ohio.

When the cheering stopped, the Baltimore & Ohio started building; it was, after all, the first railroad of any consequence, and everything had to be learned by trial and error. The first part of the roadbed, following the English model, was built for the ages: solid, level, its rail originally mounted on stone blocks, its bridges, like the Carrollton Viaduct above, masterpieces of masonry which still stand. Most of its construction engineers were famous men—Jonathan Knight, the chief, Stephen H. Long, the western explorer, Major George Washington Whistler, the husband of the lady in his son's famous painting of "Whistler's Mother" (he acquired the first engine with a steam whistle, although this is debated, and he afterward built a railroad for the czar from Moscow to St. Petersburg), his West Point friend Captain William G. O'Neill, and Benjamin H. Latrobe, son of the noted architect of the National Capitol. Ross Winans, who later became the builder and advocate of "camelback" locomotives (so called because the cab sat atop the boiler like a hump), devised a kind of wheel axle bearing. So little friction remained that a half-pound weight, suspended over a pulley so that it would drop, could pull a small, four-hundred-pound car which Winans set up on the floor of the Baltimore Exchange to prove his point. Old Charles Carroll was prevailed upon to come out again and ride in the magic little car, to his great delight.

Experimentally at least, steam came to the Baltimore & Ohio before it appeared at Charleston when Peter Cooper, another tinker and inventor cut from much the same plain honest cloth as George Stephenson, appeared on the scene just as progress with the railroad was slowing down. Self-educated, a former carriage maker's apprentice, then a grocer and glue manufacturer, Cooper had bought real estate in Baltimore and started making iron there. How better to protect his investment than to help the city grow? Here is how he told the story himself, fifty-two years later, in the *Boston Herald:*

"The Baltimore & Ohio Railroad had run its tracks down to Ellicott's Mills, thirteen miles, and had laid 'snakehead' rails, as they called them, strap rails, you know, and had put on horses. Then they began to talk about the English experiments with locomotives. But there was a short turn of 150 feet radius . . . and the news came from England that Stephenson said that no locomotive could draw a train on any curve shorter than a 900-foot radius.... The directors had a fit of the blues. I had naturally a knack of contriving, and I told the directors that I believed I could knock together a locomotive that would get the train around....

"So I came back to New York and got a little bit of an engine, about one-horse power (three and one-half-inch cylinder and fourteen-inch stroke) and carried it back to Baltimore. I got some boiler iron and made a boiler about as big as an ordinary washboiler, and then how to connect the boiler with the engine I didn't know.... I had an iron foundry, and had some manual skill in working in it. But I couldn't find any iron pipes. The fact is, there were none for sale in this country. So I took two muskets and broke off the wood part, and used the barrels for tubing to the boiler.... I went into a coachmaker's shop and made the locomotive, which I called the 'Tom Thumb,' because it was so insignificant. I didn't intend it for actual service, but only to show the directors what could be done. I meant to show two things; first, that short turns could be made; and secondly, that I could get rotary motion without the use of a crank. I changed the movement from a reciprocating to a rotary motion. I got steam up one Saturday night; the president of the road and two or three gentlemen were standing by, and we got on the track and went out two or three miles. All were delighted, for it opened up new possibilities for the road. I put the locomotive up for the night. All were invited to a ride Monday—a ride to Ellicott's Mills.

"Monday morning, what was my grief and chagrin to find that some scamp had been there and chopped off all the copper from the engine and carried it away, doubtless to sell to some junk dealer. The copper pipe that conveyed the steam to the pistons was gone. It took me a week or more to repair it. Then ... we started—six on the engine, and thirty-six on the car. It was a great occasion, but it didn't seem so important then as it does now. We went up an average grade of eighteen feet to the mile, and made the passage . . . to Ellicott's Mills in an hour and twelve minutes. We came back in fifty-seven minutes. Ross Winans, the president of the road, and the editor of the Baltimore Gazette made an estimate of the passengers carried, and the coal and water used, and reported that we did better than any English road did for four years after that. The result of the experiment was that the bonds were

In Peter Cooper's vain 1876 race for President, his posters remembered Tom Thumb.

sold at once and the road was a success."

Peter Cooper did not say a word about the famous race with a horse on the way home, when the stage people hitched a fine grey to a carriage on a parallel track and challenged the *Tom Thumb*. The tiny locomotive was soon in the lead when its primitive blower failed, the fire cooled, and the horse swept by

to victory—its last. Popular folklore to the contrary, Peter Cooper was not the father of steam locomotion in America, or even a significant contributor to the science. But he was a picturesque popularizer, and after his demonstration, the Baltimore & Ohio did buy some very practical steam engines for its long struggle to the West.

2. On to the Western Waters

2. On to the Western Waters

This stagecoach broadside of 1815 indicates an average speed of about six miles per hour; even the most primitive early trains did twenty and better. One early railroad traveller, the irrepressible Davy Crockett, found out the hard way, by opening a window. "I can only judge of the speed by putting my head out to spit," he said, "which I did, and overtook it so quick that it hit me smack in the face." Sensible people spat on the floor. According to the nearly unanimous report of European visitors of the era, the wholesale public expectoration of our citizenry was second only, as a natural wonder, to the mighty Niagara Falls.

PRECEDING PAGES: *This fine early photograph, while faded in spots, heralds the appearance of the railroad enthusiast. It is 1858, at Relay, Maryland, with a flag-bedecked locomotive of the B&O line hauling an excursion for artists.*
SMITHSONIAN INSTITUTION

America is a land of quick enthusiasms and quick rejections. Transportation in the early 1800's underwent one revolution after another: the early turnpikes with their wagons and stages were barely in place before the country was swept by a new passion for canals and packets. By 1840 there were some thirty-three hundred wonderfully picturesque but slow miles of these "expensive gutters." On the rivers, with equal suddenness, sails and drifting rafts gave way to steamboats. Viewed beside these increasingly palatial craft, which provided many plain people with their first glimpse of elegance and luxury, the primitive puffing railroads of 1830 and 1831 may have seemed like mere toys.

A different and more farseeing view soon began to prevail among the merchants, however. The businessmen of Baltimore, for instance, learned in 1832 that the new railroad's freight charges between that city and Ellicott's Mills were down to one quarter of the old turnpike levy. A similar shaft of commercial light burst upon the prudent Yankee businessmen of Boston when they discovered that the new rail line to Worcester cut costs to a third of the old wagon rate. Canal rates were often cheaper, but speed along the Erie, for example, was four miles per hour downstream, and two miles up, and the shallow water froze over during the winter. Crude as they were, railroads could run in all seasons and every day (except Sunday, of course!), and they could be built almost anywhere, without having to cling to river valleys and flat country. Railroads brought into being business which had not existed before. One could move rather perishable products, like milk or fruit, for example, and all kinds of raw material and manufactured goods which had previously cost too much to ship. The new Erie Railroad had barely opened its first few miles in the 1840's when one train brought eighty thousand boxes of strawberries to delight the palates of New Yorkers.

"Railroad fever" became widespread overnight in the United States. Behind the more sober merchants there lurked a multitude of promoters and speculators and dreamers, each with a glittering prospectus in his hand. By the time the very considerable financial Panic of 1837 struck down the weaker lines, there were some two hundred railroad projects afoot, over forty in New York State alone, each with its charter from a legislature, each with its optimistic stock salesmen, its mass meetings, its beguiling orators, its subsidized allies extolling its wonderful benefits in the press and the pulpit. Most of the enthusiasm and the money was raised in the hundreds of small towns and cities. The fever spread to the new midwestern states, to Kentucky, Ohio, Indiana, and Illinois; in 1837 the last-named, when its population was 380,000, authorized thirteen hundred miles of railroad. State funds poured in by the millions, so much that Michigan's investment later bankrupted the state.

Of the provenance of this photograph we know nothing, but the bustling railroad riders seem by their attire to date to the 1850's.

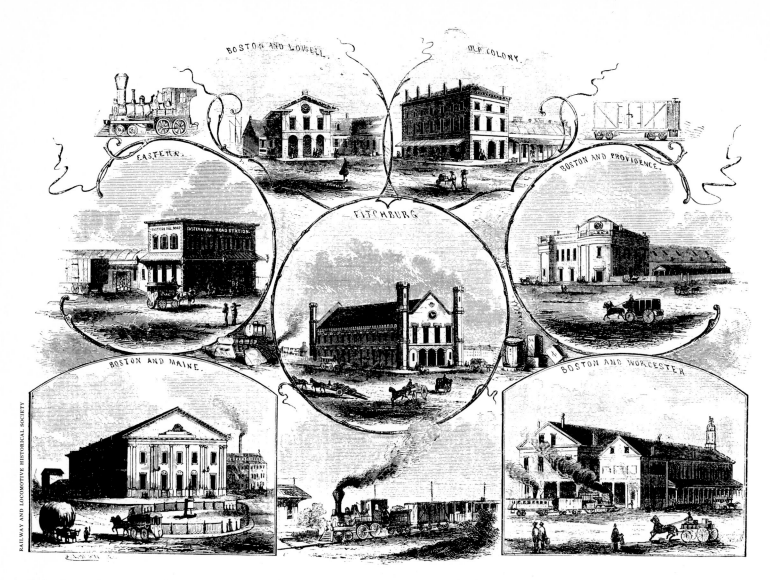

Only two rail companies limp into dilapidated stations in today's Boston, but in 1856, seven railroads boasted these seven stations.

The opposition, naturally enough, was bitter. As business melted away on the turnpikes and canals, teamsters, as tough-minded in that day as in their huge trucks today, turned violent, aided and abetted by tavern-keepers and "canawlers" and the turnpike stockholders. Tavern men in Philadelphia assembled a mob and simply tore up a section of track in that city, and teamsters in New York State took to beating up the crews of stalled trains, or stoning or shooting them from ambush. Besides this physical violence, there was the majesty of the law as made by legislatures under anti-railroad influence. If railroad charters were easy to get—legislators rarely say no directly—there were provisions in many of them that made them almost worthless. A new railroad might not enter within certain city boundaries, and thus link up with other lines. It could not carry freight when a competing canal was open, or charge a lower freight or passenger rate. In some cases it had to pay to the state anything earned over 10 percent, no matter how long an investor might have waited for his first dividend. Or it must agree to allow the state to take back the line after, say, twenty years. In one New England state, charters required railroads to pay every landowner the valuation he himself set on any land taken by eminent domain. Many a small canal or turnpike town which in some similar foxy way drove the railroad away lived to regret the day, if it lived at all.

Yet despite its enemies and overly-optimistic friends, despite the follies of inexperienced railroad builders, three thousand actual miles of track had been laid by 1840, and they swelled threefold by 1850. Mankind was on the move, impelled unconsciously by the Industrial Revolution and political events both near and far away. Hard-working Germans swarmed to the New World after the unsuccessful revolution of 1848; in their wake came hard-fisted Irish driven across the seas by famine and poverty. Connecticut swarmed with inventive tinkers, Massachusetts and Pennsylvania with new industry, for which coal and iron at reasonable prices would soon be a necessity. Farmers, weary of the stony, hardscrabble farms of New England, were heading for the rich soil of the Middle West. Gold, its value only recently enhanced by its very scarcity in the Panic of 1837 (which lasted, by the way, for some years), was discovered in faraway California and uprooted still more thousands. The race for the West was on; it was the prize for which the great ports of the East contended, each with its own iron horses.

Baltimore was the first great port, as we observed in the last chapter, to start building a railroad toward the western waters, a goal she would reach only after great delays and financial travails, at Wheeling, then in Virginia, in 1852. All enterprises looked in one way or another to a connection with the Great Lakes or the river system of the Midwest. Massachusetts, her seaborne trade badly hurt by the British blockade of the War of 1812, entered the race for the back country trade early, with railroads radiating in many directions out of Boston: to Lowell, to Worcester, with a connection there on another railroad to Norwich, Connecticut, to Portland, to Providence. The last of these routes, the start of the now all-important shore line which is the route of the so-called "Northeast Corridor" today, languished in the face of rivers then thought too difficult to bridge. One completed the trip to New York from Norwich, or Providence, or later Stonington, Connecticut, by steamboat. Boston, supported by her most eminent citizens—Adamses, Quincys, Hales—built westward in slow, deliberate steps, and reached the Hudson River opposite Albany, for a link by ferry with the Erie Canal and her primitive river railroads, before New York City's rival lines got there. By laying tracks northward to Montreal, despite mountains and weather, both Boston and Portland acquired gateways to the products of Canada, and to her

Harper's Weekly, MAY 28, 1859

CONVENIENCE OF THE NEW SLEEPING CARS.
(Timid Old Gent, who takes a berth in the Sleeping Car, listens.)
BRAKEMAN. "Jim, do you think the Millcreek Bridge safe to-night?"
CONDUCTOR. "If Joe cracks on the steam, I guess we'll get the Engine and Tender over all right. I'm going forward!"

Sleeping cars of a primitive sort came in very early, but they were no place for squeamish or apprehensive wayfarers. This cartoon comes from a Harper's Weekly *magazine of 1859.*

Engine and train crew pose proudly with their locomotive on the Fitchburg Railroad (now Boston & Maine) sometime in the 1860's or 1870's.

RAILWAY AND LOCOMOTIVE HISTORICAL SOCIETY

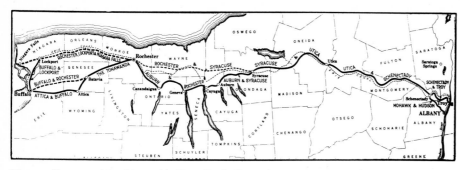

The ten lines combined into the New York Central in 1853 appear above in solid lines. Large dashes show shortenings of the main line, small ones the Erie Canal. The two Lockport routes led to the Falls Bridge. The Auburn line became the "Old Road."

seaborne trade during the period of winter when the St. Lawrence River is icebound. Wool, cotton, leather, and other raw materials streamed into southern New England spinning mills and shoe factories and returned to the interior in the form of manufactured goods.

By the time the Western Railroad of Massachusetts, as it was called then, reached Albany, New York State, although it lagged behind in the race because of its waterways, had a railroad of sorts from Albany to Buffalo. It was a combination of seven short, independent companies, the first of them the Mohawk & Hudson, on which the *DeWitt Clinton* made her debut. Next one got aboard the Utica & Schenectady, and there were changes between trains and railroads thereafter at such places as Utica, Rome, Syracuse, Auburn, Rochester, and Attica. The line often diverged, for reasons of policy and politics, far from the Erie Canal route, and was 328 miles long, compared with its modern 297. There was an absolute four-block break in Rochester, at the behest of the local livery and cab interests. The lines ran on wooden rails capped with strap iron, which had a regrettable tendency to break loose and send sharp ends called "snakeheads" shooting upward through wooden car floors. There was no through baggage or ticketing, and because of the two-train-a-day schedule of 1842 (for which modern Amtrak seems long to have suffered an atavistic affinity) the trip required twenty-four very taxing hours. By 1849, improvements and better rail had shortened the time to fifteen hours, but it was not until 1853 that the seven lines were consolidated, along with three other connecting railroads, into the New York Central. The man who put them together was the strong-willed Erastus Corning of Albany, nail maker, ironmonger, and for twenty years president of the Utica & Schenectady. He took no pay from the railroad, at least until 1856, and instead openly got rich by supplying everything the line needed in the way of iron.

At Albany six steamboat companies, with some twenty boats a day, went down the Hudson to New York City, a trip steeped in history and romance. Freight, which cares nothing about romance, tended to move by rail toward Boston, especially when a bridge was built at Troy to link the Central with the lines across Massachusetts. At the western end of the New York Central, John A. Roebling in 1855 completed the first large railroad suspension bridge in the world across the Niagara rapids. It was, one might say, his rehearsal for building the Brooklyn Bridge years later, and it was started, humbly enough, by flying a kite over the gorge far below. The string was used to pull over a cord, then a heavier cord, then ropes, and finally the cables. This new wonder, operated jointly with the Great Western Railway of Canada, gave the New York lines a connection with the Dominion, and eventually a northern route to Detroit and Chicago. Meanwhile, the Erie Canal, although it continued to operate a profitable freight business, stopped carrying passengers.

Rival Pennsylvania had proceeded even more sensibly than New York in

Behind the lounging gentlemen in the foreground an

early train passes over John Augustus Roebling's great Niagara Falls Suspension Bridge, built in 1855. It was 821 feet long.

The great Horseshoe Curve of the Pennsylvania Railroad, rising on a 1.8 percent grade from left to right, was a key portion of the route over the highest point of the Allegheny Mountains which replaced the old system of inclines in the 1850's. This old picture, whose panoramic process distorts the curve in the foreground too sharply, was taken after this section was four-tracked in 1899. In the distance are successive dams of the Altoona water system, and at far right is what may be a helper engine, or the transportation which brought the photographer to the site. At this spot today stands a preserved Pennsylvania K-4S, a Pacific-type locomotive, a tribute to all the steam that worked the curve until the mid-1950's.

the business of reaching the western waters, after a false start. Under state auspices a combination of railroads, canals, inclined planes, and rivers had created a transportation system of sorts, called the "Main Line of Improvements," between Philadelphia and Pittsburgh. First there was a railroad to Columbia on the Susquehanna with an inclined plane at each end; the tracks were built like a public highway, which anyone might use (until the absurdity of the arrangement became manifest). The second stage was the Middle Division Canal, which followed the Susquehanna to Harrisburg and then the Juniata Valley westward, with thirty-three aqueducts and 111 locks over a space of 172 miles. At the end, in Hollidaysburg, passengers and freight transferred to the Allegheny Portage Railroad, opened in 1834. The canal had carried the line up 585 feet; now the Portage, with a series of five inclined planes in ten miles, went up another 1,398 feet to the summit at Blair's Gap, whence four more planes dropped the traffic down 1,172 feet to Johnstown, on the Conemaugh River. Between the planes, which were operated by steam engines at the top, pulling trains up by rope or wire in about five minutes, horses and later steam engines moved them along the intervals of level going. The Portage was doubletracked, so that the weight of a train ascending could always be balanced against another one being lowered at the same time. The final part of the journey was on the Western Division Canal, some 104 miles down the valleys of the Conemaugh, Kiskiminetas, and Allegheny rivers, via sixteen aqueducts, a tunnel one thousand feet long, and sixty-six locks. Because a water supply was a steady problem, a dam had to be built on the Conemaugh, the same dam which later wiped out the town of Johnstown.

Simply to describe this complex, ambitious work makes evident its endless loadings and unloadings, its tedium, and its disadvantages, even without

reckoning the problems of freezing over, or of floods or expense. It cost a monumental eighteen million dollars and had accumulated forty million in debts by the time it was knocked down for $7,500,000 to its commercial successor. What slowly replaced it, under the skilled hand of Chief Engineer John Edgar Thomson, was the Pennsylvania Railroad. Thomson had visited George Stephenson, had helped lay out the Camden & Amboy, and had built the Georgia Railroad. He spanned the wide Susquehanna with a great bridge, and variously tunnelled and fought his way across the mountains. His triumph, which is still one of the great sights in railroading, was the famous Horseshoe Curve, five miles west of Altoona, where the line crosses the highest point of the mountains by doubling back across the Kitanning Valley in a great rising U-turn. Long before the first through train reached Pittsburgh—the Portage Railroad remained, for a time, in use—Thomson, now president, was already planning the further extensions of the line through the Old Northwest to Chicago. For more than a century, the Pennsylvania Railroad would be the greatest and best-managed in America, the great rival of the New York Central. It never missed a dividend, or engaged in the frenzied finance of the era.

Before any of these relatively sensible companies had crossed the Appalachians, another railroad had done it and shown them how—or how not to. In 1851, the six-foot-wide tracks of the New York & Erie Railroad reached Lake Erie in one of those grand pageants and feasts of oratory and gastronomy without which nothing could be started or ended in the early nineteenth century. From the Hudson River a special train of guests had made its way across the southern tier of New York counties, gaped at the rails winding through valleys and mountains, looked respectfully down from the great

This handbill, issued in 1837, advertises the old route to Pittsburgh, and connections west.

In the pantheon of railroad founders, Eleazar Lord, first, third, and seventh president of the Erie, must be marked as the maker of truly big mistakes. He put through the Erie's unique six-foot gauge, partly because a wide track would supposedly support the stronger power he would need to cross high country, but mostly because New York did not want other railroads to be able to interchange with it and take trade away from the state. Eventually, in 1878–85, it cost the Erie $25,000,000 to standardize its gauge. It was Lord who decided to build the line on long oak pilings driven deep into the earth. He believed that this odd elevated structure would avoid snowdrifts and the tedium of grading roadbeds, and one hundred expensive miles of piling were set in place by special steam machinery. But they were neither sturdy nor practical and no piece of track was ever laid on them. Lord and one of his hand-picked successors then made the monumental error of passing up a chance to buy, for a paltry $90,000, the stalled New York & Harlem Railroad before Vanderbilt got his hands on it. With a short ferry ride from Piermont on the other side of the Hudson and a few more miles of track laying, the purchase would have given the Erie an all-important entrance into New York City instead of a terminus in the boondocks, twenty-five miles away. One could sell bad ideas but not good ones to Eleazar Lord.

BOTH: EDWARD H. MOTT, *Between the Ocean and the Lakes,* 1899

stone Starrucca Viaduct, stared from the high Cascade bridge, received sixty hand-embroidered flags from ladies' groups along the way, and wound up at Dunkirk, New York. In the party were the weary President of the United States, Millard Fillmore, and four of his cabinet, including the Secretary of State, the silver-tongued old Daniel Webster. Hoarse from making endless trackside "remarks," rheumy from riding, as he had insisted, in an easy chair strapped to a flat car (for a better view), and sodden from too many restoratives, Webster could not enjoy the spectacular party somehow staged by the tiny, eight-hundred-soul village of Dunkirk, nor the whistles, the gunfire, the bands, the oxen roasted whole. But everyone knew a great event had taken place, and the Board of Aldermen back in New York produced the handsome scroll on the facing page to pay its tribute to "THE WORK OF THE AGE."

It was a work of genius, of grit, and of folly. It must have been the only railroad ever born of a pamphlet, a document written back in the 1820's by a well-travelled Yankee harness maker named William C. Redfield, who had perceived a route to the West through, successively, the valleys of the Delaware, the Susquehanna, the Chemung, the Tioga, the Genesee, and the Allegheny to Lake Erie; if the towns along the way had little population, they would grow. It was certainly the first big railroad built from almost nowhere to nowhere, for it started at a marsh called Tappan Slote (now Piermont) on the Tappan Zee portion of the Hudson, twenty-five miles upriver from Manhattan, and wound up in little Dunkirk. In later years, of course, it bypassed Dunkirk on its way to Chicago (and to Buffalo, and many other places, until it was some 2,600 route miles of railroad) and gave up Piermont altogether. Piermont, perhaps by coincidence, was the seat of Eleazar Lord, a well-meaning and honest former student of divinity (and friend of Redfield) on whom the hand of destiny most inappropriately settled for president of the Erie when it was organized in 1833. His twelve years in and out of office were a constant, heartbreaking battle for funds. Progress was slow and his errors (see caption at left) astonishing. Eventually, with mountainous debts and $201.33 in the treasury, the Erie passed to a really able man, Benjamin Loder, who in eight more years drove the road to conclusion. Besides attempting something never done before for which there was no experience—how steep should a grade be, how sharp a curve, how strong a bridge?—President Loder had to deal with a sinking treasury and rising snowfalls, with grasping landowners and rowdy crews of immigrant Irish construction workers, whose members divided into factions from Cork, Tipperary, and County Down and battled among themselves, or with a small but sturdy group of Germans. Their fighting had such deadly effect that all work once stopped at a place called Shin Hollow and the militia, in full dress uniform (it had no others) and equipped with a cannon, had to be called out. The Irish dispersed, not realizing that none of the militiamen knew how to fire their big brass guns.

Loder eventually broke his health in overcoming the shaky Erie's problems, but not before he had installed a first-class superintendent, Charles Minot (see page 52), and civil engineers, of whose work, a Harper's guidebook commented in 1855: "It crosses mountains deemed impossible; it goes over valleys which timid men said it would cost millions to fill in; it leaps valleys where bold engineers paused, shook their heads, and turned back."

Now merged with its rival Lackawanna, which is basically a coal road, and bankrupt once again, the Erie still rolls across the same Starrucca Viaduct over a century later. The building of the line, the adventures of Lord and Loder, make in many ways as great a story as that of the Pacific Railroad, but all this was forgotten when the Erie, the weakest financially of the new railroads, found not only fame but infamy as the tool of the robber barons. Watered, rigged, and squeezed, the Work of the Age never recovered.

EDWARD H. MOTT, Between the Ocean and the Lakes, 1899

The Alderman's tribute spared no expense to show (from top) the terminal dock at Piermont, the Cascade Bridge, and the Starrucca Viaduct.

While great companies struggled for the West, America back East, especially in the Northeast, took ever more to locals, branches, and other

shorter railroads like the Morris & Essex, as shown in E. L. Henry's painting of the crowded South Orange, New Jersey, station in 1864.

TWENTYFIVE TON PASSENGER ENGINE.
LAWRENCE MACHINE SHOP
LAWRENCE MASS.

ENGINES OF THIS PLAN WEIGHING FROM 37000 TO 64000 LBS.
M. W. BALDWIN & CO, LOCOMOTIVE BUILDERS,
PHILADELPHIA.

THE HINKLEY LOCOMOTIVE WORKS, BOSTON.

The Builders' Pride

Something of the sheer joy that early railroad men took in their creations comes through in their locomotives of long ago. Before the days of ornate stations, crack trains, and "palace" cars, which came after the Civil War, they expressed themselves in a heraldry of bright colors, shining brass, ornamental scrollwork, and even painted pictures. All this the new locomotive builders, ten of them by 1840 and some forty by 1850, proudly exhibited to the trade in handsome lithographs like those on these two pages. Valuable as they are to collectors today, they were given away free, to be hung in offices and shops of railroad men, a constant reminder of the sterling qualities of each and every company. To the engineer, as much a folk hero in his time as the bold aeronaut in another, his machine was his prized possession; many roads gave steady custody of an engine to one man, as the Navy bestows a ship on its captain. Engine crews and roundhouse men no doubt wasted time wiping and polishing these gorgeous objects, although in the days of the woodburner—supreme through the Civil War—one was usually dusting off clean dry ash rather than wiping the stains of greasy coal or oil. When Commodore Vanderbilt, as good at pinching pennies as he was at extracting millions from anything he touched, painted the engines black and ruled out the shiny brass on his newly acquired railroads, the bright colors soon disappeared. It was perhaps symbolic of the triumph of finance capitalism over the more individualistic and, we dare say, romantic era of railroading.

The early Pegasus in his coat of many colors breathed steam at every pore, struck off sparks despite the arrester in the huge stack, heaved and panted, and was obviously a living thing. Little wonder, therefore, that it usually bore a name, whether for its very newness, like *Novelty,* its size, from *Tom Thumb* to *Goliath,* or its aspirations, like the *Best Friend of Charleston.* Was it fast?

The Lawrence *of 1853 includes a nattily garbed fireman or engineer, but the Baldwin* Tiger, *with a ribbon on the tender, its namesake under the window, and a jungle scene on the headlight, undoubtedly is the gaudiest. It was one of a set of four built for the Pennsylvania Railroad in 1856 and 1857. The elegant* Hinkley, *dating to the 1870's, was produced by a relatively small shop. The boilers, modern modelmakers ought to observe, were left in the natural shiny metal color. Only the working parts and a little brass on fittings escaped the black paint of later years.*

Call it *Rocket, Racer, Lightning, Velocity, Stampede,* or *Cyclone.* Was it strong? Then name it *Hercules, Ajax, Samson,* or *Giant.* One could not omit governors, from *Bradford* on down to the most commonplace current occupant (whose favor might be needed), big shippers, like *J. C. Ayers,* the patent medicine king, and generals, national heroes, cities and towns, railroad presidents, or locomotive builders themselves. Even humbler railroad men occasionally won the accolade. There were Indian names, easy, like *Uncas* or *Hiawatha,* and hard, like *Ammonoosuc, Wannalancet, Carrabassett, Senecawanna, Musconetcong,* and *Wawayanda.* Mythology supplied *Jupiter, Adonis, Atalanta, Jason;* history, *Hannibal, Attila,* and rows of more recent personages; and there were animals, girls, and a thousand oddities as well, of which we might mention *Frugality* (management's policy), *Trustee* (bankruptcy was frequent), and *Right Arm*—which is Bay State slang for Cape Cod, after its obvious shape on the map, but has other connotations.

By the 1850's, railroads had settled in most cases on one basic design, the so-called "American" type shown in our lithographs, known in later years as a "4-4-0." These numbers describe the wheel arrangement according to a system of steam locomotive classification devised around 1900 by an engineer named Frederic M. Whyte. The first number indicated the number of wheels in the leading truck (two on each side here but four altogether); the second lists the driving wheels (four again); the last number was for the wheels on a trailing axle (none in this, or other early designs, but needed in many later engines with larger fireboxes requiring support).

The new design was light and flexible and strong enough to do most of the work required by railroads of the day; it dominated the scene for many decades. The American embodied all the discoveries of twenty years, among them Jervis' leading pivoted truck, necessary for following the curving and lightly built American railroads, and the "four-coupled" arrangement of

The Amoskeag Manufacturing Company of Manchester, New Hampshire, posed one of its woodburners, fully loaded and manned, before the factory buildings of the great Amoskeag textile mills, which also built engines. It was 1856, when, estimates John H. White, Curator of Transportation at the Smithsonian Institution, four to five million cords of wood were devoured annually in American locomotives.

drivers invented in 1836 by Henry R. Campbell, which linked the four wheels that did the pulling into a single unit. It made the "single," that is, single-axle, two-wheel engine, obsolete in America, although that design continued to be popular in passenger service on the fine, level rails in England, often with giant wheels as high as eight or nine feet. In terms of power at the drawbar, which hauls the train, large wheels mean less strength but much greater speed once a train gets going: good for fast passenger service. Wheels with a much smaller diameter gain in tractive effort for freight as they lose in speed. The American style struck a rough, efficient balance; it would handle both, and take grades once thought impossible.

Still another important feature of the design was the equalizing lever, devised in 1838 by Joseph Harrison, Jr., another Philadelphian, who wished to cure the inevitable tendency of one or more of the rigid sets of four-coupled driving wheels to slip or spin on even slightly uneven track. His equalizer allowed the wheels on each side to move up and down while resting their entire weight at a center point. With an equalizer on each side, and the flexible forward truck weighing on its single pivot, he succeeded in setting the whole locomotive on three points, in the manner of a three-legged stool,

SMITHSONIAN INSTITUTION

Matthias William Baldwin, shown with his first full-size locomotive, *Old Ironsides*, in this ancient tribute, began life as a jeweller's apprentice, and then a toolmaker in Philadelphia, where he became a fast friend of Franklin Peale, one of the talented seventeen children of the noted painter and jack-of-all-trades Charles Willson Peale. Baldwin had built a small stationary steam engine for his tool work when Peale got him to make, from what he could read of the Rainhill Trials, a little locomotive for a miniature indoor train to pull about visitors to Peale's Museum. This was 1831, and the toy was such a success that the Philadelphia, Germantown & Norristown Railroad (which was almost shorter than its name) commissioned Baldwin to build a real outdoor locomotive, which appears above. A disappointment on its first trip, when it went exactly one mile an hour with much hand-pushing by Baldwin and a friend, it was soon altered and doing twenty-eight miles an hour. The PG&N, which had hesitated, sold its horses. In 1834, Baldwin built five engines, in 1835 fourteen, one thousand by 1861, and he and his successors forty thousand by 1913. They worked, as might be expected, like jewels. A man of wide interests, he was an early art collector, a member of the American Philosophical Society, and a strong Abolitionist who founded a school for black children. As tempers grew sharp, his engines were boycotted in the South—to its loss when war came, since the Confederacy had few locomotive-building facilities.

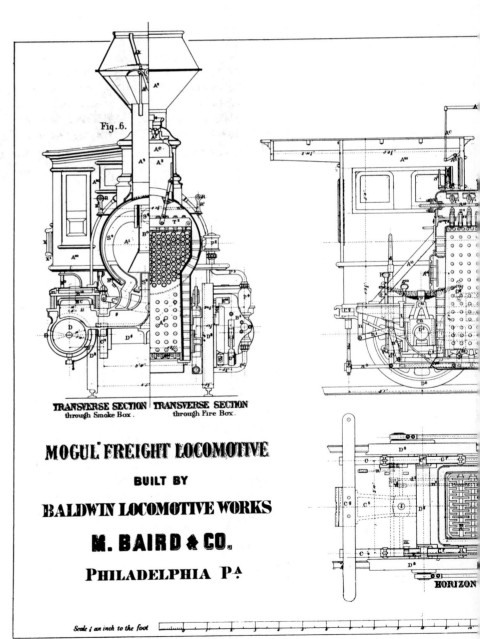

Fig. 6.

TRANSVERSE SECTION through Smoke Box. TRANSVERSE SECTION through Fire Box.

HORIZON

MOGUL FREIGHT LOCOMOTIVE

BUILT BY

BALDWIN LOCOMOTIVE WORKS

M. BAIRD & CO.,

PHILADELPHIA PA.

Scale ½ an inch to the foot

which will stand firm on any uneven surface, just as a rigid chair will not.

There were many triumphs for the early builders. William Norris of Philadelphia sent his *George Washington,* pulling a train of more than its own weight, up a 7 percent grade and won himself an export business replacing English inclines and their stationary engines. James Brooks built *America,* the first of the American type. The *Gowan & Marx,* Harrison's locomotive on which he installed his new equalizing levers, hauled 101 little freight cars weighing forty times as much as the engine without a murmur. It was named for British bankers who were large investors in the Philadelphia & Reading Company. The shop of Thomas Rogers of Paterson, New Jersey, whose factory was an ancestor of the giant American Locomotive Company, is generally credited with combining many new ideas of the time, including spread trucks, the wagon-top boiler, and a lower center of gravity, into the standard woodburner of the era. And Matthias Baldwin, whose firm would become dominant, discovered how to make metal joints so steam-tight that pressure could go as high as 120 pounds. There have been many passing fads and many real developments since, but nothing quite as suitable to all purposes in its time as the faithful 4-4-0.

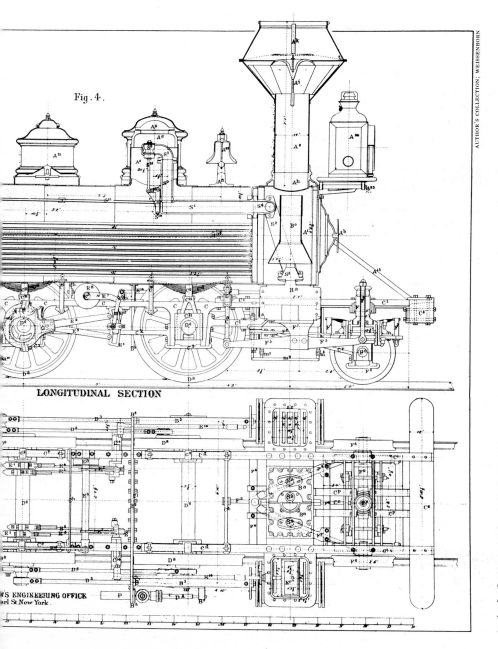

Fig. 4.

LONGITUDINAL SECTION

S ENGINEERING OFFICE
rl St. New York.

In the early 1860's, the "Mogul" freight locomotive came along to supplement the sturdy 4-4-0. One appears at left in plan and elevations. It was, in the Whyte system, a 2-6-0, with the truck wheels reduced to two, and more of the weight and hence power distributed over six-coupled driving wheels. This particular design is taken from Weissenborn's American Locomotive Engineering, *a noted book of plans published in 1871. It clearly exhibits the array of flue tubes and the arrangement of the firebox and many working parts. After Baldwin's death in 1866, the works were run by his able partner, Matthew Baird.*

A Shriek and a Bell

In 1842, Charles Dickens made a celebrated tour through the settled parts of the United States. Here is the novelist's account, in *American Notes*, of a ride on the new Boston & Lowell Railroad, which both fascinated and appalled him.

"There are no first and second class carriages as with us; but there is a gentlemen's car and a ladies' car: the main distinction between which is that in the first, everybody smokes; and in the second, nobody does. As a black man never travels with a white one, there is also a negro car; which is a great blundering clumsy chest, such as Gulliver put to sea in, from the kingdom of Brobdingnag. There is a great deal of jolting, a great deal of noise, a great deal of wall, not much window, a locomotive engine, a shriek, and a bell.

"The cars are like shabby omnibuses, but larger: holding thirty, forty, fifty, people. The seats, instead of stretching end to end, are placed crosswise. Each seat holds two persons. There is a long row of them on each side of the caravan, a narrow passage up the middle, and a door at both ends. In the centre of the carriage, there is usually a stove, fed with charcoal or anthracite coal; which is for the most part red-hot. It is insufferably close; and you see the hot air fluttering between yourself and any other object you may happen to look at, like the ghost of smoke.

"In the ladies' car, there are a great many gentlemen who have ladies with them. There are also a great many ladies who have nobody with them: for any lady may travel alone, from one end of the United States to the other, and be certain of the most courteous and considerate treatment everywhere. The conductor or check-taker, or guard, or whatever he may be, wears no uniform. He walks up and down the car, and in and out of it, as his fancy dictates; leans against the door with his hands in his pockets and stares at you, if you chance to be a stranger; or enters into conversation with the passengers about him. A great many newspapers are pulled out, and a few of them are read. Everybody talks to you, or to anybody else who hits his fancy. If you are an Englishman, he expects that the railroad is pretty much like an English railroad. If you say 'No,' he says 'Yes?' (interrogatively), and asks in what respect they differ. You enumerate the heads of difference, one by one,

I like to see it lap the miles,
And lick the valleys up,
And stop to feed itself at tanks;
And then, prodigious, step

Around a pile of mountains,
And, supercilious, peer
In shanties by the side of roads;
And then a quarry pare

To fit its sides, and crawl between,
Complaining all the while
In horrid, hooting stanza;
Then chase itself down hill

And neigh like Boanerges;
Then, punctual as a star,
Stop—docile and omnipotent—
At its own stable door.
— Emily Dickinson

"The Fitchburg Railroad touches the pond about a hundred rods south of where I dwell. I usually go to the village along its causeway, and am, as it were, related to society by this link. The men on the freight trains, who go over the whole length of the road, bow to me as to an old acquaintance, they pass me so often, and apparently they take me for an employee; and so I am. I too would fain be a track-repairer somewhere in the orbit of the earth....

When I meet the engine with its train of cars moving off with planetary motion...; when I hear the iron horse make the hills echo with his snort like thunder, shaking the earth with his feet, and breathing fire and smoke from his nostrils (what kind of winged horse or fiery dragon they will put into the new Mythology I don't know), it seems as if the earth had got a race now worthy to inhabit it."

Henry David Thoreau, from *Walden*

and he says 'Yes?' (still interrogatively) to each. Then he guesses that you don't travel faster in England; and on your replying that you do, says, 'Yes?' again (still interrogatively), and it is quite evident, don't believe it. After a long pause he remarks, partly to you, and partly to the knob on the top of his stick, that 'Yankees are reckoned to be considerable of a go-ahead people too;' upon which *you* say 'Yes,' and then *he* says 'Yes' again (affirmatively this time); and upon your looking out of window, tells you that behind that hill, and some three miles from the next station, there is a clever town in a smart lo-ca-tion, where he expects you have concluded to stop. Your answer in the negative naturally leads to more questions in reference to your intended route (always pronounced rout); and wherever you are going, you invariably learn that you can't get there without immense difficulty and danger, and that all the great sights are somewhere else.

"If a lady take a fancy to any male passenger's seat, the gentleman who accompanies her gives him notice of the fact, and he immediately vacates it with great politeness. Politics are much discussed, so are banks, so is cotton. Quiet people avoid the question of the Presidency, for there will be a new election in three years and a half, and party feeling runs very high: the great constitutional feature of this institution being, that directly the acrimony of the last election is over, the acrimony of the next one begins; which is an unspeakable comfort to all strong politicians and true lovers of their country: that is to say, to ninety-nine men and boys out of every ninety-nine and a quarter.

"Except when a branch road joins the main one, there is seldom more than one track of rails; so that the road is very narrow, and the view, where there is a deep cutting, by no means extensive. When there is not, the character of the scenery is always the same. Mile after mile of stunted trees: some hewn down by the axe, some blown down by the wind, some half fallen and resting on their neighbours, many mere logs half hidden in the swamp, others mouldered away to spongy chips. The very soil of the earth is made up of minute fragments such as these; each pool of stagnant water has its crust of vegetable rottenness; on every side there are the boughs, and trunks, and stumps of trees, in every possible stage of decay, decomposition, and neglect. Now you emerge for a few brief minutes on an open country, glittering with some bright lake or pool, broad as many an English river, but so small here that it scarcely has a name; now catch hasty glimpses of a distant town, with its clean white houses and their cool piazzas, its prim New England church and school-house: when whir-r-r-r! almost before you have seen them, comes the same dark screen: the stunted trees, the stumps, the logs, the stagnant water—all so like the last that you seem to have been transported back again by magic.

"The train calls at stations in the woods, where the wild impossibility of anybody having the smallest reason to get out, is only to be equalled by the apparently desperate hopelessness of there being anybody to get in. It rushes across the turnpike road, where there is no gate, no policeman, no signal: nothing but a rough wooden arch, on which is painted 'WHEN THE BELL RINGS, LOOK OUT FOR THE LOCOMOTIVE.' On it whirls headlong, dives through the woods again, emerges in the light, clatters over frail arches, rumbles upon the heavy ground, shoots beneath a wooden bridge which intercepts the light for a second like a wink, suddenly awakens all the slumbering echoes in the main street of a large town, and dashes on haphazard, pell-mell, neck-or-nothing, down the middle of the road. There—with mechanics working at their trades, and people leaning from their doors and windows, and boys flying kites and playing marbles, and men smoking, and women talking, and children crawling, and pigs burrowing, and unaccustomed horses plunging and rearing, close to the very rails—there—on, on, on—tears the mad dragon of an engine with its train of cars; scattering in all directions a shower of burning sparks from its wood fire; screeching, hissing, yelling, panting; until at last the thirsty monster stops beneath a covered way to drink, the people cluster round, and you have time to breathe again. . . .

"I returned at night by the same railroad and in the same kind of car. . . . glancing all the way out the window from the corners of my eyes, I found abundance of entertainment for the rest of the ride in watching the effects of the wood fire, which had been invisible in the morning but were now brought out in full relief by the darkness: for we were travelling in a whirlwind of bright sparks, which showered about us. . . ."

The Talking Wires

Ezra Cornell

Charles Minot

Charles Francis Adams, Jr.

It is one thing to build a railroad, and quite another to operate it, which is the job of the superintendent. One of the great ones in the early days was Charles Minot of Haverhill, Massachusetts. He was a judge's son and trained for the law, but got more pleasure out of learning telegraphy or surveying, and operating locomotives. Minot was a big, hot-tempered, venturesome man who had risen to superintendency on the Boston & Maine when he was hired by President Benjamin Loder of the Erie as general superintendent.

Thus it was Minot who presided as the line was finished, and managed the great celebration of 1851 described earlier in these pages. A democratic sort, Minot made no use of the special car or flunkies usually employed by men of his rank; instead he rode the locomotive or the pay car, or sometimes an old coach pushed ahead of the engine, for better visibility. Along the lines he got to know everybody, hired hands, stubborn Dutch farmers, wily Indians. (One group of the latter demanded a high price for some rocky land. It was pointed out to them that it was useless for farming, and would grow neither corn nor potatoes. The chief thought a moment and said, "It pretty good for railroad." The Erie settled.)

One character Minot got to know was a shabby eccentric named Ezra Cornell, whom he spotted stringing telegraph lines near the tracks at Goshen. The sight gave him an idea. When the big Morse telegraph company refused him, Minot got Cornell to place wires along Erie poles on the eastern division of the line; Cornell and the Erie formed the New York & Erie Telegraph Company. Later they acquired the use of Morse patents and changed the company name to the New York & Western Union Telegraph, which made Cornell a wealthy man, and brought a noted university into existence. It was on September 22, 1851, that Minot made his move. The story is well told by Edward Harold Mott, author of the enormous (nine-pound) classic work, *Between the Ocean and the Lakes; the Story of Erie,* published in 1899:

"W. H. Stewart was running the westbound express train on the day when Superintendent Minot made his astounding innovation in railroading, he happening to be going over the road on that train. The train, under the rule then existing, was to wait for an east-bound express to pass it at Turner's, 47 miles from New York. That train had not arrived, and the westbound train would be unable to proceed until an hour had expired, unless the tardy east-bound train arrived at Turner's within that time. There was a telegraph office at Turner's, and Superintendent Minot telegraphed to the operator at Goshen, fourteen miles further on, and asked him whether the east-bound train had left that station. The reply was that the train had not yet arrived at Goshen, showing that it was much behind its time. Then, according to the narrative of the late W. H. Stewart, given to the author in 1896, Superintendent Minot telegraphed as follows, as nearly as Stewart could recollect:

To Agent and Operator at Goshen:
    Hold the train for further orders.

    Chas. Minot, *Superintendent*

"He then wrote this order, and handed it to Conductor Stewart:

To Conductor and Engineer, Day Express:
    Run to Goshen regardless of opposing train.

    Chas. Minot, *Superintendent*

" 'I took the order,' said Mr. Stewart, relating the incident, 'showing it to the engineer, Isaac Lewis, and told him to go ahead. The surprised engineer read the order, and handing it back to me, exclaimed:

" ' "Do you take me for a d--n fool? I won't run by that thing!" '

" 'I reported to the Superintendent, who went forward and used his verbal authority on the engineer, but without effect. Minot then climbed in the engine and took charge of it himself. Engineer Lewis jumped off and got in the rear seat of the rear car. The Superintendent ran the train to Goshen. The east-bound train had not yet reached that station. He telegraphed to Middletown. The train had not arrived there. The west-bound train was run on a similar order to Middletown, and from there to Port Jervis, where it entered the yard from the East as the other train came into it from the West.'

"An hour and more in time had been saved to the west-bound train, and the question of running trains on the Erie by telegraph was once and forever settled."

Despite this achievement, Minot was too democratic for a new Erie administration, and he refused to enforce a set of strict, indeed needlessly strict, work rules drawn up by an upstart divisional superintendent, Daniel C. McCallum. Minot was replaced in

1854 by McCallum, but the new man's disciplinary methods soon brought on the Erie's first strike, and another bankruptcy soon ensued. McCallum went and Minot, who had been running the Michigan Southern, returned to his old job. It was ironic, or perhaps merely suitable, that in 1862 Secretary of War Stanton would call on McCallum to run the United States Military Railroads.

It would be pleasant to relate that with Minot's demonstration all railroads thereafter adopted telegraphic operation and that no more delays or accidents could be ascribed to its lack. But, in fact, almost exactly twenty years later, one of the most memorable wrecks in history took place at Revere, north of Boston, for that very reason. The Eastern Railroad of Massachusetts indeed had telegraphic installations in most stations, but its independent superintendent, Jeremiah Prescott, would have no truck with them, sticking to his rules and timetables and leaving the telegraph for such members of the public as might want to send telegrams.

On a humid, foggy evening in August, 1871, obstinate attention to Prescott's rules made it possible for one badly delayed branch-line train from Lynn to cause a pile-up of three crowded passenger trains at Everett Junction; the Lynn train had broken down, which no one knew, but nothing could move onto the branch until it made its belated appearance. The blockade at Everett in turn held up a northbound main-line local, a fact unsuspected back in Boston and, worse still, unknown to the engineer of the *Bangor Express*, heading north at high speed on the same tracks. Everett was clear now, and the switch tender waved his lantern at the passing express to confirm the fact. But pounding through the fog several minutes later, the engineer suddenly saw two dim red lights—they had no reflectors—dead ahead and very close at hand. They were the rear lamps of the local, unloading at Revere. He whistled for brakes, reversed his engine, and dove out of the cab. He survived, but twenty-nine died and fifty-seven were injured. Boston seethed with outrage, and Wendell Phillips, the great orator of Abolition, discovered a new cause. The Eastern Railroad never recovered from the infamy or the lawsuits, eventually disappearing into the Boston & Maine.

The best comment was offered eight years later by Charles Francis Adams, Jr., the wisest contemporary commentator on railroading: "A simple message to the branch trains to meet and pass at any given point other than that in the schedule would have solved the difficulty; but no!—*there* were the rules, and all of the rolling stock of the road might gather at Everett in solemn procession, but, until the locomotive at Lynn could be repaired, the law of the Medes and the Persians was plain: and in this case it read that the telegraph was a new-fangled and unreliable auxiliary."

Giant Erie broad-gauge engine No. 144, *built by Danforth, Cooke in 1853, dwarfs Engineer Henry Carbaugh at Paterson, New Jersey, depot in 1867.*

The Greatest Junction of All

Railroads made Chicago, and Chicago made railroads; it was the greatest junction of all. It was a muddy village of some three hundred rag-tag-and-bobtail settlers where lake boats stopped in the 1830's; a German immigrant passing through rejected a chance to buy three hundred acres of its low-lying sandy waterfront at sixteen cents an acre. Its merchants were happy with their lake trade and aspired only to make plank roads over the mud on which farmers might drive their produce to town. And when a promoter from the East named William B. Ogden came talking railroads, and wheedled the outlying farmers into emptying their mattresses to buy stock in his Galena & Chicago

Union Railroad, the town passed an ordinance forbidding it to build a depot in the town. But when the little railroad, with its all-secondhand equipment, began to deposit grain by the trainload just outside the city in 1848, the merchants awoke to the knock of opportunity. The grain elevators expanded their business 900 percent almost overnight. Ogden kept extending his railroad west; eventually it became the Chicago & Northwestern.

Yet by 1851, just as the Erie was reaching Dunkirk back in New York, a strange and depressing situation prevailed in the new western states. Barely one hundred miles of railroad radiated out of Chicago. Also, head-

ing south, were eight miles of embankment wholly innocent of track, which the state had started building just in time for the Panic of 1837. With this, like Indiana and Michigan, Illinois was trying the old notion of railroads as common highways, but she ran out of money. Her state debt of $17,000,000 was selling at eighteen cents on the dollar; Indiana's and Michigan's were bringing a thin twenty each. Meanwhile, immigration from the East had deposited some three million new settlers in a wilderness devoid of roads.

The new immigrants began demanding that government do something soon. The answer was the first railroad land grant, 2,595,000 acres of federal land, six alternate even-numbered sections of unpre-empted land for every mile built, to be issued to fund the building of the Illinois Central by a private company—seven hundred miles north and south through the state, with a "branch" to Chicago. The contract said that it should be completed in six years and that 7 percent of the company's *gross* should be paid to the state in perpetuity, certainly the best deal that dead-beat Illinois had ever made. Uncle Sam was permitted to set his own charge for carrying troops, freight, and mail, and eventually settled on 50 percent for the first two and 80 percent for the mail. (Over the years the government discovered, propaganda to the contrary, that it had made a great bargain.) Not without a struggle was money raised, and from sources as various as Boston and Salem shipping kings, William Ewart Gladstone, Richard Cobden, Wendell Phillips, and even Harriet Beecher Stowe. Stephen A. Douglas helped put through the land grant and Abraham Lincoln became an Illinois Central lawyer. The "IC," then the longest line in the world, was completed exactly three days before the deadline set in the contract, in 1856.

(The story is told that Lincoln once submitted it a bill for a fee of $2,000, to be told by the superintendent, an ex-Army officer, "Why, sir, this is as much as Daniel Webster himself would have charged. We cannot allow such a claim." Lincoln may have been a provincial, frontier lawyer, but he had won

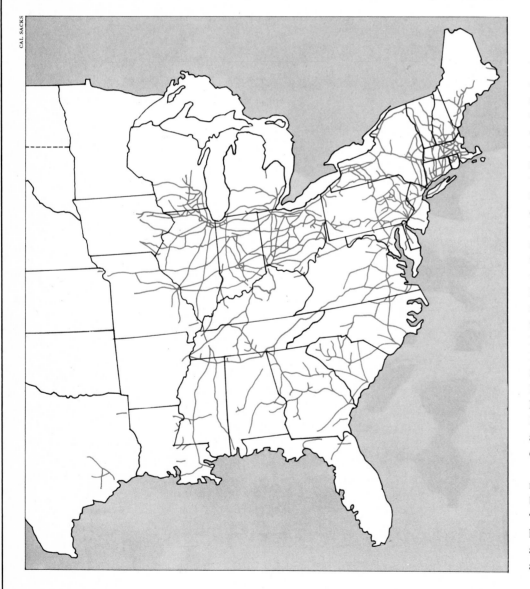

CAL. SACKS

The predominance, by two to one, of northern railroads over southern on the verge of the Civil War is made clear above. Except mainly for the Erie and its connections, the North was standard gauge or close to it (four feet nine or ten), the South below Richmond mainly five feet. There were no direct rail routes between them, save by ferries across the Ohio or the Potomac.

With a fortune made in the China trade before he was twenty-four, John Murray Forbes, shown on the facing page, became the ablest railroad builder of the Middle West.

54

railroad cases, and helped the Chicago, Rock Island defend its bridge across the Mississippi from the steamboat interests. And so he took his bill back and mailed a new one for $5,000. After suing in court, he collected. The superintendent who had refused him was George Brinton McClellan, and Lincoln would encounter him again.)

Alone of the great eastern cities, Boston had failed to build a railroad empire into the West, although it had once had an opportunity to buy the New York Central before Vanderbilt got it. (Men from Springfield, Massachusetts, including President Chester W. Chapin of the Western Railroad of Massachusetts, espied the chance, went to Boston to lay the matter before the great men of the city, but failed because in that stiff Brahmin society they did not know how to get introduced to the right people—it could only have happened in what was once known, without much conscious humor, as the Hub of the Universe.) But the Bostonians made up for their omissions under the astute financial leadership of John Murray Forbes, a friend of Lincoln and of Ralph Waldo Emerson, a Yankee hewn out of granite who had sailed in clipper ships to Canton and made a fortune in the China trade while still a young man. In the world of nineteenth-century railroading he was a rare bird indeed, a man so honest that Emerson said that Forbes was "not likely, in any company, to meet a man superior to himself." Persuaded by another Yankee, John W. Brooks, Forbes led a financial group that bought the ailing Michigan Central and, using only the best rails, drove it to Chicago. There he looked westward and bought a bankrupt affair only twelve miles long called the Aurora Branch. He extended it, acquiring other small lines until he reached Quincy, Illinois, and a place just opposite Burlington, Iowa, on the Mississippi, whereat the branch became the great Chicago, Burlington & Quincy. Thus Boston got itself a railroad empire at a remove. Other roads arrived until, in 1860, Chicago had eleven different railroads. There were stations everywhere like the one at right, where all the races and classes of America seem to be bustling by. As the map on page 54 shows, the northern states in the East were now linked to the new West by iron rails, while river traffic to the South declined. All of this was an augury of victory in the war to come.

3.The First Railroad War

3. The First Railroad War

John Brown in 1859

The first great act of violence which, in hindsight, announced the coming of the Civil War, took place rather prophetically on a railroad. In the small hours of the morning of October 17, 1859, a Baltimore & Ohio express, eastbound from Wheeling, Virginia, ground into the station at Harper's Ferry, Maryland, stopping in the usual fashion just before crossing the fine, long bridge across the Potomac. As they looked out, the conductor, A. J. Phelps, and his engineer, William McKay, were astonished to see the tracks lined with armed men swinging lanterns and torches. The baggagemaster, attempting to get off, was stopped by two men with guns; in the distance a few rifles spoke. Then there was some shooting nearby at the depot. Phelps presently found the leader of this unexpected force holding up the train, a bearded man who called himself Captain Anderson. The conductor explained with some heat that he was carrying the United States Mail and that no one had the right to stop him. To this Anderson after a time agreed, but not before he had told the conductor a story that made his jaw drop. Next morning, that story went by telegraph to the railroad's master of transportation, William Prescott Smith:

W. P. Smith   Monocacy, 7:05 A.M., Oct. 17, 1859
    Baltimore

  Express train bound east under my charge was stopped this morning at Harpers Ferry by armed Abolitionists. They have possession of the bridge and of the arms and armory of the United States. Myself and baggagemaster have been fired at and Hayward, the colored porter, is wounded very severely.... They are headed by a man who calls himself Anderson and number about 150 strong. They say they have come to free the slaves, and intend to do it at all hazards.

  The leader of these men requested me to say to you that this is the last train that shall pass the bridge, either east or west. It has been suggested that you had better notify the Secretary of War at once. The telegraph wires are cut east and west of Harpers Ferry and this is the first station that I could send a despatch from.   A. J. Phelps.

Perhaps thinking his conductor had taken leave of his reason, Smith took two hours to reply. Or, at any rate, his messenger to the telegraph office took his time. And he sent this rather sharp reply to Ellicott's Mills, much nearer to the train's destination:

A. J. Phelps   Baltimore, Oct. 17, 1859. 9 A.M.
    Conductor of the Express East at Ellicotts Mills

  Your despatch is evidently exaggerated and written under excitement. Why should our trains be stopped by Abolitionists and how do you know that they are such and that they number a hundred or more? What is their object? Let me know at once before we proceed to extremities.   W. P. Smith.

"See where the cannon ball went!" the man at right seems to be saying. But his companion looks bored by such an everyday event of the war.

Situation normal in Northern Virginia: The engine Commodore, *derailed by the Confederate troops, awaits being righted while the track gang seen*

in the distance works to restore the line.

That would calm the man down, he must have thought. But Conductor Phelps, his temper barely under control, stuck to his guns in this reply:

W. P. Smith   Ellicott's Mills, Oct. 17, 1859
   Baltimore
   My despatch was not exaggerated, neither was it written under excitement, as you suppose. I have not made it half as bad as it is. The Captain told me that his object was to liberate all the slaves and that he expected a reinforcement of 1500 men to assist him. Hayward, the negro porter, was shot through the body and I suppose by this time is dead. The Captain also said that he did not want to shed any more blood.
   I will call at your office immediately on my arrival and tell you all. One of my passengers was taken prisoner and held as such for some time. I will bring him to see you also.
                                                            A. J. Phelps.

This time Smith believed him and went to President John W. Garrett, the able man who struggled throughout the war to keep the much-put-upon Baltimore & Ohio running. Then Garrett telegraphed the Secretary of War. Certainly there can be found no more vivid a description of how the news of John Brown's raid reached the outside world than in these telegrams unearthed by that railroad's great historian, Edward Hungerford. Anderson, of course, was "Old Brown of Osawatomie," the fanatic (or saint, if you prefer, as Emerson did) who came with eighteen followers to capture the government arsenal and distribute its arms to slaves—who, contrary to his expectations, failed to rise. The telegrams remind us of the first of many ironies in that tragedy, that Brown's first victim was a black man, Hayward Sheppard, an inoffensive porter. It is another irony that the railroad soon brought Robert E. Lee with a company of United States Marines to recapture the arsenal and, a little later, Thomas Jonathan (later "Stonewall") Jackson to command a Virginia company at John Brown's execution—for the same offense which these two eminent gentlemen would later commit, Jackson, indeed, against the very same place. On April 18, 1861, he was back in Harper's Ferry, commanding some Virginia Militia who took over as Union forces burned the arsenal again, and retired. The war was young and uncertain; mails, steamboats, and even railroads operated for a time between the opposing sides. At first Jackson let the trains keep operating, then he complained to Garrett in Baltimore that the big coal trains rolling east at night were keeping his men from sleeping, and set short daylight hours, grudgingly accepted by the railroad, during which they might operate. When this ruse had concentrated enough equipment within the area he controlled, Jackson pounced. Eventually he managed to confiscate over forty engines and three hundred cars. Knowing the South's shortages, Jackson sent a dozen or more of the locomotives southward over the roads, a long trip in which it often took forty horses to haul them. On grades they were often pushed as well by up to one hundred sweating men. No railroad ever had a more effective enemy than Stonewall Jackson, at least until the era of the robber barons. In less than a year, for example, he destroyed twenty-three bridges. It was going to be a hard war for border railroads.

In particular it would be hard for a railroad operating out of Baltimore, a city divided in its loyalties. It was the further misfortune of Garrett's railroad that the city, like so many others in the early days of railroading, possessed no connections between lines, or almost none. One changed stations, as one still does in New York or Chicago, although nowadays freight cars at least can be physically exchanged. Although Baltimore was the hub through which lines from the north—from Harrisburg or Philadelphia—converged to head south for Washington on the all-important Baltimore & Ohio "branch," the only connection was a single track through the city's streets to the latter's

CITY DEPARTMENT..

AMERICAN TELEGRAPH COMPANY,

GENERAL OFFICE, 145 BROADWAY.

TERMS AND CONDITIONS ON WHICH THIS AND ALL MESSAGES ARE RECEIVED BY THIS COMPANY FOR TRANSMISSION.

CAMBRIDGE LIVINGSTON, Sec'y.   E. S. SANFORD, Pres.

Received at N. Y. & N. H. R. R. Depot, 27th St.   1863.

Dated _____ 1863.

No. 1   C. Vanderbilt Esq
         pres't N.Y & H RR.

Your letter of the nineteenth has just been rec'd. the Engines referred to were seized by order of this Dept from an absolute & paramount necessity for the supply of the armies on the Cumberland they are absolutely essential for the safety of those armies & the order cannot be revoked whatever damages your Company may sustain the

---

CITY DEPARTMENT.

AMERICAN TELEGRAPH COMPANY,

GENERAL OFFICE, 145 BROADWAY.

No. 2   Gov't. is responsible for but the Military operations & the supply of the arms at Chattanooga in the judgment of this Dept & no doubt also in your judgment are superior to every other consideration Nothing but a Controlling necessity would induce the Dept to interfere with the business of any individuals or Companies this however is a Case when the safety &

CITY DEPARTMENT.

AMERICAN TELEGRAPH COMPANY,

GENERAL OFFICE, 145 BROADWAY.

No. 3   Support of an army depends upon the exercise of the authority of the Gov't & prompt acquiesence by loyal citizens. I hope then that you will not only throw no obstacle in the way of a speedy forwarding of these Engines to Louisville but that you will use your well known energy in aid of the government to hurry them forward
         Edwin M. Stanton
         Sec'y of War

By telegraph Secretary Stanton struggles to instill a little patriotism into Cornelius Vanderbilt, who had whined about his commandeered engines.

Mounted on a flatcar, the mortar "Dictator" comes up on the Military Railroad to pound Petersburg with two-hundred-pound exploding shells.

Camden Station. No locomotive crossed town but cars were dragged, one at a time, along this track by teams of horses.

Because of a supposed plot on his life, President-elect Lincoln was persuaded to give up his announced public progress through the city in early 1861, and instead passed through the city unheralded in this fashion at three in the morning in an ordinary sleeping car, unknown even to the employees. Mrs. Lincoln and her sons made the planned trip the next day, and were well received, but by April 19, when the Sixth Massachusetts Regiment made a well-advertised appearance on its way to help defend Washington, southern sympathizers in Baltimore turned ugly. The train was uncoupled and the first nine of thirty-five cars were drawn safely along Pratt Street across the city, bothered by nothing more than boos and groans, but the tenth was stoned and turned back. Then the crowd pushed forward and barricaded the tracks with bricks and sand. It would have astonished Boston to have seen a volunteer group of Negro sailors from southern ships in the harbor dragging up two huge anchors to complete the work of obstruction, cheering as they did for the South and "Massa Jeff Davis."

In detachments the rest of the Sixth, guns loaded with powder and ball, began marching along the streets to Camden Station, led by the mayor of the city. The mob pressed, stones flew, and a quick march became a run. But when several Massachusetts men fell, the troops wheeled and fired. A dozen or so of the mob were killed.

So the work of destruction began. In heavily fought-over areas like Northern Virginia, armies swept back and forth, rebuilding as they came, tearing down as they left. Winchester, Virginia, changed hands sixty times. Large parts of the Baltimore & Ohio, though steadily and doggedly rebuilt, were out of business for months at a time, and the same was true, in the West, on the Louisville & Nashville, torn up by southern armies, repaired, maimed again and again by southern guerillas.

As it soon became evident to everyone except a few generals, it was a railroad war, and the first one in which the new means of transportation would play a significant role. And the northern victory was in no small degree made possible by the fact that it possessed twice as much rail mileage as the Confederacy—some twenty thousand to nine thousand. The westward drive to the Middle West in the years before the war had linked the new states commercially, physically, and it turned out, militarily, to the northern cause. And their track, equipment, personnel, and sources of supply were far superior. The Erie and the Pennsylvania alone had more locomotives than the Confederacy, which, in addition, had almost no plants in which to build more, save mainly the Tredegar Iron Works at Richmond, which the southern government converted instead to the manufacture of ordnance.

Except for the border lines, American railroads had never known such prosperity. They carried troops, supplies, and ordnance. Cars of the private companies like Adams Express brought parcels to the soldiers, and, more somberly, took their bodies home. The Wilmington & Weldon Railroad of North Carolina was so busy that it declared a 31 percent dividend in 1863. The Illinois Central, despite the cut rates a land-grant road had to give the government, paid 8 percent in 1863 and raised it to 10 percent in 1865. Even the perpetually out-of-pocket Erie paid its first dividend. The prosperity in the South, however, was short-lived as shortages and inflation took their toll. Lubricating oil rose from $1 to $50 a gallon, coal from 12¢ to $2 a bushel, wheels for cars from $15 to $500 each. The states of the Confederacy produced only a minute fraction of their own iron rails (steel had not yet come into use), importing them from the North or from England. Some of their lines were still strap-iron on wood. Cut off from their suppliers by war and

Scottish-born Major General Daniel C. McCallum, once superintendent of the Erie, inventor of a kind of arched truss bridge that made him well-to-do, and, on the side, a once-popular poet, became the stern director of railroads in the United States, with the power to seize and operate any he needed. Starting with only a short section of one line in 1862, he eventually controlled over two thousand miles of lines in the war zones. His greatest achievement was the supply over long distances and shaky lines of Union troops in the West, especially during Sherman's advance on Atlanta. He was a desk man and a martinet, but a man of great organizing skill.

General Herman Haupt, railroad construction chief in Virginia, scouts a bridge site.

blockade, the southern railroads began to tear up branch lines to secure the rails for more important routes, and the government at Richmond had whole railroads it regarded as non-essential taken up in Florida, Texas, and Georgia, and moved to strategic locations.

One telling gauge of the ability of Civil War generals was their understanding, or lack of it, in dealing with this immensely important new means of rapid movement. The tale is told of one general who stopped an important train at a farmhouse so that his wakeful wife might get some sleep, and there is another of a commander who, during the Second Battle of Bull Run, halted a Union supply train heading for the front, on the theory that he might need the train to move his men. And the train sat motionless for twenty-four hours, blocking all traffic, while he made up his mind. The general whom others disliked was Herman Haupt, whom Secretary of War Edwin M. Stanton had put in charge of construction and repair of railroads in the eastern theater of war. "Be as patient as possible with generals," Stanton had told the then Colonel Haupt. "Some of them probably will trouble you more than they will the enemy."

Early in the war, however, General Lee and Stonewall Jackson had discovered the speedy possibilities of trains for shifting whole brigades and armies in lightning movement back and forth between the defenses of Richmond and the Shenandoah Valley. In the summer of 1862, General Braxton Bragg moved his whole Army of the Tennessee, some thirty thousand men, from Tupelo, Mississippi, over 770 miles to Chattanooga, in about a week. Driven out of that city to the south, Bragg was hard-pressed during the Battle of Chickamauga in September, 1863, when a whole corps of the Army of Northern Virginia under General James Longstreet was sent to reinforce him by rail. The puffing troop trains took a roundabout nine-hundred-mile excursion through Wilmington, Augusta, and Atlanta but arrived in time to save Bragg and send his opponent, Union General William S. Rosecrans, reeling back to Chattanooga. There he came under siege, much to the distress of the government at Washington, which only recently had been exulting over the Union victories at Gettysburg and Vicksburg. Rosecrans appealed for help. Would his whole Army of the Cumberland be lost? The available reinforcements were with the Army of the Potomac, then inactive but over a thousand miles

(Continued on page 70)

Always in the field, Haupt (in the black hat at right)

inspects track work on the Orange & Alexandria Railroad near Bull Run in 1863. The locomotive was named for him.

During McClellan's Peninsular campaign in 1862, which brought him almost to the gates of Richmond, federal troops took over the Richmond & York River Railroad. General McCallum brought locomotives and cars by ship from Baltimore and started running trains that at one point came as close as four miles to the Confederate Capital. This photograph shows a bridge under work, workmen and a photographer's field darkroom in the foreground (photographs in that era had to be developed wet and at once), and a locomotive arriving on a ship in the background. The place is supposedly White House Landing, on the Pamunkey River, where the line began. But all of it was lost when McClellan's ponderous campaign fizzled.

U.S. SIGNAL CORPS PHOTO (BRADY COLLECTION) IN THE NATIONAL ARCHIVES

Great skills, some of them almost fiendish, were applied by both sides in the destruction of railroads. At top are rails bent the simple way: One end is anchored against a firm rail, and a pin set in a tie for a fulcrum, whereupon a horse pulls the rail until it bends. Another method twisted them as well, leaving them beyond repair. The most satisfying trick to the troops, shown at right, was to place rails over a pile of crossties, which was then set afire until the centers of the rails grew red hot and dropped at both ends. If there was time, one grabbed the cool ends and wrapped the rails around trees; Union men called the resulting tangle "Sherman's neckties."

to the east. In between, blocking any direct access by rail, were the armies of the Confederacy.

Secretary Stanton began calling in his generals. George Gordon Meade, who commanded the Army of the Potomac (and had let Lee get away after Gettysburg), did not know what to do. Next came General Halleck, then top of the Army heap. How soon, he was asked, could some sixteen thousand men be moved from Virginia to Tennessee? Halleck guessed about three months, but was uncertain. The chief of the Army telegraphic corps, T. T. Eckert, who knew something about railroads, was asked his opinion. He thought it would take less than three months, but asked for a chance to go study some maps and timetables. Returning, he ventured sixty days, and then, gaining confidence, reduced it first to forty and then, throwing caution to the winds, to fifteen days. Despite the problem of a round-about route through Maryland, Ohio, and Indiana, the question of crossing the unbridged Ohio River, the problems of feeding and supplying, Stanton was off to see Lincoln and a session of the War Cabinet, at 1:00 A.M. In the wee hours the issue was debated. "Fighting Joe" Hooker thought it could not be done, but Stanton was vehement, and Lincoln gave his reluctant consent.

Before the great movement was done there were thirty trains and about six hundred cars, and not sixteen thousand but twenty-five thousand men, together with ten batteries of artillery. They moved by rail up to Washington, then over the Baltimore & Ohio, via Relay House and Martinsburg, to just below Wheeling. There were passenger cars and boxcars of every known variety, the latter fitted out with crude seats. To get a view and a little ventilation, the soldiers in the boxcars knocked out a board here and there. At Wheeling, men and wagons marched across a pontoon bridge, and took new trains to Columbus, and Indianapolis, and still another change down to Jeffersonville, Indiana. There a bridge of coal barges carried them to Louisville and fresh trains south to their destination. It took eleven and a half days.

No one doubted the effectiveness of railroads in war any longer. Put another way, they had become a necessity, and hence a prime target. While Grant battered Lee's army in Virginia, General William Tecumseh Sherman to the west set out in the spring of 1864 to march south to Atlanta, the South's principal rail hub. His line of supply for a hundred thousand men and thirty-five thousand animals deep in enemy country strung back up the single-track Western & Atlantic to Chattanooga, then the Nashville & Chattanooga and the Louisville & Nashville, altogether 472 miles. The Western & Atlantic had seen more than its share of destruction and adventure, going back all the way to the daring Andrews Raid of 1862 (pages 74–77). Reconstructing and maintaining that railroad in the wake of Sherman's army was the hardest task that faced the military organization in the whole war, not to mention defending it against constant raids and attacks by Confederate forces, yet the reassuring scream of the locomotive whistle was never far behind the troops.

Finding the bridge over the Oostanaula River at Resaca destroyed and still burning, Sherman is reported to have asked his chief construction engineer how long it would take to fix it. Four days, he was told. "Sir," snapped Sherman, "I give you forty-eight hours or a position in the front ranks." With two thousand men, the engineer made it in seventy-two hours, the delay excused because the iron rods in the bridge were at first too hot to handle. Still more bridges went up like magic, including one 780 feet long and ninety-two feet high in four and a half days. Ties by the thousands and timber for bridges were cut in the nearby woods by platoons of soldiers; others passed water by bucket brigades to still the thirst of locomotives. And the day after Sherman's first troops entered smoldering Atlanta the trains arrived. When Confederate

This spidery wooden bridge over Potomac Creek on the Richmond, Fredericksburg & Potomac Railroad was thrown up by Herman Haupt in less than two weeks, despite totally inexpert labor. It won fame when President Lincoln visited it and reported, "I have seen the most remarkable structure that human eyes ever rested upon. That man Haupt has built a bridge across Potomac Creek, about four hundred feet long and nearly a hundred feet high, over which loaded trains are running every hour, and, upon my word . . . there is nothing in it but beanpoles and cornstalks." Destroyed by retreating Union troops, to Haupt's intense irritation, it was rebuilt three times.

Sherman's men tear up rail at Atlanta in 1864.

General Hood, driven out of Atlanta and operating in Sherman's rear, destroyed thirty-five miles of track and 455 feet of bridges, not to mention supply depots, Sherman's men restored it all in thirteen days. And then, when he set to march from Atlanta to the sea, to destroy the war-making power of the Confederacy, and to live off the country, Sherman had the Western & Atlantic, so carefully restored, so painfully rebuilt, torn up once again—to protect his rear.

The still photographs of Civil War railroads, whether recently repaired or newly in ruins, are always quiet and almost unreal. Such was the state of the art of the camera. But the trains that seem almost like toys and the men posed so stiffly were a fury of activity, and the men in charge were legends. There was Herman Haupt, West Pointer turned railroad man, for instance, who ran the Military Railroads in Virginia, the angry enemy of interfering generals who became the first of many miracle bridge builders (out of nothing but "beanpoles and cornstalks," as Lincoln admiringly put it). We must add his former assistant, E. C. Smeed, who developed a way of not only bending but twisting rails to destroy them—and could build bigger bridges even faster than his old boss. Where he had passed a-building no trees grew. There was Grenville Dodge, who rebuilt the Mobile & Ohio and once, under Grant's orders, repaired one hundred miles of track and 182 bridges in forty days, a good rehearsal for his later job of building the Union Pacific. The most remarkable of all was that harsh disciplinarian from the Erie Railroad, Daniel McCallum. When the federal government started taking over captured railroads, with only six miles from Washington to Alexandria at the start, McCallum was put in charge by Secretary Stanton. By the end of the war he controlled over two thousand miles of the United States Military Railroads, mostly in Northern Virginia and the Chattanooga area, with 419 locomotives of all descriptions and thousands of cars, most of this mighty array in the West. Without McCallum's sleepless crews, Sherman said, the Atlanta Campaign "would have been impossible."

In a sense, the war ended as it began, with a railroad episode, when on April 8, 1865, Lee's last supply trains, which had just rolled into Appomattox Station to feed his hungry troops, were seized by Union cavalry in a raid led by Major General George Armstrong Custer. With all hope gone, the man who had captured John Brown now surrendered to General Grant.

How Confederate General Hood left Atlanta rail yards for Sherman: This was an ordnance train.

The Great Locomotive Chase

One of the greatest railroad stories in the annals of war, told and retold with many an embellishment by writers and film makers, is that of the Andrews Raid. In April, 1862, part of a Union army, led by General O. M. Mitchel, was moving on Huntsville, Alabama, with the further intention of then turning east and attempting to seize Chattanooga, Tennessee, which was not strongly held at the time because the major opposing armies in that theater were fighting and fencing for position farther west. James J. Andrews, a spy and contraband runner known

would bring to fame was the *General*, a classic "American" type woodburner built in 1855 by Rogers, Ketchum & Grosvenor of Paterson, New Jersey. We pick up the story as it was told after the war by a participant, the Reverend William Pittenger; then he was just Private Pittenger, Company G, Second Ohio Volunteers:

"The soldiers for this expedition, of whom the writer was one, were selected from the three Ohio regiments belonging to General J. W. Sill's brigade, being simply told that they were wanted for secret and very danger-

Georgia, more than 200 miles away, the evening of the third day after the start. When questioned, we were to profess ourselves Kentuckians going to join the Southern army.

"On the journey we were a good deal annoyed by the swollen streams and the muddy roads consequent on three days of almost ceaseless rain. Andrews was led to believe that Mitchel's column would be inevitably delayed, and as we were expected to destroy the bridges the very day that Huntsville was entered, he took the responsibility of sending

WILBUR G. KURTZ

In the scene above, the raiders scatter from the General, *her fuel now completely gone and steam pressure rapidly falling, as the* Texas, *running backward, catches up. The painting was made by Wilbur G.* Kurtz, Sr., *a devoted lifelong student of the Andrews Raid, whose meeting with such survivors as Captain Fuller of the stolen train led to his marriage with the Captain's daughter, Annie Laurie Fuller.*

to Mitchel, came to him with his scheme. With twenty-four men in civilian clothes he would penetrate deeply into rebel lines, seize a train, and effectively put the railroad between Chattanooga and its supply and reinforcement base at Atlanta out of action. Moving from south to north and cutting the wires behind him as he burned bridges, he would pass by Chattanooga and rejoin Mitchel by rail, thus signalling his success and making Mitchel's chance of victory (if indeed it was very strong) much greater. The railroad he would attack was the single-track Western & Atlantic, then operated as the Georgia State Railroad. The engine he

ous service. So far as known not a man chosen declined the perilous honor. Our uniforms were exchanged for ordinary Southern dress, and all arms, except revolvers, were left in camp. On the 7th of April, by the roadside about a mile east of Shelbyville, in the late twilight, we met our leader. Taking us a little way from the road he quietly placed before us the outlines of the romantic and adventurous plan, which was: to break into small detachments of three or four, journey eastward into the mountains, and then work southward, travelling by rail after we were well within the Confederate lines, and finally meet Andrews at Marietta,

word to our different groups that our attempt would be postponed one day—from Friday to Saturday, April 12th. This was a natural but a most lamentable error. . . .

"One of the men was belated and did not join us at all. Two others were very soon captured by the enemy, and though their true character was not detected, they were forced into the Southern army, and two, who reached Marietta, failed to report at the rendezvous. Thus, when we assembled, we were but twenty, including our leader. All preliminary difficulties had been easily overcome, and we were in good spirits. But some serious obstacles had been revealed on our ride from Chattanooga to Marietta the previous evening. The railroad was found to be crowded with trains, and many soldiers were among the passengers. Then the station—Big Shanty—at which the capture was to be effected had recently been made a Confederate camp. To succeed in our enterprise it would be necessary first to capture the engine in a guarded camp, with soldiers standing around as spectators, and then to run it from 100 to 200 miles through the enemy's country, and to deceive or overpower all trains that should be met—a large contract for twenty men! Some of our party thought the chances of success so slight, under existing circumstances, that they urged the abandonment of the whole enterprise. But Andrews declared his purpose to succeed or die, offering to each man, however, the privilege of withdrawing from the attempt—an offer no one was in the least disposed to accept. Final instructions were then given, and we hurried to the ticket office in time for the northward bound mail train, and purchased tickets for different stations along the line in the direction of Chattanooga.

"Our ride as passengers was but eight miles. We . . . soon saw the tents of the forces camped at Big Shanty (now Kennesaw Station) gleam white in the morning mist. . . . When we stopped, the conductor, engineer, and many of the passengers hurried to breakfast, leaving the train unguarded. Now was the moment of action! Andrews, our two engineers, Brown and Knight, and the fireman hurried forward, uncoupling a section of the train consisting of three empty baggage or box cars, the locomotive and tender. The engineers and fireman sprang into the cab of the engine, while Andrews, with hand on the rail and foot on the step, waited to see that the remainder of the band had gained entrance into the rear box car. . . . A sentinel, with musket in hand, stood not a dozen feet from the engine watching the whole proceeding, but before he or any of the soldiers and guards around could make up their minds to interfere, all was done, and Andrews, with a nod to his engineer, stepped on board. The valve was pulled wide open, and for a moment the wheels of 'The General' slipped around ineffectively; then, with a bound that jerked the soldiers in the box car from their feet, the little train darted away, leaving the camp in the wildest uproar. . . .

"According to the time-table, of which Andrews had secured a copy, there were two trains to be met. These presented no serious hindrance to our attaining high speed, for we could tell just where to expect them. There was also a local freight not down on the time-table, but which could not be far distant. Any danger of collision with it could be avoided by running according to the schedule of the captured train until it was passed; then, at the highest possible speed, we would run to the Oostenaula and Chickamauga bridges, lay them in ashes, and pass on through Chattanooga to Mitchel, at Huntsville, or wherever eastward of that point he might be found, arriving long before the close of the day. It was a brilliant prospect, and, so far as human estimates can determine, it would have been realized had the day been Friday instead of Saturday. On Friday every train had been on time, the day dry, and the road in perfect order. Now the road was in disorder, every train far behind time, and two 'extras' were approaching us. But of these unfavorable conditions we knew nothing, and pressed confidently forward.

"We stopped frequently, at one point tore up track, cut telegraph wires, and loaded on cross-ties to be used in bridge burning. Wood and water were taken without difficulty, Andrews telling, very coolly, the story to which he adhered throughout the run, namely, that he was an agent of General Beauregard's running an impressed powder train through to that officer at Corinth. There was a wonderful exhilaration in passing swiftly by towns and stations through the heart of an enemy's country in this manner. . . .

"At Etowah Station we found the 'Yonah,' an old locomotive owned by an iron company, standing with steam up; but not wishing to alarm the enemy till the local freight had been safely met, we left it unharmed. Kingston, thirty miles from the starting-point, was safely reached. A train from Rome, Ga., on a branch road, had just arrived and was waiting for the morning mail—our train. We learned that the local freight would soon come also, and, taking the side track, waited for it. When it arrived, however, Andrews saw to his surprise and chagrin that it bore a red flag, indicating another train not far behind. Stepping to the conductor, he boldly asked, 'What does it mean that the road is blocked in this manner when I have orders to take this powder to Beauregard without a minute's delay?' The answer was interesting but not reassuring: 'Mitchel has captured Huntsville and is said to be coming to Chattanooga, and we are getting everything out of there.' He was asked by Andrews to pull his train a long way down the track out of the way, and promptly obeyed.

"It seemed an exceedingly long time before the expected 'extra' arrived; and when it did come it bore another red flag! The reason given was that the 'local,' being too great for one engine, had been made up in two sections, and the second section would doubtless be along in a short time. This was terribly vexatious; yet there seemed nothing to do but wait. *For an hour and five minutes* from the time of arrival at Kingston, we remained in this most critical position . . . until the whistle of the expected train from the north was heard; then, as it glided up to the depot, past the end of our side track, we were off without more words.

"**B**ut unexpected danger had arisen behind us. Out of the panic at Big Shanty two men emerged, determined, if possible, to foil the unknown captors of their train. There was no telegraph station, and no locomotive at hand with which to follow; but the conductor of the train, W. A. Fuller, and Anthony Murphy, foreman of the Atlanta railway machine shops, who happened to be on board of Fuller's train, started on foot after us as hard as they could run! Finding a hand-car they mounted it and pushed forward till they neared Etowah, where they ran on the break we had made in the road and were precipitated down the embankment into the ditch. Continuing with more caution, they reached Etowah and found the 'Yonah,' which was at once pressed into service, loaded with soldiers who were at hand, and hurried with flying wheels toward Kingston. Fuller prepared to fight at that point, for he knew of the tangle of extra trains, and of the lateness of the regular trains, and did not think we would be able to pass. We had been gone only four minutes when he arrived and found himself stopped by three long, heavy trains of cars headed in the wrong direction. . . . So, abandoning his engine, he, with Murphy, ran across to the Rome train, and, uncoupling the engine and one car, pushed forward with about forty armed men. As the Rome branch connected with the main road above the depot, he encountered no hindrance, and it was now a fair race. We were not many minutes ahead.

"Four miles from Kingston we again

stopped and cut the telegraph. While trying to take up a rail at this point we heard the whistle of a pursuing engine! With a frantic pull we broke the rail and all tumbled over the embankment with the effort. We moved on, and at Adairsville we found a mixed train (freight and passenger) waiting, but there was an express on the road that had not yet arrived. We could afford no more delay, and set out for the next station, Calhoun, at terrible speed, hoping to reach that point before the express, which was behind time, should arrive. The nine miles which we had to travel were left behind in less than the same number of minutes! The express was just pulling out, but, hearing our whistle, backed before us until we were able to take the side track; it stopped, however, in such a manner as completely to close up the other end of the switch. The two trains, side by side, almost touched each other, and our precipitate arrival caused natural suspicion. Many searching questions were asked which had to be answered before we could get the opportunity of proceeding. We, in the box car, could hear the altercation. . . .

"Fuller and Murphy saw the obstruction of the broken rail, in time to prevent wreck, by reversing their engine; but the hindrance was for the present insuperable. Leaving all their men behind, they started for a second foot-race. Before they had gone far they met the train we had passed at Adairsville and turned it back after us.

"But Andrews had told the powder story again, with all his skill, and had added a direct request in peremptory form to have the way opened before him, which the Confederate conductor did not see fit to resist; and just before the pursuers arrived at Calhoun we were again under way. Stopping once more to cut wires and tear up the track, we felt a thrill of exhilaration to which we had long been strangers. The track was now clear before us to Chattanooga; and even west of that city we had good reason to believe that we would find no other train in the way till we had reached Mitchel's lines. If one rail could now be lifted we would be in a few minutes at Oostenaula bridge, and, that burned, the rest of the task would be little more than simple manual labor, with the enemy absolutely powerless. We worked with a will.

"But in a moment the tables were turned! Not far behind we heard the scream of a locomotive bearing down upon us at lightning speed! The men on board were in plain sight and well armed! Two minutes—perhaps one—would have removed the rail at which we were toiling; then the game would have been in our own hands, for there was no other locomotive beyond that could be turned back after us. But the most desperate efforts were in vain. The rail was simply bent, and we hurried to our engine and darted away, while remorselessly after us thundered the enemy.

"Now the contestants were in clear view, and a most exciting race followed. Wishing to gain a little time for the burning of the Oostenaula bridge we dropped one car, and shortly after, another; but they were 'picked up' and pushed ahead to Resaca station. We were obliged to run over the high trestles and covered bridge without a pause.

"The Confederates could not overtake and stop us on the road, but their aim was to keep close behind so that we might not be able to damage the road or take in wood or water. In the former they succeeded, but not the latter. Both engines were put at the highest rate of speed. We were obliged to cut the wire after every station passed, in order that an alarm might not be sent ahead, and we constantly strove to throw our pursuer off the track or to obstruct the road permanently in some way so that we might be able to burn the Chickamauga bridges, still ahead. The chances seemed good that Fuller and Murphy would be wrecked. We broke out the end of our last box car and dropped crossties on the track as we ran, thus checking their progress and getting far enough ahead to take in wood and water at two separate stations. Several times we almost lifted a rail, but each time the coming of the Confederates, within rifle range, compelled us to desist and speed on. Our worst hindrance was the rain. The previous day (Friday) had been clear, with a high wind, and on such a day fire would have been easily and tremendously effective. But to-day a bridge could be burned only with abundance of fuel and careful nursing.

"Thus we sped on, mile after mile, in this fearful chase, around curves and past stations in seemingly endless perspective. Whenever we lost sight of the enemy beyond a curve we hoped that some of our obstructions had been effective in throwing him from the track and that we would see him no more; but at each long reach backward the smoke was again seen, and the shrill whistle was like the scream of a bird of prey. The time could not have been so very long, for the terrible speed was rapidly devouring the distance, but with our nerves strained to the highest tension each minute seemed an hour. On several occasions the escape of the enemy from wreck seemed little less than miraculous. At one point a rail was placed across the track so skillfully on a curve that it was not seen till the train ran upon it at full speed. Fuller says that they were terribly jolted, and seemed to bounce altogether from the track, but lighted on the rails in safety. . . .

"Before reaching Dalton we urged Andrews to turn and attack the enemy, laying an ambush so as to get into close quarters that our revolvers might be on equal terms with their guns. I have little doubt that if this had been carried out it would have succeeded. . . .

"Dalton was passed without difficulty, and beyond we stopped again to cut wires and obstruct the track. It happened that a regiment was encamped not a hundred yards away, but they did not molest us. Fuller had written a dispatch to Chattanooga, and dropped a man with orders to have it forwarded instantly while he pushed on to save the bridges. Part of the message got through and created a wild panic in Chattanooga, although it did not materially influence our fortunes. Our supply of fuel was now very short, and without getting rid of our pursuer long enough to take in more, it was evident that we could not run as far as Chattanooga.

"While cutting the wire we made an attempt to get up another rail, but the enemy, as usual, were too quick for us. We had no tool for this purpose except a wedge-pointed iron bar. Two or three bent iron claws for pulling out spikes would have given us such superiority, that, down to almost the last of our run, we would have been able to escape and to burn all the Chickamauga bridges. . . .

"We made no attempt to damage the long tunnel north of Dalton, as our enemies had greatly dreaded. The last hope of the raid was now staked upon an effort of a different kind. A few more obstructions were dropped on the track and our speed was increased so that we soon forged a considerable distance ahead. The side and end boards of the last car were torn into shreds, all available fuel was piled upon it, and blazing brands were brought back from the engine. By the time we approached a long covered bridge the fire in the car was fairly started. We uncoupled it in the middle of the bridge, and with painful suspense awaited the issue. Oh, for a few minutes till the work of conflagration was fairly begun! There was still steam-pressure enough in our boiler to carry us to the next wood-yard, where we could have replenished our fuel, by force if necessary, so as to run as near to Chattanooga as was deemed prudent. We did not know of the telegraph message which the pursuers had sent ahead. But, alas! the minutes were not given. Before the bridge was extensively fired the enemy was upon us. They pushed right into the smoke and drove the burning car before them to the next side-track.

"With no car left, and no fuel, the last scrap having been thrown into the engine or upon the burning car, and with no obstruction to drop on the track, our situation was indeed desperate.

"But it might still be possible to save ourselves if we left the train in a body and took a direct course toward the Union lines. Confederate pursuers with whom I have since conversed have agreed on two points—that we could have escaped in the manner here pointed out; and that an attack on the pursuing train would likely have been successful. But Andrews thought otherwise, at least in relation to the former plan, and ordered us to jump from the locomotive, and, dispersing in the woods, each to save himself.

"The question is often asked, 'Why did you not reverse your engine and thus wreck the one following?' Wanton injury was no part of our plan, and we could not afford to throw away our engine till the last extremity. When the raiders were jumping off, however, the engine was reversed and driven back, but by that time the steam was so nearly exhausted that the Confederate engine had no difficulty in reversing and receiving the shock without injury. Both were soon at a stand-still, and the Confederates, reenforced by a party from a train which soon arrived on the scene—the express passenger, which had been turned back at Calhoun—continued the chase on foot. . . .

The hunt for the fugitive raiders was prompt, energetic, and successful. Several were captured the same day, and all but two within a week. Even these two were overtaken and brought back, when they supposed that they were virtually out of danger. Two who had reached Marietta, but had failed to board the train . . . were identified and added to the band of prisoners.

The last reunion of veterans of the Andrews Raid was photographed in front of the memorial in the Chattanooga National Cemetery. Andrews and the others lie behind it. Left to right, John R. Porter, who overslept at Marietta, missing the ride but not capture; William Knight, engineer who ran the General *for Andrews; raiders William Bensinger and Jacob Parrott; Henry Haney, fireman of the* Texas; *Anthony Murphy, Fuller's fellow-sprinter; and Daniel Dorsey, another raider. Porter lived longest, until 1923, proving once again the importance of getting enough sleep.*

"Now follows the saddest part of the story. Being in citizens' dress within an enemy's lines, the whole party were held as spies. A court-martial was convened, and the leader and seven out of the remaining twenty-one were condemned and executed. . . . Of the remaining fourteen, eight succeeded, by a bold effort,—attacking their guard in broad daylight,—in making their escape from Atlanta, Ga., and ultimately in reaching the North. The other six, who shared in this effort, but were recaptured, remained prisoners until the latter part of March, 1863, when they were exchanged through a special arrangement made by Secretary Stanton. All the survivors of this expedition received medals and promotion. The pursuers also received expressions of gratitude from their fellow Confederates."

The decorations the survivors received were the first Congressional Medals of Honor ever awarded; then the men were taken in to talk with President Lincoln. Those who paid with their lives were reburied in 1891 at the Chattanooga National Cemetery behind a memorial given by the State of Ohio and topped with a likeness of the *General* (see picture), but, alas! as she looked when converted to a coal-burner, without her bonnet stack. She was damaged in the explosion of an ammunition train during Hood's evacuation of Atlanta in 1864 (a great moment as re-created in *Gone With the Wind*), but was repaired. In the 1890's, barely escaping the scrapyard, she was "restored" somewhat for exhibition at the World's Fair of 1893 at Chicago. She has scarcely missed an exposition since, and in the 1960's was "shopped" again by her owners, the Louisville & Nashville, so that she could run around a united country again under her own power, pursued only by railroad buffs. Air brakes were hidden in her tender so as not to spoil her "period" appearance. How much of the *General* today is original it is hard to say, but after many adventures, including latter-day seizures and lawsuits between towns contending to keep and exhibit her, she may be seen, at least *pro tem*, at Big Shanty Museum, in Kennesaw, Georgia. The *Texas*, the last of her pursuing engines, is now on exhibit in Atlanta, but the *Yonah* and the other engine, the *William R. Smith*, have crossed over Jordan.

A Trip to Gettysburg

Railroads had played an important role in the Battle of Gettysburg in July of 1863. Herman Haupt, who had lived in that town, figured prominently in organizing and repairing the railroad routes into that area—lines like the Northern Central and the Hanover Branch Railroad. He fought hard to get out trains of wounded over routes blocked by stalled supply shipments. Haupt had been a classmate at West Point of General George G. Meade, which did not stop him from rushing to Washington in a special night train to urge vainly that Meade be pressed to pursue and strike the retreating Confederate Army.

Over five months after the battle, when the dead had been buried in a new national cemetery, a special train took Abraham Lincoln to the consecration. On the way the President once again passed through Baltimore, but this time openly in the light of day, with cheers ringing in his ears as the teams of horses drew his car through the streets from Camden Station to the Bolton Station of the Northern Central.

The special paused at Hanover Junction, where the branch to Gettysburg turned off. The scene at right is of the Junction. So is the picture above, showing ladies, photographers, and military men on hand for the Lincoln special. The unsettled argument is whether the tall figure on the platform, in characteristic stovepipe hat, is Abraham Lincoln, and whether these mere coaches are his train, which started from Washington with four more elegant cars. Did he change? Why two dapper men—guards, perhaps?—are standing on the deck roof no one knows, but it is evident that the whole company, engineer and fireman included, are posing for the distant photographer, who must be standing atop another car. And we have a good view of contemporary station architecture and a fine, boxlike little locomotive with a cap stack and a shiny pair of signal lanterns hanging out in front.

Abraham Lincoln Goes Home

This private car, with handsome staterooms and extra-length beds, was built for President Lincoln but used by him only in death, its rich brown woodwork draped in black crepe, its guards wearing mourning. Carried near the end of the train, the car is out of the picture below, taken on the lakefront at Michigan City, Indiana. The care and precautions the many railroads used for this occasion are exemplified in the Hudson River line's special instructions seen at top right.

The assassination of Abraham Lincoln and his funeral journey home put a Shakespearian ending to the tragedy of the American Civil War. After the week of services and lying-in-state in Washington, the nine-car funeral special pulled out on the Baltimore & Ohio at eight in the morning of April 21, 1865, a Negro regiment lined up along the tracks as an honor guard. The bodies of the President and his little son Willie, who had died in 1862, were in the special car, and the rest of the train housed his grieving family and a large party of civil and military mourners. To the sound of minute guns and tolling church bells this sad procession moved, generally at a deliberate twenty miles per hour, along the long route that Lincoln had followed when he came east in 1861 on his way into history, leaving out only Cincinnati. At places like Baltimore, Harrisburg, Philadelphia, New York, and major cities all the way to its final resting place in Springfield, Illinois, Lincoln's body was taken off his car to lie in state and be seen by sorrowing crowds. The trip took a week, in an almost symbolic rain.

INSTRUCTIONS.

This train has the right of track over all other trains bound in either direction, and trains must reach Stations at which they are to meet, or let Special pass, at least ten minutes before Special is due.

A "Pilot Engine" will leave New-York 10 minutes in advance of Special Train, running 10 minutes ahead of published time to East Albany. Pilot Engine has same rights as Special, and at Stations where trains meet or pass it, they must wait for Special.

The train will run at a Slow rate of speed through all Towns and Villages.

Train No. 10 will, on this day, leave 30th Street at 4.15 P. M.

All Station Masters, Trackmen, Drawbridge Tenders, Switchmen and Flagmen will be governed by the General Rules and Regulations of the Company.

J. M. TOUCEY,
Ass't Sup't.

Leave New-York, (30th Street)	4.00 P. M.
" Manhattan	4.20 "
" Yonkers	4.45 "
" Dobbs' Ferry	5.00 "
" Irvington	5.07 "
" Tarrytown	5.15 "
" Sing Sing	5.30 "
Arrive PEEKSKILL	5.57 "
Leave PEEKSKILL	6.00 "
" Garrison's	6.26 "
" Cold Spring	6.33 "
" Fishkill	6.50 "
" New Hamburgh	7.06 "
Arrive PO'KEEPSIE	7.25 "
Leave PO'KEEPSIE	7.40 "
" Hyde Park	7.56 "
" Staatsburgh	8.08 "
" Rhinebeck	8.24 "
" Barrytown	8.40 "
" Tivoli	8.52 "
" Germantown	9.10 "
" Catskill	9.27 "
Arrive HUDSON	9.38 "
Leave HUDSON	9.41 "
" Stockport	9.52 "
" Coxsackie	10.00 "
" Stuyvesant	10.07 "
" Schodack	10.26 "
" Castleton	10.35 "
Arrive EAST ALBANY	10.55 "

4. The Race to Promontory

4. The Race to Promontory

Theodore Dehone Judah, born in Bridgeport, Connecticut, in 1826, was the true father of the Central Pacific Railroad, although, even before his early death in 1863, it was taken away from him by the "Big Four" who completed the job.

PRECEDING PAGES: *The Union Pacific construction crews have crossed Green River, Wyoming, in 1868 on a temporary bridge and masons are setting out piers for a more permanent replacement. A. J. Russell's photo also shows Citadel Rock.*

If the Pacific Railroad, the greatest physical achievement of nineteenth-century America, had been built in the age of fable, it would in the natural course have been converted into a kind of *Iliad* or *Aeneid*, celebrated, half believed, and endlessly interpreted; Shakespeare would have recast it; Hollywood at length would have made the epic again (indeed, it tried) with the usual cast of thousands; and no one would have done it justice. As in a true epic, the narrative concerns an immense challenge, that of throwing rails across endless plains and terrifying mountain ranges the like of which neither Homer nor Virgil could have imagined. By way of prologue, prophets and visionaries appear as heralds. Then the vast stage is taken over by two great antagonists, two companies racing toward each other in bitter rivalry, one from the east, one from the west, to meet somewhere in the wilderness. Since there are great financial rewards for every mile laid, each seeks to outbuild the other, and sometimes to undo the other's work. The hordes of workmen are like two armies—in fact, they are armies, as great as most in antiquity—and different races contend as well: white men against red men on one hand, Irish tracklayers for the Union Pacific against Chinese for the Central Pacific on the other. And while this heroic cast struggles in the field, other more powerful and occasionally sinister figures who direct the armies or profit from them scheme and battle for advantage in the background. Generals, lawgivers, and at least four Presidents of the republic, present or future, make appearances. If there is no Helen of Troy, there are plenty of lesser temptresses along the way, and there is a tremendous prize, the empire of the West. There is wealth for some and poverty and death for others, and the rewards are not necessarily given to the deserving, as is the habit of history.

Have we pushed the epic image too far? To travel the route of the very first transcontinental railroad today, or such of its 1,780 miles as Amtrak services, to experience its long tunnels, high bridges, deep cuts, and spectacular mountain scenery, is to wonder whether we are today the equals of men who with their bare hands laid these long ribbons of metal over a century ago. It is a thought reinforced for those with long memories by the announcement in 1974 by New York administrators under Mayor Abraham Beame that it would take until 1980 to complete a three-thousand-foot connection from the existing Long Island Railroad to Kennedy Airport. Three thousand *feet*! The Union Pacific located and laid 568 miles in one year; the track gangs of the Central Pacific once did ten between sunup and sundown. When the rails were linked in 1869, America went wild with celebration. Yet, a few years later, when investigators had probed the financial machinations, the national mood changed. As a respected Massachusetts senator, George Hoar, put it: "When the greatest railroad in the world, binding together the continent and uniting two great seas which wash our shores, was finished, I have seen our national triumph and exaltation turned to bitterness and shame."

The Great West was barely purchased from Napoleon and the railroad invented when men began to dream of linking the Atlantic to the Pacific. In 1845 Asa Whitney, a Connecticut Yankee, put before Congress his idea of setting aside a sixty-mile-wide strip of land from the Mississippi to the Pacific at the Columbia River; the railroad would pay for itself by selling land, timber, and minerals and by developing cities along the way. By the 1850's, after the Mexican War, the acquisition of California and the Southwest, and the Gold Rush, the fever to go west rose in intensity. Under Jefferson Davis as Secretary of War, Army topographical engineers surveyed five different general routes across the West over which a railroad might be constructed. In view of the fierce sectional rivalry of the era, it is not surprising that Southerners favored southern routes and Northerners northern ones; in any case nothing could be agreed on; and besides, the Army had not in fact actually attempted to lay out roadbeds.

In 1854, however, there arrived in California, newly hired to engineer a short railroad from Sacramento into the Sierra foothills, a twenty-seven-year-old native of Bridgeport, Connecticut, named Theodore Dehone Judah. He had surveyed railroads in New England, and built one along the Niagara Gorge, but in California his sense of mission, or monomania, fell upon him. Why should a man spend six months by sailing ship around the Horn, or several months in steamboats and a land trip across Central America (as he had just done with his young wife), or risk the dangers of a wagon train or the overland coaches, to get to California? Judah would instead drive rails across the Sierras eastward, and build a railroad across America. Everywhere he went, and to everyone whom he met in that vigorous new state, Judah talked his great idea, so tirelessly and persistently that he came to be known as "Crazy" Judah.

The idea itself was popular, however tiresome at times its propagandist, and Judah played a part in bringing about a Pacific Railroad Convention in San Francisco in September, 1859. Enough enthusiasm was generated to send him to Washington to try to sell the convention's idea to the government.

In the Capital Judah talked to everyone who would listen; he wrote; he opened a kind of little museum on his favorite subject, but Buchanan's Washington, preoccupied with its troubles over slavery and secession, gave him no encouragement. Judah and his wife made the long journey home while he assured her that his railroad "will be built, and I'm going to have something to do with it." Back in California, Judah submitted the most modest expense account in history for such an expedition ($40 for printing his bills and circulars) and struck off for the summer to survey a railroad route in the Sierra Nevada, the wide range of forbidding, snow-capped mountains which shuts off the California plain from Nevada and the east. Perhaps with more precise figures and a possible route, he decided, he could be more persuasive.

Moving up from the mining settlement of Dutch Flat, Judah came upon the famous Donner and Emigrant passes, only a couple of miles apart. An old wagon route led through them into the gorge of the Truckee River and the flatlands of Nevada and the sites of new mining strikes. That autumn of 1860, he returned during the first snowfall to Dutch Flat and in the store of his friend, a druggist named Dr. Daniel Strong, drew up the "Articles of Association of the Central Pacific Railroad of California." And the two men set out to raise money for the 115 miles of proposed rails from Sacramento to the Nevada state line. To be incorporated under California law, they had first to obtain pledges of at least $1,000 for each mile of track. Some was raised at Dutch Flat, but little elsewhere. Disappointed in San Francisco, Judah went

Grenville Mellen Dodge, born in 1831 in Danvers, Massachusetts, took up railroad surveying, made a distinguished record in the Civil War. He built not only the Union Pacific but many other railroads, dying full of fame and honor in 1916.

The Central Pacific crews hit mountainous country long before the rival Union Pacific. Here is Bloomer Cut, eight hundred feet long and all blasted out

of a dense mass of aggregate, in 1865.

The U.P. grade stretches to infinity behind Construction Superintendent Samuel Reed.

to Sacramento where, one June night of 1861 in a room over a hardware store, destiny awaited him. It took an unlikely form. There were perhaps a dozen local men on hand as Judah unrolled his maps, his estimates, and his profiles. And that night he was wise enough to restrain his tongue, saying little about a railroad across America and a great deal about a practical way for Sacramento merchants to move their goods to the new Nevada mining camps, to expand their businesses, to get government help, and to wind up with a monopoly over the route.

Judah's message, which must have been eloquent that night, stirred four merchants particularly. One was a slow-spoken, ponderous wholesale grocer with political ambitions named Leland Stanford, one an overweight drygoods man named Charles Crocker, and the other two ran the hardware store over which the meeting was taking place. One of these was the reedy and frugal bookkeeper Mark Hopkins (not ever to be confused with the noted educator of the same name), and the other his younger, chunkier partner, Collis P. Huntington, a transplanted Connecticut Yankee who had (outside of Judah) most of the brains in the room. They would become the famous and infamous "Big Four" who risked their modest fortunes to make Judah's vision come true. Over the years they would enrich themselves beyond the dreams of avarice and turn the Central Pacific, and its mammoth stepchild, the Southern Pacific, into the so-called "Octopus." According to one's point of view, that company either helped to build or tyrannized California for four decades. All this lay in the future, however, as they incorporated the company with themselves as officers and resolved at once to send their Chief Engineer Judah back once again to Washington to lobby for aid.

Although anything to do with government takes time, aid was forthcoming. With a war on, with no more Southerners around to wrangle over the route, with the recognized need to keep California and the West in the Union, with an army of lobbyists, and without any real opposition, a Pacific Railroad Act went through Congress and was signed by President Lincoln on July 1, 1862. It provided that two companies would build the great project: A new one called the Union Pacific would lay track westward from Omaha, Nebraska, just across the Missouri River from Council Bluffs; and the Central Pacific Company would start east from Sacramento to meet them at the California-Nevada boundary. And it provided the financial aid without which the roads could never have been built. Each company was given a right-of-way strip, plus any land needed for yards and other facilities and five alternate land sections (a section is 640 acres) per mile built, on each side of the track, or ten altogether. The land, such of it that was arable, possessed no value then except to the Indians, who were not consulted although occasionally mollified with small gifts and free rides behind the iron horse when they came making the peace sign. The grants would have value only when linked to the outside world. What counted most were the loans that the federal government offered each company for construction, as a kind of first mortgage on the properties. They took the form of thirty-year bonds at low interest and were to be issued on a kind of scale of difficulty—$16,000 per mile of track in the flatlands, $48,000 per mile in mountainous areas, and $32,000 per mile in the intermediate plateaus between mountain ranges. Each company had one to cross, the Union Pacific over the Rockies and the Central across the Sierras. Judah wired the news of his triumph back to his partners in Sacramento: "We have drawn the elephant. Now let us see if we can harness him up."

Judah arrived back in California to discover that the Big Four were taking over his dream. Stanford, elected governor of the state in 1861, lobbied through various local bond issues and loans which eventually brought the Central Pacific an additional $3,000,000. And he found experts, including Professor Josiah Whitney, the state's first official geologist, to swear that the Sierras began not in their real foothills but in the very slowly rising plain twenty-two miles east of them, just outside Sacramento. The Interior Department back in Washington, which knew little about it, approved, and California Representative Aaron Sargent persuaded Lincoln to consent, which allowed the Central Pacific to collect the mountain rate of $48,000 for that almost flat trackage. "Here, you see," Sargent jested afterward, "my pertinacity and Abraham's faith moved mountains." One mountain, the highest in the state, was named for the professor. When construction began, rather slowly, in early 1863, the Big Four who ran the railroad incorporated themselves in the person of Crocker as the contractors to build it, at great profit to themselves whatever the fortunes of the stockholders in the railroad itself. Conflict of interest indeed surrounded the Central Pacific like a cocoon, but so it did the building of nearly all great railroads in the mid-nineteenth century. The horrified Judah was soon eased out, and given $100,000 for his stock. Returning east hoping, it is believed, to find some other financing to back him in regaining control, he contracted yellow fever while crossing the Isthmus of Panama and died soon after reaching New York. Stanford became the political front for the company in California, Hopkins the treasurer, and Crocker, accompanied by a Chinese valet and carrying saddlebags full of gold coin to reward the diligent, took over as the construction boss in the field. At this, for all his vast girth, he turned out to be enormously successful. The quiet Huntington, the real boss, went to Washington to handle the all-important lobbying. Their risks were great, but the money tree was in position, and four eager men were ready to shake it.

The rival Union Pacific had no such harmony or tidy financial arrangements as the Big Four's. It was chartered by Congress in 1862 with an authorized capital of $100,000,000, with 162 federal commissioners—noted railroad and financial men—whose real job was to get its stock sold and its management organized. There was a nominal president, a well-known general named John A. Dix, but the real enterprisers were financial sharks. The most important and its first chief lobbyist was a nonpracticing physician and

The Big Four who ran the Central Pacific consisted of Leland Stanford (upper left), Charles Crocker (upper right), Collis P. Huntington (lower left), and Mark Hopkins. Of their partnership, Huntington said, "We were successful, we four, because of our teamwork. Each complemented the other in something the other lacked. There was Stanford, for instance, a man elected senator and governor, a man who loved to deal with people. He was a good lawyer. There was Mark Hopkins. He was a fine accountant and understood the value of everything. He was a thrifty man. Then, there was Crocker, the organizer, the executive, the driver of men." Huntington, the real boss, handled the behind-the-scenes work in the East, and outlived all the others. Their cooperation among themselves stood in marked contrast to the squabbling within the Union Pacific.

"I have found," said the Crédit Mobilier's Congressman Oakes Ames, "there is no difficulty in inducing men to look after their own property."

railroad promoter, Dr. Thomas C. Durant. There was a colorful propagandist and drumbeater, the noted eccentric George Francis Train. There was a front man, Sidney Dillon, later the railroad's president, and there were the Massachusetts shovel makers, Oakes and Oliver Ames, the so-called "Boston Crowd" that at one point elbowed aside the Durant crowd. Durant—aided by Collis Huntington—persuaded Congress and the President in 1863 to sweeten the deal in the original Pacific Railroad Act of the year before, doubling the land grants at a stroke and, more significantly, reducing the per-mile bonds from a first- to a second-mortgage issue. Railroad bonds sold better than stocks; only $218,000 of the U.P.'s original stock issue could be placed. But now it could issue its own first-mortgage bonds.

It was Train, a man who looked like Mephistopheles and was given to such bombastic statements as "The Pacific Railroad is the nation, and the nation is the Pacific Railroad!" (he thought of himself as its true father), who devised for Durant the infamous Crédit Mobilier, the titular construction company which contracted to build most of the Union Pacific. Train named it for the French joint-stock company of the Second Empire which had started out making loans on movable personal (that is, mobile) property, and which, before its collapse in the midst of scandal in 1871, had become a major force in banking in that wheeling and dealing era. Like the Big Four, the men in financial control of the Union Pacific employed themselves to build it, paying their Crédit Mobilier considerably more than the true cost of construction and materials. The real construction work, of course, was done by others. Durant's first chief engineer, the honest Peter A. Dey, had estimated his per-mile cost out of Omaha at $30,000. Durant then asked him to prepare his figures on the basis of better grades and wider roadbeds, upon which Dey pondered and raised the sum to about $50,000. Through a predecessor deal to the Crédit Mobilier, contractor Durant billed railroad vice president Durant for $60,000, and ordered the line built to the original cheap standard. The idea, as the Doctor neatly put it, was to "grab a wad from the construction fees—and get out." But it was Dey who got out.

If the Ames brothers of Easton, Massachusetts, had been content to sell their shovels to the Union Pacific, they would have made money enough. But Oakes was a member of Congress from 1863 to 1873, and important in the committee on railroads. Presently he was a heavy investor in the Crédit Mobilier; and beginning in 1867, seeking, as he incautiously wrote a friend, "more friends in this Congress," he began distributing stock to key politicians for much less than its true value. His gifts descended "where they will do us the most good," he said, to men as noted as Vice President Schuyler Colfax, Speaker James G. Blaine, Representative James A. Garfield, and two future Vice Presidents, Henry Wilson and Levi P. Morton. Then, in December, 1867, he cut a melon—a 100 percent dividend on the capital. Sidney Dillon went in as president of the Crédit, replacing Durant, who was, however, still vice president of the railroad. Oliver Ames became the Union Pacific president. Things went smoothly for a time; the Pacific Railroad had no trouble in a Congress on which both the Crédit Mobilier and the generous Mr. Huntington of

This simplified map shows the main lines of the Central and Union Pacific railroads to their meeting at Promontory, Utah, with some but not all of the construction camps and other sites indicated. On this scale the map cannot show the route's twists and turns. The branch to Salt Lake City was built in 1869 to mollify Brigham Young, who had wanted the main line to come there. Nevada became a state in 1864, Nebraska in 1867, and Wyoming Territory was broken off from Dakota Territory in 1868, all while the Pacific Railroad was building. A more complete map of the same lines in 1893 appears on pages 250–51.

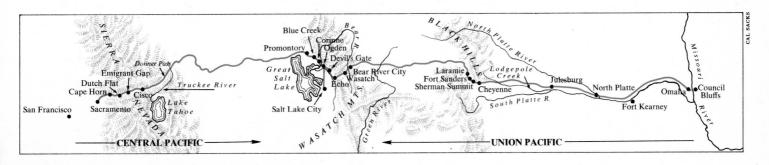

Here in all its glory, with a bar every few feet, is Bear River City, near the Utah-Wyoming border, one of the Union Pacific construction towns known as "Hell on Wheels" for their moral atmosphere and their habit of soon moving on to the next base, leaving only litter and graves behind. Opposite below, construction boss Jack Casement poses before his huge work train. It fell to him to purge such towns as this of the criminal element.

California showered so many blessings. Its stock, of course, was distended with water, and there were those who grasped what was happening. In 1869, according to that pillar of rectitude, Charles Francis Adams, Jr., the grandson and great-grandson of Presidents and (which would have astonished him at the time) later president of the Union Pacific himself, the Crédit Mobilier "is another name for the Pacific Railroad ring. The members of it are in Congress; they are trustees for the bondholders; they are directors; they are stockholders; they are contractors; in Washington they vote the subsidies, in New York they receive them, upon the plains they expend them. . . . Ever shifting characters, they are ubiquitous; they receive money into one hand and pay it into the other. . . ."

Eventually, as we ought to know from Teapot Dome and Watergate, someone blows the whistle on any scandal in which many are involved. That happened in 1872. A man who was squeezed out of the Crédit Mobilier went to court, and damaging letters from Ames came to light. Many reputations were stained and some were destroyed. Oakes Ames, who some commentators believe had not entirely selfish motives but a blind moral eye to his favorite project, named names and figures. While their peers in the Congress strained to explain away their "misunderstandings" and innocent "indiscretions," the House censured both Republican Oakes Ames and Representative James Brooks, a Crédit Mobilier investor who had the misfortune to be a Democrat. The vote, one sardonic newspaper observed, was a warning "to corrupt

Congressmen against turning State's evidence." Both Ames and Brooks, broken by the scandal, died within weeks. It is easy, however, to play muckraker, especially a century later—or even a few years later. Seas are not discovered by the scrupulous, nor continents conquered by mild churchgoers; there was risk at every step in building the Pacific Railroad, and most of those who undertook the job did it with the hope of gain. At one point the Ames shovel fortune was mortgaged to keep paying Union Pacific bills.

Out on the plains and mountains, quite another story was being enacted as General Grenville Dodge, who succeeded Peter Dey as chief engineer, actually built the railroad. Even before the war, he had been its advocate and he knew from firsthand experience as a surveyor the route along which he would begin—out the broad valley of the Platte from a start at Omaha on the Missouri River. One day in August, 1859, after he had just returned from a surveying trip, he was resting after dinner on the stoop of the Pacific House in Council Bluffs when Abraham Lincoln sat down beside him; Lincoln was then well known, of course, but not yet candidate of the Republican party for President. He had come, in fact, to make a speech and to look into some property he had acquired. "By his kindly ways," Dodge wrote much later, Lincoln "soon drew from me all I knew of the country west, and the result of my reconnaissances. As the saying is, he completely 'shelled my woods,' getting all the secrets that were later to go to my employers."

Lincoln was a believer in the railroad, and would run on a platform with

(Continued on page 96)

Memories of the Crédit Mobilier

Through a dummy construction company called the Crédit Mobilier, Thomas C. Durant, the real financial power in the Union Pacific, and his cronies paid themselves inflated prices for the work and supplies required by the advancing railroad, at least until Durant's power was seized by Congressman Oakes Ames. At right are a certificate of Crédit stock issued to the railroad; a visit in a private car, with Durant (second from right) flanked by two other directors, John Duff on his left and Sidney Dillon on his right; and the New York Sun headline when one disgruntled insider blew the whistle on the Crédit and Ames' gifts of its stock to his cooperative fellow legislators.

INCORPORATED UNDER A SPECIAL ACT OF THE STATE OF PENNSYLVANIA.

THE CREDIT MOBILIER OF AMERICA

No. 58

454 SHARES

This Certifies that Union Pacific Ry Co. is entitled to Four hundred fifty four Shares in the Capital Stock of the **Credit Mobilier of America** on which have been paid $200 on each share transferable on the Books of the Company in person or by Attorney at the office of the Treasurer in the City of Philadelphia, or at any Transfer Agency established by the Company, only upon surrender of this Certificate and payment of all instalments then due.

Witness the signatures of the President and Secretary of the Company Dated at the Transfer Agency in the City of New York this 18 day of December 1869

Benjamin F. Ham Auth Secretary

President

CAPITAL $25,000,000 IN 25,000 SHARES OF $100 EACH WITH POWER TO INCREASE TO $10,000,000.

ONE HUNDRED DOLLARS PAR VALUE OF SHARES

Stamp

At Fort Sanders, Dakota Territory, in 1868, General Grant came out to settle the argument between Dodge, at far left, and Durant, slouching at

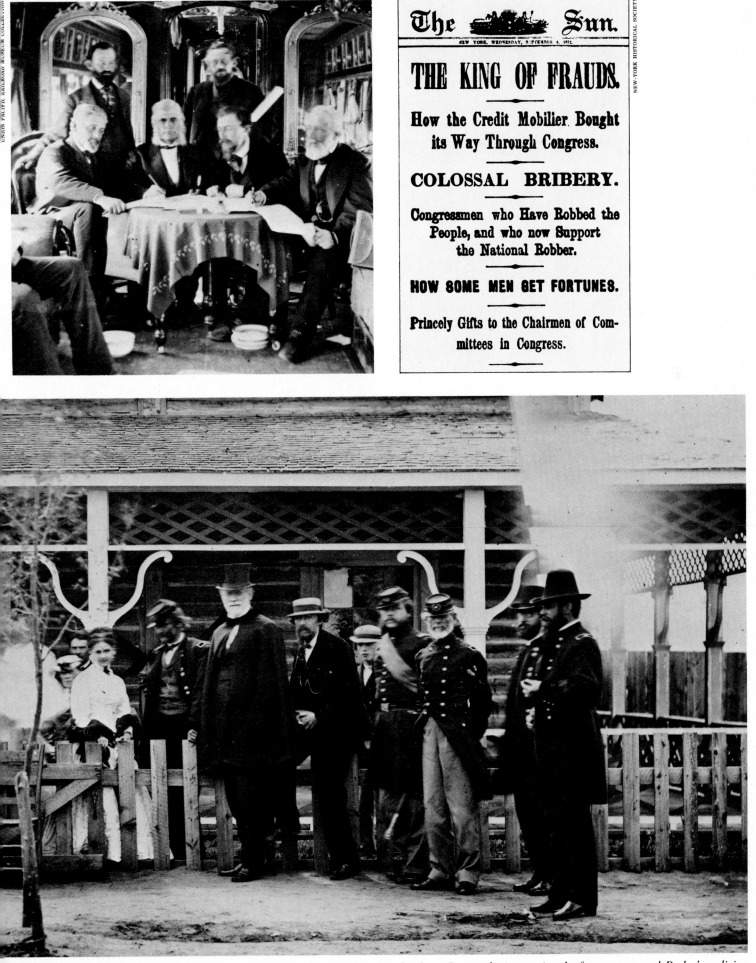

The Sun.

NEW YORK, WEDNESDAY, SEPTEMBER 4, 1872.

THE KING OF FRAUDS.

How the Credit Mobilier Bought its Way Through Congress.

COLOSSAL BRIBERY.

Congressmen who Have Robbed the People, and who now Support the National Robber.

HOW SOME MEN GET FORTUNES.

Princely Gifts to the Chairmen of Committees in Congress.

right next to top-hatted General Harney. General W. T. Sherman is framed in the door. Grant, who is grasping the fence, supported Dodge's policies.

With a crude crane to handle the stone, Union Pacific masons put together the footings for the permanent bridge over the Green River, at the same site shown on pages 82–83. The shadow of the official railroad photographer, A. J. Russell, appears at right foreground; he is standing on the temporary wooden bridge over which the tracks first passed. His sharp, clear views, eight hundred in all, are an unmatched historical achievement.

a strong plank on that subject. In the spring of 1863, when Dodge was a general with a fine record both as a combat officer and a military railroad builder, President Lincoln sent for him again. Dodge feared that he was about to be reprimanded for having taken the much criticized step of arming Negroes in his command for guard duty, but Lincoln wanted to talk Union Pacific again. There was a question as to which Missouri River town was to be the terminus, and the two men settled on Omaha, even though no railroad had yet reached across Iowa to Council Bluffs, the town on the other side of the river. As the conversation proceeded, Dodge ventured the opinion that the government should build the Union Pacific, saying private enterprise could never handle it. To that Lincoln replied that he had his hands more than full with the war, and that he would have to see that private enterprise got the support it needed. All this Dodge reported to Durant in New York, which certainly contributed to the passage of the amended Pacific Railroad bills in their more generous form.

Since he enjoyed the confidence of both Generals Grant and Sherman, as soon as the war ended Dodge was sent out west to conduct the Indian campaigns of 1865 and 1866, which was a convenient opportunity to clear out the hostiles from the proposed railroad line and seek out passes with gentle grades through the Black Hills and the Wasatch Mountains. While returning from the Powder River campaign, he rode up Lodgepole Creek one day to the summit of Cheyenne Pass, then struck south along the crest of the mountains for a good look at the country. He had six troopers and a scout with him while his main body of troops and train were moving to the east at the base of the mountains, although within occasional sight of smoke signals. At noon Dodge's small party was set upon by Indians coming up between them and the troops. Racing to the top of a ridge, Dodge's small party dismounted and started eastward down it, holding the enemy at bay with their Winchesters, hoping to catch the eye of a relief force with a signal, which only happened just before nightfall. On the way Dodge could not help noticing that the ridge descended gently without a break. If they saved their scalps, Dodge told the scout, this would be a fine place for a railroad to cross the Black Hills, the only good one he had found in years of hunting. There the line eventually went, and the pass was named for General Sherman, who was good enough to release Dodge from his command in 1866 in order to head the construction of the Union Pacific.

Dodge took charge on May 1, 1866, and by the time winter halted construction that year he had built 293 miles to put his new base construction camp at North Platte, Nebraska. Each year thereafter the pace speeded up even more while Dodge organized his vast project like an army, numbering about ten thousand men and as many draft animals. Hundreds of miles ahead were the surveying parties, consisting of a chief engineer, his assistant, rodmen, flagmen, and chainmen, plus axemen, teamsters, and hunters, with a small military escort posted on the flanks. Following them came the location men to stake out the exact grades and curves and then the grading crews, working several hundred miles ahead of the tracklayers. For these thousands of hard-handed graders steady processions of wagon trains had to haul supplies and provisions in enormous quantities, not to mention herds of cattle to provide the regular diet of beef. Little of the ubiquitous buffalo meat was used. Bridge-building gangs worked some five to twenty miles ahead, sometimes putting up fairly flimsy structures, but the track crews rarely had to wait for a bridge or an embankment. The logistics behind all this effort are fascinating to contemplate, for the plains offered neither wood nor iron nor food, nor any means of fabrication. Everything had to be brought from the east over a single line of track from Omaha. And since no railroad reached Council Bluffs and Omaha until late 1867, those same supplies had to come up the Missouri in steamboats during the few months that navigation was possible, up that shallow river which, Senator Thomas Hart Benton said, was too thick to swim in but not thick enough to walk on.

The greatest sight on the Union Pacific, according to all who witnessed it, was the tracklaying. Dodge's construction bosses, the brothers Jack and Dan Casement, had put together a work train of twenty or more cars which carried everything: carpenters' and machine shops, feed stores and a saddlery, kitchens, offices, telegraph, a general store, water cars, and sleeping accommodations for all ranks. The work itself functioned like an assembly line. A supply train would come up the single track behind the construction train and dump off thousands of rails, ties, fishplates, spikes, rods, switch stands, and everything needful. It would then head back east and the construction train would also back up to just behind the pile of new supplies.

Little flatcars, pulled by a horse and usually driven by some urchin, would load up, and move up on the last finished rails. Out ahead the ties went down, five to a twenty-eight-foot length of rail. Then the "iron men," five to a rail on each side of the track, would pull on command, hefting the five-hundred-to seven-hundred-pound iron forward and, at the word "Down!," dropping it right in place, or so close that it was soon "lined" to the gauge. The little car would already be moving forward on it while clampers and spikers were still fastening it down—three strokes to the spike, ten spikes to a rail, four hundred rails to a mile. When the little flatcar was emptied, it would be wrestled off the tracks to make way for another, then rerailed and rushed back for another load. By late spring of 1866 the work became so precise and efficient

As the tracklayers neared Promontory, bitter enmity sprang up between the Central Pacific's Chinese crews (above, with an American foreman) and the Union Pacific's Irishmen (below), who went after the "heathen" Chinese as though they were Protestants in Ulster. First mules and then a few workmen were killed as the rivals contended. But then the government ended the competition by setting the specific meeting point.

that laying a mile a day became the rule, later stepped up to two and three.

The performers in this muscular ballet, indeed all of Dodge's army, carried rifles as well as their other tools. From the omnipresent Confederate gray and butternut trousers, as well as Union blue, it was obvious that many men who knew how to use them were on hand. There were also freed slaves, hordes of tough Irishmen from the eastern cities, Germans, English adventurers, and that usual miscellany of tight-lipped characters who tend to join foreign legions and any moderately well-paid enterprise that promises adventure. As the base camps moved westward, setting up shop at places like Fort Kearney, North Platte, Julesburg in Colorado Territory, Cheyenne, and at other locations long since forgotten, a movable city accompanied them, a Gomorrah of gamblers, saloonkeepers, and painted women who went to work almost as the first train appeared. "Hell-on-Wheels," it was called, and Dodge did little to interfere until even harder characters began to take over—pimps, gunmen, thieves, and other prototypes of latter-day Chicago and New York criminals. Drinking and women and loaded dice were one thing, but murdering his men was another, and Dodge had Jack Casement clean up in vigilante style.

The Plains Indians, who saw the handwriting on the wall all too clearly, on occasion picked off advance parties and wrecked a few trains. Into the flaming wreckage of one they tossed the tomahawked bodies of the crew. Military escorts were small, and as one officer observed, it is hard to surround three Indians with one cavalry trooper. Nevertheless, the red men were not as troublesome to Dodge as the money men from New York and the visitations of Dr. Durant, who at one time sought to force Dodge to lengthen his route unnecessarily—to increase the amount of subsidy. It took the personal intervention of General Grant, then the shoo-in candidate for President, to put Durant in his place.

Dodge's greatest rival, in truth, was Crocker, who had driven the Central Pacific through the Sierras in the face of deep snows, solid rock, and incredible difficulties. And the rivals of Dodge's predominantly Irish crews were the great gangs of Chinese whom Crocker, in the face of incredulity and hostility, had rounded up in San Francisco and later in China itself. Tired of native Americans, who seemed to sign on only as a cheap trip to the gold and silver mines, where they departed, he tried a group of fifty Orientals. If they were little fellows weighing only 110 pounds or so, Crocker argued defensively that they had built the Great Wall of China, hadn't they? They proved docile, well behaved, and industrious, chipping away by hand at tunnels at a rate as slow as eight inches a day (seven tunnels in one two-mile stretch), laboring under vast falls of snow, hanging over precipices in baskets to drill holes for explosives, and erecting the long snowsheds without which the line could not have made it over the Sierras to the plateau country of Nevada and Utah. An amendment to the Pacific Railroad Act had left the meeting place of the two companies indefinite. As a result, and until the point was fixed at Promontory, Utah, west of Ogden, rival surveying and grading crews pushed past each other on parallel lines for hundreds of miles. As the grading crews began working close to each other, the Irish began rolling boulders down on Chinese crews, or setting charges near them without warning, but the Chinese gave as good as they got. As usual there were casualties, but everything comes to an end, and so, by order of Washington, did the great railroad race.

On May 10, 1869, two official trains, one from each railroad, stood on each side of a one-rail gap in the track. The private cars carried officials and even real ladies. Out of the ramshackle saloons and bawdyhouses of Promontory poured a motley crowd of workmen while the celebrities and their guests gathered to watch Durant and Leland Stanford drive a ceremonial spike of gold. There were actually a number of other special spikes as well, just as

Grant's Vice President Schuyler Colfax, who had stock in the Crédit Mobilier, it turned out later, visits Echo Canyon with a party of guests in 1869.

there are always many pens used by Presidents to sign important bills; as a nation we tend to overdo things. The real last spike was of polished steel, since it was wired to the telegraph line and would conduct an electric charge when struck, and thus give the world the news. An Army detachment lined up to clear a space before the speakers, to the joy of the photographer, A. J. Russell, and the band played while one Chinese crew and one Irish crew laid down the last two connecting rails. There was a brief flurry of excitement when someone, wishing to urge on the photographer, yelled "shoot!" Knowing only one meaning for that word and oppressed by the large Irish presence, the Chinese dove for cover.

While this matter was being composed, America hung over the telegraph. From coast to coast parades waited to start, church bells prepared to ring, signs waited to be unfurled (San Francisco's read "CALIFORNIA ANNEXES THE UNITED STATES"), and cannoneers stood to their fieldpieces, lanyards at the ready. The telegrapher at his special table near the track conversed with Omaha. It was fortunate that on this occasion no Indian cut some wire for a bracelet, as so often happened, and no buffalo chose that moment to scratch his back so violently against a pole as to interrupt communication, which also happened frequently. Here is the transcript of what the talking wires said:

Omaha Telegraph (to all Western Union stations):
TO EVERYBODY: KEEP QUIET. WHEN THE LAST SPIKE IS DRIVEN ... WE WILL SAY "DONE." DON'T BREAK THE CIRCUIT, BUT WATCH FOR THE BLOWS OF THE HAMMER.
Promontory Telegraph:
ALMOST READY. HATS OFF. PRAYER IS BEING OFFERED.
Chicago Telegraph:
WE UNDERSTAND. ALL ARE READY IN THE EAST.
Promontory Telegraph:
ALL READY NOW. THE SPIKE WILL SOON BE DRIVEN. THE SIGNAL WILL BE THREE DOTS FOR THE COMMENCEMENT OF THE BLOWS.

Payday for construction crews at Blue Creek Station, Utah, in April, 1869, was a little less formal but more open than the payoff to men like Colfax. This is a detail from a Russell photo.

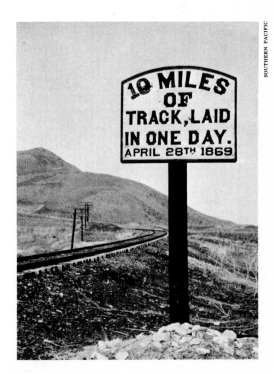

This all-time record on the Central Pacific was made to meet a wager between Crocker and Durant: track was laid at one mile an hour.

Flanked by the Central Pacific's engine Jupiter, *left, and the Union Pacific's* No. 119, *dignitaries at Promontory, Utah, prepare to drive the last spike on May 10, 1869, while A. J. Russell takes their photograph. The telegrapher's table is visible near the track, and another camera at right foreground. This is the penultimate moment.*

In his best gubernatorial manner, Leland Stanford stepped forward with a shining silver hammer and drew it back. A hush fell over the assembled politicians, dignitaries, gandy dancers, soldiers, mountain men, gamblers, ladies, soiled doves, impassive Chinese, and all that incredible company. No sound but the hiss of two locomotives leaking steam. Stanford swung.

He missed.

As the roar of laughter died, Dr. Durant took the hammer and also missed, whether out of clumsiness or tact no one will ever know. In his excitement the telegrapher sent his "Dot, dot, dot" anyway. Dodge, watching from one side, now stepped forward and drove the spike home. Then the two locomotives moved up gently to touch their pilots. The engineers of each stepped forward and broke a bottle of champagne over the other's locomotive. For the photographers, Dodge shook hands with Samuel Montague, chief engineer of the Central Pacific. Crocker and Huntington did not bother to come, although Stanford later had an imposing painting made which mended these and other omissions, and carefully removed the waving bottles in the interests of respectability. Bret Harte wrote a poem which began:

> *What was it the engines said,*
> *Pilots touching—head to head,*
> *Facing on a single track,*
> *Half a world behind each back?*

They might have said, scandal is forgotten and achievement remains. Long freights still roll today doing America's business over the great route which Theodore Judah dreamed of and Grenville Dodge sketched out on the hotel stoop for Mr. Lincoln ten long years before.

The spike driven, the engines come together, bottles appear, and Dodge and Montague shake.

5. Building a New Nation

The sign on the horse reads:

My Name Is
NIC
I Have Drawn The Iron Car
750 Miles

5. Building a New Nation

A decaying wooden bridge not far from Promontory looked like this when photographed for American Heritage *by David Plowden in 1967, two years before the centennial of the driving of the golden spike. The tracks were lifted in World War II when a cut-off was built across Salt Lake.*

PRECEDING PAGES: *Northern Pacific workers halt for their picture near present-day Miles City, Montana, in 1881. The same horse, "Old Nig," took part in the NP's last spike ceremony in 1883.*

On the morning after the driving of the last spike, the residents of Promontory suffered a giant, collective hangover. But this was nothing, however, to the larger indisposition which developed when the government looked into the shell game which had left the Union Pacific Railroad a financial cripple, ready for the raiding parties from Wall Street. No similar investigation of the Big Four and their Contract and Finance Company was possible, if only because a convenient fire destroyed that profitable company's books in the early 1870's. Nor did the Big Four make the mistake of falling out among themselves.

In another sense, too, the completion of this first shaky transcontinental line ended in a kind of letdown. Just as the ceremony closed word came that De Lesseps had finished the Suez Canal, which meant that much of the trade of Europe with the Orient, which the Pacific Railroad had hoped to carry, would never pass across North America. Places like Denver and Salt Lake City (which had provided much sturdy Mormon labor to the rival building crews) were aggrieved at being left off the main line. The expected volume of traffic, after a brief initial flurry, fell off until some trains were moving little freight and only a handful of travellers. Burdened with debt for the government loans, Union Pacific stock, originally 100 points, went down steadily. It was at 9 before the Crédit Mobilier scandal broke. The shakily constructed line had to endure more decades of depredations by such predators as Jay Gould and Russell Sage; it had to undergo heavy rebuilding and improvement over the years. In 1904 a trestle twelve miles long was built across the Great Salt Lake, connecting Lucin and Ogden, which shortened the old Central (now Southern) Pacific route by forty-four miles and left Promontory itself on a secondary freight route. Then in the steel scarcity of World War II the tracks were torn out, leaving nothing around this celebrated point except a weather-beaten frame building, rotting ties and trestles, and a modest monument to mark the spot where the whole United States was originally united by rail. At length, the National Park Service moved in and put up a museum.

Yet Promontory was a true beginning in the settlement of the Great West. Those like Horace Greeley and Abraham Lincoln who had once thought that this predominantly bare and arid two-thirds of the United States would take a century or more to settle were proved wrong by the energy of the railroad builders. Within half a century, in 1912, the last of the forty-eight continental states had been taken into the Union and the twelve thousand miles of railroad in the trans-Mississippi area in 1870 had multiplied tenfold. Much of this represented the filling in of the tier of states from Minnesota down to Texas, but the most spectacular lines were the transcontinentals.

While the Union Pacific was building across Nebraska and Wyoming, the tracklayers of a parallel route to the south, the Kansas Pacific, which the same Pacific Railroad Acts of 1862 and 1864 had created, were constructing a line to Denver, and thence the Denver Pacific headed north to meet the Union Pacific at Cheyenne. Far to the north a second transcontinental railroad had been separately chartered by Congress in 1864 to follow the 47th–49th Parallel route surveyed in 1853–54 by Army engineers. But construction on this Northern Pacific line commenced only in 1870, and completion of a sort—from Lake Superior to the lower Columbia River—took place in 1883.

During the immediate postwar period other heroic enterprises were afoot. The years 1882 and 1883 witnessed the completion of major sections of such other important lines as the Denver & Rio Grande across Colorado, the Texas & Pacific westward to El Paso, the Santa Fe across Kansas and Colorado to Albuquerque, and the Southern Pacific southward from San Francisco to Los Angeles and eastward across southern Arizona, New Mexico, and Texas to New Orleans. Slowly but more certainly the Burlington pushed its conservative way through Iowa, Missouri, and Nebraska under the leadership of John Murray Forbes. His successor, Charles Elliott Perkins, carried the line to Denver in 1882 and to Billings, Montana, in 1894. Far to the north the remarkable James J. Hill was slowly building what became his Great Northern toward the coast, which it reached in 1893. Scarcely any of these enormous accomplishments were brought into being without towering feats of engineering, backbreaking work, fast financial footwork, and (except for the Burlington) a generous amount of double-dealing. Great fortunes accumulated. In a few cases the men whose faces fill the pious histories and whose names dot the maps of the roads they built had their men fight for routes and even resort to gunplay; yet all their rivalries would eventually be adjudicated politely, over cigars in eastern boardrooms.

History seems to work in waves, if not in spasms. In the years following the Civil War, railroad building became almost an article of faith with the American people. Lines were expanding everywhere, whether needed or not, but the mania was most severe in the West. It did not seem to matter much where one actually built. The big thing was to get tracks down; where they might go eventually, what their connections might be—all too often these were matters of little consequence. The railroad did not seek business but created it. It was all very different from Europe, or the settled East. The town or valley or trading post on the prairie through which a railroad passed knew it had a future, but the place without a railroad was headed for oblivion. Great care had to be taken to attract the favor of the railroad company and to avoid its wrath, to confer land and privileges, and, when pressed, raise money for it.

A western city could indeed be a sometime thing: there is a Union Pacific story that is much to the point, told by an Englishman who saw a long, shambling freight train pull up at a new construction site in Wyoming Territory. The cars were laden with walls, tents, lumber, signs, and everything that denotes American culture from pianos to billiard tables. The conductor emerged from his caboose and announced to the crowd at the new station, with an expressive wave of his hand, "Gentlemen, here's Julesburg."

Most of Julesburg, a construction camp then left behind, had simply picked up and followed business, which was the way things went in a country fairly intoxicated by the prospect of every new dawn. The construction crews had merely to pause for the dealers in town lots to appear, staking out streets and avenues. And if the engineers decided that here might be erected a roundhouse, a repair shop, a sawmill, or anything apt to give a little shade or protection from the wind, someone was sure to get out beautifully rendered "views" of this great city-to-be, its broad avenues lined with hotels, parks,

The financiers who played so large a role in filling the West with over-capitalized railroads and the poorhouses with incautious investors range from honest supersalesmen, like Jay Cooke (above), to unscrupulous manipulators, like Jay Gould (below), who once stated as his policy, "I don't build railroads. I buy them." America's most powerful banker until J. P. Morgan's time, Cooke had ably served the Treasury during the Civil War, selling hundreds of millions of bonds which the government could not move. When the disaster with the Northern Pacific, described in the text, forced such a respected banking house as his to close its doors, it was natural for a panic to follow. Cooke's main fault was optimism, a belief that things would go only up. How could the West fail? But Gould the corrupt speculator knew that everything that goes up also goes down, especially when nudged, and he made money either way. After milking the Union Pacific dry, he bought and expanded the Missouri Pacific, and then took on other lines until he controlled well over eight thousand miles, or half the lines in the Southwest, including the Texas & Pacific and the St. Louis Southwestern. Back in New York he bought the elevated railways, Western Union, the New York *World*, and a great estate, Lyndhurst, where he died, not widely mourned, in 1892. Cooke, who kept his popularity, later recouped some of his fortunes and his estate through successful mining investments, and died aged eighty-four in 1905.

Rivers in the West were even less well behaved than those in the East. The picture at top left shows what happened to a stretch of track on the Denver, South Park & Pacific narrow-gauge railroad near Waterton when Goose Creek Dam gave way. At top right the noted photographer F. Jay Haynes has captured the moment when the spring flood of the Missouri in 1881 broke up the ice over which for some years the Northern Pa-

opera houses and opulent mansions. Displayed back east, such inspiring lithographs produced results; and life, a bit shabbier, perhaps, would in time imitate art.

Grandiose dreams on the part of the builders and touching faith in the securities markets of New York, London, and Amsterdam worked well for a while. Consider, for example, the second great transcontinental railroad, the Northern Pacific, which was only a gleam in the eye of certain senators from Minnesota and Wisconsin until it took corporate if not corporeal shape at the hands of an old Yankee named Josiah Perham. His regular business was promoting popular railroad excursions, and he carried in his hand a charter to build from Lake Superior to the Pacific Ocean. Since it had been given him by the legislature of the faraway state of Maine, it may have lacked conviction. Congress paused during the Civil War long enough to supersede that preposterous document and bestow on Perham a charter of its own, duly signed by President Lincoln in 1864. Because the area was so desolate and so unpromising that General Sherman called it "as bad as God ever made," the act doubled the land grant of the Union and Central Pacific lines, and awarded the Northern Pacific forty alternate sections through the Territories, which is to say 25,600 acres, per mile. Indian titles to any of that total of forty-seven million acres were, in the cavalier phrase of the white man's law, "extin-

F. JAY HAYNES: HAYNES FOUNDATION COLLECTION

guished." That is also fifteen times the size of Connecticut, which its natives like to think of as the largest of the modest-sized states. But there were no government loans and Perham was not allowed to mortgage either his lands or his railroad: the result was that no one would buy his stock, and he died in 1868 without laying any track. When a new president came in, he got the charter revised to permit the necessary mortgaging and allow the railroad to issue $100,000,000 in construction bonds. In that era, people bought bonds, and distrusted stock, which usually fell into the hands of promoters and gave them voting control.

To take on the bond-selling, the great firm of Jay Cooke & Company, fresh from its successes in helping finance the Civil War, stepped forward in 1869, and in effect assumed control of the company. Two teams of surveyors hit the trail, one in the Columbia River area, the other working across the upper Missouri River toward the Rockies. Meanwhile, full of his perennial hope and enthusiasm, sure of success, convinced that the lands were worth at least four times the $100,000,000 in gold bonds, Cooke launched a large advertising campaign extolling the rich soil, the priceless forests, and the mild climate, which his press agents compared to Paris and Venice. They let it be rumored that orange groves had been found in this great empty land, which wits began to call "Jay Cooke's Banana Belt." His agents soon raised

cific ran its trains between Mandan and Bismarck, North Dakota, during winter months. In the summer, the railroad used the ferry arrangement above to carry its trains across at the same place. An 0-4-0 switcher is dragging freight cars off the big side-wheeler used in 1879. At bottom opposite, a Southern Pacific train creeps through the flood-swollen waters of the Imperial Valley past a breakwater of protective sandbags in 1905.

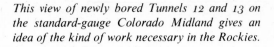

This view of newly bored Tunnels 12 and 13 on the standard-gauge Colorado Midland gives an idea of the kind of work necessary in the Rockies.

This picture of the Royal Gorge on the Denver & Rio Grande Railroad was taken by the noted photographer W. H. Jackson. The gorge runs more than four miles through the canyons of the Arkansas River, between granite walls as high as a thousand feet. One can see the famous hanging bridge, originally installed because no firm footings could be found; the crossover had to be suspended with steel beams from the sides.

$30,000,000 in the United States, and he had negotiated the sale of $50,000,000 more in Paris when the Franco-Prussian War began and the deal fell through. Cooke plunged on, laying track from both ends. Construction costs, particularly on the western end where everything was necessarily brought by sea, rose steadily. The eastern part of the road had reached the Missouri at Bismarck, North Dakota, when in 1873 no more money could be found in overtaxed financial markets and, after a few desperate efforts, Jay Cooke & Company, unable to meet its debts or interest, had to close its doors, precipitating the worst panic since 1837. Construction came to an end.

Stalled for some years, the Northern Pacific gradually recovered and with fresh financing from a banking syndicate was quietly building again in 1881, at which point there entered into its affairs that unusual promoter, Henry Villard, who had observed Gould at close range and matched wits with him. With the possible exception of Charles Francis Adams, Jr., he was the best educated of all the railroad kings. Born Ferdinand Heinrich Gustav Hilgard, of a noted family in Speyer, Baden, and educated at the universities of Munich and Würzburg, he sympathized as a youth with the 1848 revolutionists and, on emigrating to the United States, took the surname of a French friend to avoid being found and brought back. He became a newspaper reporter, first in the German-language and then in the American press, a friend of Greeley and Lincoln, a traveller in the West, writing a guide to the Pikes Peak gold regions when he was only twenty-five. He married the daughter of that fiery abolitionist William Lloyd Garrison.

In the Civil War Villard grew famous as a war correspondent and afterward, in 1868, took a position as secretary of the American Social Science Association, which got him into the investigation of banking and railroad finance. Travelling in Germany for his health in 1873, he came into contact with a committee representing the anxious bondholders of the Oregon and California Railroad Company, which engaged him to go to the scene. There were many such worried committees in that era of wide European investment in this "developing country." While rescuing the interests of the bondholders, Villard became fascinated by the Northwest and took up financing himself, acquiring control of a ship line and then organizing a railroad eastward from Portland up the south bank of the Columbia River, called the Oregon Railway and Navigation Company. It was his hope to connect with some westbound transcontinental, but it appeared that the Northern Pacific, the first to show up, intended to go straight through the towering Cascade Range to a much better terminus on Puget Sound itself; its officials declined to use his easier river route. And so Villard, the pygmy, set out to buy the giant. He distributed a confidential circular to some fifty of the wealthy and trusted friends he had made in twenty-eight years in America, asking them to put up $8,000,000 for a purpose which was not revealed. This "Blind Pool," as it became known, was a unique transaction, a testimony to his reputation, and so successful that it was eventually oversubscribed by $12,000,000.

With this money, Villard won control of the battered Northern Pacific. In the face of danger that Congress might take away the huge land grant, which had already in theory expired, he undertook to build the unfinished nine hundred miles in two years. Huge gangs of Chinese were hired on the western end as laborers, with Mormon grading contractors; from the east Swedes and Irish labored mightily. In the Rockies, new feats were necessary: there were 130 miles of heavy rock cutting, a trestle eighteen hundred feet long and many shorter ones, not to mention a 3,850-foot tunnel through Mullan Pass. This last was so hard to complete that it had to be bypassed with a temporary track, of outrageous curvature and grade.

The ceremonies at Promontory paled beside the great party that Villard

threw for the completion of the Northern Pacific in 1883. Not without attention to fund raising, he had invited a vast crowd of celebrities for the final spike driving in September at Gold Creek, Montana. It took four trains to bring large delegations of politicians like Secretary of State William Marcy Evarts, former President U. S. Grant, Carl Schurz, and brigades of governors and mayors. There was also a sizeable party of titled Englishmen that included most notably, as it turned out later, the then untitled historian James Bryce (see page 133), and not a few *Hochwohlgeborene* from old Germany, including among the newsmen a German editor named Nicolaus Mohr, who left behind an entertaining account of the endless parades, celebrations, banquets, and ear-deadening speech-makings with which the party made its slow progress westward from St. Paul and Minneapolis. At various points such celebrities as President Chester A. Arthur and Sitting Bull made willing or unwilling appearances. The old chief seemed bored by everything except the bright red shirt worn by one of the workmen.

As the trains approached Gold Creek on the temporary tracks over Mullan Pass, there were several incidents, one of which Editor Mohr witnessed. His train had started downhill when the conductor, looking out the end of one car, saw that the lounge car and the cars behind it had become uncoupled and were fast disappearing behind. He signalled the engineer to stop, only to have the lost cars, now gathering speed from gravity, come crashing into the forward ones. There was considerable damage but no one, fortunately, was injured.

At the ceremony itself Villard stood up, raised his arm, and cried, "I have no golden spike, but an iron one." It was the same piece of iron that had been used when the first tracks were laid years before, and after endless tributes to

How rapidly the West filled up with railroads in the twenty-one years after Promontory is made clear in this map. The transcontinentals completed up to that year are indicated by their initials, plus the approximate route of the Great Northern main line, finished only in 1893. The map, based on one kindly provided by the Association of American Railroads, shows how thickly webbed with rails the eastern plains had become, and it suggests the number of narrow-gauge lines in Colorado. In 1890 the total number of American railroad route miles, excluding yards and extra tracks and the like, was 163,597. The network grew to its greatest extent, 254,037 miles, in 1916, and has thereafter steadily declined.

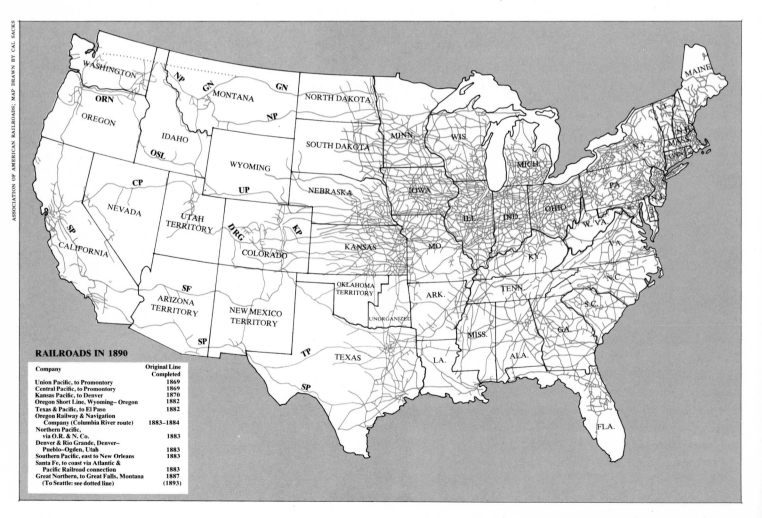

RAILROADS IN 1890

Company	Original Line Completed
Union Pacific, to Promontory	1869
Central Pacific, to Promontory	1869
Kansas Pacific, to Denver	1870
Oregon Short Line, Wyoming–Oregon	1882
Texas & Pacific, to El Paso	1882
Oregon Railway & Navigation	
Company (Columbia River route)	1883–1884
Northern Pacific,	
via O.R. & N. Co.	1883
Denver & Rio Grande, Denver–	
Pueblo–Ogden, Utah	1883
Southern Pacific, east to New Orleans	1883
Santa Fe, to coast via Atlantic &	
Pacific Railroad connection	1883
Great Northern, to Great Falls, Montana	1887
(To Seattle: see dotted line)	(1893)

all the famous people present (and to Cooke, who was not), everyone had a whack at the spike, including Grant, Evarts, Villard, a parade of politicians, a Crow Indian chief, who said something no one could understand, and Villard's three-month-old son—who really only touched the handle as the blow was struck. Then the band played "Yankee Doodle," "God Save the Queen," and "Die Wacht am Rhein," and America had a second transcontinental railroad.

If Henry Villard thought all his ceremonies, whose cost was criticized by the stockholders, would help bring in more investment, he miscalculated. The railroad's deficit grew so huge that he was forced to resign in 1884. But he returned to the Northern Pacific board later on and retired as chairman in 1893. Within a few years, the Northern Pacific did build its own line over the Cascades, via Stampede Pass, in weather as bad as anything Crocker and his Chinese had encountered in the Sierras twenty years before, and made a grand entry into Seattle.

Railroads are all to some degree monopolistic, unless men are fatuous enough to lay them down parallel to each other, side by side through the same towns—which has happened, to be sure, until one company has put the other out of business. The struggles for territory were generally settled with decorum in banks or offices, however the parties felt about each other. But down in the Rocky Mountains of Colorado and New Mexico in the late 1870's two railroads clashed in the manner one usually finds in shoot-'em-up "Wild West" motion pictures, for the very elementary reason that two railroads cannot both go through a mountain pass that has barely room for one.

One such pass, the Raton, sat astride the only gateway from the Colorado plains to the high plains of New Mexico, in the mountains above Trinidad, disturbed by nothing more than a wagon toll road kept by an old scout named Wootton. He ran a kind of tollhouse and bar half way up. A little but growing Kansas railroad, originally the Atchison & Topeka, founded by an old Free-Soiler of prewar days named Cyrus K. Holliday, had been inching across the state toward the Colorado border, which it just barely made by the necessary date to get its relatively modest land grant of three million acres. On the way it created one fabled cow town after another— Newton (called "Shootin' Newton" after the carefree conduct of cowhands who brought their steers there); then legendary Dodge City, which needed a lock-up so soon after the steam cars arrived that, for lack of lumber, a large, penitential hole was simply dug in the ground. Meanwhile the company had added "& Santa Fe" to its name and developed transcontinental yearnings. It headed toward Pueblo, in southern Colorado, where it met the rails of the new Denver & Rio Grande. Thence General Manager William B. Strong, the able Santa Fe boss, intended to push south for the Raton Pass.

And that, he discovered, was exactly what the Rio Grande meant to do as well; its chief, a smooth operator named William Jackson Palmer, who had been a cavalry general in the late war, aimed to fulfill the company's title by crossing New Mexico to that very river. His tracks already reached below Pueblo to a place called El Moro, on the way to Raton.

Two railroads building to the same pass! Strong hastened to New Mexico to get the usual necessary legislation, and found that the Southern Pacific, which also aimed to monopolize that territory, had just got a local law put through, its ink still wet, to prevent a "foreign" railroad from entering. Overnight Strong rounded up a few local men and set up a special New Mexico company. At the Wootton tollhouse at the pass, a friendly sheepherder appeared and hung about making himself agreeable to the lonely old proprietor. Meanwhile, Strong sent his chief engineer, one Albert Robinson, posthaste to

The rival chieftains in the war of the Rocky Mountain passes, at Raton and the Royal Gorge, were William Barstow Strong (left) of the Santa Fe and General William Jackson Palmer of the Denver & Rio Grande. Born in Vermont, Strong was a hard-nosed, experienced railroad operating man during whose active direction (1877–89) the Santa Fe grew from a prairie grain and cattle carrier a little over 780 miles long to a great transcontinental extending from Chicago to the Pacific and the Gulf of Mexico. The more cultivated and elegant Palmer came from Delaware, and started in railroading as private secretary to the noted Pennsylvania Railroad president J. Edgar Thomson. As a cavalry officer in the Civil War he received a Congressional Medal of Honor, and then went surveying railroads west of the Rio Grande. He took on the building of the latter part of the Kansas Pacific, in the pre-Gould days, laying 150 miles of track in ninety-two days. To get fresh meat for his men, he hired a young hunter, William F. Cody (later "Buffalo Bill"), at $500 a month to kill twelve buffalo a day and see that they were cut and dressed and ready for the cooks each evening. To raise needed funds, he also ran buffalo hunts for eastern sportsmen, if that is the word for men who sat on a slow-moving train potting away at the huge and stupid creatures, not even stopping to pick up the kill. The railroad completed, Palmer took on the Rio Grande in its struggle to find southern and western connections for Denver. He helped develop Colorado Springs, and in later life built much of the Mexican National Railway.

Riflemen of the Denver & Rio Grande in the Royal Gorge await rival tracklayers from the Santa Fe during the hostilities of 1878–79.

run a line through Raton and stake it out first, possession in that area being nine points of the law. In a Rio Grande smoker, rattling south from Pueblo to the end of track at El Moro, Robinson spotted his opposite number, the Rio Grande's Chief Engineer J. A. McMurtie. They nodded distantly, each suspecting the other's purpose. At El Moro, both got off, McMurtie stopping to round up, arm, and equip a force to go hold the pass. But Robinson, keenly conscious of his orders, mounted a horse and rode hell-for-leather for Trinidad. That ancient settlement, which was being bypassed by the Rio Grande, was only too happy to aid a man who promised to bring *his* railroad through it. In short order he had a force of volunteers armed with rifles, shovels, and stakes, and they raced for the pass. Reaching Wootton's they were greeted warmly by the old man and his sheepherder friend, who had been a Santa Fe advance man all along. At four in the morning, the story goes, guards posted, they began staking out a roadbed. Half an hour later, McMurtie's party arrived. There were hot words but no gunplay, and the Santa Fe got its first train through in late 1878, by a switchback. Later the tunnel was built through its summit, known to all riders of the *Chief.*

General Palmer had long since announced his intention to push westward from Pueblo right into the Royal Gorge of the Arkansas River, a pencil-thin canyon three thousand feet deep through the Rockies, to the rich silver mines of Leadville, so far served only by wagon freight. Then in the spring of 1878 he learned, because his railroad controlled the telegraph, that Strong, too, was aiming at the Royal Gorge and was sending an engineer to Cañon City, on the way into the Gorge, to organize a force to hold the site. Palmer dispatched a hundred armed men in by train, but the Santa Fe force got around behind them and set up in business, a few men shovelling but most of them looking down rifle barrels as the Rio Grande men approached, thought better of it, and withdrew. Then Palmer got together another force, to sneak around even farther up the canyon than the Santa Fe men. The result was a standoff. To everyone's surprise, the discouraged Palmer leased his railroad to the Santa Fe for a time, then reclaimed it by force when the Santa Fe broke the agreement.

The matter dragged on in the courts, without a decision, and then real warfare broke out, during which a trainload of Rio Grande partisans killed and wounded a few Santa Fe men. The latter road had hired the celebrated marshal "Bat" Masterson of Dodge City, with a crowd of his hangers-on as deputies, to defend a Santa Fe strong point. On being approached under a flag of truce by the Rio Grande's treasurer with a valise full of money, however, the noted gun toters made a deal and drifted away. A guerilla war of some months' duration eventually ended with the Rio Grande in possession and certified legally so by the Supreme Court of the United States. In later years, both roads shared the Denver-Pueblo-Cañon City lines, along with the Colorado & Southern.

Blocked from crossing the Colorado ranges, the Santa Fe struggled westward through New Mexico only to clash again, this time with Jay Gould's Texas & Pacific and Collis Huntington's Southern Pacific, now in league with each other and determined to stop the rival. Eventually on a complex of owned and leased lines, Strong got to California, but the railroad fell thereafter into trouble and receivership, to be rescued much later and turned into one of the nation's best.

Most of the railroads of the West had been built to standard gauge, thanks to Lincoln's original action with the Pacific Railroad, so that four feet, eight and one-half inches was becoming a more and more universal width on big railroads everywhere. But in the Colorado ranges, which the Denver & Rio Grande made its domain, the high ridges, passes, and steep defiles were less

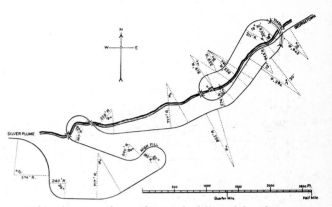

This diagram shows the track followed by the famous Georgetown Loop of the Georgetown, Breckenridge & Leadville, a Union Pacific subsidiary, and everywhere indicates the degree of curvature. The figures, for example "574' R." at the far left, indicate the radii of the circles of which each curve would form part of the circumference. The longer the radius, the gentler the curve. The sharpest on the line is marked "High Fill," at 30 degrees. Around sharp curves the little short trains naturally had to creep; nowadays the Denver & Rio Grande holds its degree of curvature to 2! On the other hand, it can run its trains around them at seventy miles per hour. To climb 623 feet in a straight route would require a prohibitive grade of 6 percent between Silver Plume and Georgetown. Therefore, it was necessary for the tracks to loop over each other in this fashion to stay within an average grade of 3 percent. Four and one-half miles of track had to be laid to go a distance of only two miles.
The Railroad Gazette, NOVEMBER 27, 1885

OVERLEAF: *This excellent panorama of the Georgetown Loop, taken in 1884 by W. H. Jackson, just before regular passenger service began, shows four trains at once. There is a one-car special in the foreground, from which the photographer has undoubtedly climbed up to the vantage point of "High Fill" (see diagram above) to point his camera toward Georgetown. Next behind is a double-headed freight on the trestle over Clear Creek. In the far distance, above on the high bridge, is another freight, and passing beneath it one can make out a passenger train.*
COLORADO STATE HISTORICAL SOCIETY, LIBRARY

These triple-decked dormitory cars were used by Jim Hill's construction crews as the track swept westward across the plains. The cars are marked with the initials of the St. Paul, Minneapolis & Manitoba Railroad, the name of Jim Hill's railroad at the time; it became the Great Northern in 1890 when all the parts were pulled together in one whole. The men belong to construction crews working for a contractor named Donald Grant, who is standing at left in the rear behind other officials, the camp doctor with his bag, and a visiting Indian. The timekeeper, another Grant, is seated in the buckboard, and a buffalo skull and deer antlers can be seen on the car in the foreground. When these trains got to the mountains and their tunnels, the upper decks had to be sawed off to get through. At a scene like this, one could never tell whether old Jim Hill himself might show up, to criticize or to lend a hand, or just to make sure no one was taking a bad grade up ahead. He saw to everything.

hospitable to normal railroading. The long, gentle curves preferred in fast standard-gauge operation were hard to place and expensive to build, and so General Palmer's railroad and many others turned to the narrower width of three feet, a measure that became for years the standard of mountain railroading in the West. There were more three-foot and three-foot-six lines in the East, especially in Pennsylvania, and others in Britain, not to mention the wide use of various slim gauges on the Continent. And, of course, there were other back-country "narrow gauges," including Maine's diminutive two-footers, and other oddities. Not all of them worked mountain routes, but all were cheaper to build. The word "narrow" is relative. In its days of six-foot-wide tracks, the Erie used to refer disparagingly to the competing New York Central (four feet, eight and one-half inches) as "the narrow-gauge route."

In 1876 Palmer's engineers had pushed a line westward into the Rockies in southern Colorado by way of Alamosa, Antonito, and Durango to the mines in the remote San Juan and Uncompahgre mountains. The history of Colorado in this period is of continual discoveries of precious metals in areas that only a mountain goat could penetrate. There were great finds around Silverton, toward which Denver & Rio Grande crews rushed northward from Durango through the spectacular canyon of the Rio de las Animas Perditas, or River of Lost Souls. Its smooth vertical walls dropped as much as a thousand feet, down which men dangled on ropes to drill, blast, and chip out a narrow shelf to accommodate the miniature track. The Durango-Silverton line, still operated for tourists by the Rio Grande, is one of the last survivors of all the spectacular narrow-gauge lines built not only by that railroad but by many others in Colorado, Utah, California, Nevada, and other western states. It has a number of locations where the faint-hearted would be well advised to look away from the windows. It is isolated now, for its connection with the rest of the system has been abandoned in recent years. Yet as recently as 1942, when America's narrow-gauge mileage had dwindled from over ten thousand to only fourteen hundred, 770 of it was still running in the Centennial State.

The original main line of the Rio Grande, through the contested Royal Gorge, Leadville, and other mining areas, eventually went on over Marshall Pass and the Gunnison River to Salt Lake City and Ogden. Later it was supplanted by the shorter Moffat Tunnel route west of Denver, although the Royal Gorge still carries freight. Even before that it was converted, by the addition of a third rail, to both narrow- and standard-gauge operations.

In the great days of these wonderful, toy-like railroads there was nothing like their diminutive engines and rolling stock, complete with slender Pullman sleepers, dining cars, and the gaudy if Lilliputian private or "business" cars of railroad officials, in several of which the author was privileged to ride from Antonito to Durango and Silverton some ten years ago. Of one of these cars a contemporary account in *The National Car Builder* (January, 1880) said, "There is an entire absence of gilding, which enhances the effect of the exquisite inlay work in leaves and flowers, outlined after the Queen Anne style. The ceiling is in figured white oak, beautifully paneled and decorated with vines and flower pieces.... At one end of the car are the ladies' toilet, a large linen closet and a Baker heater and at the other end are the gentlemen's lavatory and saloon. Narrow mirrors occupy the spaces between the windows; the sections are richly upholstered.... Each car is lighted with five Hicks & Smith's two-light hurricane lamps suspended from the ceiling. The outside panels are in the usual chocolate color relieved by gilt designs in the Queen Anne style. The windows are polished French plate glass."

The narrow gauge had its luxury trains as well as its palace cars, and the riders dined superbly on the local trout and wild fowl, with fine wines imported from France to aid the digestion of the new-rich mining kings, previously nursed on humbler liquids like rotgut "Injun" whiskey. The Rio Grande's *San Juan*, the last elegant narrow-gauge train, came complete with railway post office, express cars, and two tiny Pullmans.

When the diggings gave out, the narrow gauges disappeared, or were, if needed, converted to standard, but more often they can be traced only by evocative scars across the mountainsides where once the cars swayed along with their rich cargoes. But they left behind an enduring legend and a well-organized company of mourners. Each of the famous old lines, whether it is the Cripple Creek, the Rio Grande Southern, or the rugged Denver, South Park & Pacific, or some of the great Nevada or California lines, has its scholars and historians whose knowledge, inch by inch, of their beloved topic would make a Bancroft or a Prescott drop his eyes in envy.

The Georgetown Loop, shown on pages 114–115, was spectacular but no more so than many another location, especially on the lines of the Denver, South Park & Pacific, regarded by many as the greatest of all those in the Colorado memory book, which started off in 1873 for the mines to the west and southwest of Denver. In the dry phrase of Professor Stuart Daggett in a study of the Union Pacific he made in 1908 in his book *Railroad Reorganization*, the South Park was "the last of Mr. Gould's gifts to the parent line." In the time-honored traditions of western railroad financing, Jay Gould had taken a quarter interest in one of the construction companies building this line, and he received stock in the railroad company itself as a dividend on this investment. Next, he had the Union Pacific, then under his power, buy the stock of the South Park from himself at par. Its real value was much less.

Of this little railroad, Charles Francis Adams, Jr., during his brief but vain attempt to repair the fortunes of the wounded Union Pacific, wrote, "The chief source of revenue was in carrying men and material into Colorado to dig holes in the ground called mines, and until it was discovered that there

An older Jim Hill, squinting with his one good eye at his manuscript, makes the opening address at the Alaska-Yukon-Pacific Exposition in 1909 in Seattle (at top). Still chunky but powerful, ready at any moment to tap in a ceremonial spike (below) or offer a quote from Burns or Pilgrim's Progress, *Hill was now enormously wealthy, the owner of banks, of a castle, and of one of the then great collections of modern French painters.*

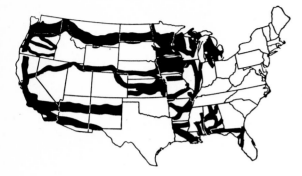

There is a quite unjustified but widely believed legend about the amount of government land given away to encourage colonization. The exaggerated map above, widely reproduced in American history textbooks, reflects the distortion on this topic which Robert Selph Henry of the Association of American Railroads once found in twenty-three out of twenty-four texts he examined (Mississippi Valley Historical Review, September, 1945). Based on a bitter Democratic party election poster of 1884, it shows in black about four times the actual lands granted. In fact, these are only the areas within which grants might have been made, not only to railroads but also to wagon roads and river-improvement projects. It ignores the fact that grants were assigned in a checkerboard or alternate-section pattern. And most of the shaded area is actually the so-called "in lieu" areas; often when land grants included already pre-empted or homesteaded sections, the railroad would receive in their place others farther from the tracks. Of all the 155,504,994 acres originally bestowed, some were forfeited when projected roads were not completed; 131,350,534 were actually taken up. Three million acres of spectacular timber land were repossessed in 1915 from the Southern Pacific.

One of the great coups in colonizing western land grants was that of C. B. Schmidt, a German-speaking agent of the Santa Fe, who managed to talk thousands of hard-working Mennonite farmers into leaving Russia and settling in villages like this one. Despite many minor but fierce sectarian differences, the Mennonites were united in their strict pacifism. Once welcomed to the Russian steppes by Catherine the Great, they were being persecuted by czarist officials when Schmidt, moving elusively through Russia, persuaded them of the opportunity and freedom in America. They arrived laden down with gold pieces sewn in their

was nothing in those mines, the business was immense." Despite this jaundiced view, and the Gouldish chicanery in its background, the Denver & South Park was a marvel of mountain engineering as it wound its perilous way through some of the most stunning scenery in the world. In its slow demise, spanning fifty years, it has become the subject of vast nostalgic attention by enthusiasts, most notably M. C. Poor and his collaborators in a kind of full gospel called *Denver South Park & Pacific,* and a new testament called the *Pictorial Supplement* thereto.

The last of the great western empire builders, and the man to whom the phrase stuck, was James Jerome Hill. Everyone referred to him as "Jim," at least when they were being polite. He was hard; he was tough; he was sometimes mean and vindictive; but he was the most resourceful and successful. Alone in this yeasty company, Jim Hill laid down his transcontinental, the northernmost yet built, without a land grant, never went into receivership, and never lost control.

Hill was a Scottish-Canadian of humble but literate background who had intended to be a doctor until as a boy he lost an eye in an accident with an arrow. The other eye was both sharp and commanding. At eighteen Hill's imagination was stirred by the thought of going to the Orient to make a fortune; one day in 1856 he arrived at the new little town of St. Paul, Minnesota, hoping to join one of the brigades of westbound trappers and traders. Because he was just too late, he remained in St. Paul, which became his headquarters for the rest of his life. Down at the steamboat landing he got a job as a clerk for a line of packets and made himself something of an expert in trading, shipping, and the setting of freight rates. In 1865 he ventured into business for himself as a freight forwarder and in time became an agent for the St. Paul & Pacific Railroad. Within a few years he was in the steamboat business for himself, running up the Red River into Manitoba in partnership with a former Hudson's Bay Company official, Norman W. Kittson, out of which he began to make his first real money.

During the Panic of 1873 the little St. Paul & Pacific Railroad, which was badly built and tremendously overcapitalized, went into receivership and Hill saw an opportunity. Raising funds from three fellow Canadians—his longtime friend Norman Kittson, Donald A. Smith, an official of the Hudson's Bay Company, and George Stephen, president of the Bank of Montreal—Hill was able in 1878 to acquire control of the railroad. The Dutch holders of its defaulted bonds were happy enough to sell at Hill's low valuation although many tears were wept over their fate by the muckrakers of later times. Hill had risked every cent he owned, and was soon busy rehabilitating the track,

then extending it to the Canadian border and a connection with Winnipeg.

This original line, to be sure, did have a land grant, but its extension eventually into a transcontinental, generally parallel to and competing with the Northern Pacific, was financed by the wizardry of Jim Hill. He built for less, and he built his lines where he knew trade would appear. In Minnesota, Hill came into control of a heavy lumber business. In the Red River valley to the west he foresaw a new wheat field for the world, and an even greater one beyond in the Dakotas. While his main line crossed North Dakota he threw out spurs at short intervals to the north until the map of his lines in that state looked like a comb with its teeth turned northward. All of these branches helped him to get the carloads of wheat that made Minneapolis the center of milling in America—after which he carried the flour. He reached Great Falls, Montana, in 1887, and Seattle in 1893. The line was now called the Great Northern. In Montana he ran extensions to local coal fields to provide cheap coal for his locomotives. No hurry; wait for business; don't run empty freight cars. By the time his "Pacific Extension" reached Puget Sound and its great stands of timber, the East and Midwest were clamoring again for lumber; Michigan was a stubbly clearing, and Wisconsin and Minnesota were nearly stripped of their forests; these were the days before anyone cared much about conservation. In the empties, heading back west, he shipped cotton for Japan.

In his younger days, Hill had gotten to know Minnesota on horseback and on snowshoes, often sleeping out alone in the open. No office man, he followed his tracks westward in anything around from a handcar or a caboose to his private car. He inspected the grades and the work with the economical eye of a Scot. One day, a story goes, he discovered a brand new track spike lying loose on the roadbed. In some heat he set off to find the wasteful section foreman. But the latter, according to a story in *A Treasury of Railroad Folklore*, must have been a quick thinker. As he saw Hill bearing down, he hurried forward. "Thank goodness you found that spike, Mr. Hill," he said. "I've had three men looking for it for nearly a week."

Hill knew many of his men by name, and was not above getting off his private car to lend a hand in the heavy work. Once, during a driving snowstorm, the grizzled old man spelled the shoveling crew one at a time for three hours, sending them into the car for coffee and a little relaxation. This of course is the way to build morale on a railroad. On the other hand, Hill expected hard work and instant obedience in return, and he could be so capricious as to fire an office man because he could not stand his surname. (It was Spittles.) Complaint only infuriated him. When the citizens of the small resort town of Wayzata in Minnesota objected to all-night switching near

(Continued on page 122)

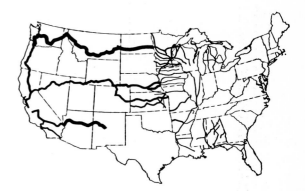

This map represents the land grants in their true proportion. Some 8 percent of the total mileage of American railroads was built on or with land grants, mostly the big transcontinentals. (That the big land-grant lines all went bankrupt at some time or other and that Jim Hill's grant-free Great Northern did not, fascinated the late Stewart Holbrook, although he added, "I am not sure what this proves." Our maps are reprinted from his Story of American Railroads.) Speaking for the Illinois Central grant back in 1850, Senator William R. King, later Vice President, said all our western lands, if not developed or gotten at, would "never command ten cents." The 131,350,534 acres actually given, in the best official estimate of modern times, were worth when granted about $126,000,000. In 1945 the Committee on Interstate and Foreign Commerce of the House of Representatives figured that Uncle Sam had gotten back, in free or low-rate carriage of freight and government personnel, military and civilian, a round $900,000,000. That was double the amount the railroads received for lands they sold and the current value of the lands they still held. Uncle Sam had done so well, after all, that Congress voted to give up the land-grant rate reductions permanently after October 1, 1946.

clothing, but the most valuable baggage they carried, besides their own dauntless character, was the little bags of red winter wheat with which they made the prairie bloom. Some eighteen thousand left Russia for America in the ten years following 1873. Eight thousand went to Manitoba and the largest part of the remainder to Kansas where, it turned out, neither drought nor grasshoppers really hindered them. They gave their villages pretty names like Gnadenau (Meadow of Grace), Blumenfeld (Field of Flowers), and Hoffnungsthal (Valley of Hope), which were, in view of the results, good prophecies. They still prosper today.

We might call the pictures on these two pages "the myth and the reality." The German-language "Guide to Southern Minnesota and Eastern Dakota" describes a region "which has no equal for agriculture." The sod house, so typical of treeless Nebraska, gave way to wood when the family prospered. This family is unidentified.

On and on the railroads beckoned, and in vast crowds the emigrants followed. That the more southerly plains also attracted them is attested by the pictures on these two pages, especially the siren song below of the Missouri, Kansas & Texas Railway, everywhere known as the "Katy." The large center picture shows what the photographer described as "the first crowd that came to buy town lots" at Horton, Kansas, September 20, 1888. The station is not quite finished.

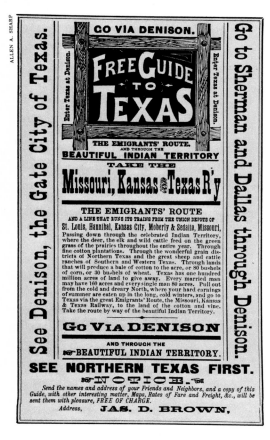

their summer houses, Hill tore down the station and set it up a long, inconvenient two miles away.

Jim Hill's stormy life, which lasted until 1916, bridges the era from early railroad building to the last climactic financial wars, which are discussed in the next chapter. He was, looking backward at all the contradictory accounts, a sharp trader but likeable. And he shared in the dream of filling all those vast empty spaces, "the Garden of the West," with cities, farms, and ranches; indeed he went further than some who simply dumped their settlers on the prairie and steamed off. He imported specially bred cattle, just as he did Englishmen, Scotsmen, Norwegians, and Swedes. His cattle were good for both beef and milk production, and he gave the animals away to people along the line. In Great Northern country, with no land grant, you homesteaded a government quarter section for as little as $20 in fees at the land office.

Whichever railroad you took to the West, however, you were in for some nasty surprises. Getting there was not half the fun, as the travel ads have it today. That part, described by an eyewitness, Robert Louis Stevenson, on pages 130–131, was only the beginning. The life of the "sodbuster" was hard, and that of his wife almost unendurable. The wind never stopped blowing and the ceiling of the sod house, built because there was at first no timber, never stopped raining dirt on her table and all her works. It took much more land to support a family than it had back east, and everything, in the end, depended on the price one got for a cash crop. That was set, often lower every year, by mysterious markets and forces thousands of miles away. Meanwhile, all too many of the railroads that had succeeded in enticing the

The crowded train below, so reminiscent of scenes of fleeing refugees in India or Eastern Europe, is packed with homesteaders awaiting the gun for the opening of the Cherokee Strip in Oklahoma in 1889, the last major land rush in the West. As the deadline approached, the Chicago, Rock Island & Pacific carried many thousands to Caldwell, Kansas; having used up the passenger equipment, it fell back on cattle cars jammed far beyond capacity with eager homesteaders.

settler to "the great temperate zone" charged him all the traffic would bear.

Temperate! It was bare and harsh, buffeted by cruel winters, baked by torrid summers. Rain, when it came, was a destructive torrent. Droughts occurred at regular intervals. The first twenty thousand settlers who poured into the Dakota Territory after the Civil War had barely erected roofs over their heads when the great spring blizzard of 1873 blew in on Easter Sunday, when the prairie was just turning green, and covered their homesteads with snow that fell for three days. It was a storm so terrible that farmers lost their way between the kitchen and the chicken house, to be found frozen to death days later. In 1874, with most railroad construction halted by the financial panic of 1873, the grasshoppers struck, eating every growing thing from the Canadian border to northern Texas. A Union Pacific train at Kearney was stalled in a three-foot drift of 'hoppers.

But the mania was hard to kill, especially in an area that held so many surprises. It was the heyday of the miner, the cowboy, the train robber, and the bad man, any and all of whom you might find riding the plush or the wooden slats of the steam cars. In 1875–76 there was a new gold rush into the Black Hills in the Dakotas, followed by a population boom. In 1883 there was a silver strike in Idaho. The buffalo began to disappear, the cattle to multiply. As the tracks headed west and south in Kansas, the great cattle drives came to an end, and beef moved to market by rail. The sections and townships filled with a mixed crew of westering Americans and new European arrivals, and the oldest race of all, the Indians, fell back, although not without a few moments of pathetic resistance, ending each time in defeat—

Railroads filled the West with people but emptied them of game, especially the buffalo. Here is a private hunting party with its bag on the car City of Worcester *about 1884.*

for the warlike Sioux under Crazy Horse and Sitting Bull in 1876, for the Nez Percé under Chief Joseph farther west a year later, and finally for the Sioux at Wounded Knee in 1890. Reservations and Indian lands, treaties and promises to the contrary notwithstanding, opened up steadily to the white man, even in the former "Indian Territory," in wild "boomer" land rushes like that which populated Oklahoma City with ten thousand people in an afternoon.

Of course, we know now, it was all too prodigal, too wasteful, too dog-eat-dog. Not only did we slaughter the buffalo, we plowed up the famous prairie grass on which it fed, the wonder of the early explorers, the grass that held the soil. We plowed so deep and so often that the soil eroded and bestowed on us the sky-darkening horror of the dustbowl. Jim Hill overpopulated his high plains—it is easy to slip into that possessive—and many a dispirited Montana or Dakota farmer eventually gave up the unequal fight. Too many railroads were constructed at too much cost, which recalls the comment of one western rail baron, Darius Ogden Mills, on one of his properties, a luckless line of some three hundred miles. "Either we built it three hundred miles too long," he complained, "or three hundred years too soon." The penalty for this reckless railroad policy, or lack of it, is being paid today.

For all the men who were broken and women who were dried to leather by the frontier, for all the slaughter and waste of resources, for all the unrealized dreams, the promise of the West was nevertheless fulfilled. Its mines produced the ore and precious metals that helped make America a rich nation. The upland forests resounded to the crash of the axe, the hum of the saw, and the shrill whistle of little geared logging engines hauling their enormous cargo to the railheads. Although the farmer who really succeeded in time was the big mechanized one, the prairie did produce the Corn Belt, one of the great granaries of the world. Whole new cultures as different as Grant Wood's Iowa, the Mormon Commonwealth of Utah, and the new civilization called California prospered out of the unlikely mixture of immigrant and old American stock. The government-lent bonds were paid off with interest. The land grants, for all the propaganda unloosed against them over the years, turned out a good investment for America—not only for the people who settled them and the railroads that later discovered in them unsuspected oil and mineral wealth, but for the United States Treasury as well, just as the first grants had, way back in Illinois, in less than one lifetime.

The Kansas Pacific promoted buffalo-hunting parties;

here the official taxidermist displays stuffed heads outside the railroad's general offices in 1870. The bleached bones were left on the prairie.

O. Henry on Holding Up a Train

O. Henry, who did time himself under his real name of William Sidney Porter, puts his story of how easy it was to rob the steamcars into the mouth of a cowboy out of work. He is one of four fairly hard characters. The place is Oklahoma.

"The first 'stick-up' I was ever in happened in 1890. Maybe the way I got into it will explain how most train robbers start in the business. Five out of six Western outlaws are just cowboys out of a job and gone wrong. The sixth is a tough from the East who dresses up like a bad man and plays some low-down trick that gives the boys a bad name. Wire fences and 'nesters' made five of them; a bad heart made the sixth. . . .

"We selected a place on the Santa Fe where there was a bridge across a deep creek surrounded by heavy timber. All passenger trains took water at the tank close to one end of the bridge. It was a quiet place, the nearest house being five miles away. The day before it happened, we rested our horses and 'made medicine' as to how we should get about it. Our plans were not at all elaborate, as none of us had ever engaged in a hold-up before.

"The Santa Fe flyer was due at the tank at 11:15 P.M. At eleven, Tom and I lay down on one side of the track, and Jim and Ike took the other. As the train rolled up, the headlight flashing far down the track and the steam hissing from the engine, I turned weak all over. I would have worked a whole year on the ranch for nothing to have been out of that affair right then. Some of the nerviest men in the business have told me that they felt the same way the first time.

"The engine had hardly stopped when I jumped on the running-board on one side, while Jim mounted the other. As soon as the engineer and fireman saw our guns they threw up their hands without being told, and begged us not to shoot, saying they would do anything we wanted them to.

"'Hit the ground,' I ordered, and they both jumped off. We drove them before us down the side of the train. While this was happening, Tom and Ike had been blazing away, one on each side of the train, yelling like Apaches, so as to keep the passengers herded in the cars. Some fellow stuck a little twenty-two calibre out one of the coach windows and fired it straight up in the air. I let drive and smashed the glass just over his head. That settled everything like resistance from that direction.

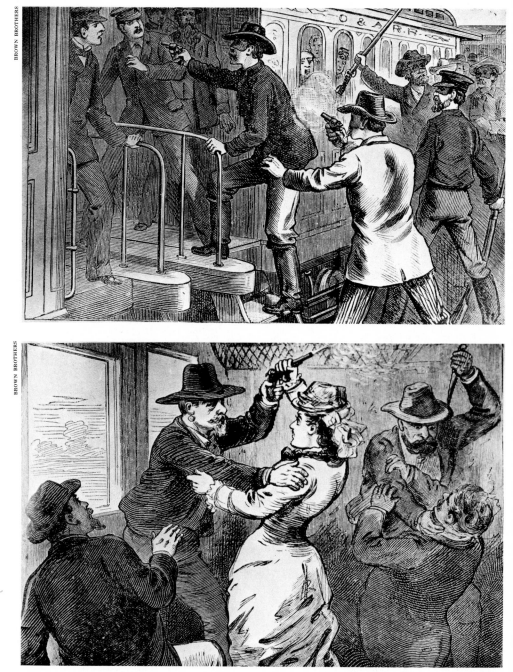

Robbing the steamcars in a small way, as opposed to the wholesale methods of a Fisk or a Gould, was regarded as criminal but endlessly diverting. There was a kind of delicious excitement in it which could be enjoyed vicariously by readers of such elevating publications as The National Police Gazette, and by students of their titillating illustrations. There seemed to be little difficulty in stopping and boarding trains, and it was rarely necessary to subdue the passengers with the force shown above; they could usually be expected to contribute liberally when looking into the barrel of a pistol. Feminine virtue was in less danger than the strongboxes in the express cars, as the tale told in the adjoining columns by O. Henry indicates. Their depredations brought a kind of fame to a number of organized bands of train robbers, beginning with the Reno boys of Indiana, who were eventually hanged by vigilantes. Jesse and Frank James and their partners the Younger boys proved successful for a long time on trains in Iowa, Kansas, and Missouri until Jesse was shot. They won a certain sympathy from a public that felt little or no liking for the railroads. With the coming of all-steel cars, faster trains, and more sophisticated police work, the picturesque train robbers of the songs and the dime novels joined the highwayman of old in limbo.

"By this time all my nervousness was gone. I felt a kind of pleasant excitement as if I were at a dance or a frolic of some sort. The lights were all out in the coaches, and, as Tom and Ike gradually quit firing and yelling, it got to be almost as still as a graveyard. I remember hearing a little bird chirping in a bush at the side of the track, as if it were complaining at being waked up.

"I made the fireman get a lantern, and then I went to the express car and yelled to the messenger to open up or get perforated. He slid the door back and stood in it with his hands up. 'Jump overboard, son,' I said, and he hit the dirt like a lump of lead. There were two safes in the car—a big one and a little one. By the way, I first located the messenger's arsenal—a double-barrelled shotgun with buckshot cartridges and a thirty-eight in a drawer. I drew the cartridges from the shotgun, pocketed the pistol, and called the messenger inside. I shoved my gun against his nose and put him to work. He couldn't open the big safe, but he did the little one. There was only nine hundred dollars in it. That was mighty small winnings for our trouble, so we decided to go through the passengers. We took our prisoners to the smoking-car, and from there sent the engineer through the train to light up the coaches. Beginning with the first one, we placed a man at each door and ordered the passengers to stand between the seats with their hands up.

"If you want to find out what cowards the majority of men are, all you have to do is rob a passenger train. I don't mean because they don't resist—I'll tell you later on why they can't do that—but it makes a man feel sorry for them the way they lose their heads. Big, burly drummers and farmers and ex-soldiers and high-collared dudes and sports that, a few moments before, were filling the car with noise and bragging, get so scared that their ears flop.

"There were very few people in the day coaches at that time of night, so we made a slim haul until we got to the sleeper. The Pullman conductor met me at one door while Jim was going round to the other one. He very politely informed me that I could not go into that car, as it did not belong to the railroad company, and, besides, the passengers had already been greatly disturbed by the shouting and firing. Never in all my life have I met a finer instance of official dignity and reliance upon the power of Mr. Pullman's great name. I jabbed my six-

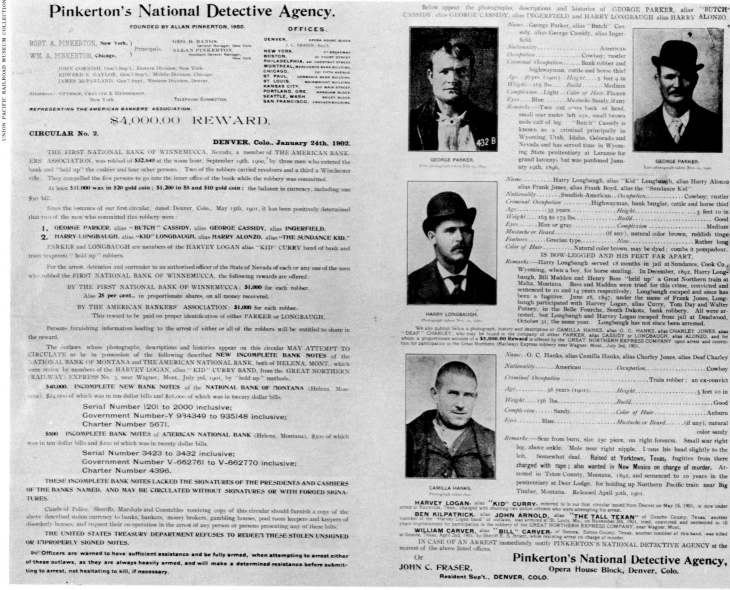

For the last famous gang, Butch Cassidy's "Wild Bunch," the Pinkertons got out this unflattering but interesting "wanted" poster in 1902.

shooter so hard against Mr. Conductor's front that I afterward found one of his vest buttons so firmly wedged in the end of the barrel that I had to shoot it out. He just shut up like a weak-springed knife and rolled down the car steps.

"I opened the door of the sleeper and stepped inside. A big, fat old man came wabbling up to me, puffing and blowing. He had one coat sleeve on and was trying to put his vest on over that. I don't know who he thought I was.

"'Young man, young man,' says he, 'you must keep cool and not get excited. Above everything, keep cool.'

"'I can't,' says I. 'Excitement's just eating me up.' And then I let out a yell and turned loose my forty-five through the skylight.

"That old man tried to dive into one of the lower berths, but a screech came out of it and a bare foot that took him in the bread-basket and landed him on the floor. I saw Jim coming in the other door, and I hollered for everybody to climb out and line up.

"They commenced to scramble down, and for a while we had a three-ringed circus. The men looked as frightened and tame as a lot of rabbits in a deep snow. They had on, on an average, about a quarter of a suit of clothes and one shoe apiece. One chap was sitting on the floor of the aisle, looking as if he were working a hard sum in arithmetic. He was trying, very solemn, to pull a lady's number two shoe on his number nine foot.

"The ladies didn't stop to dress. They were so curious to see a real, live train robber, bless 'em, that they just wrapped blankets and sheets around themselves and came

out, squeaky and fidgety looking. They always show more curiosity and sand than the men do.

"We got them all lined up and pretty quiet, and I went through the bunch. I found very little on them—I mean in the way of valuables. One man in the line was a sight. He was one of those big, overgrown, solemn snoozers that sit on the platform at lectures and look wise. Before crawling out he had managed to put on his long, frock-tailed coat and his high silk hat. The rest of him was nothing but pajamas and bunions. When I dug into that Prince Albert, I expected to drag out at least a block of gold mine stock or an armful of Government bonds, but all I found was a little boy's French harp about four inches long. What it was there for, I don't know. I felt a little mad because he had fooled me so. I stuck the harp up against his mouth.

" 'If you can't pay—play,' I says.

" 'I can't play,' says he.

" 'Then learn right off quick,' says I, letting him smell the end of my gun-barrel.

"He caught hold of the harp, turned red as a beet, and commenced to blow. He blew a dinky little tune I remembered hearing when I was a kid:

Prettiest little gal in the country—oh!
Mammy and Daddy told me so.

"I made him keep on playing it all the time we were in the car. Now and then he'd get weak and off the key, and I'd turn my gun on him and ask what was the matter with that little gal, and whether he had any intention of going back on her, which would make him start up again like sixty. I think that old boy standing there in his silk hat and bare feet, playing his little French harp, was the funniest sight I ever saw. One little red-headed woman in the line broke out laughing at him. . . .

"Then Jim held them steady while I searched the berths. I grappled around in those beds and filled a pillow-case with the strangest assortment of stuff you ever saw. Now and then I'd come across a little pop-gun pistol, just about right for plugging teeth with, which I'd throw out the window. When I finished with the collection. I dumped the pillow-case load in the middle of the aisle. There were many watches, bracelets, rings and pocket-books, with a sprinkling of false teeth, whiskey flasks, face-powder boxes, chocolate caramels, and heads of hair of various colors and lengths. There were about a dozen ladies' stockings into which jewellery, watches, and rolls of bills had been stuffed and then wadded up tight and stuck under the mattresses. I offered to return what I called the 'scalps,' saying that we were not Indians on the warpath, but none of the ladies seemed to know to whom the hair belonged.

"One of the women—and a good-looker she was—wrapped in a striped blanket, saw me pick up one of the stockings that was pretty chunky and heavy about the toe, and she snapped out:

" 'That's mine, sir. You're not in the business of robbing women, are you?'

"Now, as this was our first hold-up, we hadn't agreed upon any code of ethics, so I hardly knew what to answer. I replied: 'Well,

This grim armed company set out after the Cassidy gang in a special train on the Union Pacific.

not as a specialty. If this contains your personal property you can have it back.'

" 'It just does,' she declared eagerly, and reached out her hand for it.

" 'You'll excuse my taking a look at the contents,' I said, holding the stocking up by the toe. Out dumped a big gent's gold watch, worth two hundred, a gent's leather pocket-book that we afterward found to contain six hundred dollars, a 32-calibre revolver; and the only thing of the lot that could have been a lady's personal property was a silver bracelet worth about fifty cents.

"I said: 'Madame, here's your property,' and handed her the bracelet. 'Now,' I went on, 'how can you expect us to act square with you when you try to deceive us in this manner? I'm surprised at such conduct.'

"The young woman flushed up as if she

had been caught doing something dishonest. Some other woman down the line called out: 'The mean thing!' I never knew whether she meant the other lady or me.

"When we finished our job we ordered everybody back to bed, told 'em good night very politely at the door, and left. We rode forty miles before daylight and then divided the stuff. Each one of us got $1,752.85 in money. We lumped the jewellery around. Then we scattered, each man for himself.

"That was my first train robbery, and it was about as easily done as any of the ones that followed. But that was the last and only time I ever went through the passengers. I don't like that part of the business. Afterward I stuck strictly to the express car. During the next eight years I handled a good deal of money. . . . "

R.L.S. on the Emigrant Train

Harper's Weekly, NOVEMBER 13, 1886

This scene, sketched on the spot by the painter Rufus Zogbaum, shows passengers on the hard seats of a Union Pacific emigrant car in 1886.

Unfortunately for him but fortunately for posterity, a great writer rode an emigrant train from Omaha to California in 1879 and left behind an imperishable account of its rigors. Ill and almost penniless at twenty-nine, cut off financially by his family, who disapproved of the woman he was going to join, Robert Louis Stevenson rode the hard way. These are excerpts from his account, *Across the Plains*, published in 1892 when he was famous (and had married the lady).

"I suppose the reader has some notion of an American railroad-car, that long, narrow wooden box, like a flat-roofed Noah's ark, with a stove and a convenience, one at either end, a passage down the middle, and transverse benches upon either hand. Those destined for emigrants on the Union Pacific are only remarkable for their extreme plainness, nothing but wood entering in any part into their constitution, and for the usual inefficacy of the lamps. . . . The benches are too short for anything but a young child. Where there is scarce elbow-room for two to sit, there will not be space enough for one to lie. Hence . . . the company's servants, have conceived a plan for the better accommodation of travellers. They prevail on every two to chum together. To each of the chums they sell a board and three square cushions stuffed with straw, and covered with thin cotton. The benches can be made to face each other in pairs, for the backs are reversible. On the approach of night the boards are laid from bench to bench, making a couch wide enough for two, and long enough for a man of the middle height; and the chums lie down side by side upon the cushions with the head to the conductor's van and the feet to the engine. When the train is full, of course this plan is impossible, for there must not be more than one to every bench, neither can it be carried out unless the chums agree. It was to bring about this last condition that our white-haired official now bestirred himself. He made a most active master of ceremonies, introducing likely couples, and even guaranteeing the amiability and honesty of each. The greater the number of happy couples the better for his pocket, for it was he who sold the raw material of the beds. His price for one board and three straw cushions began with two dollars and a half; but before the train left, and, I am sorry to say, long after I had purchased mine, it had fallen to one dollar and a half.

"[An] afternoon was spent in making up the train. I am afraid to say how many baggage-waggons followed the engine, certainly a score; then came the Chinese, then we [the single men], then the families, and the rear was brought up by the conductor in what, if I have it rightly, is called his caboose. The class to which I belonged was of course far the largest, and we ran over, so to speak, to both sides; so that there were some Caucasians among the Chinamen, and some bachelors among the families. But our own car was pure from admixture, save for one little boy of eight or nine who had the whooping cough. At last, about six, the long train crawled out of the Transfer Station [at Council Bluffs] and across the wide Missouri river to Omaha, westward bound.

"It was a troubled uncomfortable evening in the cars. There was thunder in the air, which helped to keep us restless. A man played many airs upon the cornet, and none of them were much attended to, until he came to *Home, sweet home*. It was truly strange to note how the talk ceased at that, and the faces began to lengthen. I have no idea whether musically this air is to be considered good or bad; but it belongs to that class of art which may be best described as a brutal assault upon the feelings. Pathos must be relieved by dignity of treatment. If you wallow naked in the pathetic, like the author of *Home, sweet home,* you make your hearers weep in an unmanly fashion; and even while yet they are moved, they despise themselves and hate the occasion of their weakness. It did not come to tears that night, for the experiment was interrupted. An elderly, hard-looking man, with a goatee beard and about as much appearance of sentiment as you would expect from a retired slaver, turned with a start and bade the performer stop that 'damned thing.' 'I've heard about enough of that,' he added; 'give us something about the good country we're going to.' A murmur of adhesion ran round the car; the performer took the instrument from his lips, laughed and nodded, and then struck into a dancing measure. . . .

"There were meals to be had by the wayside. . . . rarely less than twenty minutes for each; and if we had not spent many another twenty minutes waiting for some express upon a side track among miles of desert, we might have taken an hour to each repast and arrived at San Francisco up to time. . . . Civility is the main comfort that you miss. Equality, though conceived very largely in America, does not extend so low down as to an emigrant. Thus in all other trains, a warning cry of 'All aboard!' recalls the passengers to take their seats; but as soon as I was alone with emigrants, and from the Transfer all the way to San Francisco, I found this ceremony was pretermitted; the train stole from the station without a note of warning, and you had to keep an eye upon it even while you ate. The annoyance is considerable, and the disrespect wanton and petty.

"Many conductors, again, will hold no communication with an emigrant. I asked a conductor one day at what time the train would stop for dinner; as he made no answer I repeated the question, with a like result; a third time I returned to the charge, and then Jack-in-office looked me coolly in the face for several seconds and turned ostentatiously away. I believe he was half ashamed of his brutality; for when another person made the same inquiry, although he still refused the information, he condescended to answer, and even to justify his reticence in a voice

loud enough for me to hear. It was, he said, his principle not to tell people where they were to dine; for one answer led to many other questions, as what o'clock it was? or, how soon should we be there? and he could not afford to be eternally worried.

"It had thundered on the Friday night, but the sun rose on Saturday without a cloud. We were at sea—there is no other adequate expression—on the plains of Nebraska. I made my observatory on the top of a fruit-waggon, and sat by the hour upon that perch to spy about me, and to spy in vain for something new. It was a world almost without a feature; an empty sky, an empty earth; front and back, the line of railway stretched from horizon to horizon, like a cue across a billiard-board; on either hand, the green plain ran till it touched the skirts of heaven. Along the track innumerable wild sunflowers, no bigger than a crownpiece, bloomed in a continuous flower-bed; grazing beasts were seen upon the prairie at all degrees of distance and diminution; and now and again we might perceive a few dots beside the railroad which grew more and more distinct as we drew nearer till they turned into wooden cabins, and then dwindled and dwindled in our wake until they melted into their surroundings, and we were once more alone. . . .

"To cross such a plain is to grow home-

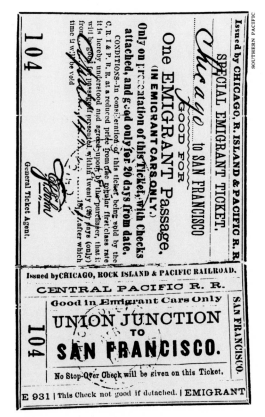

sick for the mountains. I longed for the Black Hills of Wyoming, which I knew we were soon to enter, like an ice-bound whaler for the spring. Alas! and it was a worse country than the other. All Sunday and Monday we travelled through these sad mountains, or over the main ridge of the Rockies, which is a fair match to them for misery of aspect. Hour after hour it was the same unhomely and unkindly world about our onward path; tumbled boulders, cliffs that drearily imitate the shape of monuments and fortifications—how drearily, how tamely, none can tell who has not seen them . . . and for sole sign of life, here and there a few fleeing antelopes; here and there, but at incredible intervals, a creek running in a cañon. The plains have a grandeur of their own; but here there is nothing but a contorted smallness. Except for the air, which was light and stimulating, there was not one good circumstance in that God-forsaken land.

"And yet when [the next] day came, it was to shine upon the same broken and unsightly quarter of the world. . . . And when I think how the railroad has been pushed through this unwatered wilderness and haunt of savage tribes, and now will bear an emigrant for some £12 from the Atlantic to the Golden Gates; how at each stage of the construction, roaring, impromptu cities, full of gold and lust and death, sprang up and then died away again, and are now but wayside stations in the desert; how in these uncouth places pigtailed Chinese pirates worked side by side with border ruffians and broken men from Europe, talking together in a mixed dialect, mostly oaths, gambling, drinking, quarrelling and murdering like wolves; how the plumed hereditary lord of all America heard, in this last fastness, the scream of the "bad medicine waggon" charioting his foes; and then when I go on to remember that all this epical turmoil was conducted by gentlemen in frock coats, and with a view to nothing more extraordinary than a fortune and a subsequent visit to Paris, it seems to me, I own, as if this railway were the one typical achievement of the age in which we live, as if it brought together into one plot all the ends of the world and all the degrees of social rank, and offered to some great writer the busiest, the most extended, and the most varied subject for an enduring literary work. If it be romance, if it be contrast, if it be heroism that we require, what was Troy town to this? . . ."

Humbugs and Oligarchs

The most wonderful satire on the high-pressure railroad promotions of the time is contained in a speech made in a most unlikely place, on the floor of the House of Representatives in Washington in 1871 by a thitherto little-known Democratic representative from Kentucky, J. Proctor Knott. What apparently roused him to his great effort were the preposterous claims advanced on behalf of an obscure bill then before the House to charter a company to be called the St. Croix & Lake Superior Railroad, which was to run from Hudson, Wisconsin, to Superior, Wisconsin, which was near the then muddy little village of Duluth (pop. 3,000). As Knott warmed to his subject, word passed through the corridors and cloak rooms of the House until the floor was jammed with lawgivers who never forgot the occasion. The railroad was killed, although, we scarcely need mention, Duluth survived, and even forgave the orator. In this small space we can only give fragments of Knott's humorous speech.

"Years ago, when I first heard that there was somewhere in the vast *terra incognita*, somewhere in the bleak regions of the great Northwest, a stream of water known to the nomadic inhabitants of the neighborhood as the river St. Croix, I became satisfied that the construction of a railroad from that raging torrent to some point in the civilized world was essential to the happiness and prosperity of the American people, if not absolutely indispensable to the perpetuity of republican institutions on this continent. I felt instinctively that the boundless resources of that prolific region of sand and pine shrubbery would never be fully developed without a railroad constructed and equipped at the expense of the Government—and perhaps not then. . . . I was utterly at a loss to determine where the terminus of this great and indispensable road should be, until I accidentally overheard some gentleman the other day mention the name of 'Duluth.' Duluth! The word fell upon my ear with peculiar and indescribable charm, like the gentle murmur of a low fountain stealing forth in the midst of roses, or the soft, sweet accents of an angel's whisper in the bright, joyous dream of sleeping innocence. Duluth! 'Twas the name for which my soul had panted for years, as the hart panteth for the water brooks. But where was Duluth? Never, in all my limited reading, had my vision been gladdened by seeing the celestial word in print. And I felt a profounder hu-

James Proctor Knott

miliation in my ignorance that its dulcet syllables had never before ravished my delighted ear. I was certain the draughtsman of this bill had never heard of it, or it would have been designated as one of the termini of this road. I asked my friends about it, but they knew nothing of it. I rushed to the Library and examined all the maps I could find. I discovered in one of them a delicate hairlike line, diverging from the Mississippi near a place marked Prescott, which I supposed was intended to represent the river St. Croix, but I could nowhere find Duluth.

"Nevertheless, I was confident it existed somewhere, and that its discovery would constitute the crowning glory of the present century, if not of all modern times. I knew it was bound to exist in the very nature of things; that the symmetry and perfection of our planetary system would be incomplete without it, that the elements of material nature would long since have resolved themselves back into original chaos if there had been such a hiatus in creation as would have resulted from leaving out Duluth. . . . Just as the agony of my anxiety was about to culminate in the frenzy of despair, this blessed map was placed in my hands; and as I unfolded it a resplendent scene of ineffable glory opened before me. . . . There, for the first time, my enchanted eye rested upon the ravishing word 'Duluth.'. . .

"I find by reference to this map that Duluth is situated somewhere near the western end of Lake Superior, but as there is no dot or other mark indicating its exact location I am unable to say whether it is actually confined to any particular spot, or whether 'it is just lying around there loose.' I really cannot

tell whether it is one of those ethereal creations of intellectual frostwork, more intangible than the rose-tinted clouds of a summer sunset; one of those airy exhalations of the speculator's brain, which I am told are ever flitting in the form of towns and cities along those lines of railroad, built with Government subsidies, luring the unwary settler as the mirage of the desert lures the famishing traveler on, and ever on, until it fades away in the darkening horizon, or whether it is a real, bona fide, substantial city, all 'staked off,' with the lots marked with their owners' names. . . . I am satisfied Duluth is there, or thereabout, for I see it stated here on this map that it is exactly thirty-nine hundred and ninety miles from Liverpool, though I have no doubt, for the sake of convenience, it will be moved back ten miles, so as to make the distance an even four thousand.

"Then, sir, there is the climate of Duluth, unquestionably the most salubrious and delightful to be found anywhere on the Lord's earth. Now, I have always been under the impression, as I presume other gentlemen have, that in the region around Lake Superior it was cold enough for at least nine months in the year to freeze the smoke-stack off a locomotive. But I see it represented on this map that Duluth is situated exactly halfway between the latitudes of Paris and Venice, so that gentlemen who have inhaled the exhilarating airs of the one or basked in the golden sunlight of the other may see at a glance that Duluth must be a place of untold delights, a terrestrial paradise. . . . Nevertheless, sir, it grieves my very soul to be compelled to say that I cannot vote for the grant of lands provided for in this bill. . . . There are two insuperable obstacles in the way. In the first place, my constituents, for whom I am acting here, have no more interest in this road than they have in the great question of culinary taste now perhaps agitating the public mind of Dominica, as to whether the illustrious commissioners who recently left this capital for that free and enlightened republic would be better fricasseed, boiled, or roasted, and in the second place these lands, which I am asked to give away, alas, are not mine to bestow! My relation to them is simply that of trustee to an express trust. And shall I ever betray that trust? Never, sir! Rather perish Duluth! Perish the paragon of cities! Let the freezing cyclones of the black Northwest bury it forever beneath the eddying sands of the raging St. Croix!"

James Bryce, the British scholar-statesman who often understood America better than the Americans (and was ambassador here, 1907–13), attended the completion of the Northern Pacific, below, in 1883. These comments on railroad magnates are from his *American Commonwealth* (1888).

"War is the natural state of an American railway towards all other authorities and its own fellows, just as war was the natural state of cities towards one another in the ancient world. . . . The president of a great railroad needs gifts for strategical combinations scarcely inferior to those of a great war minister. . . . He must so throw out his branches as not only to occupy promising tracts, but keep his competing enemies at a distance; he must annex small lines when he sees a good chance, damaging them first so as to get them cheaper; he must make a close alliance with at least one other great line, which completes his communications with the East or with the farther West, and be prepared to join this ally in a conflict. . . .

James Bryce

These railway kings are among the greatest men, perhaps I may say are the greatest men, in America. They have wealth, else they could not hold the position. They have fame, for every one has heard of their achievements; every newspaper chronicles their movements. They have power, more power—that is, more opportunity of making their personal will prevail— than perhaps any one in political life, except the President and the Speaker, who after all hold theirs for only four years and two years, while the railroad monarch may keep his for life. When the master of one of the greatest Western lines travels towards the Pacific on his palace car, his journey is like a royal progress. Governors of States and Territories bow before him; legislatures receive him in solemn session; cities and towns seek to propitiate him, for has he not the means of making or marring a city's fortunes? Although the railroad companies are unpopular, and although this autocratic sway from a distance contributes to their unpopularity, I do not think that the ruling magnates are themselves generally disliked. On the contrary, they receive that tribute of admiration which the American gladly pays to whoever has done best what every one desires to do."

Hatless Henry Villard poses on the footboard of a shining eight-wheeler, ready for the "last-spike" ceremonies on his Northern Pacific.

6. The Age of Bare Knuckles

*"The Great Race for the Western Stakes, 1870"
is Currier and Ives' somewhat labored cartoon on
the rivalry of Jim Fisk's heavily rigged Erie and
the two parts of Commodore Vanderbilt's new
railroad empire, its stock recently "watered."*

PRECEDING PAGES: *"Let Them Have It All, And
Be Done With It"* *is the caption for this* Puck
*cartoon of 1882, in which the railroad kings of
the moment divide up Manhattan. They include
William H. Vanderbilt, Jay Gould, Russell Sage
(Gould's moneylending partner and the scourge of
railroads around Chicago), and Cyrus Field, the
Atlantic Cable man who was briefly involved in
buying up the New York elevateds with his brother
David Dudley Field and Jay Gould.*

It was the roughest age in the history of American capitalism, those years right after the Civil War, and the place to see it in action was not the plains, plateaus, and passes of the West but an ugly little brownstone, five stories high, at 22 Broad Street in New York City. This was the crowded Wall Street branch of Delmonico's Restaurant, just a few doors from the Stock Exchange. Here was the home of "corners" and thimblerigging, the place where booms and panics were engineered; up and down the adjacent streets were the main offices of the railway kings whose imperial power and imperious ways so impressed the historian James Bryce. Railroads were our first "Big Business," and the main concern of Wall Street. Anyone who doubted that needed only to step into Delmonico's lobby and watch the anxious men at the ticker tape, or look in the eating rooms and see the men of the hour.

These were not the men who built railroads, to paraphrase Jay Gould's remark, but the men who bought and sold them. That would be Gould himself, the dark little fellow in the black beard who ate so sparingly, almost an ascetic in that company of trenchermen. Though he was barely thirty in 1867, people were afraid of him; it was said he had outsmarted his associates in a leather business and driven one to suicide. Recently he had been taken onto the board of directors of the troubled Erie Railroad.

The man who had brought that about, the new power in the Erie, Daniel Drew, could usually be found in the cheapest part of Delmonico's, according to Lately Thomas, the historian of that noted establishment. That was the downstairs lunch counter among the messenger boys and clerks, where he would munch a sandwich after first saying grace over it, as was his unvarying custom. An eccentric among eccentrics, he had the manner and speech of a hayseed. Reputedly, he was only partially literate, and he did nothing to discourage the story. Looking at the famous old manipulator, it was hard to credit the undoubted fact that the pockets of his seedy black clothes usually bulged with securities or greenbacks. In another pocket would be his Bible, from which he occasionally puzzled out apt quotations, and a large bandanna handkerchief. Sometimes, as he pulled out the latter to perform its office at his sharp nose, he would drop, seemingly unnoticed, a slip or two of paper, indicating some stock he might be selling or buying, or perhaps a desired price. But these crudely written bits of information, when surreptitiously retrieved, would be about as helpful to the finders as the false lights once set by the professional shipwreckers of Block Island.

"Uncle Dan'l's" rustic public personality was topped off by an old drover's cap, recalling the fact that he had spent a great many of his more than seventy years driving cattle to market. He had bought his first herd with $100 received as a bounty for joining the Army in the War of 1812, and he had won fame for his habit of salting his animals and then letting them drink their prodigious fill just before they were weighed in by the buyers. From "watering stock," a good preparation for railroad finance in that era, he had graduated to running his own cattle yards and then into steamboating on the Hudson and on Long Island Sound, in cutthroat competition with another poor boy made good, Commodore Cornelius Vanderbilt. One could often find them racing their great side-wheelers *Drew* and *Vanderbilt*; modesty was not their long suit. Now their battle had shifted from that ring to railroads although they were friends of a sort, like pugilists taunting each other between matches.

Not that Drew or any other patron of Delmonico's would be apt to find the old pirate, tall and distinctive in his fur-lined greatcoat and out-of-fashion high stock, in that den of speculators. Even if he had a stomach for lunch after his customary breakfast—three lamb chops, eight or nine eggs (yolks only), and tea with twelve lumps per cup—the Commodore spent just an hour or so downtown in the morning and then drove home to enjoy the afternoon racing his fine horses. The boy who had started out as a ferryman in New York Harbor with $100 lent by his mother and an old sailing barge called a periauger was now worth some twenty millions, very likely the largest American fortune at the time. Bluff, hearty, and energetic, he was now determined to dominate the railroads heading from New York to the West. Among others, Drew stood in his way. Indeed, his bitterest rivals were Drew, his quiet young friend Gould, and his even more impossible ally in the so-called "Erie Ring," the brassy and bumptious Jim Fisk.

Fisk was what is sometimes called "an original," a born promoter whom people variously called "Jubilee Jim" or "The Prince of Erie," although he preferred "Admiral," from his steamboat activities. At Delmonico's one would find the flashily dressed Fisk in one of the costly upstairs rooms, arranging anything from a swindle to a seduction, with appropriate wines and flowers; he was no more to be seen with his mentor Uncle Dan'l at the cheap lunch counter than J. P. Morgan would be at a hot dog stand, at least after he

At the indicator in Delmonico's Broad Street restaurant, speculators follow the ups and downs of Erie stock during the frenzied days of 1868–69.

William H. Vanderbilt's twin Fifth Avenue houses

William K.'s château and W. K., Jr.'s (right)

Cornelius II's castle at Fifty-Seventh Street

That railroading could be a rewarding line of work was amply demonstrated by the massive Vanderbilt presence on Fifth Avenue in New York. Their showy town houses, built by the leading architects, ran with few interruptions from Fifty-First Street to Fifty-Eighth. The above is only a sampling. The prolific and prodigious Vanderbilts, ranging from dukes and polo players to inventors and one full-fledged Communist, were all descendants of the Commodore's dutiful son William Henry, who doubled the family inheritance, the last actively to manage the spreading railroad system. Thereafter they were directors.

"arrived." That interesting process had led from Pownal, Vermont, to peddling tinware and travelling with Van Amberg's circus, which was a good place to learn something about trimming the suckers. Then he went to Jordan Marsh's big store in Boston, and did so well that he was made the store's salesman of necessaries (and unnecessaries) to the Army, emerging with a tidy bankroll. Wall Street attracted him like a magnet, and quickly relieved him of his savings, but he made a connection there with Daniel Drew, for whom he was able to perform little services; one was to set up a group of unwary Boston speculators on whom Drew unloaded a small railroad, the Providence & Stonington, for which he had no further need.

Drew's new concern, the Erie, had attracted his interest not long after its completion to Lake Erie back in 1851. "The Work of the Age" had been in trouble ever since. Battered by floods, beset by wrecks, bedeviled by strikes, it had already gone bankrupt once; then, as a kind of climax, Drew became a stockholder and a director. On a movie sound track, one might expect here a chord of doom. Because he could lend money obtainable nowhere else, and endorsed Erie loans of $980,000, they made him treasurer, which was like installing a fox to guard a henhouse; in effect he had control. The Erie, which was overcapitalized but basically a good earner, served Drew as a handy tool in his favorite game of short selling. In the treasury he found twenty-eight thousand shares of unissued stock and $3,000,000 worth of convertible Erie bonds; he took them as collateral against loans of $3,500,000 he made to the railroad. Then, in a rising market, he began going short on his own account in Erie stock. When the stock reached 95, he converted the bonds into common stock, and with those and the other twenty-eight thousand shares he began to flood the market. The price of Erie stock slipped and then, as brokers panicked, plunged to 50, and Drew made an enormous personal profit.

Such tricks would not work, of course, in the case of "corners," in which speculators would trap their short-selling rivals. Those who had gone short were the "bears," who had undertaken to deliver in the future stocks they did not own but planned to buy at low prices if the stock went down. The "bulls" on the other hand bet the stock would go up, so that they would collect, in effect, a profit on every share the discomfited short seller would have to deliver. Bulls seeking a "corner" in some company would try to acquire, as quietly as possible, all the stock outstanding. When thereafter the bears tried to buy to cover their commitments there would be almost no stock to be had. In their frantic search these short sellers would have to bid the price up, sometimes hundreds of dollars per share, all to the enormous profit of those holding the corner. In this very kind of trap, Drew himself was twice caught by Commodore Vanderbilt.

In 1862 Vanderbilt began to buy stock in the somewhat unpromising New York & Harlem Railroad, which extended from Twenty-Third Street, the north end of what was then the city, up Fourth (now Park) Avenue, crossing the Harlem River and heading north by an inland route to Chatham, New York, and a connection to Albany. A year later the Commodore persuaded New York to pass an ordinance allowing his line to connect over new tracks with the downtown area. The stock shot up when that permission was given and Drew of course saw an opportunity to make a coup. He sold the stock short. Then he induced his corrupt Tammany allies on the City Council to rescind the ordinance, which would normally drive the stock down. When the ordinance was cancelled, however, the stock did not fall as far as Uncle Dan'l expected. Soon it started up. Vanderbilt bought every share offered, and Drew discovered to his horror that he had contracted to deliver more shares than existed outside the Commodore's pocket. The price now took off into the sky. In order to settle, Drew sustained a heavy loss. "Pay up or shut up," said the Commodore heartlessly when Drew approached him seeking mercy.

Vanderbilt next acquired the other line that headed for Albany, the Hudson River Railroad, later the picturesque main line northward but then very feeble. While he was trying to combine the two lines into a single company by means of a bill in the legislature, Drew essayed to buy the defeat of the bill, go short, and recoup his previous losses. Yet once again Vanderbilt and his friends cornered him and left him smarting in defeat.

Triumphant, the Commodore turned his attention to the New York Central Railroad, which Erastus Corning had put together between Albany and Buffalo. Although Vanderbilt's railroads had been connected with it in 1866 by a bridge over the Hudson to Albany, the Central transferred its freight and passengers to his tracks only when the river was frozen and their favored competing boat lines could not operate. This displeased the Commodore, a bad man to cross. Besides, he had ideas. One cold day in January, 1867, he unexpectedly halted train service on the east, or far side of the bridge. Passengers would simply have to make a two-mile hike across the bridge and through the snow. Freight could scarcely move. Consternation and indignation ruled in Albany and a committee of the legislature, egged on by the Central, waited upon Vanderbilt. Why would he not keep operating his trains into Albany Station?

The Commodore was ready for them; in fact he was eager to answer. He had discovered, he said, a law that prohibited his railroad from running trains across the river. Yes, a very old law. Here was a copy. This act of the legislature had been passed long ago when the New York Central in its early days had been trying to block any competition from other routes to the east. To be sure, the law had never been used and had been quite forgotten, but he, a law-abiding citizen, would not violate it. Speechless, the legislators departed.

The stock of the wounded New York Central went down and Vanderbilt started buying. In late 1867 he acquired full control, and eventually united both roads, creating the single line on which the *Empire State Express*, the *Twentieth Century Limited*, and many other great trains would eventually roll. He put a great deal of money into improving the lines; he was a more constructive man than his opponents. Perhaps the improvements justified the fact that he watered the stock at that moment by some $42,000,000. In the course of the consolidation, in fact, he awarded himself a "bonus" of $6,000,000 in cash and $20,000,000 in stock. With these added millions in his pocket, the old monopolist set out in 1868 to buy the Erie.

The Erie was the bouncing ball of the stock market, thanks to Drew's financial gymnastics, but Vanderbilt bought its shares relentlessly, investing many millions. No doubt he meant to corner it just as he had done so successfully before, but there seemed to be no end of shares, and no information on how many ought to exist. This time, as he learned later, he faced a printing press. Behind it cranking furiously stood the Erie Ring of Drew, Gould, and Fisk. There was somehow always more stock for sale. The trio had many devices, from fresh Drew loans against convertible bonds to the issuing of good—well, reasonably good—Erie stock in exchange at par for the worthless paper of other small railroads, which the Ring picked up with one hand and unloaded on the Erie with the other. Tammany joined the Ring, and Boss William Marcy Tweed sat down on the once proper and dignified Erie board. The Ring threw perhaps a hundred thousand shares of this fraudulent stock onto the market, an enormous amount in that deflated era. To stop the issuance of stock on which the ink was scarcely dry, Vanderbilt got an injunction from a tame judge, George Bernard. The Erie Ring got a counter injunction from another judge, but Vanderbilt's judge ignored it and ordered the arrest of Drew, Gould, and Fisk. As word reached them late one evening at

Newport: the Breakers, Cornelius II's "cottage"

The New Jersey place of a daughter, Mrs. Twombly

Asheville: G. W. Vanderbilt II's Biltmore

Scarborough, New York: Daughter Margaret's house

These little hideaways are four of the many great country estates of Vanderbilt heirs made possible by the New York Central Railroad. There were, of course, others in Newport, like William K.'s Marble House, which cost $2,000,000 to build and $9,000,000 more to decorate, and Fred's Rough Point. Of all the Vanderbilt houses that grew up in the watering places of America, the most beautiful was George Washington Vanderbilt II's stunning palace, Biltmore, designed after Chambord and Blois in France by Richard Morris Hunt, landscaped by Frederick Law Olmsted, and endowed with forests by Gifford Pinchot.

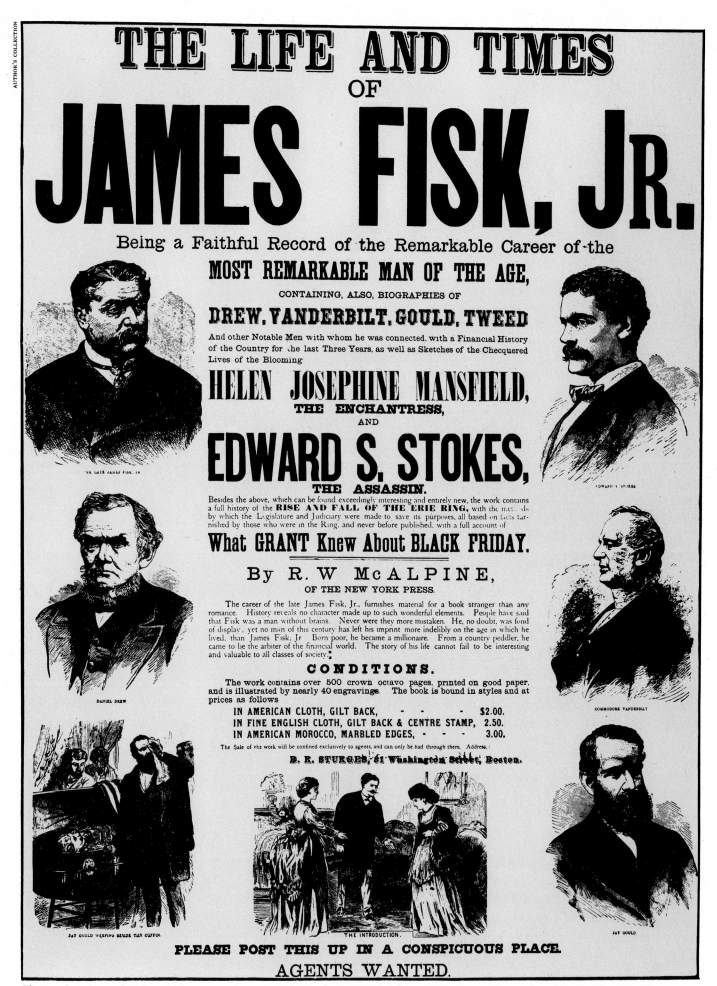

The gaudy career of Fisk and his associates was gobbled up by readers of the popular press and sensational books like this one.

the Erie's offices in New York that a *force majeure*, ordered by Bernard, was coming for them, the salty trio, guarded by more than a hundred hired thugs, dashed madly for the ferry to New Jersey. After a brief scuffle at the ferry slip with the outnumbered sheriffs, they made good their escape to Jersey City, well beyond Judge Bernard's jurisdiction. With them they carried the Erie's books and papers and $6,000,000 in greenbacks, proceeds of the stock unloaded on the raging Commodore.

Taking over and heavily guarding the Taylor Hotel in Jersey City, which Fisk, enjoying this quasi-military operation, renamed Fort Taylor, they succeeded in breaking Vanderbilt's corner. He had lost millions. Injunctions flew back and forth. Vanderbilt had his judge appoint a receiver, a Vanderbilt son-in-law, for some one hundred thousand shares of illegally issued stock. Another judge promptly enjoined the son-in-law from acting. Then a Tammany politician named Peter B. Sweeney was appointed receiver instead. Although anything he might "receive" was safely across the river and out of his clutches, he was paid $150,000 for his arduous services.

The battlefield shifted to Albany, where the Drew forces sought to bribe the legislature into legalizing their recent stock issues. But Vanderbilt outbid them and the Drew bill was defeated. Next Gould boldly appeared in person in Albany, with half a million dollars of persuading money in his valise. Of course he was arrested under Bernard's earlier court order, brought back before him in Manhattan, and put in charge of a sheriff. But somehow the sheriff was persuaded to accompany Gould, satchel still in hand, back to Albany, where the latter took a hotel room and the former sat outside. Inside Gould announced that he was too sick to move or see anyone including the sheriff. The sheriff camped there while someone who looked very like Gould was able to get out and visit enough members of the State Senate to buy the enactment of the original bill legalizing the stock.

But now, while the lower house of the people's representatives eagerly awaited its turn at the satchel, there came horrifying news. The two sides had made a kind of treaty. In effect, Uncle Dan'l handed his old friend "Corneel" the money he might have spent on the legislators, plus enough more to cut the Vanderbilt losses to a more modest amount. Drew bought back the stock he had sold Vanderbilt, although at a compromise price. The stock itself went back to the Erie treasury, the lawgivers were left hungry, and the Erie Railroad itself was some $9,000,000 poorer for the settlement.

But the Erie had not yet escaped. The Ring had barely begun its looting. Gould's safe was filling up; an interesting piece of high Victorian steel and cabinetwork, it may be viewed today in the cathedral hush of his old estate at Lyndhurst overlooking the Hudson, preserved by the National Trust just as though the little monster had been some kind of public benefactor. With Vanderbilt out of the way, Gould took over the presidency of the Erie in October, 1868, and soon there were more issues of dubious stocks and bonds, more injunctions, more bribes, more corners. In one of them Gould and Fisk bankrupted and drove out their mentor, Drew, leaving him to be supported by the charity of his poor relatives, occasioning no noticeable change in his already parsimonious life style.

In the spoils Fisk got Drew's Fall River Line of steamboats—which was the way to go to Boston in the Gilded Age, before all the river mouths of the Connecticut shore line had been bridged by the railroads (and for many of the nabobs, long after that). Drew had ordered and Fisk got in 1869 the new three-thousand-ton floating palaces *Bristol* and *Providence*. Their walking beams ran paddle wheels thirty-eight feet across; the decks were alternate strips of black walnut and yellow pine, they slept over eight hundred souls in a luxury not available today. In the early morning, having raced up the Sound

Jim Fisk toasts President Grant in the course of an entertainment aboard his palace steamer Bristol, *shown below. This was not, as Grant thought, purely a social occasion, for Fisk was then busily plotting his notorious corner on gold. Grant's brother-in-law Abel Corbin had been cut in to the deal in return for trying to prevent the President from releasing government-held gold stocks—a move that at any time could break the corner. Grant, like Harding at a later time, was surrounded by fast operators, but when he learned what was up he had the gold released. The resulting crash on September 24, 1869, was Black Friday, as described in the accompanying text.*

by night from New York to Fall River, travellers boarded the special boat train to Boston, breakfasting in more luxury. Fisk filled the boats with thick carpets and fine fixtures. There were orchestras, and in the two ships some 250 canaries in cages, each personally named by Fisk, a man of prodigious fancies. "If Vanderbilt's a Commodore," he announced, "I can be an Admiral," and got himself a fancy uniform, and another one for his mistress, an untalented actress named Josie Mansfield with whom for a time he lived quite openly, although there was a real Mrs. Fisk in Boston, where his picture, no doubt, was turned to the wall. On the other hand, flanking the stairs of one of these great white ships were portraits of Fisk and Gould. "There are the two thieves," a stockbroker is said to have remarked, "but where's Christ?"

The headquarters of the Erie was in a New York opera house that Fisk had acquired to be near his friends in the chorus, who were set up in a house next door. The Prince of Erie, now grown fat but jovial as ever, charged the railroad $75,000 a month rent for the ornate offices from which the Erie Ring began a series of financial raids. They took on the United States Express Company, and then an unfortunate railroad called the Albany & Susquehanna. Their most outrageous feat was an attempt to corner the gold market, a coup that failed but brought on the infamous "Black Friday," September 24, 1869. Many businesses were ruined in the ensuing panic, and public amusement with the well-publicized antics of the Erie Ring turned to anger. An unchastened Gould went before a congressional committee. What had happened to certain monies owed to creditors? Gone, he said. Gone where? "Gone where the woodbine twineth," said the boy financier. It was also he who commented on another occasion, "Nothing is lost save honor."

Fisk's brazen career ended suddenly on January 6, 1872, when he was shot dead on the stairs of the Grand Central Hotel by Edward Stokes, a young rival for the favors of Josie Mansfield. The Prince of Erie, denounced from every pulpit at his demise, was nevertheless so entertaining to the populace that his public funeral, staged by Tammany in the truly grand manner, was the great event of the year. There was a band of two hundred pieces, a long column of blue-coated guardians of the law, the entire Ninth Regiment (into which he had bought his way) parading behind Colonel Fisk's riderless horse, a vast concourse of the curious, and a special train to carry him back in style to Brattleboro, Vermont, and a great marble tomb. America loves a cheerful scoundrel, and besides, he had supported his aged parents.

In 1872 Gould was thrown out of the Erie, which he had brought to bankruptcy again. When he hesitated to resign, the Civil War hero General Daniel Sickles, representing a combination of unhappy English stockholders, cynically persuaded him by saying that his very departure would raise the price of Erie stock. Always receptive to good ideas, Gould agreed, bought heavily, submitted his resignation, and made his last coup in Erie stock—after which, as we know, he teamed up with Russell Sage, to turn their destructive talents on western railroads like the Union Pacific. His touch, they said, was death.

By that time Commodore Vanderbilt and his able son William were transforming the New York Central & Hudson River Railroad, through purchases of other lines throughout the Midwest, into one of America's major railroad properties. At last in 1877 the rugged old ferryman died, with his wife playing the organ and the family intoning his favorite hymn, "Come All Ye Sinners, Poor and Needy." He left about $100,000,000. Amid the many mourners at the grave in New Dorp, Staten Island, were noticed a number of honest men like Peter Cooper. They must have recognized in Vanderbilt some kind of creative force, for all his buccaneering. Even old Dan'l Drew turned up, threadbare, skinny, clutching his worn umbrella, a living ghost from the bareknuckle period of American railroading.

The Commodore's son William enjoyed a bad press, as in the cartoon above showing him ravishing Liberty, or some other noble abstraction. It was he who uttered the phrase "The public be damned," even if it was torn out of context. He seemed to care most about his great race horse, Maude S., whom he kept in a private pasture on the present site of the Biltmore Hotel, handily in view of his office window in the old Grand Central Terminal. Yet he was an able man, honest by the lights of his time, who vastly expanded and improved the New York Central—it was now, note the phrase, a "system" filling the Middle West. He died in 1885, only eight years after his father.

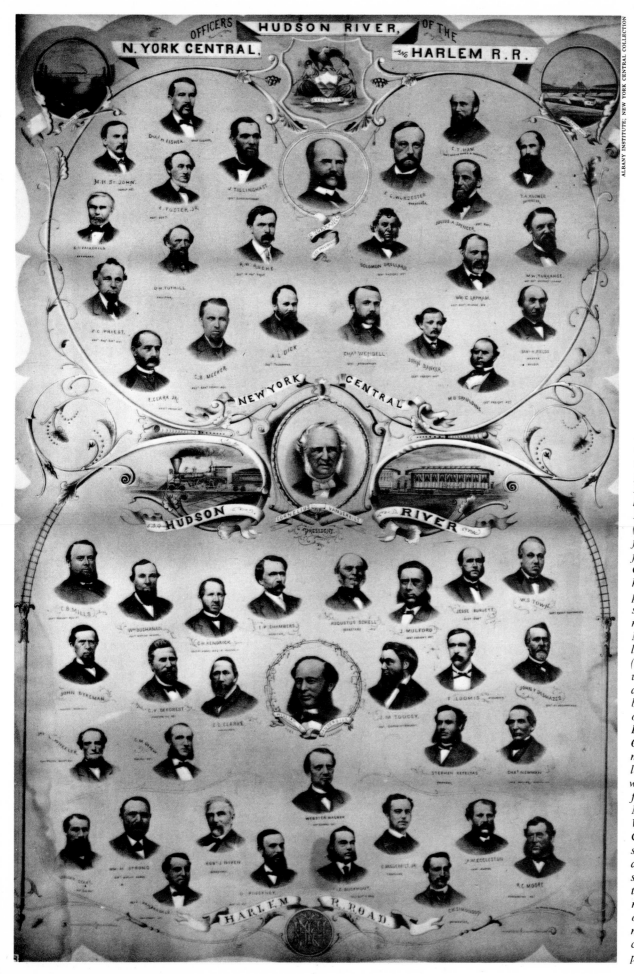

A proud lithograph of the new Vanderbilt railroad empire about 1869 displays not only the great Niagara Bridge (upper left) and the disputed Hudson River Bridge (upper right) but strong family presence in the officialdom. Seen below the Commodore at center is his son William, a vice president. Above is his son-in-law Daniel Torrance, a vice president. Near the bottom is William's son Cornelius II (mislabelled Jr.), a treasurer. (His son-in-law Horace Clark does not appear but he was president of the Vanderbilt-owned Lake Shore Railroad.) One may also find the noted Chauncey Depew, later president of the whole enterprise, the famous superintendent J. M. Toucey, and Webster Wagner, who built the Central's parlor and sleeping cars, like the one at center. The locomotive shown is the Vanderbilt, the only one which remained colorfully decorated when the Commodore, in the age of coal, ordered all others painted a funereal black.

The greatest standardizer, in another sense, was thrifty, pious John D. Rockefeller, of whom his sister said, "When it was raining porridge, John's dish was always right side up." No small part of the success of Standard Oil was due to the large freight rebates which John D.'s partner Henry M. Flagler forced on the railroads, beginning in the 1860's. From Ohio the rate for shipping oil was 35¢ a barrel. Standard used its power to get a special rate for itself of 10¢. Then Rockefeller associates devised the "drawback": The railroad was forced to refund to Standard the 25¢ difference the competitors had paid. In a year and a half, John F. Stover says, four railroads had to pay Standard Oil drawbacks amounting to $10,000,000. These were among the methods which helped Rockefeller drive his competitors to the wall and build his great fortune, taxing not only the railroads but every American home with kerosene lamps. The unconscionable practices of the oil and other trusts ironically helped bring on more real regulation of railroads than of themselves. Old John D. himself had just retired in the odor of sanctity when this picture was taken in 1910; he could never understand why people were so angry with his sensible methods.

The Standardizers

By 1880, although the railroad kings continued their colorful wars, the lines they played with had grown astonishingly. The thirty-five thousand miles of railroad at the end of the Civil War had expanded to ninety-three thousand, and in the next decade, a time of tremendous construction, to 164,000. Construction was particularly heavy in the neglected South and in the West, and the Midwest was covered by a spider web of rails. Nor was this vast growing network any longer the fragile, bumpy sort of road the wartime armies knew, interrupted at every big river and in many cities with freight and passengers shifting at each change in gauge. Strong albeit light steel rails, first used in 1863 on the Pennsylvania, covered a quarter of the lines in 1880 and four-fifths of them only ten years later. Air brakes and better couplers (see pages 188-189) were coming in, and the South's five-foot gauge was disappearing. On two days in 1886, May 31 and June 1, thirteen thousand miles of remaining five-foot gauge in the South were standardized, half the roads on one day, the remainder on the next. With track gangs stationed along every mile of track, all traffic was halted. Between 3:30 A.M. and 4 P.M. on each day, one rail was everywhere moved the necessary inches closer to its mate.

Several generations have grown to adulthood supposing that time itself has always been what it is today, four zones loping across the land in the path of the sun, but before November 18, 1883, time was a fairly chaotic affair, set locally by cities and towns, quite independently of any other place. The growth of railroads made the confusion impossible, as the illustration at far right indicates. When solar time was noon in Chicago, as railroad historian Stewart Holbrook recorded, it was 12:31 in Pittsburgh, 12:24 in Cleveland, 12:13 in Cincinnati, 12:09 in Louisville, 12:07 in Indianapolis, 11:50 in St. Louis, 11:48 in Dubuque, 11:41 in St. Paul, 11:27 in Omaha. There were, for example, thirty-eight different times in Wisconsin. There were three different clocks in the Buffalo station and six different times in Pittsburgh, depending on the railroad. That such nonsense had to stop was obvious, and the change was brought about by William Frederick Allen, a member of the staff of the *Official Guide of the Railways and Steam Navigation Lines*, the hardy perennial Bible of railroaders, whose practical rather than theoretical time boundaries were adopted by the General Time Convention and put into effect by the railroads, despite a certain amount of resistance from conservatives and the kind of clerics who used to resist Sunday trains. With no lobby to push it, and no money in it, Congress did not bestow its blessing on the system that railroads gave us until 1918.

Standardization of time and gauge, followed by steady improvements in engines, rolling stock, signal and control systems, and the like, converted a lot of little railroads, no matter who owned them, into a nationwide system. A man might travel almost anywhere by rail, but more importantly, he could ship anything anywhere. If he was in a hurry, there were fast-freight lines, born after the Civil War. Operated over many railroads by private companies that owned their own cars, they gave way—because of abuses, and because they left the railroads themselves only the less desirable shipments—to fast freights managed by groups of railroads operating pools of cars. One could ship a carload lot anywhere by the "Continental" or the "Green Line" or the "Great Western Dispatch," or dozens of other lines.

The American economy, its markets suddenly nationwide, underwent a revolution; the railroad created industries, and did it wholesale. It carried coal everywhere in new hopper cars, and burned the product itself. An iron and steel industry made its rails, and long trains carried the ore. Lumber, livestock, food, and manufactured products of all sorts began to move by rail, and the businessman no longer thought merely of carrying his product to some nearby town. All America was his potential buyer. A thousand ordinary things that had been woven or sewn or churned or ground or preserved in the home could suddenly be bought in a store that the world supplied. And this gift from the steam engine transformed the life of American women. Luxuries became necessities, and they had to be carried too. It is estimated that ton-miles of freight—that is, tons of freight multiplied by the number of miles they moved by rail—rose from ten billion in 1865 to seventy-nine billion in 1890: eight times as much (and thirty-six times as much just before World War I). Everything in America was growing—population, cities, immigration, business, consumption, national wealth—and the railroads led the way.

For all these achievements, nevertheless, the railroads, once welcomed into every town and village, were cordially hated by the victims of their rates, their wrecks, and the high-handed methods of men who ran what were supposed to be services in the public interest as though they were private fiefdoms. It was long believed by Populists and reformers that the railroads enjoyed the anarchy that prevailed among them, and that they abhorred the very thought of regulation. Yet many railroad managers longed for some sort of stability, some kind of control over rates, and some protection against raids and ruthless competition. It was a yearning born not out of any social conscience, in most cases, but out of common sense. That very kind of stability was waiting in the wings. It would not be the work of government but of a single man.

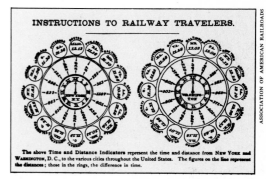

Sample "Time and Distance Indicators" from Appleton's Railway & Steam Navigation Guide *for October, 1873, show how travellers had to set their watches in the days before the railroads introduced standard time zones. They are figured from either New York City or Washington, D.C., at precise noon, the settings appearing in the little outside circles. Noon in Washington was twelve minutes later than in New York City.*

From the standpoint of the general public at the time, the three most dramatic moments in American railroad history were the driving of the spike at Promontory, the adoption of standard time, and the day on which the major railroads of the North and South were united for all practical purposes by the same gauge of track. That last occasion was hailed in the fine drawing at left by Thomast Nast, published in Harper's Weekly *on June 5, 1886. In actual fact the southern lines adopted four feet, nine inches rather than the true standard gauge of four feet, eight and one-half inches, mainly because that was the width of the Pennsylvania Railroad, which sent the most freight into the southern states. The difference was so small that the two gauges were compatible for most practical purposes; some years later, of course, the half-inch difference was dropped.*

J. P. Morgan repels the press photographers, without full success. The man at right may be a chauffeur, dressed for his outdoor post.

The Heritage of Ill Will

He had no use for newspapermen, as the angry photograph at left shows, and not much more for photographers who came by permission. Edward Steichen was allowed exactly two minutes; as the piercing eyes burned into the camera lens the young photographer could think of nothing but the headlights of an express train bearing down upon him. Everything about J. Pierpont Morgan, from his impressive physique to his peremptory manner, was commanding, and even his partners tiptoed by him like office boys. He spoke in ultimatums. He was the greatest banker in Christendom, an imperial presence who overawed not only railroad kings but governments. He was aristocratic in manner and regal in his way of life, travelling either by private train or in a succession of imposing steam yachts all called *Corsair*. Was the name a conscious irony? He collected art as he collected corporations, and for leisure moments seemed to enjoy the company of bishops of the Episcopal Church, in whose affairs he was a prominent lay member. Lawyers could be hired in brigades to outwit or confuse the enemy. Politicians he despised either because they could be bought or because they could not comprehend his kind of high finance. As for sentimental twaddle about the public interest, his opinion is best summed up in his famous remark, "I owe the public nothing."

In his time Morgan was a kind of one-man Federal Reserve System: When America's gold reserve was in danger, President Cleveland in 1895 called Morgan to the rescue. It was duly rescued, although at considerable profit to Morgan. When banks were about to close their doors in the Panic of 1907, everyone turned to Morgan to save them, including the Secretary of the Treasury. Marshalling the leaders of finance, he succeeded, although not without wounds and losses for many; certain of his maneuvers at the time are still wrapped in mystery. In his person also, he might be said to have anticipated the Securities & Exchange Commission. In the financial jungle of the times Morgan-managed securities were usually sound, and he saw to it that they paid. As an international banker in what was, in the late nineteenth century, still a "developing" country, he worried about the faith and trust that Europeans would have in the securities of American business.

In 1879 he had helped William H. Vanderbilt to sell almost half his holdings in the New York Central to English investors, to avoid disturbing the market and lowering the price, and he was all the more distressed when in the early eighties the steady dividends of the New York Central declined. The cause of this untidy situation was a typical example of railroad wars of the era. Along the opposite bank of the Hudson River from the Central, and then parallel to it all the way to Buffalo, had been built a rival called the New York, West Shore & Buffalo. It was partly financed by George Pullman, out of spite against Vanderbilt for using Wagner sleeping cars instead of his own. The Pennsylvania Railroad, then managed by an able buccaneer named Thomas A. Scott, acquired a commanding interest in the West Shore.

In classic situations of this sort, the trick was to slash one's rates, drive the new competition to the wall, and take over—although such schemes did not always work. When the Central had fought with the Erie in this same fashion years before, for example, it had cut the cattle rate from Buffalo to New York to $1 a head. Canny Jim Fisk had bought every bit of livestock he could lay hands on in Buffalo and shipped it over the rival road at this giveaway figure, making a tidy profit off the Commodore. This time, however, the contestants

Morgan had given and raised campaign funds for President Theodore Roosevelt (the latter is seen tub thumping here in a railroad yard), and was irritated by subsequent Administration actions like the suit against his and Jim Hill's Northern Securities Corporation. The way to settle matters quietly, he had suggested to Roosevelt, was to have "your man" (the Attorney General) talk it out with "my man" (the Morgan lawyer), as though they were rival sovereign powers. TR was only an on-and-off Progressive, perhaps, but too radical nevertheless for the great financier. When Roosevelt left the White House to William Howard Taft and set out on a well-publicized big-game safari in Africa, Morgan said to a friend, "I hope the first lion he meets does his duty."

J. P. Morgan needed able if subservient lieu-tenants. One such was a professional railroad man named Charles S. Mellen. During the Hill-Har-riman struggles, the banker decided he needed his own representative as president of the Northern Pacific, and he rang Mellen on the telephone. Here is the illuminating conversation:

MORGAN: **Is that you Mr. Mellen?**
MELLEN: **Yes.**
MORGAN: **Anybody hear what we say?**
MELLEN: **No.**
MORGAN: **Will you take the Northern Pacific?**
MELLEN: **Yes.**
MORGAN: **Will you leave it all to me?**
MELLEN: **Yes.**
MORGAN: **Good-bye.**

Morgan made Mellen president of the financially sound New Haven in 1903, and employed him to build the monopoly. But Mellen was to keep in his place. Once when the New Haven was about to pay many unnecessary millions for two almost worthless competitors (consolidated as the New York, Westchester & Boston), Mellen asked Morgan about a note for the purchase drawn up by Morgan's lawyer Francis Lynde Stetson.

MELLEN: **Can you give me a few moments?**
MORGAN: **Certainly.**
MELLEN: **This note is not in the form it should be; there should be additional informa-tion given.**
MORGAN: **Did Mr. Stetson draw that note?**
MELLEN: **Yes, I suppose so.**
MORGAN: **Do you think you know more about how it ought to be done than he does?**

During a subsequent investigation we have this colloquy before the ICC:

COUNSEL: **Were you Mr. Morgan's man as presi-dent of the New Haven?**
MELLEN: **I have been called his office boy. I was very proud of his confidence. I regard the statement that I was his man as a compliment.**

were more evenly matched. Vanderbilt, striking back at Scott, organized the "Southern Pennsylvania Railroad." Just a little to the south of Scott's main line, huge crews began grading, levelling, and tunnelling an entirely new railroad all the way from Philadelphia to Pittsburgh.

To Morgan all this was sheerest waste and folly, and he decided to knock heads together. He invited both parties to a conference in the comfort of the *Corsair*. George Roberts, who had just succeeded Scott as president of the Pennsylvania, Chauncey Depew, the clever lawyer who served Vanderbilt as the actual president of the New York Central, and several others steamed back and forth around New York Harbor and the lower Hudson for a whole afternoon and evening. There was, in a literal sense, no escape from Morgan's forceful arguments. Each railroad should buy out its "nuisance" competitor. It was very foolish for gentlemen to continue such a fruitless battle, he pointed out. Depew agreed. Roberts objected that Pennsylvania state law for-bade him to take over a competitor in his own state, but Morgan brushed this aside; what were lawyers for? Later in the evening all agreed to his terms. The New York Central acquired the West Shore, and Roberts the uncompleted South Pennsylvania Railroad. Morgan got somewhere between $1,000,000 and $3,000,000 for his efforts. It is interesting to note that many years later the unused, grass-grown rights of way and long tunnels of the South Pennsyl-vania became significant parts of the Pennsylvania Turnpike.

In the competitive jungle, Morgan was the lion, the most active force in consolidating and reorganizing railroads. He had straightened out the affairs of one line after another—the Philadelphia & Reading in 1886, the Chesa-peake & Ohio in 1888, and then, following the Panic of 1893 when no fewer than 156 railroads collapsed, he restored the Erie, the Lehigh Valley, the Nor-folk & Western, and others. In the South, which was still recovering from the devastation of the Civil War, lay a great grab bag of shaky iron pikes which had been impoverished in various ways, often by a systematic looting that began during Reconstruction. Perhaps as many as fifty different railroads in the area—merging, falling apart, reforming in new combinations—had reached a financial nadir when they came to Morgan in despair. Reorganiza-tion by Morgan could be a painful experience. Railroads could not prosper if overburdened with debt, and so stockholders would be assessed to pay off bonds. Sometimes they were simply wiped out. Profitable lines would be repaired and worthless ones disposed of. When he got through, Morgan had created the Southern Railway, which developed into the present well-run and profitable system.

It had been after the turn of the century that Morgan undertook his most majestic operations. He put together the United States Steel Company, the largest corporation in the world; he financed the International Harvester Company. In the West he became involved in the greatest railroad battle the country was yet to witness.

In 1894, when the Northern Pacific went into receivership, Jim Hill, aided by his old Canadian associate George Stephen, now Lord Mount Stephen, had taken over control of that long-time rival and Morgan had reorganized it; the property was held by an effective although minority stock ownership. But at about the same time, Morgan also made an error. Attempts were made to interest him in the similarly bankrupt Union Pacific, but he dismissed it as "a streak of rust." He was unmoved when that unimpressive-seeming younger man, Edward Henry Harriman, called to ask his assistance. Morgan disliked him and sent him away. Harriman had built his success in taking over and reviving the Illinois Central; now he had conceived the bold venture of buy-ing up the Union Pacific, which had gone broke, thanks to the long control of Gould and Russell Sage, in the Panic of 1893. Its stock was cheap. The same idea had occurred to Jacob H. Schiff, head of the banking house of Kuhn, Loeb & Co. Schiff and Harriman bought it together, and the latter was in full charge of the company from 1898 until he died in 1909. Soon Harriman was restoring not only the tracks and rolling stock of the Union Pacific but its financial fortunes as well. In 1900 Collis Huntington died and an era ended in the Southwest; for the Union Pacific Harriman by 1901 managed to purchase his Central and Southern Pacific railroads—the Pacific Railroad of old was now finally united, at least for Harriman's lifetime.

It would be useful, Harriman thought, to pick up now the old, conservative Chicago, Burlington & Quincy, which was particularly strong in states like Iowa, Nebraska, and Montana, to carry his influence northward. Even more importantly, the Burlington would give his now completed Pacific Railroad an entry into Chicago and St. Louis; the Union Pacific still started at Omaha. Then in March, 1901, to his dismay, he learned that Hill and Morgan had snatched it out from under his nose. Hill also needed an outlet to Chicago, and he would also be able now to ship his North Coast lumber south to the lower plains, and link up at last with Denver, Kansas City, and St. Louis.

With the Hill lines now mightily expanded, Morgan set out for Aix-les-Bains for a little vacation and art-buying; Jim Hill went out to Seattle. But then in April, reading the financial pages, he noted suspiciously that Northern Pacific shares were for some strange reason moving up sharply. Supposedly he controlled that railroad, but only through the minority position that was normally sufficient. Day by day Northern Pacific kept rising, and the troubled Hill headed east on a record-breaking run in a special train. Arriving in New York, he went in his direct way to see Jacob Schiff at the offices of Kuhn, Loeb. Was Mr. Schiff doing the buying for Harriman? The banker was equally direct and admitted that his client, now barred from the Burlington, intended to take over the Northern Pacific. After all, he said, Mr. Hill did not control it. In fact, he said, Mr. Harriman now did—but this was not quite true yet, for he still lacked about forty thousand shares of a majority.

Hill now went to Morgan's partners and broke the bad news; a cable flew to Aix-les-Bains asking permission to buy. It was Friday. In those days, the market was open Saturday mornings. On Saturday, while Hill and his partners waited word from abroad, Harriman, brooding about his needed forty thousand shares, called Schiff's office to place the order. But Mr. Schiff was at the synagogue, and the order was not executed. Meanwhile, at the opening on Monday morning, the Morgan bankers bought all the Northern Pacific shares they could lay hands on, enough to deal Harriman one of his few defeats, driving the prices higher and higher and creating a minor panic.

Morgan, as usual, preferred peace and a community of interest. It was arranged to give Harriman a role on the Northern Pacific board. Then all the parties joined together in what they were pleased to call the Northern Securities Company. But it was the Progressive Era, the Roosevelt Administration brought suit, and the Supreme Court had heard the election returns. In 1904 it outlawed that celebrated holding company and ordered its dissolution. This was accounted a great victory over the bloated interests, although in fact it meant that, instead of working through a holding company, the individuals simply held the various securities themselves and operated the three railroads exactly as they had intended.

By about 1906, consolidations had organized some two-thirds of American railroads (150,000 out of 228,000 miles in all) into seven great and several minor systems. There were the Vanderbilt roads (22,500 miles), the Pennsylvania system (20,000), Gould lines in the Mississippi valley (17,000 miles controlled by Jay's son George, at least for a few years), E. H. Harriman's empire (21,000), the Hill lines (21,000), the Rock Island system (15,000), and

(Continued on page 152)

Few men fought J. P. Morgan and came off unscathed, but he underestimated Edward Henry Harriman, who had been a Wall Street office boy at fourteen and in his fifties had taken over the Union Pacific, the Southern Pacific, the Illinois Central, the Central of Georgia, and enough other roads so that he personally managed twenty-five thousand miles of line and controlled another thirty-five or forty thousand. Using the UP treasury as though it were an investment bank, Harriman acquired a large voice in the New York Central, and he even took control of the Erie. (*Everyone* at some point owned that unhappy company.) Harriman also had control of thirty-five thousand miles of steamship lines. No one had ever had such power. How big could he grow? In its public investigation of 1906 the ICC questioned him about his plans. He had bought heavily into the Santa Fe. Did he mean to take the rest?

HARRIMAN: If you will let us I will go take the Santa Fe tomorrow.

QUESTION: Then it is only the restriction of the antitrust law that keeps you from taking it?

HARRIMAN: I would go on as long as I live.

QUESTION: . . . You would also take the Northern Pacific and Great Northern, if you could get them?

HARRIMAN: If you would let me.

QUESTION: And your power, which you have, would gradually increase as you took one road after another, so that you might spread not only over the Pacific coast but over the Atlantic coast?

HARRIMAN: Yes.

As Peter Lyon says in his book *To Hell in a Day Coach*, which contains many nuggets of this kind, such frankness amounted to provocation. Roosevelt called Harriman "an enemy of the public" and the Supreme Court eventually broke apart Harriman's empire after his death. On balance, it must be said that he is the man who finally made the great Pacific Railroad strong and healthy.

In heavy black lines this map shows the routes owned and controlled by the New York, New Haven & Hartford Railroad in the Morgan-Mellen days (not counting their hand in connecting systems like the Boston & Maine, the Maine Central, and the New York, Ontario & Western). The lines running generally south from Boston had been the Old Colony Railroad; running west in the north of Connecticut, the Central New England crossed the great Poughkeepsie Bridge. It too had once been a competitor, as was the New York & New England with its route from Boston to New York via Willimantic. In the great days nearly every line shown ran passenger service of some sort. The map does not show the vast congeries of New Haven-owned streetcar and interurban lines covering

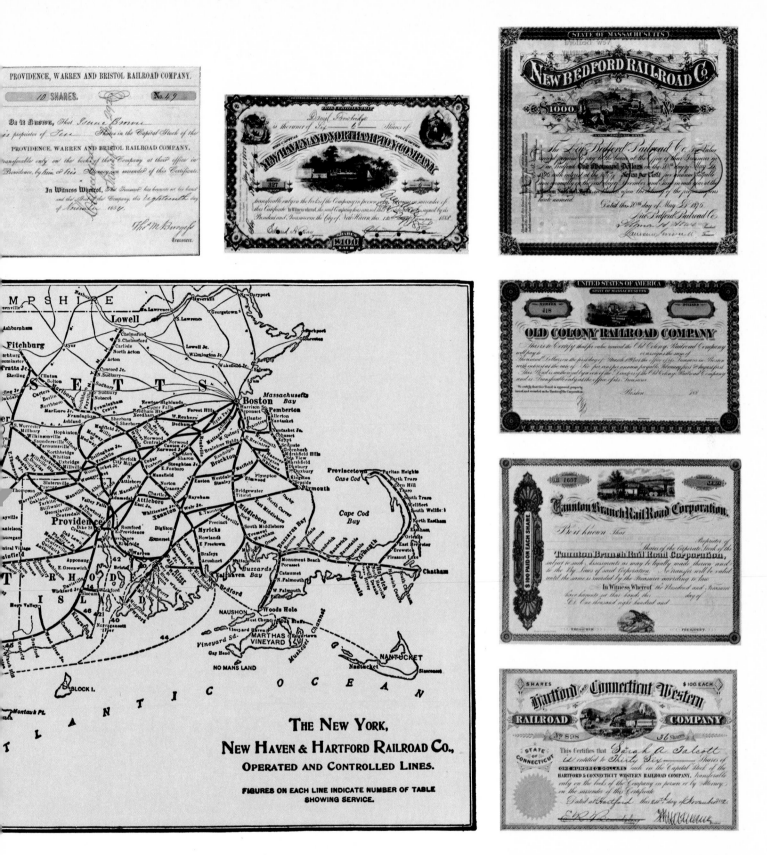

most of the same cities, but it indicates their steamboat lines to Bridgeport, New Haven, Hartford, New London, Providence, Fall River (with its special connecting trains to Boston), and New Bedford, where one could take the company's service to Woods Hole, Martha's Vineyard, and Nantucket. As the stock certificates around the border indicate, many parts of this system were once independent, and their routes can be traced by the curious. Yet these are only a handful of the three hundred corporations engorged at various times by the New Haven, which was itself swallowed up later on in the disastrous Penn Central combine. None of the steamboat lines and only a pitiful skeleton of the railroad service now survive out of a system which once seemed powerful and eternal.

CERTIFICATES FROM THE COLLECTIONS OF ALLEN A. SHARP AND CHARLES CASE

No one had welcomed the railroads more than the new western farmers, and no one came to hate them so bitterly. Totally dependent on the rails to carry their products to market, they found them extortionate as well as discriminatory middlemen. At one point, for example, when the grain rate from many Minnesota towns to St. Paul was 25¢ a hundredweight, it would be only half that for the longer distance from St. Paul to Chicago. Farmers paid the high short-haul rate, but the middlemen in the cities, where railroads competed, could obtain much better long-haul terms. As John F. Stover points out, farmers who were getting 15¢ in Iowa for corn that was selling at $1 a bushel in the East preferred to burn it for fuel. The farmer was at the mercy of the local grain elevator, often owned by the railroad. The country store he patronized charged him high prices since it also paid heavy shipping charges. The motto of the roads was "all the traffic will bear." In an era of falling prices and depression, the farmers fought back through an organization called the Patrons of Husbandry, organized in "granges." By 1874 there were twenty thousand granges. This cartoon, "The Grange Awakening to Sleepers," a pun on a familiar synonym for railroad crossties, shows how the new political force made itself felt. In most of the plains states its political pressure passed many "granger" laws outlawing rate discriminations, the giving of free passes to politicians, and other abuses. The railroads resisted, but the Supreme Court, to the industry's surprise, upheld the Granger laws in 1877.

Morgan's own collection of 18,000 miles. It must be understood that each system contained many different railroads, nearly all operating under their own names—romantic to read as the freight cars rolled by—but they were all controlled beneath the surface by one or the other of the two great money powers of the time. One was grouped around Harriman and Kuhn, Loeb money, the other around Morgan and his allies.

What Lord Acton said of power, and the corruption it brings, was fatally true in the high noon of the "Money Trust," a phrase we owe to a Minnesota congressman, Charles A. Lindbergh, the father of the flier. The sizable resources of J. P. Morgan & Co., private bankers, were only the center of a circle of widening power that through interlocking directorates controlled most of the larger corporations in the country. At one point, eleven Morgan partners held seventy-two directorships in forty-seven of the largest companies; they were allied with Standard Oil through William Rockefeller, the quiet acquisitor's jolly brother, with George F. Baker's First National Bank, with the National City, the Guaranty Trust, the Banker's Trust, the Chase, the life insurance companies, the Baldwin Locomotive Works, American Telephone & Telegraph . . . but there is no end to it. Here is the way one perceptive commentator, Louis D. Brandeis, later a Supreme Court justice, put it at the time:

"J. P. Morgan (or a partner), a director of the New York, New Haven & Hartford Railroad, causes that company to sell to J. P. Morgan & Co. an issue of bonds; J. P. Morgan & Co. borrow the money with which to pay for the bonds from the Guaranty Trust Company, of which Mr. Morgan (or a partner) is a director. J. P. Morgan & Co. sell the bonds to the Penn Mutual Life Insurance Company, of which Mr. Morgan (or a partner) is a director. The New Haven spends the proceeds of the bonds in purchasing steel rails from the United States Steel Corporation, of which Mr. Morgan (or a partner) is a director. The United States Steel Corporation spends the proceeds of the rails in purchasing electrical supplies from the General Electric Company, of which Mr. Morgan (or a partner) is a director . . ." (and so on endlessly).

Dispassionate historians, looking at the great banker in terms of the ethics of his time, find nothing personally corrupt in Morgan's imperial dealings. But the questions still arise. How can one man act for so many opposing economic forces? Which of the conflicting interests is being protected, and which, inevitably, sacrificed? And what of the public interest that underlies all? These are only the beginning of a whole series of questions that arise in considering Morgan's "last hurrah" in railroad finance, his misadventure with the once prosperous New York, New Haven & Hartford Railroad.

For decades this railroad, put together from many smaller and rival lines, had served southern New England; it operated a busy network of 2,037 miles of road in 1903; for years it had paid a regular dividend of at least 8 percent, and was esteemed as an investment by fiduciaries, colleges, and conservative investors. Everyone called it, for short, "the New Haven," everyone except Morgan, who called it "the Hartford," because he was born there and had a sentimental feeling about it. In fact, Morgan decided, it must be a major railroad, strong enough to resist grabs from outside, indeed strong enough to do some grabbing itself. In 1903 he put in his own man, Charles S. Mellen, a man whose name would eventually become anathema to millions, a colorful fellow who liked to associate with showy types like the noted gourmand and squire of Lillian Russell, Diamond Jim Brady, who also sold railroad equipment. Brady gave Mrs. Mellen diamonds, and was always ready to serve as a silent, unquestioning director in "dummy" corporations set up by the New Haven. Morgan would not have entered the same room with Brady, but in Mellen he had a properly subservient tool.

With Morgan backing and urging, Mellen set out on one of the most ambitious expansion schemes of any railroad, at least in relation to the size of the territory involved. The steamboat lines that plied the protected waters of Long Island Sound and beyond—to Fall River, Providence, New Bedford, and other ports—were competitors. They could slash rates below the railroad's to the same places, and had done so since Jim Fisk's day. Mellen bought them, without much argument about the price. Observing this, other operators started new lines just to sell them to the openhanded New Haven. It was known that the seafaring Mr. Morgan liked boats.

The next competitors to be gathered in were the trolley lines. The present generation, if it has seen a streetcar at all, may wonder how this purely city form of transportation could trouble a railroad, but it must be realized that electric traction had been perfected only a few years before and had spread like wildfire not only over city streets but between towns and cities. The trolleys cut badly into the local passenger service of railroads in heavily populated areas like the New Haven's. By night the trolleys carried freight, often to the customer's door, and that was competition too, the first since the days of the freight wagon and the stagecoach. And Mellen bought almost all of these lines in Connecticut, about a thousand miles worth, and many more in Rhode Island, paying hugely inflated prices (in Rhode Island to Senator Nelson Aldrich, who had gathered them together and doubled his money). The stocks had already been watered, and were watered once again, with one issue after another sold to a trusting public as the trolleys were reorganized and integrated into the New Haven system. In New York State, Mellen bought the New York, Ontario & Western Railroad as a westward link.

So far, so good. But it was in Massachusetts that Mellen ran into trouble. Despite the plain language of a state law that prohibited any railroad from acquiring directly or indirectly the stock of any other railroad company, he began to buy up trolleys and interurbans in the central and western parts of the Bay State. The angry governor called for legislative action, whereupon the New Haven brazenly suggested that the acquisitions be subjected to a test case in the courts. Properly "influenced," the lawgivers agreed. Such matters could be dragged out interminably, and decisions purchased. Meanwhile he promised to buy no more railroads. The legislators had barely gone home when Mellen brazenly bought four more streetcar companies and, in small, quiet purchases, Massachusetts' own Boston & Maine Railroad, controlling most of northern New England.

"Great Scott!" E. H. Harriman once said, when apprised of that hitherto healthy and independent company, "is there anything like that still left out of doors?" As the sardonic contemporary critic Charles Edward Russell put it, the Boston & Maine was a company that "by some chance had not been loaded to the guards with the common stock, preferred stock, debentures, first, second, and consolidated mortgages, notes and refunding certificates that now adorn the greater part of our admired railroad structure."

At length the Massachusetts Supreme Court ruled that the New Haven had to divest itself. Suddenly the trolley lines were taken over by a "voluntary association" that was allowed to issue stock but not required to make any financial reports; its members were principally Brady and various directors of the New Haven. That board, a social and financial register of the times, included William Rockefeller, Morgan, George F. Baker, G. MacCulloch Miller, Lewis Cass Ledyard . . . but it is too long and painful to list in full. The shares of the Boston & Maine, worth approximately $14,000,000, were suddenly "sold" to a Meriden, Connecticut, coal dealer named John L. Billard, whose net worth on the tax rolls, according to New Haven historian John L. Weller, was $30,000, plus a horse, a buggy, and a piano. Obligingly, Mr.

Collis P. Huntington reacted characteristically to the Grangers; he called them "communists." By 1896, when this cartoon of him by James Swinnerton appeared in the San Francisco Examiner, *he was the last survivor of the Big Four, still in absolute charge of the great Central Pacific-Southern Pacific monopoly. The "Octopus," as it was commonly known to its opponents, seemed to rule not only the legislature and the courts of California but also its shippers, its business, its lands, and the lives of many of its people. While other railroads held large areas in their grasp— like the New Haven in New England—none was more overwhelming than the Southern Pacific. Crafty old Huntington died in 1900 and the company passed into the equally strong but more reasonable hands of E. H. Harriman: He was public-spirited enough to rescue the Imperial Valley from the flooding Colorado River and to send all available help by rail to San Francisco in the devastating earthquake and fire of 1906. The Big Four left behind their giant showplaces on Nob Hill and a mixture of legacies, including Stanford University and the famous Huntington Library in San Marino. In a strange match, Huntington's widow married his nephew Henry Huntington, who built not only the library but the great Pacific Electric Railway System of Los Angeles, the most useful combination of city and interurban transit any American city ever possessed. California foolishly let it be destroyed by "freeways" and the new twentieth-century octopus, the automobile industry and the highway trust.*

FRANK LESLIE'S
ILLUSTRATED
NEWSPAPER

Entered according to the Act of Congress, in the year 1877, by FRANK LESLIE, in the Office of the Librarian of Congress at Washington.

No. 1,140—VOL. XLIV.]   NEW YORK, AUGUST 4, 1877.   [PRICE, 10 CENTS. $4.00 YEARLY. 13 WEEKS, $1.00.

THE SCENE AFTER THE FIRST VOLLEY.

CARRYING OFF THE DEAD.

THE MOB ATTACKING THE SOLDIERS AT THE ARMORY.

THE MOB ASSAULTING A MEMBER OF THE SIXTH.

THE MOB FIRING THE CAMDEN STREET STATION.

MARYLAND.—THE BALTIMORE & OHIO RAILROAD STRIKE—SCENES AND INCIDENTS OF THE CONFLICT BETWEEN THE SYMPATHIZERS WITH THE STRIKERS AND THE FIFTH AND SIXTH REGIMENTS MARYLAND MILITIA, IN BALTIMORE, JULY 20TH.—FROM SKETCHES BY OUR SPECIAL ARTISTS.

Mellen and Mr. Morgan "introduced" him to the National City Bank, which
loaned him money against the stock he bought. After this disguise was no
longer necessary, he sold the stock not to a railroad (illegal, of course) but to
the New England Navigation Company. A canny Yankee, Billard held out
for a profit—how could the New Haven sue and bare the facts?—collecting
$2,913,648 on an investment of nothing at all. The Navigation Company, nat-
urally, was a New Haven subsidiary. In turn it "sold" the shares to a new
holding company in Boston, a blind for New Haven control, and Mellen
became president of the Boston & Maine—and the Maine Central, too. In
the New Haven system there were three hundred corporations entwined and
entangled in the great monopoly, like so many polliwogs in a pail. They
bought and sold each other in maneuvers so bizarre that a lady stenographer
was once for a day or so president of a company. A Yankee handyman
named Grover Cleveland Richards was taken on another memorable occasion into the Bank of Manhattan, where James S. Hemingway, a New
Haven director, handed him a check made out to him for $3,000,000. Then he
was asked to endorse it over on the spot to a Hartford lawyer, who took it to
a teller's window and then had Richards sign two more checks, for $1,450,000
and $1,500,000. Richards asked no questions, and was sent home the next day
with a new suit for his trouble.

Mellen had swallowed buying Aldrich's trolleys—worth about $6,000,000
—for over $19,000,000, but he objected mildly when his financial master made
him buy two "nuisance" competitors for Westchester County commuters, railroads not even built yet, which finally cost the New Haven $36,000,000 for a
little over eighteen miles of track when it was all laid. Called the New York,
Westchester & Boston, it lost over $1,000,000 a year from the start, and was
eventually torn up in the 1930's. The great man snubbed Mellen's questions
(see caption on page 148). Large sums are believed to have gone to politicians, and some could never be found at all. Records had unaccountably
caught fire again. And the foolish purchase is still unexplained.

It has been suggested that Morgan was "using" the New Haven as he did
other solvent corporations in his famous struggle to save the banks in the
1907 Panic—in effect, making them buy at high prices worthless stocks held
by troubled banking firms that might otherwise go under. One might call it
robbing Peter to get Paul off the hook. Perhaps success had gone to Morgan's
head, perhaps he was unaware of Mellen's structure of subsidiaries, which
the ICC, after its great investigation of 1914, said "were seemingly planned,
created, and manipulated by lawyers expressly retained for the purpose of
concealment or deception." According to the government, the total capitali-
zation of the New Haven system in the ten years between 1903 and J. P.
Morgan's death in 1913 rose from $93,000,000 to $417,000,000, of which
staggering increase only about $136,000,000 had gone into electrifications,
equipment, and the railroad itself. Of the remainder, even after allowing for
buying concrete items like steamboats, trolleys, and other railroads, millions
could not be accounted for. The only certainty was that all that water—
enough, if Long Island Sound had gone dry, to operate the company's
steamers—was also enough to cripple forever and eventually bankrupt the
once healthy New Haven Railroad.

In their earliest days the railroads were bedevilled by petty local laws
requiring such foolishness as having trains preceded by horsemen to warn of
their approach, or by restrictions imposed by the canals or other rivals. But
these were soon swept away, and nothing hindered the rails thereafter until by
their own folly in the late 1860's and 1870's they brought down on their heads
the wrath of the western farmers. The fast-talking promoters had brought
these people to their new homes which, unlike the old farms back east or in

NEW YORK PUBLIC LIBRARY

*When the strikes reached the always troubled
Erie, loyal workers were sometimes dragged off
trains. At Hornellsville and elsewhere, armed citizens, doubtless enjoying the derring-do, came
along to protect the train crews, which they are
doing here. The fireman is clearly a person of
standing, perhaps a Harvard man. (Playing at
railroading is fun under almost any circumstances.) Strikers retaliated by stopping trains
with greased rails. One captured train, its crew
taken off, was sent hurtling down a grade toward
a busy yard, where only fast work at the switches
by an alert yardmaster prevented a disaster.*

Before order was restored in Pittsburgh, some $5,000,000 worth of damage had been done by the strike of 1877 to rail and other property. The picture above is from an unpublished stereographic photo of tracks damaged by fire near Sixteenth Street. The crowd is looking down at the destroyed underpinnings. At right, in a companion stereo, are the smoking ruins of the roundhouse.

Europe, were far away from towns and markets. They had even been sold railroad stock—crinkly, beautifully engraved, but all too often, worthless paper. Overcharged to ship their crops, the farmers formed social-political clubs called "Granges," which pushed through middle-western legislatures strong laws against rate discrimination.

There were many other abuses as well, and many other victims in the age of the robber barons. Railroad money spoke powerfully in state legislatures, in courtrooms, and in newspaper offices; indeed many newspapers were controlled or owned outright by men like Huntington, Gould, and Mellen. It was easy enough to see that new stock issues, either free or at a low price, were distributed where they would do the most good. Railroad rates for many years were never published, often changing overnight. William H. Vanderbilt admitted that he gave special rates constantly to big customers; it was inevitable.

Small in a way but enormous in its impact was the custom of giving free passes to anyone whose good will the railroads sought. Such a gift would often mollify a clergyman opposed to Sunday trains, soothe a judge, and please a governor. Legislators got them also until a pass became regarded in most parts of the country as a vested right. Sometimes, in the gaudy days of the bonanza railroads, the passes were made of silver and gold. All this fun, however, the farmers sought to end, and the first step in federal control of the railroads was to a large degree brought about by a man who had grown up on a farm on the unbroken prairie of Illinois, Shelby M. Cullom. After a distinguished career in the Republican party, he entered the United States Senate determined to establish some national control over interstate railroad methods. With the indignation of the public as his weapon, and by means of hearings held all over the country, he was able to get the Interstate Commerce Commission established in 1887. It prohibited discriminatory rates, pooling, and the kind of rebates and drawbacks that had so assisted the growth of the Standard Oil Company. Railroads were required to post their rates, which should be "reasonable and just." Yet it was not very much of a law. It did not allow the ICC to fix rates and it provided no real power of enforcement. It turned out indeed that railroads, with their batteries of lawyers, could circumvent the Act quite easily. And the ICC was dealt several defeats by the Supreme Court. By the late nineties the Commission was powerless.

The excesses of the first decade of the twentieth century nevertheless led inevitably to new laws. The Elkins Act of 1903 gave the ICC its first enforcement powers and, when that proved insufficient, the Hepburn Act of 1906, pushed by Cullom and Theodore Roosevelt, allowed the Commission power to fix the actual rates and have them apply right away instead of waiting for the long processes of the courts. It restricted the free passes. In fact, it gave the Commission a power greater than that ever imposed on any other American industry and one that would in time prove fatal.

The railway kings fought back, as might have been expected, on every possible occasion. Their answer, for example, to the Supreme Court decision on the Granger laws was to raise all the freight rates in the East by 50 percent. Later that year, 1877, four major eastern railroads—the New York Central, the Pennsylvania, the Erie, and the Baltimore & Ohio—set up a railroad pool. With the rates nicely arranged, the four railroad presidents agreed to slash the pay of their workmen by 10 percent. Others quickly joined them.

Greater folly is hard to imagine. It was a day when conductors and engineers, the aristocrats of the working force, earned about $3 for a twelve-hour day, when firemen got $2 and the lowly brakemen, $1.75. It was also a day when most of the railroads were continuing to pay their stockholders 10 percent in dividends, and the very year in which the president of one of them, William H. Vanderbilt, received his well-publicized paternal legacy of

Successful as a carbuilder but a failure as a paternalist, George Pullman (center) poses with his family in 1897, the year of his death, at Castle Rest, his place in the Thousand Islands and not, as it sounds, the name of a car. The older men are his brothers, both ministers; at left is his wife and behind her a daughter (who did not, legend to the contrary, name all the Pullman cars for a dollar a piece) and her husband, future Illinois governor and presidential aspirant Frank O. Lowden.

$100,000,000. On June 1, 1877, twenty thousand Pennsylvania Railroad wage earners took a 10 percent cut but kept on working. The Lehigh Valley, the New York Central, the Lackawanna, the Michigan Central—one after another the other railroads reduced wages. A slash on the Erie on July 1 brought grumbling, but Governor Lucius Robinson of New York, who was also an Erie director, sent state troops to patrol the lines, just in case. Everyone thought that action the most natural thing in the world. Real trouble only started when the pay cuts hit the Baltimore & Ohio. It was the second such in eight months on that line, even though the stock was also paying 10 percent.

The strike began on the B & O at Martinsburg, West Virginia, where Stonewall Jackson had, as we have seen, wreaked havoc on the railroad during the Civil War. The militia were summoned but turned out to be in sympathy with the strikers. Yet a fuse had been lit and suddenly the strikes of 1877 involved almost all the railroads that had cut wages, some two-thirds of the total. For seven to ten days all freight and most passenger service ceased. Violence broke out at Wheeling, and at the request of Baltimore & Ohio president John Garrett, the federal government sent troops to the scene of "insurrection." Whoever had caused the insurrection, the B & O was careful to bill the government and collect for transporting the rescuing troops. At places like Buffalo, Chicago, St. Louis, Omaha, and St. Paul, troops, policemen, and GAR veterans were brought in to stop the violence.

The real holocaust took place in Pittsburgh, where angry crowds of strikers and sympathizers confronted nervous armed militiamen, with the usual results. In the battles that followed, twenty-four persons were killed, a hundred locomotives and over two thousand cars destroyed, and many buildings burned. Some railroads quickly rescinded the cuts, but in general the strike was broken. Many of the participants were fired, jailed, or placed on black lists. A nervous peace was re-established.

Although the main "Big Four" brotherhoods had been organized in the

Disciplined regular army units like these on a Rock Island troop train poured into Chicago in the Pullman strike. They shot no one, but their presence helped end violence and vandalism. President Cleveland, previously a railroad lawyer, was both criticized and praised for sending them.

years during and after the Civil War, they were originally mainly mutual-insurance societies. The first powerful union, unique in our history at the time, was the American Railway Union, organized in 1893 by the fiery Eugene Victor Debs. He was zealous and active; he believed in the strike weapon. In 1894 he used it successfully to lick Jim Hill, who had thrice slashed the wages on the Great Northern. Then Debs took on George Pullman, the paternalist who had built a model company town outside Chicago named after himself. There were many pretty cottages, but his rents and rates were some 25 percent higher than in other parts of town. Pullman business was off because of depression; he could keep up profits only by reducing wages, and cut them 19 percent. A committee of workmen called upon him to seek arbitration. There was nothing to arbitrate, said the palace car builder, who fired three of the committee members. In late June, 1894, Debs moved in to help, announcing that his now huge union would not handle the cars of the Pullman Company, which was an operating as well as car-building firm. The brotherhoods did not support the strike. As the trouble mounted, strikebreakers came in, injunctions flew, militia marched, and President Cleveland sent federal troops to Chicago. He did it over the protests of Governor Altgeld of Illinois and the mayor of Chicago, who urged that no intervention was necessary. To that, Cleveland responded, "If it takes the entire army and navy of the United States to deliver a postal card to Chicago, that card will be delivered." The regulars behaved well, but sheriff's deputies, militia, and strikers are as bad a mix as oil and water. Criminals and arsonists move in on such opportunities. The strike spread, often out of Debs' control. In Chicago there was rioting, shooting, and death for twelve men—until the strike was broken on July 19. Debs, an ogre to many but an intensely likable man, went to jail to become thereafter not only a perpetual Socialist presidential candidate but a sainted figure of the Left. His union in time broke up and was replaced by more aggressive leadership in the many brotherhoods.

Eugene V. Debs had been secretary of the Brotherhood of Locomotive Firemen but it was not militant enough for him. He formed the short-lived American Railway Union and led it into the violent and disastrous Pullman strike of 1894. Subsequently he was five times Socialist candidate for President, campaigning in old-time revivalist style, the last time (1920) while in jail for his fiery pacifism during World War I. Here he is spellbinding a sea of derby hats in 1908.

A great deal of the history of labor is symbolized by the two documents at the right, the one a kind of black list from the Denver, South Park & Pacific Railroad of 1884 (then a part of the Union Pacific system), the other a poster for one of the great railroad brotherhoods, issued in 1915. Both will reward study, for the first certainly helped to lead to the other. The little scenes in the poster stress the danger of the trainman's job, the fine funeral the member may expect, and the benefits his widow will receive. The lodge meeting at bottom center is a reminder of the fraternal and social aspect of these organizations. The four original brotherhoods were the engineers, dating back to 1863; the conductors, 1868; the firemen, 1873; and the trainmen, 1883. For years in the nineteenth century they were the aristocrats of labor both as to pay and status, which placed them more in the lower professional than in the working class. Because of their power, and disinclination to strike, they won most of their requests from the railroads, especially an elaborate seniority system by which one moved up the ladder from lowly brakeman on a freight to lordly conductor on the limiteds, or from coal-pushing fireman to the best engineer's berth. For years they remained aloof from the American Federation of Labor, unlike the various railroad trades —the men in the shops, the yards, the stations, and along the tracks. All this changed in the twentieth century. Four of the operating unions today, their members reduced from the great era of railroading, are joined in one United Transportation Union, AFL-CIO. The Brotherhood of Locomotive Engineers is still independent.

Form 2512

Union Pacific Railway.

COLORADO DIVISION.

—COMPRISING THE—
COLORADO CENTRAL R. R.
DENVER, SOUTH PARK & PACIFIC R. R.
DENVER PACIFIC R'Y.
GREELEY, SALT LAKE & PACIFIC R'Y.
DENVER & BOULDER R'Y.
GOLDEN, BOULDER & CARIBOU R'Y.
GEORGETOWN, BRECKENRIDGE & LEADVILLE R'Y.
DENVER, WESTERN & PACIFIC R'Y.

A. A. EGBERT,
GEN'L SUPT.

Office of GENERAL SUPERINTENDENT.

Denver, Colo., _____ 1884.

The years up to 1913 marked the end of the great unregulated power of American railroads. In 1913, not long before his death, even the great Morgan was put on the witness stand in a congressional investigation of the Money Trust. In the following summer the ICC investigation of Charles Mellen and the affairs of the New Haven Railroad so dominated the front pages that a mere front-page reader would have been surprised when war suddenly erupted in Europe on August 4. The heritage of ill will created by the grand acquisitors—the choleric Hill, the arrogant Pullman, the pious Rockefeller, the sly Gould, the imperial Huntington, the domineering Morgan— burst forth in a stream of regulatory measures. The public interest was at long last reasserting itself. Looking backward, one may wonder why it is that men so often never understand that they are sowing the seeds of their own destruction.

Follies upon follies had now beset the railroads at the beginning of a new period in history. The unions and the regulators, like the domineering robber barons before them, would now have their day. Meanwhile, on the streets of the cities and on the dusty roads of the country had appeared the first coughing, bumpy little contributions of Henry Ford to America's future. The stage was set for the troubles that beset American railroads to this day.

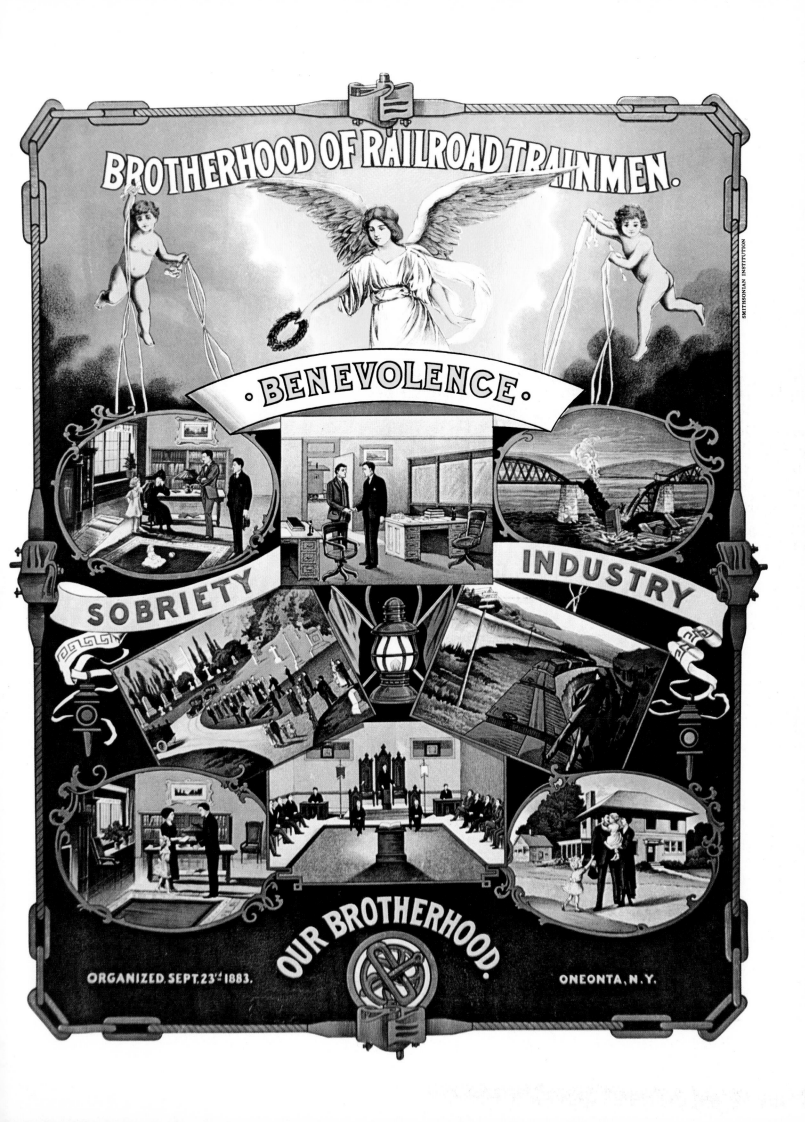

BROTHERHOOD OF RAILROAD TRAINMEN.

· BENEVOLENCE ·

SOBRIETY

INDUSTRY

OUR BROTHERHOOD.

ORGANIZED. SEPT. 23rd 1883.

ONEONTA, N.Y.

A Portfolio

7. The Romantic Image

In relating its annals of struggle and strife, it is quite easy to forget that to most people a century ago the railroad was not a bone of contention but a wonderful new physical presence. Vanderbilts and Goulds were as remote figures as popes and sultans, but the iron horse was here in plain sight in every town and village, its furnace fires flickering and its whistle screaming down the valley. The passage of a train closer at hand was a sight to stir the blood, as though the engine were a living thing, its exhaust panting and its great driving wheels and gleaming side rods moving in powerful rhythm. The railroad was the great mechanism of the nineteenth century and the people took it to their hearts. That romance, which lasted until the age of the automobile and still gives us twinges, was reflected in literature and art—as, for example, in George Inness' famous painting of the *Lackawanna Valley*, at right, with its fine feeling for the new industrial landscape.

(He painted it in 1854 for the penny-pinching first president of the Delaware, Lackawanna & Western Railroad, George D. Phelps, who offered the young artist $75 to immortalize his new roundhouse at Scranton and show all three of his locomotives, each lettered with the company's interminable name. For that price, said Inness, he could have only one, and at a distance, uninscribed.)

An even surer sign of the railroad's pervasive grip on the American imagination is to be found in lesser but more popular art forms. And so we pause here on the next few pages for a brief color sampling of instructive lithographs, advertisements, songs, and pictures for children from railroading's first century.

"THE FAST MAIL" Entered according to Act of Congress, in the Year 1875, by J.A BURCH, in the Office of the Librarian of Congress at Washington

"THE FAST MAIL".

Scene of catching and delivering the Mails on the Lake Shore & Michigan Southern Railway.

The centerpiece of the thrilling pageant was the steam locomotive, and the young boy at left is reacting in approved fashion to its passage in full cry. Oh, to be that debonair fireman, or that well-travelled mail clerk, heaving out the mail sacks, smartly hooking the pouches, or, best of all, the brave engineer, whose Masonic symbol adorns the smokebox door! The boy's mother, of course, is reacting to the noise as a Victorian lady was supposed to. As for his fearful young brother, we avert our gaze. The Fast Mail, *inaugurated in 1874 by William H. Vanderbilt over the grudging objections of his father, the Commodore, was the first special mail train in the United States, renowned for its cream and gold cars and its twenty-four-hour schedule between New York and Chicago, but it was withdrawn in a little over a year when the Post Office Department failed to pay extra for it. By 1909, when the symbolic chromolithograph below was printed to adorn schoolroom and depot walls, steam still ruled the world, undaunted by flimsy aircraft and new-fangled automobiles. Earth satellites were provided strictly by the Almighty.*

RINGLING BROS AND BARNU
COMBINED 100 RAILWAY CARS SHOWS
THESE TRAINS MORE THAN ONE AND ONE THIR LOADED WITH TEN THOUSAND WONDERS FR

New companies, indeed new nations, are boastful, and American businesses and American railroads were proud of anything big, or long, or unprecedented. What freight is more magical than clowns and elephants and ladies of the high wire? Although other circuses had used trains as early as 1856, there was nothing like the hundred-car train which resulted when Ringling Brothers took over Barnum and Bailey and the "big top" moved about the country in boxcars, passenger cars, and scores of flatcars loaded with wagons. Any sensible child got down to the rail yard at dawn to watch the animals unload and the wagons roll off the flats to form the morning parade down Main Street to the fairgrounds. Its great tents a thing of the past, Ringling's today still travels in its own fifteen-car train.

How long the record of this salt train of 1897 stood, it would be hard to chronicle, but one must admire the concept, the use of the President-elect, and the perhaps fanciful track arrangement that makes the picture possible. Underground salt deposits in upstate New York fill an area one hundred miles long by thirty miles wide, a formidable amount of which went for some years to New England via endless "specials" arranged by a super salesman named Elmer E. McGaffey, who once shipped 101 cars to one big grocer. With their sure instinct for their own jugulars, the carrying railroads put a stop to McGaffey's way of displaying his advertising on the cars, which they had to remove afterward, and the business dwindled. Worcester today is Morton's salt, which travels mainly by truck.

POOLE BROS. PRINTERS AND ENGRAVERS, CHICAGO.

Not all railroads shared Jim Hill's scornful opinion of passengers, and most of them had scarcely achieved their distant objectives when they began issuing clouds of ecstatic travel literature like that at left for the first-class passengers. Inside the folder, issued in 1885, its colors cheaply and badly printed, genteel "Alice" is staying at the Mammoth Hot Springs Hotel and writes a friend that she is still "rubbing her eyes" at the wonders of the West. (If she had ridden the coaches, full of emigrants, workmen, con men, and drummers, Alice would have met a harder but more real West.)

Another woman, "Phoebe Snow," was the great sales device of the Lackawanna Railroad, which had the shortest main-line route from New York to Buffalo and the advantage that it burned its own anthracite coal, which makes much less smoke and dirt than soft coal. At right are examples from two of the many series of jingles advertising the spotless amenities of "The Route of Phoebe Snow." There was a real Phoebe, too, Miss Marion E. Murray, who later went on the stage. Phoebe disappeared during World War I and a shortage of hard coal. The train, abandoned several times, finally ran not to Buffalo but over the combined Erie-Lackawanna lines to Chicago, winding up for good in 1966. Chicago didn't rhyme very well with "Phoebe Snow" anyway.

It was inevitable that the railroad would conquer the popular consciousness, as a symbol, a setting, and a salesman's device, long before it had overcome its last physical barriers. The locomotive creaked on stage in melodrama while the hero snatched the heroine from the track. And trains dominated the world of the dime novel. Engineers made splendid heroes despite a steady diet of ambushes, burning bridges, and collapsing tunnels. Thousands of millionaires' children were saved from onrushing limiteds by heroic but impecunious young men like Fred Fearnot, and he was but a pallid imitation of that habitual train rescuer Frank Merriwell, who at least one generation firmly believed was a real Yale football hero (if a little over age toward the end). See him finding a seat for a lady. Could this seat hog be the same lout of the immortal line: " 'You are a cheap cad,' Frank told the overdressed Harvard bully"? Time blots the memory. But no one can forget the railroad in allegory. It reached some sort of height in the hard-hitting service of temperance, of which the Inebriate's Express is a fine but not unique example (it takes an hour at least to find everything in the picture). In the service of romance, we think, Charles Dana Gibson did even better with Love's Express, the tender scene below.

Some of the romance of railroading for children comes out in The Railroad Book, *published in long-ago 1913 and given to the author as a child in 1920 by his parents. The educational psychologists with their "word-lists" had not appeared on the scene to forbid such phrases as "diminishing perspectives" (which you saw out the windows) or "ingenious transformations" (which overtook sleeping cars when the berths were folded away).*

The text of The
Railroad Book is
not very strong
meat, but the color
plates of the author,
E. Boyd Smith, are
a fine evocation of
ordinary railroad
travel in its greatest
era. There is the
busy river far below
the day coach, and
the West going by
while you eat in the
lordly dining car.
Getting home at the
depot is a bit tire-
some, but then our
rather pallid protag-
onists, depressingly
good as they are,
can at least hang
around the freight
house.

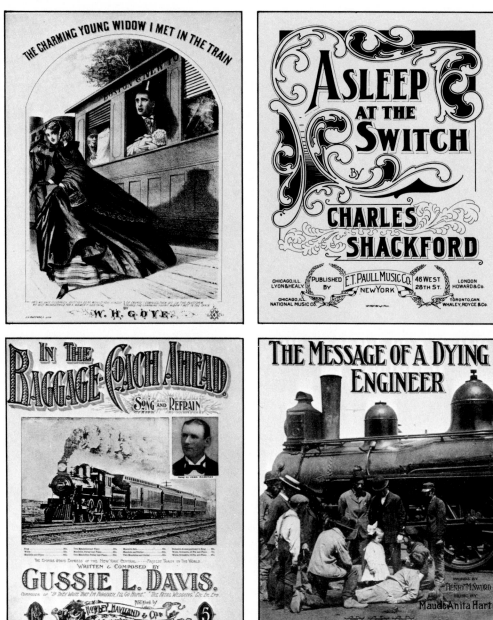

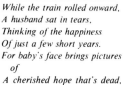

Beware of Young Widows
you meet on the railway,
Who lean on your shoulder
whose tears fall like rain.
Look out for your pockets
in case they resemble
The Charming Young Widow
I met in the train.

(She picked the rube's pockets and left him holding a
dummy baby.)

Asleep at the switch
And no warning light
To signal those trains
That rushed through the
 night. . . .

(Never mind the whole plot,
the brave daughter of the
switchman saved the train
carrying the railroad president's family, which meant
a Suitable Reward.)

While the train rolled onward,
A husband sat in tears,
Thinking of the happiness
Of just a few short years.
For baby's face brings pictures
 of
A cherished hope that's dead,
But baby's cries can't waken
 her,
In the baggage coach ahead.

(Her, of course, is Mother,
in a coffin up ahead.)

Just tell my wife
when you break the news,
I died for a child so fair,
So like our own
dear one at home,
With ringlets of
golden hair. . . .

(The child was thoughtless-
ly walking the track.)

Old-time railroading was part of a lugubrious age, so far as its songs were concerned; Tin Pan Alley habitually gave America's heartstrings a heavy going over. But smile as we may at the little selection here—lent to us from the nonpareil collection of early song covers belonging to Lester Levy, of Baltimore—railroading was a lonesome, melancholy, and often dangerous business. When you died it might very well not be in bed. Wallace Saunders, the illiterate black roundhouse man who composed the song, knew Casey Jones, who made his trip to the Promised Land in an Illinois Central engine on March 1, 1900. Dave George, the hillbilly who wrote "Old 97," had just seen the tragic wreckage of the Southern's Fast Mail, where engineer Joe Broady was found "with his hand on the throttle, and a-scalded to death by the steam." No songs are more popular with railroad men; nor could they even be imagined singing most of the Tin Pan Alley items shown here—except, perhaps, "In The Baggage-Coach Ahead," which was written by a real Pullman porter, Gussie L. Davis, and has a great climactic line: "But baby's cries can't waken her." As the late Stewart Holbrook pointed out, that "her" is held in a swelling crescendo while every man in a quartet gets in his licks, then diminishes into sliding minors and the final "in the baggage coach ahead," until there is not a dry eye in the house.

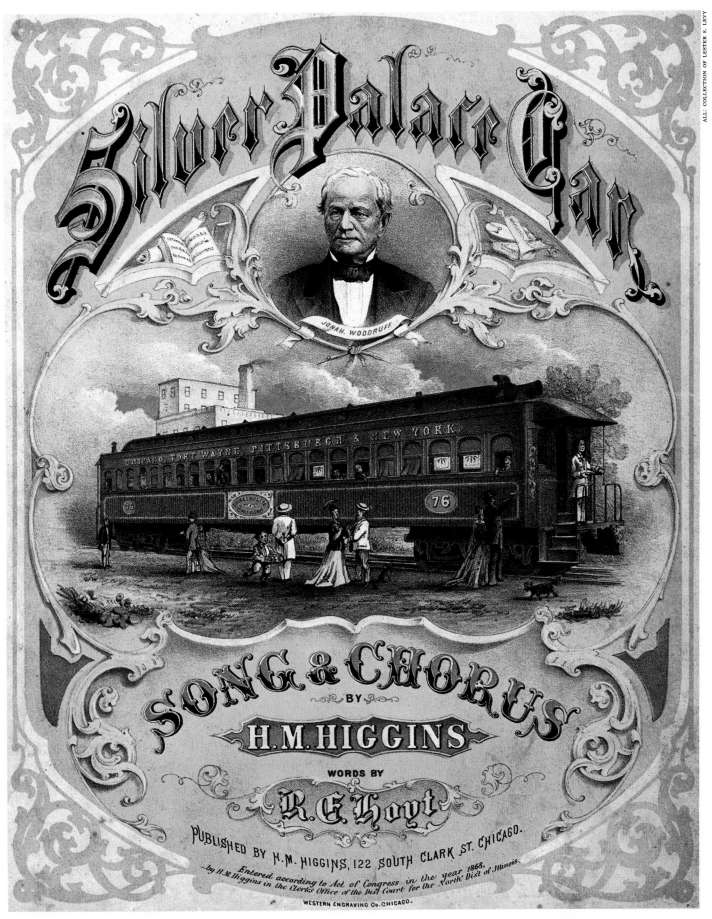

Jonah Woodruff's Silver Palace Cars were used on the Central Pacific Railroad almost from the start but rarely on eastern lines. In 1871, he organized the Woodruff Sleeping and Palace Car Company, which became a serious competitor of Pullman, but eventually sold out.

8. Down Brakes!

8. Down Brakes!

This is the dreadful moment of impact, as caught by an artist named Otto Stark. The Flying Express *was crashing into the rear of a motionless freight at Steamburg, New York, in 1888.*

PRECEDING PAGES: *When the bottom fell out of an old truss bridge at aptly named Calvary, Kentucky, in 1900, the engine, tender, and two cars of this Louisville & Nashville consist hit a dry creek bed, while the last coach teetered precariously on the verge. The usual crowd has gathered.*

I n the twentieth century, as most travellers are aware, the railroad is by a heavy margin the safest way to go. As that noted train enthusiast Rogers E. M. Whitaker ("Mr. Frimbo") of *The New Yorker* once put it succinctly to the author, "It goes through the mountains, not into them." Until very recently modern American railroads were able to boast of periods in which no passengers at all had been killed, and if the record is a little poorer recently with the debilitated equipment of the 1970's, it is still a good one compared with the early days of the iron horse. When trains today do crash, and nothing from an oxcart to a spaceship is exempt from accident, the carnage is generally small in comparison with that total annihilation imposed, say, when a trailer truck rams a Volkswagen or an Alp stops an airplane.

In this modern frame of reference, it is a little hard to recreate the horror with which mid-nineteenth-century America viewed the appalling price it was beginning to pay for the new gift of speed. If accidents were relatively few in the first two decades, the 1830's and 1840's, they began to multiply in number and degree as the trains of the 1850's went ever faster over their primitive and shoddy roadbeds. Weak iron bridges collapsed, boilers blew up, brittle iron rails broke, switches were unaccountably open, all-wooden coaches were smashed into splinters and generally caught fire from the kerosene lamps or the coal stoves which warmed them in winter. As this new terror descended on America, it was widely celebrated in newspaper articles, crude woodcuts, moralistic verse, and lugubrious ballads.

The first really bad year, as noted by Robert C. Reed, an authority on this dolorous topic, was 1853. The *annus horribilis* started slowly, with a few minor disasters, the first of which killed only three people when a Boston & Maine express was derailed in January by a broken axle at Andover, Massachusetts, and rolled down an embankment. One of the three killed was the young son of President-elect Franklin Pierce. In March, while an emigrant train paused on the Pennsylvania Railroad tracks at Mount Union, Pennsylvania, a mail train plunged into it from the rear, scalding many of the travellers, including seven who died. It was the era of the twelve-hour day: a brakeman, sent down the track to the rear to warn off approaching trains, had fallen asleep. "Human error," this is called by today's bureaucrats. In April came the worst accident yet known on American railroads, when a Michigan Central express, while passing too slowly through a railroad crossover, was hit broadside by a Michigan Southern train full of still more emigrants. Twenty-one hopeful German settlers were killed.

The prevention of accidents like this would eventually require such developments as the use of the telegraph, not to mention automatic and reasonably foolproof signals. All too often the kind of solution proposed in those days, however, would be so ultrasafe as to be self-defeating. To cope with cross-overs, for example, the state of Kansas passed this interesting enactment: "When two trains approach each other at a crossing, both shall come to a full stop and neither shall start up until the other has gone." This is no more improbable than a Washington law requiring that "a dog shall be carried on the cowcatcher of all trains. The dog is necessary to put to flight cattle obstructing the track." An Alabama law prohibited shooting at engine cabs, from which one might have inferred that it was all right to pop away at the cars.

What rivets the attention of newspapers, of course, is the fame of the victim or the bizarre nature of his demise. These two qualities were tragically combined in the most famous wreck of that year, which took place at South Norwalk, Connecticut, on May 6. The first reports had it that the distinguished Dr. Oliver Wendell Holmes, that eminent poet and surgeon of Boston, had met his death. The rumor was fortunately untrue but the 8 A.M. express which left New York that morning for New Haven, Hartford, Springfield, and Boston indeed carried a distinguished company; they were doctors who had attended a convention of the American Medical Association in New York. As the train came rapidly around the bend just east of the South Norwalk station (it had not stopped there), the engineer, who had not piloted a locomotive on the line for several years, suddenly saw that the drawbridge was open a few hundred feet ahead. He had clearly not noticed that the high ball (for "all clear") was down, and he was making somewhere between ten and fifty miles per hour, depending on whether one believed him, the victims, or the onlookers; the engineer gave the short blast of the whistle which meant "Down brakes!" but it was too late. Over the open end of the bridge and into the river went the locomotive, the baggage car, and the first two passenger cars. A third car fell part of the way and then broke apart. Two cars remained on the tracks. As the wrecked coaches piled up on top of each other in the river, forty-six persons, including five of the doctors, were killed. In one car the painter Thomas Hicks was travelling with a lady known to history only as Miss King. After the freakish manner of wrecks she was projected out onto the bank unhurt, without even getting wet, while Hicks was pinned in the wreckage. Working himself free, he searched frantically for his lost companion, giving up only after water had filled the car; there was a happy reunion afterward. If any good came of this disaster, it was the establishment of Connecticut's first Board of Railroad Commissioners, who set about making safer rules about such matters as open drawbridges. And it was also one of the few wrecks in which there has been immediately present on the scene almost more medical attention than was needed.

Only two days later two trains met head-on at Secaucus, New Jersey, the kind of senseless collision out in the open country which railroad men call a "cornfield meet." There were relatively few casualties, but the accident reminded people again that such an impact involves adding together the otherwise moderate speeds of two trains into a quite deadly total. Then in August there was another catastrophe when an excursion train and a regular train met head-on on a curve at Valley Falls Station in Rhode Island, wiping out thirteen more people.

Generally, cornfield meets resulted from miscalculations in the operation of trains in two directions over a single track on primitive timetable systems. If everyone kept on schedule, and waited on the proper siding, all went well. In fact, of course, trains were very often behind time and the question would arise as to whether one should wait or proceed. As we saw earlier in this book, the use of the telegraph, introduced in 1851 by Charles Minot on the Erie, tended to solve that problem, but in their conservative and penny-pinching way, many railroads failed to adopt telegraphic communication

No one could whip up indignation against the railroads like Harper's Weekly; *in 1887 it published "The Modern Altar of Sacrifice — The Devouring Car Stove," W. A. Rogers' cartoon above. It was the stove that usually set wooden cars afire. The 1883 cartoon below is called "Does Death Rule the Railroads and the Steamboats?"*

for as much as twenty years, causing among others the terrible wreck at Revere, Massachusetts (see page 53). Without the telegraph, cautious trains had been known to sit for hours, each waiting for the other to appear, each fearful that the other would finally have started.

It was just such a situation which prevailed on the warm morning of July 17, 1856, on a single track of the North Pennsylvania Railroad, now part of the Reading Company. At five o'clock that morning a ten-car excursion train was to leave Philadelphia laden with parochial-school children on a picnic organized by the St. Michael's Roman Catholic Church. A second load planned to pull out at eight. The trainmaster, hoping to get more of the crowd on the first train, held up its departure for some minutes, much to the displeasure of its conductor, Alfred F. Hoppel. When the train, heavily laden with men of God and young children, finally started on its way, its little engine, the *Shackamaxon*, could barely haul it and the excursion fell still further behind schedule. While regular trains followed a printed schedule, memorized by every conductor and pasted up in every engine cab, special trains like this one were given written orders. Hoppel's informed him that if he stayed on schedule, he would have a clear track all the way to the picnicground at Fort Washington. If he were more than fifteen minutes late, however, he would have to pull into a siding and permit the passage in the other direction of the first regular morning local into the city. Conductor Hoppel knew that first train's schedule very well, since it was his own normal run.

By the time he reached the only siding long enough for all his cars, at Edge Hill, Hoppel was fifteen minutes late. But he also knew that the regular down train was supposed to wait fifteen minutes at any station when an expected arrival from the other direction had not appeared, and that he could then beat the local to Fort Washington. His decision, therefore, could theoretically go either way, and he decided to proceed.

Meanwhile, the Philadelphia-bound local had started out at six that morning. It was the same time at which Hoppel's excursion train, had it remained on schedule, would have reached its destination and cleared the tracks. At 6:12 the local pulled into Fort Washington, where its young conductor, William Vanstavoren, inquired about the special. There was no sign of it. Under standard operating rules, Vanstavoren should have waited fifteen minutes and then proceeded. On the other hand, Vanstavoren assumed that, since the special had not arrived at Fort Washington on time, it must be waiting for him at Edge Hill. He discussed the matter with his engineer, William Lee, who thought they ought to wait. But Vanstavoren told him instead to proceed slowly, meanwhile steadily blowing the whistle of his locomotive, the *Aramingo*, as a warning. Thereupon the little local puffed off at about ten miles per hour, whistling so constantly that Lee could not possibly have heard the whistle of another locomotive approaching him.

Now all the conditions required for a disaster were fulfilled, with both trains approaching head-on on the not entirely foolish assumption that the other was waiting. Their combined speeds were perhaps forty-five miles per hour. Coming into Camp Hill, Pennsylvania, down a long grade and trestle with a blind curve at the bottom, Hoppel's train was beyond all hope of slowing down in any short distance. Looking forward from the cab of the local as he steamed around that very curve, Lee suddenly saw a frightening shadow speeding along the embankment ahead: only a few hundred yards separated the *Aramingo* and the *Shackamaxon*. Lee shut off his steam, threw the engine into reverse, and whistled for brakes. The fireman jumped and, when only some thirty feet remained between the trains, Lee followed him.

The ensuing crash, known to history as the Camp Hill disaster, killed about sixty and maimed as many more. Half the excursion train was consumed by

Aftermath: The inside of an overturned coach.

In dreadful human detail, and with suitable pious touches, Leslie's *magazine portrayed the "Angola Horror" of 1867 (above) showing victims who had survived their plunge off a bridge and the ensuing fire sorting out the quick and the dead. Below is the quite unexaggerated moment at Ashtabula, Ohio, in 1876, when all but the leading locomotive of the double-headed* Pacific Express *crashed through a defective bridge during a howling blizzard, killing and cremating over eighty-three passengers on the frozen creek 150 feet below. More details about this double blow to Vanderbilt's Lake Shore Railroad appear in the text.*

flames, burning many of the terrified passengers to death. In the aftermath, Vanstavoren, almost hysterical with feelings of guilt, did what he could to get help, then killed himself with arsenic. Ironically a coroner's jury later cleared him and placed the blame on conductor Hoppel of the special. Whatever the verdict, however, the real blame had to lie with a system too primitive for the speed and power of the railroad it governed.

Among the many lamentable catastrophes that beset the rails in the nineteenth century, certain ones acquired such cachet that they were forever known by an epithet. Among these the "Angola Horror" ranks high on the list. It is never referred to in any other way, and for good reason.

On December 18, 1867, the New York express of the Lake Shore & Michigan Southern Railroad was heading east at moderate speed toward Buffalo, where it would connect with the New York Central. It carried three baggage cars, and four passenger cars, of which the last was a "compromise" car from the Cleveland & Toledo Railroad. Despite the lessons learned in the recent war there were still many differences in gauge between railroads, even in the North, and it would be years before most lines would standardize at George Stephenson's four feet, eight and one-half inches. The Lake Shore tracks were four feet, ten inches apart and the Cleveland & Toledo's nearly an inch narrower. Compromise cars had wider wheel treads which permitted them, when all went well, to run on tracks of both gauges. It may be added that well-managed companies frowned on such contrivances, but no such considerations disturbed Commodore Vanderbilt, who controlled the Lake Shore.

As the express slowed a little at Angola, New York, and prepared to cross the bridge over Big Sisters Creek, a bystander observed that the narrower rear wheels of the compromise car fell off the track in crossing the frog of a switch and thereafter began bumping along the ties on the approach to the bridge. Just as the engine passed the span's standard "slow" warning signal, the emergency bell rang in the cab. Although the engineer called for brakes, it was too late for that piteously inadequate equipment to halt or slow the express, which rolled on across the span—all in safety except for the last two cars. The compromise car had dragged along the ties almost all the way across when its coupling broke and it plunged fifty feet down onto a frozen creek bed, landing upside down. Onto the shattered matchwood and over wounded passengers the stove poured its hot embers. Soon the wreckage was a holocaust, from which only three of forty-four passengers escaped with their lives. The second car from the rear also broke loose and slid down the other side of the bridge embankment, winding up on its side nearly intact. That also caught fire, but rescuers were able to put it out with snow almost at the beginning, so that only one of the passengers was killed. One of the strange features of the accident was the fact that the engineer, looking backward from his cab as he tried to stop the train, was so engulfed by steam and smoke that he could not understand what had happened until he had stopped his train on the other side of the bridge and run back along the track.

If it did nothing else, the widely publicized Angola Horror brought the use of compromise cars to an end and helped bring about the eventual standardization of gauges. It was also one more of the disasters which spurred on George Westinghouse in his efforts, patented a year or more later, to develop a better braking system based on the use of compressed air.

If faulty equipment and signalling practices caused dreadful accidents, as many more could be laid at the door of the crude and unreliable roadbed over which these primitive trains operated. Also on the Lake Shore, nine years after the Angola Horror, the *Pacific Express*, heading west at Ashtabula, Ohio, a little after 7:30 at night, broke through a bridge seventy-five feet high and consigned at least eighty-three passengers to death by fire. It had the unenviable distinction of being the worst accident up to that date, and one of the worst of all time.

Two engines had been pulling the crack train through a blizzard; the lead engineer could see only a few feet ahead as the train began to cross a bridge above Ashtabula Creek, but everything was snug if not overheated in the passenger cars behind—a smoker, two coaches, a parlor car, and three sleepers were lighted by sperm oil lamps and heated by coal. When he was nearly across, the engineer of the first locomotive, the *Socrates*, felt the structure begin to sink beneath him. Opening his throttle wide, he made the *Socrates* leap forward so powerfully that it gained the opposite bank. But his coupler snapped and behind him the other locomotive and the train fell down into the frozen creek with a loud crash.

As the first of an eventually vast crowd on the scene, the engineer of the *Socrates* came upon the driver of the other locomotive, who had been flung out of his cab in the fall and was injured but alive. As his rescuer picked him up, the other engineer remarked, "Another Angola Horror!" In his book, *Train Wreck*, Wesley Griswold describes in fearsome detail the fate of the many passengers on the *Pacific Express*, pointing out that the figure of eighty-three dead is only the wildest surmise and perhaps understates the total. There were fifty-two living passengers who either escaped or were helped out of the wreckage, but the total on the train was estimated at anywhere from 130 to 250 people. The great fire that raged unchecked did too thorough a job to make it possible to count the victims.

A great uproar followed the Ashtabula disaster and in the course of the investigation strange facts were revealed. The bridge was an iron-truss affair

(Continued on page 186)

He was going down grade,
    making 90 miles an hour
When his whistle broke into a scream.
    (Wooo! Wooo!)
He was found in the wreck
    with his hand on the throttle,
And a-scalded to death by the steam.

All railroad men know the classic ballad, "The Wreck of the Old 97," which took place on September 27, 1903, when the Fast Mail *of the Southern Railway, on its run between Monroe and Spencer, Virginia, jumped the track and went off Stillhouse Trestle near Danville. Engineer Joseph ("Steve") Broady was making up time, and the wreckage below shows what happened, not only to Broady but to both firemen, the conductor, the flagman, and eight others, mainly postal clerks.*

SOUTHERN PACIFIC

A head-on meeting created this matey scene at Batavia, New York, in 1885.

A boiler explosion left these superheater tubes looking like spaghetti.

A flash flood, a circus train, and ribbons of steel: North Dakota, 1913.

Of Freakish Disasters

That steam and momentum are both powerful and dramatic forces these pictures bear startling witness. If each in some way seems freakish, it is worth remembering that every one of these scenes can be duplicated, some of them many times. Nor can one judge the casualties by appearances. With great presence of mind, the crew of the teetering coach, shown here at Batavia, Ohio, in 1884, prevented the passengers from rushing to either end, and saved everyone on it. The Federal Express, the second train to lose its air brakes and enter Washington terrifyingly out of control (the first was a B & O express in 1887), crashed through the station's waiting room floor into the baggage room below, and not a soul was killed.

The runaway: July 8, 1905, was embarrassing for engine No. 321; *it ran*

Harper's Weekly, NOVEMBER 1, 1884

This teetering coach in Ohio was evacuated in a very gingerly way.

An explosion carried away boiler and cab but did not derail this engine.

Telescoped: sixty-four total abstainers died at Mud Run, Pennsylvania, 1888.

right through its roundhouse wall in Hartford, Connecticut.

No brakes: How the Federal came into Union Station, Washington, in 1953.

Not satisfied with the real thing, Americans turned out by the thousands in the 1890's and after to watch staged wrecks, like the one shown in the series above near Denver, which raised money for the "silver" candidate, William Jennings Bryan, in 1896. At top the mockingly named McKinley *and* Hanna *bow to each other. Having drawn apart, the engines started, the engineers jumped off, and the twain met (center), in an explosion of steam and smoke, before the camera of the noted William H. Jackson. The speed was less than promised and the two old locomotives survived rather well, as the bottom picture shows.*

following the design of William Howe, who was the brother-in-law of President Amasa Stone of the Lake Shore Railroad. It had been erected in 1863, replacing a wooden span of the same design. At the time, one of the railroad's junior engineers protested to Stone that the bridge was of dangerous design, and he was discharged for his temerity. With some misgivings the chief engineer, Charles Collins, allowed the iron bridge to be installed, even though it was an untested idea and he would have preferred a more expensive structure of stone. Although there is some question as to his culpability, two days after a legislative hearing on the disaster Collins blew his brains out with a revolver. Five years after that, brooding Amasa Stone also took his own life. In Washington, Representative James A. Garfield of Ohio introduced a bill, which had been prepared for him by Charles Francis Adams, Jr.; it proposed a procedure for investigating and reporting on every fatal railroad accident thereafter in order to find some way of preventing the slaughter. The bill failed but the idea was eventually incorporated into the Interstate Commerce Act of 1887. It is interesting to remember that Adams' grandfather, former President John Quincy Adams, had been in the first American railway accident which killed any passengers, a derailment on the Camden & Amboy. The old man had escaped unhurt but Cornelius Vanderbilt had been badly hurt. In railroading, the cast of characters changes less than one might expect.

During this same unhappy period the disaster-prone Erie had more than its share of physical trouble to complement its endless financial scandals. In 1864 it managed to run a trainload of Confederate prisoners of war head-on into a coal train, with an appalling death toll. At least fifty of some eight hundred prisoners were killed and over one hundred were wounded. A similar fate befell over one hundred of their guards, and many on both sides agreed that the wreck was worse than any battle they had seen. The blame fell on the man who had carelessly let the coal train proceed; a telegraph operator had violated the famous Rule G, which prohibits drinking on duty, or before going on duty, on all railroads.

The most famous of all Erie wrecks in this period took place at Carr's Rock on April 15, 1868, when a speeding eastbound express was just about to cross a high culvert over Carr's Rock Brook, leading into the Delaware River. Unknown to engineer Henry Green, the pounding wheels of the locomotive broke a rail on the curve where the track turned onto the culvert.

The pieces apparently stayed in place until the first of the last four cars struck the break and derailed. Momentum carried that coach and the three sleepers behind it off the track, over the bank, and down into the rocky bottom of the brook. The train had continued on for some distance when the conductor, Jasper B. Judd, patrolling his train, suddenly noticed the missing cars. By the time the express had backed up to the scene of the wreck, the last sleeper was in flames and throwing a ghastly light on the terrible scene below. Crew and passengers set about the work of rescue as fast as possible, but only two persons were saved from those in the last car and nearly everyone in the first car was killed. There were all together some forty dead. In the aftermath of the tragedy, which took place during the regime of those artful dodgers Gould and Fisk, an attempt was made to fix the blame on a supposed train wrecker called "the fiend Bowen," a half-demented man from whom a "confession" was extracted. It is more likely, however, that the miserable and brittle iron rails of the time were responsible. One acid commentator of the era, the noted diarist George Templeton Strong, wrote after the last wreck, "Another railroad accident (so-called) on the Erie Road. Scores of people smashed, burned to death or maimed for life. We shall never travel safely till some pious, wealthy and much beloved railroad director has been hanged for murder, with a 'gentleman conductor' on each side of him. Drew or Vanderbilt would do to begin with. . . ."

If the public felt vengeful toward the railroad corporations, it also created folk heroes, both real and imaginary. There was the brave engineer, personified in the steadfast John Luther ("Casey") Jones, who told his famous fireman Sim Webb to jump but stayed with his locomotive in the hope of at least slowing down his mail train as he was about to run into a freight. (John H. White, Jr., comments, "Why Jones is considered a hero I don't understand. He was running too fast and rammed into the rear of another train. His own fault.") And there was the fictional housewife flagging down the *Limited* with her red underdrawers, and the very real figure of fifteen-year-old Kate Shelley dragging herself through a storm across a damaged bridge to save a train from certain destruction. Presents, praise, and eventually a job on the railroad were her reward, and a lifetime supply of sentimental verse.

Unfortunately, however, accidents did not stop happening. As long as there were boilers, or careless inspections, they occasionally blew up. There are still

The best "after" photograph of a staged wreck is the one below, for which no certain details are available. It was taken by H. F. Pierson of Denver but the gondola car (from the Columbus, Hocking Valley & Toledo) and the landscape suggest the Midwest. In any case the wreckage was satisfying to discriminating critics, although it did not match the better if less well photographed holocaust which an official of the Missouri, Kansas & Texas (the "Katy") Railway with the marvelously apt name of William G. Crush put on in Texas in 1896. There thirty-thousand people watched two trains meet at about sixty miles an hour. Flying wreckage, which had not been counted on, killed one man and laid two photographers low.

For many years, railroad cars were coupled by the primitive link-and-pin method (above); the brakeman or switchman had to stand between the cars and drop a pin into overlapping sockets as the cars came together, a hazardous operation that killed and maimed men by the hundreds. After the Civil War, an impoverished former Confederate major, Eli H. Janney, while clerking in a dry-goods store, began experimenting with a coupler which would automatically close on impact when two came together—and could be opened from the side of a car. Observing the action of fingers crooked against each other, he whittled out a model with a jackknife, patented it, improved it, and got it used eventually in the 1870's by the Pennsylvania Railroad. A drawing of his coupler is shown below. As long as most railroad management thought workmen more expendable than money for safety devices, Janney's idea languished. It required the campaign led by Lorenzo Coffin (at far right on the opposite page) to have it adopted into federal law in 1893.

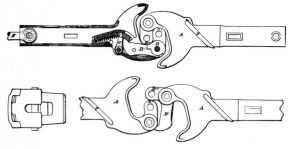

FORNEY, *The Railroad Car Builder's Pictorial Dictionary*

runaways in modern times like, for example, the *Federal Express* which crashed into the Union Station in Washington in 1953 at sixty-five miles an hour (see picture on page 185). Bridges still give trouble, if only because trains can go through them when they are open. At Atlantic City in 1906, fifty-seven people were drowned in such a miscalculation: at Newark Bay in 1958, forty-eight riders met the same fate. In the year 1875, nearly a quarter century after the first use of telegraphic train orders, there were 104 reported head-on collisions. Double track and centralized traffic control have undoubtedly reduced the toll, but, in 1953 in Conneaut, Ohio, four trains managed to meet in a horrendous tangle, including two freights, the passenger train *Mohawk*, which sideswiped one of them, and a few moments later, the *Southwestern Limited*, doing seventy miles an hour, which ran into the wreckage. Twenty-one passengers were killed, and all because a piece of pipe had fallen from one carelessly loaded gondola car onto the adjoining track.

As the years wore on, however, technology began to provide cures for many of the railroads' maladies. Beginning in the 1860's, after adoption of Bessemer's steel process in England, America began buying and eventually rolling its own steel rail, so that by about 1890 nearly all important trackage was of steel. Block signals, air brakes, electric lighting, and steam heating all played a part in reducing accidents. All-steel passenger cars made their debut in 1907 and the handsome but hazardous wooden ones were slowly retired, or wound up their days in work trains. The percentage of casualties in relation to "passenger miles" travelled fell steadily, but because for years the trackage and service kept multiplying at an astonishing rate, accidents never disappeared from the rails nor, in the more dramatic occurrences, from the newspapers (although, indeed, thousands of minor wrecks involving only freight trains never get publicized at all).

Human error, unfortunately, can never be eliminated. If the track workers who were burning brush along the line of the Toledo, Peoria & Western Railroad in August, 1887, had thoroughly put out their fires near a wooden culvert at Chatsworth, Illinois, an excursion bound for Niagara Falls would not have piled up around a fifteen-foot wooden trestle that had caught fire, and eighty-two people would have lived, and a great deal of bad poetry would not have been written. Rear-end collisions will keep taking place as long as trainmen fail to flag down following trains or engineers and firemen fail to notice their frantic signals.

The elimination of wooden cars, which were susceptible to such dreadful "telescoping" accidents as that which wiped out sixty-four members of the Total Abstinence Union in an excursion train at Mud Run, Pennsylvania, in 1888 (see page 185), did not apparently end the problem. At Mount Union, Pennsylvania, where, as we have already seen, a wooden emigrant train was struck in 1853, an all-steel car was telescoped in 1917, from the rear again, by a fast freight. Twenty people perished there in the sleeping car *Bellwood*.

One cannot prevent natural disasters, in which, generally, railroads have played heroic roles—a racing engineer attempting to warn the doomed city of Johnstown as the floodwaters rolled toward it, a Shore Line train on the New Haven Railroad nudging floating houses and boats off the track to bring passengers safely out of danger in the New England hurricane of 1938. One cannot avoid, alas, mistakes, from open switches to misread orders. Nor can we expect that even new equipment will not fail, especially in a day when trains are sometimes over-engineered in terms of the maintenance they receive. Yet, financially desperate as many American railroads are today, and much as they should be improved, the Angola Horrors and Chatsworth Wrecks of our times are taking place on mountainsides, airport approaches, and superhighways, so-called, not on the real superhighways of America, its railroads.

George Westinghouse   *Lorenzo Coffin*

George Westinghouse (left above) invented the air brake in 1869 when he was only twenty-two and eventually delivered railroad men from hazardous hand brakes, shown at left. Turned down tight, they might hold, and sometimes they might not. They were too weak for really heavy trains. In its improved form, the Westinghouse invention, shown in the plan below, stores up air in pressure tanks in both engines and cars, interconnected by a series of pipes and air hoses. Air pressure keeps the brakes *off*; the minute it is eased, they start taking hold. If the air pressure is released all at once by the engineer, or "dumped," the brakes lock. But the railroad magnates were hard to convince. "Do you pretend to tell me that you could stop trains with wind?" snapped Commodore Vanderbilt to Westinghouse. "I'll give you to understand, young man, that I am too busy to have any time taken up talking to a damn fool." It took a fanatic for railway safety, a former Civil War chaplain named Lorenzo Coffin, and a long crusade to persuade the railways of the virtues of the air brake, despite arguments and demonstrations. Eventually Coffin pushed through Congress the Railroad Safety Appliance Act of 1893, which made air brakes and automatic couplers mandatory and, ironically, made possible the heavier as well as faster trains of the twentieth century.

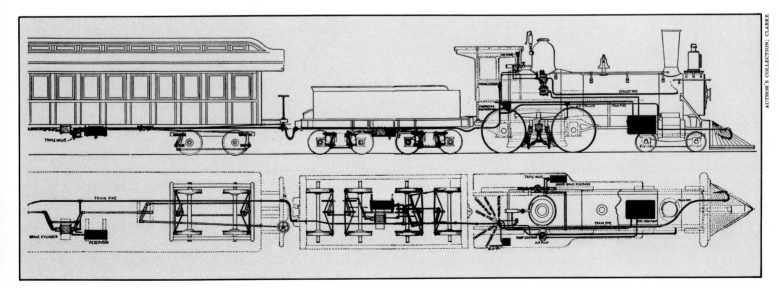

9. Boomers, Hoggers, and Brass-Pounders

9. Boomers, Hoggers, and Brass-Pounders

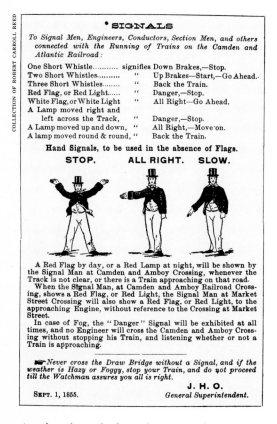

A rather elegantly dressed trainman demonstrates a variety of hand signals in this early broadside issued by the Camden & Atlantic Railroad.

PRECEDING PAGES: *With engine No. 210 of the Old Colony Railroad hitched up to the varnish and ready to go, the crew poses for the photographer at Taunton, Massachusetts, in 1884.*

By 1910, the nether end of the "golden age" of railroading, which is said to have begun around 1890, there were 1,699,420 Americans working on the railroad. Brakemen, switchmen, telegraphers, firemen, engineers, section gangs, they tended to the narrow-gauge iron of tiny lumber lines lost in the western forests, slung lightning on the complicated telegraphic arrangements of the straight, four-track New York Central, and rammed the massive decapods through the blind white passes of the Northern Route. They were colorful men doing a romantic and frequently dangerous job, and they should have left behind a bright and intricate legend. They have not; the cowboy has, and the riverboat captain, and most people with any interest in the American past can give a pretty fair description of the life of the Nantucket whaling man. But railroading, which had every bit as much deadly glamour about it as the preceding occupations, seems to be strangely inaccessible. Richard Reinhardt, in the introduction to his lively and illuminating book *Workin' on the Railroad*, suggests that this is partly the fault of the railroad men themselves. With the exception of "the Brave Engineer of fable," writes Reinhardt, the railroad man "seems to lack the solitary, fatalistic, picaresque code of behavior that gives a heroic dimension to the cowboy. Railroad men are conservative and fraternal. Their community life is introverted, closely woven, and deep-dyed with tradition. To an old-fashioned railroader, honor consists in starting young and working one's way up the ladder. In the Age of Steam, it was axiomatic that the best locomotive engineers previously had been firemen, the best conductors had risen from brakemen, and the best executives had started at the bottom as callboys, telegraphers, switchmen, or section hands. Railroading was not a temporary pastime for soldiers of fortune but a lifetime commitment for strong, dedicated men.

"At his worst, the old-time railroader was a narrow-minded, unimaginative functionary, more frightened of being fired than of dying in a flaming wreck. . . .While these institutional qualities of railroad men—including respect for authority, conformity to routine, and pride in technical skill—are admirably suited to the business of moving vehicles, they make for a formidably exclusive profession. . . ."

Whatever the reasons for the modest dimensions of generally known railroading folklore, the men who earned their living on the road were a spectacular lot. To the traveller, the most visible of the railroading fraternity was the conductor. Not only did he come through the cars collecting tickets (demanding them, an English visitor complained as early as 1854, "in a dry, callous tone, as if it would cost something to be cheerful"), he was in charge of the train. Once in a great while the engineer succeeded in cowing him and taking control, but for the most part the conductor had absolute say; in fact,

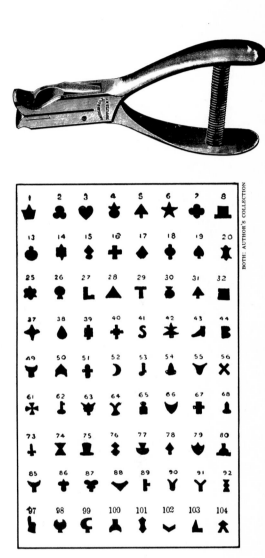

With his level gaze and steadfast posture, this Pullman conductor is as imperious as most of his breed. Ever on guard against people trying to defraud the line of the price of a ticket, the conductor knew much of human venality. Occasionally he was something of a thief himself, skimming the top off fares he collected on the train. The railroads often employed "spotters" to keep the conductors honest, but one still managed to accumulate $25,000 before retiring at fifty, and many must have done better than that. According to an ancient bit of railroad lore, conductors threw their take into the air at the end of the day, and turned over to the company all the money that stuck to the bell cord. Most conductors had individual punch designs; the sampling above is taken from a catalogue published about 1913 by the American Railway Supply Company.

We do not know the name of this engineer who is leaning with such competent ease against a driving wheel taller than he is, but it is safe to say that he was tough and capable. Undoubtedly he was also a pretty fair mechanic, since he had to answer for the condition of his locomotive when he took it out of the yards. He also had to know a great deal about all aspects of railroading rules and signals, and his job demanded that he be calm and steady in the worst situations. He had come up through the ranks, and he was doubtless hard as nails. In his day, he was a figure of unparalleled grandeur, one for which we have no modern equivalent. The pilot of a flying machine, for instance, is a pallid creature in comparison to him.

he was often called "captain" by the passengers. In the early days the conductor could dress in mufti, the only indication that he was not a passenger being the legend "conductor" spelled out on a brass strip attached to his top hat. During the opulent 1870's he added kid gloves with delicate floral hues to his costume, and frequently strode through the cars carrying a silver-plated lantern with his name and lodge emblem etched on its colored glass globe. By the nineties he was clad in the familiar blue serge suit and gold buttons, but he was still an awesome figure and, more often than not, a frightful grouch. Perhaps this was because the man, in his august position as representative of the company, had little time for trifles, and perhaps it was an understandable holdover from his early days as a brakeman.

All freight conductors and most passenger conductors began their careers as brakemen; on passenger trains long ago one could find them on the platforms at the brakes, or leaning into the cars to call station names as indistinctly as possible. On a freight a man could hardly find a tougher job. Before the railroads' dilatory adoption of the Westinghouse air brake, cars had to be stopped by hand. That was the brakeman's job; standing on the roof of a freight car, he would spin a cast iron wheel connected to a shaft that ran down to the brakes, thereby slowing or stopping the train. It was a fine job if the brakeman happened to be working a slow freight on a summer day. Then he could perch on his wheel, cooled by the constant breeze, watch the countryside roll by, and collect a day's pay at the end of his jaunt. But, as with most idylls, that was rarely the way it went. The brakeman was just as likely to find himself on top of a fast freight in the dead of winter with the roof of the car slick with ice and the wind booming down and freezing the sweat on his face. The train would be lurching around badly banked grades trying to make up for lost time, and the brakeman would be wrestling his wheel this way and that, cold and miserable and a fraction of a second away from death. Then, at the end of the line, he would hear the all-too-common story of a fellow brakeman being blown off the car in the night and found frozen to death in a drift by a section gang the next day. As a consequence brakemen were a rough lot; hard drinking, profane, violent, and arrogant. They knew they were tough, they were noisily pessimistic, and they tended to tear towns apart on payday. It was a bitter, unrewarding life that the brakeman lived, but it did start him on the way to becoming a conductor or, even better, an engineer.

Of course, nobody got to be an engineer without being a fireman first. The tallow pot (so called because it was once his job to lubricate the engine with tallow) sat just across from the engineer on the left side of the cab, but he was miles away in prestige. His was a safer job than the brakeman's, but what it lacked in danger it made up for in drudgery. It was not so bad when locomotives burned wood and the fireman had only to pitch logs into the firebox; but when coal came in, the task became a backbreaking monotony of pivoting at a crouch between tender and fire, shoveling tons of what was called, with rueful euphemism, "black diamonds." He also had to break up coal, keep an eye on the gauges, and take on water when the engine needed it. Still, this relentless work was good training for the fledgling engineer, for it required delicacy, knowledge, and skill. The fireman had to know how to scatter the coal so that the fire burned evenly and when to open the furnace door so the draught would keep the engine from tearing holes in the fire. And possibly the worst part of the job was being a perpetual scapegoat. In his book *The General Manager's Story*, Herbert E. Hamblen quotes a man who had risen through the ranks but who, after many years, still rankled over the injustices dealt him when he was a fireman. The fireman, he wrote, "bends his back, and hustles to make steam to get the train in on time, frequently with miserable fuel and an engine that ought to be in the scrap-heap. When time is lost for the want of steam, it is on the fireman's devoted head that the wrath of the engineer, master mechanic, and superintendent falls, even though it be evident to anybody that the coal is 70 percent slate and the valves and pistons blow like sieves."

But if the fireman persevered, he would in time become an engineer. At the turn of the century, that was glory, and in fact it is about the only railroading job that has survived to become something of a legend today. When most people think of old-time railroading, they think of Casey Jones roaring into eternity with his hand on the whistle cord. We have discussed Casey earlier; here is what Ted Custer, an engineer, commented: "Hard-boiled railroaders affected a withering scorn for any engineer who would stick to his post when there seemed no chance of stopping. But when emergency actually came to them, they would go into the wreck, fighting for every inch. In all my experience with thousands of engineers, I saw only one who left his post when there was the slightest chance of stopping his train."

The engineer had come up in a hard school, and he was rarely afraid to take risks. His was the judgment that determined how much a train could be pushed to make up for lost time without leaving the rails. True, the telegrapher and the conductor could "put the orders" on him—make him slow down or stop—but it was still his hand that jockeyed the locomotive. A good "hogger" was very knowledgeable indeed; for instance, a freight train pulling forty cars could burn between forty and two hundred pounds of coal per mile, and how much was consumed depended largely upon the skill of the engineer. If he used too much throttle, the locomotive would devour the fuel at an appalling rate.

Like the fireman, the engineer had to endure his share of drudgery. Every magnificent run highballing with a name train had its counterpart in horrible yard work. One gruelling example is the experience of Hamblen's hero who, coming in from a long run one evening, was immediately ordered to go back sixty miles down the line and bring up thirty cars of coal. He was tired, but there was nobody else to do it, so off he went. When he got there, he found it took four hours of switching to get his train together. Engineers did not

Fireman J. S. Miller stokes a locomotive on the New York Central, Hudson Division, above. The walls and ceiling in the cab of a locomotive seem unlikely places to find wooden planking, but it provides insulation. That cab is a poor place compared to the elegantly outfitted one to the left, which "Bat" Casey, an engineer on the Oregon & California, fixed up for himself. Casey, who is sitting at the right, spent his own money to nickel-plate the throttle, reverse lever, lubricators, and all the rest of that gleaming hardware. He also bought the linoleum on the cab floor, the mahogany seat boxes with their red plush cushions, the Seth Thomas cab clock, and of course, he provided the three-point buck deer's head.

A brass-pounder on the Erie taps out a message while a somewhat bilious apparition waits at the ticket window. It was a rare stationmaster who did not know Morse code.

get paid for switching time, and he was in a very foul mood as he finally approached the first hill with his heavy drag. Just as he got to it, the conductor stopped him—for no good reason, as it turned out—and, having lost momentum, the engineer had to split the drag into two parts to get it over the hill. By that time the locomotive was almost out of water, and died on a slight grade. The weary man rolled her back, and the last two cars came loose. He reassembled his train, cut the engine loose, and ran five miles to the next waterplug, and returned, and broke a drawbar hitching up again. By the time that was fixed he had to wait in the hole (the passing track) until the limited went by. When it did, the head brakeman materialized with an order for him to weigh all thirty cars of coal. When that was finished the engineer was so exhausted that he sent word to Chicago that he would not go on without some rest, and curled up in the cab. Just as he was about to drop off to sleep, the fireman returned from getting a drink and, in a staggering display of enterprise, began to do some noisy maintenance on the locomotive. Finally the engineer climbed to his feet and, in a daze, took the drag out early that morning, telling his fireman, "Well, we've only got about twenty miles farther to go, and I do hope we'll live to land this train in the yard—I've been with it so long that I take a kind of fatherly interest in it."

They did make it home. The engineer got down from the cab and entered on the register, "Have been fifty-two hours on duty. Do not call me until I have had eight hours' sleep.—9:30 A.M." He had been asleep in his hotel for less than forty-five minutes when a caller—an unpopular fellow whose job it was to rouse engineers—shook him awake and told him he was wanted at once for a stock train. After a sleepy refusal the caller left, but returned with an order signed by the superintendent. The engineer would not go, and, as he put it, " . . . got my medicine—thirty days suspension for refusing to obey an order. I was lucky to get off so. [The superintendent] told me that all that saved my job was the fact that an engine came in off the branch opportunely and brought the stock train through."

It is superfluous to say that this was in the days before unions were strong and safety laws forbade engineers to be on duty for more than sixteen hours at a stretch. Many engineers went to their death when, worn beyond human

Interlocking switches controlled from a central switch

tower did much to increase safety on the road, as well as add considerably to the life expectancy of the switchman.

SOUTHERN PACIFIC

The turn-of-the-century scene below gives some idea of how busy things could get for the railway mail clerk. At right is a Southern Pacific crew in their caboose on the Tucson Route in 1900.

endurance, they fell asleep at the throttle. One telegrapher recalled trying to signal a passing train at night, catching "a fleeting glimpse of the engineer in the cab window as he passed. His head and shoulders hung over the sill, his head rolling from side to side."

In such a case, all the telegrapher could do was to wire ahead down the line, but that was a great deal more than could have been done before the railroads' adoption of the telegraph. The telegraph and the railroad were so complementary that nearly every Morse telegrapher in the country worked for the road. The dispatcher was in constant touch with station operators scattered all up and down the line. If trouble developed, a telegrapher could flag down the train and pass the message. Speed was the most important attribute of the good brass-pounder; he used a baffling lexicon of abbreviations and developed a new kind of script, "op fist," which was characterized by bold curves that connected the words.

The telegrapher's job, although demanding, was relatively free from danger. When danger came, though, the lightning-slinger often proved to be as cool as the bravest engineer. Every railroad man involved in the great fire at Hinckley, Minnesota, in 1894 seems to have displayed uncommon courage, but most of the laurels must go to Tom Dunn, a telegrapher for the St. Paul & Duluth who was stationed at Hinckley. The whole town was in flames, the last train was pulling out with the paint blistering on the sides of the cars, and Dunn must have known he did not have a chance in the world of saving himself if he stayed behind. But he also knew the train would most likely never get through if he was not at his post monitoring traffic. So Dunn stayed at his key and kept the lines open until the flames consumed him.

We are told that operators always carried their Morse with them, and that they made keys out of their knives or forks and tapped out impatient messages to their wives when dinner was slow in coming to the table. They often spoke in monosyllables, for the habit of saving time ran deep. When friends were summoned to the death bed of an old operator named Charlie Phillips, he is said to have told them: "No use, boys; no battery; no current; zinc's all eaten away, and no time to galvanize now. Guess I'll have to cut off."

The switchman also shared responsibility for the safe passage of the trains, and his job was, if anything, worse than that of the brakeman. The switch-man worked in the yards, attending to the switches and coupling and un-coupling the cars. The switches were bad—their open points could take off a foot—but the couplers were downright murderous. The early couplers were link-and-pin, that barbaric device which, since it had to be set by hand, had the switchman dancing in and out between two cars as they came together. Yardmasters interviewing prospective switchmen asked to see their hands; if the men had a few fingers missing, they were marked as experienced personnel. "All through my employment as a switchman," railroad man Harry French of Kansas City recalled years later, his sister "kept one clean sheet for the express purpose of wrapping up my mangled remains." This was no mere morbid fancy on the part of his sister; French said that in the yards of the Hannibal & St. Joseph the death rate was three to five men per week. Two hundred men a year? He must have exaggerated. In the years before 1900, when the Safety Appliance Act of 1893 came into full effect, outlawing link-and-pin and re-quiring air brakes, casualty figures were hard to find. The roads were reticent; only certain states required reports. In 1880 the Census made a stab at collect-ing nationwide figures for the year, showing 924 employees killed—663 of them "through their own carelessness," it said primly. Another 3,617 were injured. It was six times more dangerous to be a workman than a passenger.

Even the men of the Railway Mail Service occasionally had their ranks decimated by violent death. The mail cars were placed at the head end of the consist, and were consequently more vulnerable in a wreck. Between 1876 and 1905 there were 5,280 casualties in the service. Moreover, the railroads often treated the clerks in a cavalier manner; as late as the 1890's many of them worked in pre-Civil War cars whose crude wooden floors might show great slices of roadbed between their uneven planking. The Railway Mail Service (which since 1949 has been known by the less satisfactory name of the Postal Transportation Service) was founded during the Civil War by a Post Office employee named George B. Armstrong. Mail had been carried in trains from the beginning, but it was Armstrong's idea to have clerks sort out the mail in

The hard cases above are the members of a sec-tion gang on the Denver & Rio Grande. The gang boss is easily recognizable—he's the one sitting down. Each gang was responsible for a section of track; the men often lived near their sections in cheap houses built by the railroad. All summer long they patrolled their five or ten miles of track by handcar, repairing and maintaining the line. All we know of the scene below is the date—the summer of 1914—and the cryptic caption writ-ten on the photograph: "Getting over the jolt."

PULLMAN STANDARD, FROM *More Classic Trains* BY ARTHUR D. DUBIN, KALMBACH PUBLISHING CO., 1975

transit. The idea was a little slow catching on in the conservative community of railroadmen, but in time the fast-mail train captured the public imagination. A song was written about mail trains, and then came a spate of a dozen plays about them. Soon there was a railway mail clerk correspondence school teaching the intricacies of sorting mail and the high drama of snatching bags of it from the depot stanchion (or, in the smaller tank towns, from the arms of the stationmaster or his wife) as the train pounded by. Speaking in behalf of his clerks, Postmaster General Thomas L. James gave a high-flown description of their taxing duties: "[A railway mail clerk] must not only be proficient in his immediate work, but he must have a general knowledge of the entire country ... so that the correspondence he handles shall reach its destination at the earliest possible moment. ... He must know no night and no day. He must be impervious to heat and cold. Rushing along at the rate of forty or fifty miles an hour, in charge of that which is sacred—the correspondence of the people—catching his meals as he may; at home only semi-occasionally, the wonder is that men competent to discharge the duties of so high a calling can be found for so small a competence, and for so uncertain a tenure. . . ."

In short, the life of the railway mail clerk was pretty much the same as the life of any other railroad man—danger, long hours, fatigue, more danger, and the constant subjugation to the inscrutable whims of the men in warm offices somewhere up the line. And yet capable men turned out, turned out by the tens of thousands, year after year, to work on the road. From switchman to engineer, from the restless boomer who drifted from job to job to the homeguard who stuck loyally by one line his whole life, all of them were beguiled by the sights and smells of the roundhouse, the raw music of railroad slang, the splendor of a 4-4-0 locomotive racing down the high iron with a mail contract at stake, and the certain knowledge that they were taking part in one of the great works of man.

Every railroad man loved to see the pay car arrive, which it generally did once a month. The one at top is an inspection and pay car on the Pennsylvania, Reading Coal & Iron, and below it men are drawing pay from the New York Central.

The apocalyptic scene opposite, at top, shows a normal day's work in an engine shop, in this case one of the New York Central's. The grimy laboring men contrast sharply with the immaculate team standing at attention below them. The latter are the crew of the Cuban Special, *an all-Pullman train which made weekly tours between Havana and Santiago from January to April, 1925. The Pullman porter attended a special school where he was taught such niceties as how to drive a fly from a car, how to hold linen, and how to wake up his charges (a shake on the curtains from without—never a knock or a word).*

At the key; in the Cab

At eighteen Andrew Carnegie, the future steelmaster, was a cocky but likable telegrapher on the Pennsylvania Railroad, and clerk as well to the Pittsburgh Division superintendent, Thomas A. Scott. This little incident from Carnegie's *Autobiography* reveals a good deal about how to get ahead in railroading, or anything else.

"Mr. Scott was one of the most delightful superiors that anybody could have and I soon became warmly attached to him. He was my great man and all the hero worship that is inherent in youth I showered upon him. I soon began placing him in imagination in the presidency of the great Pennsylvania Railroad—a position which he afterwards attained. Under him I gradually performed duties not strictly belonging to my department and I can attribute my decided advancement in the service to one well-remembered incident.

"The railway was a single line. Telegraph orders to trains often became necessary, although it was not then a regular practice to run trains by telegraph. No one but the superintendent himself was permitted to give a train order on any part of the Pennsylvania system, or indeed of any other system, I believe, at that time. It was then a dangerous expedient to give telegraphic orders, for the whole system of railway management was still in its infancy, and men had not yet been trained for it. . . .

"One morning I reached the office and found that a serious accident on the Eastern Division had delayed the express passenger train westward, and that the passenger train eastward was proceeding with a flagman in advance at every curve. The freight trains in both directions were all standing still upon the sidings. Mr. Scott was not to be found. Finally I could not resist the temptation to plunge in, take the responsibility, give 'train orders,' and set matters going. 'Death or Westminster Abbey!' flashed across my mind. I knew it was dismissal, disgrace, perhaps criminal punishment for me if I erred. On the other hand I could bring in the wearied freight-train men who had lain out all night. I could set everything in motion. I knew I could. I had often done it in wiring Mr. Scott's orders. I knew just what to do, and so I began. I gave the orders in his name, started every train, sat at the instrument watching every tick, carried the trains along from station to station, took extra precautions, and had everything run-

ning smoothly when Mr. Scott at last reached the office. He had heard of the delay. His first words were: 'Well! How are matters?'

"He came to my side quickly, grasped his pencil, and began to write his orders. I had then to speak, and timidly said: 'Mr. Scott, I could not find you anywhere and I gave these orders in your name early this morning.'

"'Are they going all right? Where is the Eastern Express?'

A general dispatcher monitors the road.

"I showed him the messages and gave him the position of every train on the line—freights, ballast trains, everything—showed him the answers of the various conductors, the latest reports at the stations where the various trains had passed. All was right. He looked in my face for a second. I scarcely dared look in his. I did not know what was going to happen. He did not say one word, but again looked carefully over all that had taken place. Still he said nothing. After a little he moved away from my desk to his own, and that was the end of it. He was afraid to approve what I had done, yet he had not censured me. If it came out all right, it was all right; if it came out all wrong, the responsibility was mine. So it stood, but I noticed that he came in very regularly and in good time for some mornings after that. . . .

"I was feeling rather distressed about what I had done until I heard from Mr. Franciscus, who was then in charge of the

freighting department at Pittsburgh, that Mr. Scott, the evening after the memorable morning, had said to him: 'Do you know what that little white-haired Scotch devil of mine did?'

"'No.'

"'I'm blamed if he didn't run every train on the division in my name without the slightest authority.'

"'And did he do it all right?' asked Franciscus.

"'Oh, yes, all right.'

"This satisfied me. Of course I had my cue for the next occasion and went boldly in. From that date it was very seldom that Mr. Scott gave a train order."

A small boy's dream came true for the whimsical poet and novelist, the late Christopher Morley, when he rode the engine cab of the *Twentieth Century Limited*, an experience he brought to vivid life in these excerpts from a piece called "On Time," from his book *Internal Revenue* (1933). From Grand Central Station the power was electric to suburban Harmon, but there the great train picked up its giant Hudson engine for the run to Albany.

"Not less decorously than a bride made ready for her groom is the Century inaugurated for departure. A strip of wedding carpet leads you down into the cathedral twilight of that long crypt. Like a bouquet of flowers her name shines in white bulbs on the observation platform. In the diner waiters' coats are laundered like surplices. Mr. Welch, the veteran conductor, carrying his little box of official sancta, has the serene benignant gravity of some high cleric. And as you walk by that long perspective of windows, you are aware they are not just a string of ten Pullman cars. They are fused by something even subtler than the liaison of airy pressure that holds them safe. They are merged into personality, become a creature loved, honored, and obeyed. . . .

"Gently she steals out along a corridor of that dusty underground forest where colored lights gleam like tropic birds. 'Green!' 'Green!' you hear Brady and his helper saying aloud to each other, checking up each signal as soon as it comes in view. The electric engine has fascination and efficiency of its own, but in this ceremony one is bound to regard it as the father who takes the bride up the aisle on his arm. The father may be (I dare say usually is) more of a man than the groom; but the groom gets the romantic applause. So the electric is not a personality: just a miracle, smooth and swift. . . . Looking out you see the Second Section spinning along, just abaft your stern, on the adjoining track. There's a little boy, perhaps four years old, who comes down to Spuyten Duyvil station every fair afternoon, with his nurse, to see the Century spin by. It's a part of an engineer's job to know his roadside clients and salute them. When Brady waves, the nurse-maid can set her watch. It's 3.05. The bell chimes musically overhead, and again one feels that there is some sort of religion in all this. And I suppose (come to think of it) that isn't a bad sort of religion either: Getting There when you said you were Going To.

"But what a moment, when you glide into Harmon and see waiting for you ... what you came to see: one of the 5200's. Of course all that talk about the groom is nonsense, for at once you adore her as She. There's only one phrase adequate for her: Some Baby! Sharp work here: it must have been a couple of minutes, but in memory it seems only a few seconds of golden excitement. . . . Have you seen the Central's 5200's? This was 5217 and I shan't forget her. She seems as big as an ocean liner when you're in the cab.

"They hand up a slip of paper to George Tully, the engineer. If you're the engineer of the Twentieth Century they don't tell you to get anywhere by a certain time. They tell you *not* to get there *before* such and such. The message, signed with 2 sets of initials, was 'Do not arrive Albany before 5.38.' . . . It's 3.36 and we're off.

"I suppose the greatest moments in life are those when you don't believe it's yourself. It *can't* be you, in that holy of holies of small-boy imagination, the cab of an engine —and such an engine. More than that, made so welcome and at home by George Tully and Tom Cavanagh that you feel you belong there. Perhaps the simple truth is that if men have something they're enormously proud of, it's pure joy to show her off. And they are never so lovable as in their honest rivalries. 'Well,' Tom roared in my ear, as he explained the automatic stoking, 'I wonder if the Pennsy's got anything better than this?' For the first thing that puzzles you is two big canted cylinders in the cab. They revolve in spasms. These feed the coal into the firebox. A man couldn't shovel fast enough by hand

to keep the pressure she needs (she eats up four tons between Harmon and Albany). The fireman sits comfortably, with his eye on the steam gauge, and regulates the coal-feed by turning a handle. I could tell you a lot about the marvel of that firebox, and the 'butterfly-door' that opens in two wings to show you her fierce heart, full of flame and hardly anything else. The coal is practically consumed by the time it reaches the floor of the furnace. I fed her myself for quite a way. 'Keep the gauge at 220,' Tom said. 'No black smoke, and don't let the safety valve lift. Every time she lifts that means 20 gallons of water wasted—costs 3 cents.' 'Keep her hot,' George Tully shouted to me, grinning. 'We've got 5 minutes to make up.'

"That was part of the fun of this ride: I had a chance to see how things go when the breaks are against you. For there's a lot of work doing along the line: four-trackage being put in, the new tunnel at Storm King, and unavoidable slow-downs. 'We'll be knocked out 6 minutes before we reach Beacon,' Tully said. 'We'll get it back.'

"Astonishing how soon one adjusts one's judgments. Leaning from the cab window, watching the flash of her great pistons, watching the 2500-ton train come creaming along so obediently behind us, one soon began to think anything less than 60 mere loitering. All the imaginations that the cab might be uncomfortable riding were bosh. There is hardly—at any rate in those heavy 5200's—any more sway or movement than in the Pullmans themselves. The one thing a constant automobile driver finds disconcerting is the lack of steering. As you come rocketing toward a curve you wonder why the devil George doesn't turn a wheel to prevent her going clean off. And then you see her great gorgeous body meet the arc in that queer straight way—a constantly shifting tangent—and—well, you wish you could lay your hand on her somehow so she'd know how you feel. When George began to let her out a bit, beyond Beacon, I just had to go over and yell at him that I thought this 5217 of his was a good girl. With the grave pleasure of the expert he said, 'They're right there when you need 'em.' He let me blow the whistle, which makes one feel an absolute part of her. . . .

"Alive, shouting, fluttering her little green flags, she divided the clear cool afternoon. Looking out into that stream of space I could have lapsed into dream. I came closer

than ever before to the actual texture of Time whereof our minds are made. This was not just air or earth that we flew upon, this was the seamless reality of Now. We were abreast of the Instant. It was Time that we fed into the flaming furnace, it was Time that flickered in the giant wheels. This was the everlasting Now, we kept even pace with it and so the mind was (literally) in its own element, motionless and at ease. Terribly great, senseless, ecstatic, mad with her single destiny, yet with queer pathos in her whole great mass, so much at our command. Her cab looked like a clockshop, so many gauges and dials. But there is no clock in an engine cab. She makes her litany to one god only— the intent man who sits leaning forward so gravely. And he verifies himself by the other little god—the tiny one in his pocket. . . .

"Green! Green! they kept repeating to one another across the cab. Tom and I sat on the port side where I could see the whole panorama of the Hudson, and far down a curve of the river a white plume where the Second Section came merrily behind us, keeping her 3 mile distance. And, with Tom, I waved to the regular clients—the 'Pig-Woman'; the two priests in cassocks and birettas, near Poughkeepsie; the Cleary Girls in Hyde Park, whose husband and father is the flag-man at that crossing; and many more. And then Tom said suddenly, after a glance at his watch, 'We've got the dope on 'em now. 49 minutes to do 45 miles.' I began to see that when chance works against him, the engine-man instinctively personifies the unforgiving minutes into mysterious enemies who are trying to spoil things. . . . These men live with Time in a way we rarely dream of. Time is not their merry wanton, as she is to some of us. She's their wife, for better for worse. There was a truly husbandly griev-ance in George's eye when, just outside Albany, we had to slow almost to a standstill. Number 7—which left Grand Central 45 minutes earlier—was right ahead of us. There was the accent of King Tamburlaine in 5217's whistle as she shouted a blasphemy in steam. We came to a stop in Albany at 5.42. And as she wasn't due to leave there till 5.49, everything was jake. But I saw Tom, who is young and proud, taking a last look at his watch as he pulled his little black satchel out of the locker. There was about fifty seconds just outside Albany that 'they' had put over on us."

10. Turrets, Towers, and Rain Sheds

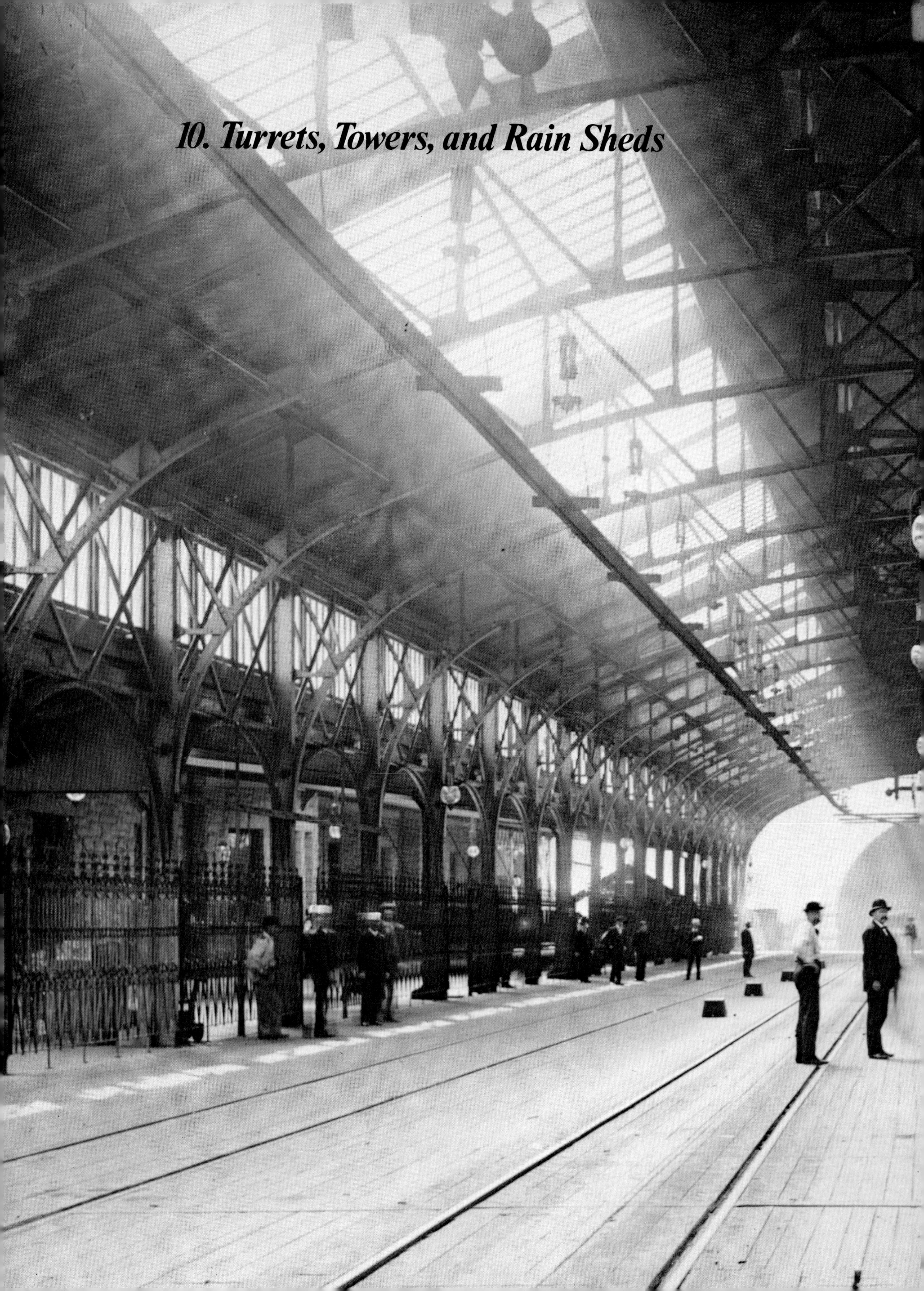

10. Turrets, Towers, and Rain Sheds

Built in 1883–85, Chicago's Dearborn Station was designed by C. L. W. Eidlitz, who liked to stick a single massive tower on his creations.

PRECEDING PAGES: *This noble arcade is the train shed of the B & O's Mount Royal Station. A primitive electric engine is towing in the train so that it will not blow coal smoke over the glass and metal; indeed, the big place does look clean. Fortunately the station has been taken over and preserved by the Maryland Institute College of Art.*

In 1875, the architectural magazine *Building News* made a resonant statement: "Railway termini and hotels are to the nineteenth century what monasteries and cathedrals were to the thirteenth century. They are truly the only real representative building we possess. . . . Our metropolitan termini have been leaders in the art spirit of our time." By 1875 the statement was true enough, although America came very late to the game of building impressive temples to the Olympian iron horse.

Almost as soon as there were railroads in England and on the Continent, they were being served by imposing, solemn stations and huge train sheds. But the English and Europeans were not faced with the baffling problems that confronted builders in America, where hundreds of miles of track ran between distant coastal cities and back into the Midwest over rough and broken terrain. Every penny of available capital in that primitive era had to go into bridges, tunnels, track, and equipment. Simply getting the rails to their destination was undertaking enough: there was no money left over for a palace at the end of the line. For decades passengers had to make do with taverns or even general stores which were near the tracks. In the National Capital, for instance, the Baltimore & Ohio bought a three-story brick house to serve as its depot in 1835. A tailor and cabinetmaker had to be moved out, the two lower floors were converted into a single room, and in a forlorn attempt to give this makeshift structure some dignity, a belfry was stuck on the roof. That was the B & O's Washington, D.C., station for fifteen years.

The same line had built America's first railroad station five years before at Mount Clare, Baltimore. During the next century and a quarter some forty thousand more passenger depots were erected. Timber was plentiful and cheap and in the beginning, therefore, most of them were made of wood. This turned out to be risky; Schenectady Station burned when it was less than a decade old, and a station in East Boston had the unhappy distinction of burning to the ground on the day it opened.

Not all the early stations were firetraps, however. Boston, the nation's first railroad center, had seven separate buildings for all of its main lines. Even in the 1830's these were fairly elaborate affairs of brick or stone. Gradually, American stations began to become more ambitious and diversified in design. In 1848 the architect Henry Austin designed New Haven Station (an ornate predecessor of the present one—now closed); it was the first important example of what later came to be called "the railroad style." The author of *Benham's City Directory and Annual Advertiser* knew a fine building when he saw one, and provided a rhapsodic description of it: "The beautiful edifice . . . is situated on Union Street and occupies the entire square from Chapel to Cherry Street being 300 feet in length. The style of architecture is Italian . . .

with a tower at each end. . . . On either side of the main hall or platform, are extensive Parlors, that on the left side being for the accommodation of ladies and is furnished with a profusion of rich and costly sofas, divans, chairs, ottomans, mirrors, etc., with convenient dressing rooms attached. Obliging servants are always in attendance. . . . The Ticket Office is on the left side of the grand hall, with ornamental windows of ground glass. . . . The design of this beautiful structure . . . reflects the highest credit on the architect. . . . Its cost to the railroad was upwards of $40,000. Long may it stand as an enduring monument to the taste, the liberality and the enterprise of its projectors." Benham notwithstanding, the station did have its drawbacks. The building was at street level; trains ran through a cut, and passengers had to descend to narrow, smoky, and inadequate platforms in order to board them. A small boy, getting off the cars into the steam and gloom, remembered his Calvinist upbringing and asked his father, "Is this hell?" "No, my son," replied his father, "New Haven."

By the late 1850's various styles of station architecture had been tried; the unsuccessful attempts were discarded and the successful ones studied and refined. One element, however, was absolutely essential to architects of the era —the tower, which, when grand enough, becomes a campanile. Whether Italian villa or Norman, every station had to be adorned with at least two; even the tiny station in Jersey City, which was scarcely more than a train shed, had legitimacy conferred upon it in the form of a pair of small decorative towers. More significant structurally was the arch; a number of stations were built with a great arched train shed roof which covered the waiting rooms and ticket offices as well as the trains, a severe and simple design. For the most part, though, architects were beguiled by European fashions, and produced widely eclectic buildings. Even in their occasional failure to achieve architectural coherence, these structures took on a peculiarly American charm.

Not everyone thought so, of course. On the eve of the Civil War, Henry Hudson Holly, author of the first American pattern book to include plans for a depot, wrote: "In Britain, stations are beautiful and tasteful, just as their trains are safe and luxurious." But in America, Holly went on, stations were "uninviting or ridiculous, beggarly or pretentious. . . ." It is hardly surprising that Holly offered his own design—an Italian villa pepped up with a dash of English Victorian Gothic—as a solution to this gloomy situation. Such a station, he claimed, would "set a good architectural example and result in improving the taste of the community."

If Holly disliked pretension in railroad stations, he was soon to endure unprecedented assaults on his taste. When after the Civil War the northern railroad barons found themselves very wealthy indeed, they set about building shrines to themselves and their works. These took the form of the increasingly grandiose passenger stations of the latter half of the nineteenth century. (Commodore Vanderbilt even built a triumphal frieze surrounding a statue of himself; only the statue survives, above the roadway which now surrounds Grand Central.) A source of pride to the cities they adorned, as well as to their builders, these massive edifices were often wonderful confections of brick and stone, extravagantly ornamented, and studded with ells and wings and towers. Some of the greatest architects of the day had a hand in them— Louis Sullivan, H. H. Richardson, Stanford White, and the highly influential D. H. Burnham. At their best, the great stations were supremely fine structures. The story of all of them can pretty well be told in the story of one— Grand Central Station in New York is not the largest railroad station, and it never was; nor was it ever the busiest. But it is the most famous of them all, and for years it was unquestionably the center of the world.

When, at the age of seventy-six, Cornelius Vanderbilt consolidated his

The ravishing structure above is a drinking fountain, designed by Theodore C. Link for the St. Louis Union Station in 1891. The jocular face below ornamented the building's exterior. Into the station's forty-two stub tracks ran the trains of eighteen different railroads. Four tracks survive.

The busy scene at the Harrisburg Station, above, was photographed just after the Civil War. The top-heavy structure was a union station in the true sense of the word; the four trains visible here were operated by four separate roads—the Pennsylvania, Northern Central, Cumberland Valley, and Philadelphia & Reading. Although it looks like part of a college campus, the dignified building above opposite is Broad Street Station in Richmond, Virginia. Designed by John Russell Pope, the architect of the Jefferson Memorial and the National Gallery, and completed in 1919, it is still a working station. Not so the Chicago & North Western station below it; it has gone and in its place Chicago has the Merchandise Mart.

companies into a new railroad—the New York Central & Hudson River Railroad—he celebrated by breaking ground for a new station at Fourth (now Park) Avenue and Forty-Second Street. It was 1869, Forty-Second Street was still unpaved, and everyone thought it was a great joke, building a station so far uptown. The newspapers christened it the "End-of-the-World Station," but Vanderbilt called it the Grand Central Depot.

It was a fine gaudy building, a cross between the Louvre and a cast-iron toy bank. Critics complained that it was wanton to slap a slate mansard roof onto a Renaissance building, but it is highly unlikely that the Commodore was disturbed by this sort of carping. Grand Central opened in 1871, and by the next year it was really three separate stations in one L-shaped building— the New Haven's, the Harlem's, and the New York Central & Hudson River's. All these operations shared a common train shed, a magnificent arched structure of cast-iron and glass. The Commodore had meant it to be a locomotive terminal, but when he saw it all fresh and new and sunny he decided that no locomotive would enter it to smudge it up with corrosive smoke. This meant some very tricky railroading when the trains came in. The floor of the shed was tilted so that departing trains had only to release their brakes and coast out to where the engines were waiting; but arriving trains had to be "switched on the fly." As the train approached the station the engineer braked a little to give the brakeman some slack at the couplers. At a signal from the whistle the brakeman pulled the pin, uncoupling the train from the engine, which darted over onto an adjacent track. The open switch swung shut behind the engine, and the cars coasted up into the station. This maneuver was every bit as dangerous as it sounds, yet we are told that there was never an accident.

Twelve tracks ran into the terminal, and they were not enough for the traffic they had to handle. Even for 1871, Grand Central was, despite its imposing façade, a rather puny station. And then there was the problem with the

(Continued on page 213)

The fallen angel above, lying ignobly in a New Jersey meadow, was once part of McKim, Mead & White's monumental Pennsylvania Station in New York City. A visible incarnation of the power of the great Pennsylvania Railroad, the station covered twenty-eight acres when it was completed in 1910. The huge waiting room at left (with no seats on which to wait) was derived from —and dwarfed—the tepidarium of the Baths of Caracalla in Rome. Some architectural critics were dismayed by the gratuitous waste of space, and one was astonished that "so judicious a creature as the Pennsylvania Railroad could heavily increase its corporate debt in order to hide the steel roofs of its stations under the vaults of Caracalla." Overblown it may have been, but it was magnificent. When the station was pulled down in 1966, The New York Times *commented that we will "be judged not by the monuments we built, but by those we have destroyed."*

"terminal fan." A terminal fan is, simply, the tracks fanning out from the main line in a rough triangle so that trains can be fed into the station. The one at Grand Central was scrupulously well managed, but it had a low "altitude"; that is to say, it could not extend laterally beyond Forty-Ninth Street where the trains entered the Park Avenue tunnel, a mere four hundred yards away. In 1876 the Commodore added six more terminal tracks, but this made the fan even more crowded and difficult. Sooner or later something would have to be done, but nobody knew quite what, and when it was done, it turned out to be the wrong thing.

In 1899 the controversial mansard roof was pulled off, the ornamentation stripped from the brick walls, and the walls themselves made three stories higher and covered with granite. The three stations were consolidated into one, and three more tracks were crowded in. The renovated station opened in 1901. It had cost $5,000,000 but, the authorities glumly realized, it still handled the rail traffic in the old, inadequate way.

The smoke in the Park Avenue tunnel was frightful. From time to time an engineer would pass out from the coal gas, and often the firemen lay flat on the footplates during the passage, avoiding the most virulent of the fumes. Moreover, the smoke often obscured the red and green signal lights. Early in 1902, at the peak of the morning rush, a New Haven commuter train was halted at a red signal when a New York Central express came groping blindly through the smoke on the same track. Seventeen people died in the wreck, and there was a great uproar in the papers. Spurred by the protests that followed, the New York State Legislature passed a law decreeing that after the first of July, 1910, no steam locomotive could enter Manhattan on any track used mainly for passenger service. The railroad had eight years in which to electrify Grand Central.

So it was that a man named William J. Wilgus stood looking over that crowded fan on a September day in 1902. Wilgus was Grand Central's chief engineer, and a great one, as events would prove. He not only had to electrify

When Commodore Vanderbilt's Grand Central Depot, opposite, opened in 1871, people complained that it was actually closer to Albany than to New York City. Within a few years, though, the city had teemed north around it. The train shed, below, had two acres of glass in its roof. Vanderbilt's architects disguised its entrance, above, so successfully that one would never guess that the façade concealed splendid steel arching.

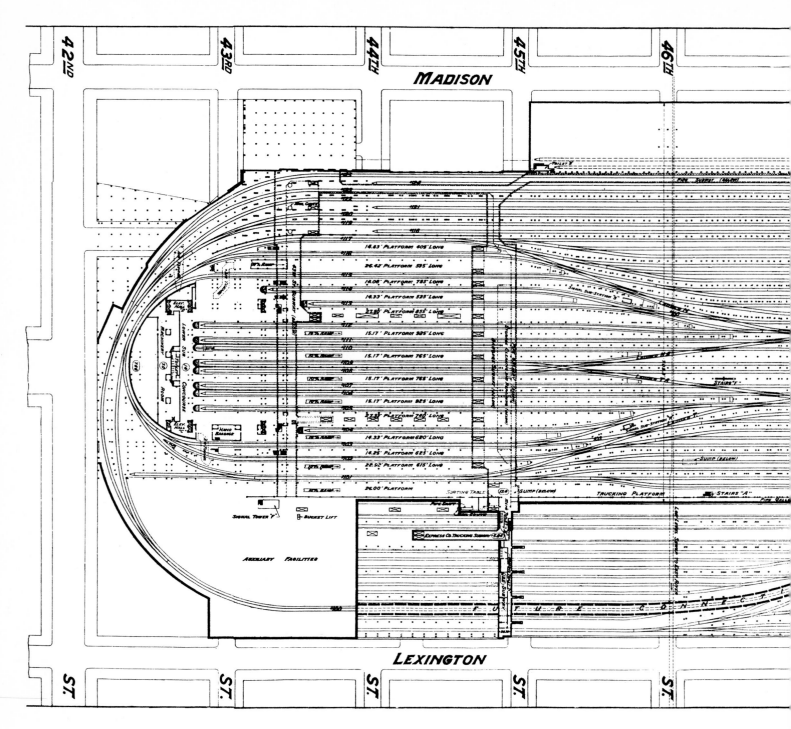

The heart of Grand Central is its unique two-level terminal fan, which was designed to accommodate one hundred million passengers a year. Traffic never did get quite that heavy, but in 1946, during the high-water mark of railroading that followed the Second World War, sixty-five million people passed through the station. The upper level of the fan was once used for the great limiteds, while the lower level, whose labyrinthine track plan is shown above, handled commuter traffic. Grand Central Terminal was essential in the development of New York City's suburbs, and today forty million commuters use the station each year. The trains that carry these people are controlled by a vast system of interlocking switches, watched over from a number of signal towers. Between Forty-Ninth and Fiftieth streets, six men staff a multilevel tower that has jurisdiction over the more than thirty miles of terminal track.

the station, but to expand it, and this seemed impossible. Bounded on the west and east by Vanderbilt and Lexington avenues, and on the north and south by Forty-Ninth and Forty-Second streets, Grand Central Station was locked into its forty-eight acres. Wilgus sketched and pondered and then an idea came to him in what he later described as "a flash of light." He would build two fans, one on top of the other; it had never been done before, but it was possible. Then, since all was to be electrified and there was no need for smoke ventilation, he would build skyscrapers above the upper fan. The fan could be extended by cutting back farther north, far beyond the Forty-Ninth Street limit. The ground there was solid granite, and it would cost a fortune to excavate, but the cost could be partly defrayed by the revenue coming in from the new buildings. And, finally, loop tracks could be introduced.

And that, in essence, is just what happened. Wilgus convinced the board of directors, and his plans were distributed among some of the nation's foremost architects, who sent in their proposals. Stanford White of New York and Samuel Huckel, Jr., of Philadelphia both wanted the job, but the prize went

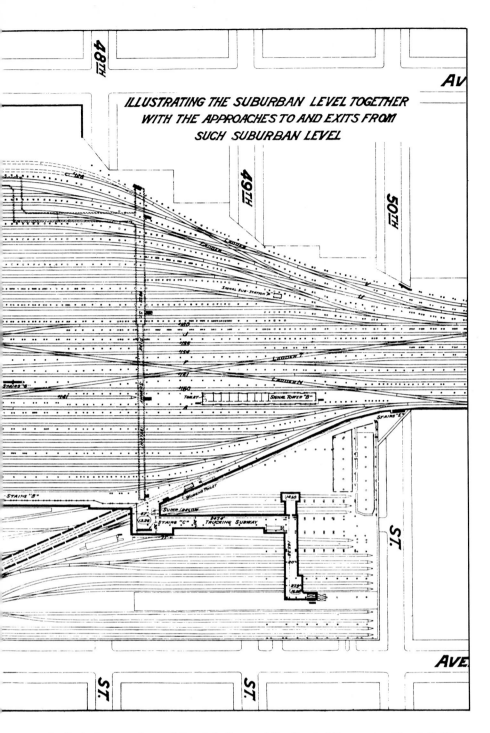

ILLUSTRATING THE SUBURBAN LEVEL TOGETHER
WITH THE APPROACHES TO AND EXITS FROM
SUCH SUBURBAN LEVEL

Grand Central is our greatest example of what architectural historian Carroll L. V. Meeks has called the "megalomania" era of railroad station design. At the top is the station as it appeared before the fifty-nine-story Pan Am Building dwarfed it. When it was opened in the mid-sixties, Pan Am poured twenty-five thousand additional people into the station, yet Grand Central had been so well designed that it easily handled the traffic.

to the little-known firm of Reed & Stem of St. Paul, Minnesota. Reed & Stem had proposed a stately building where, for the first time in America, ramps were to be used instead of stairways.

Wilgus went to work, tearing down the Commodore's fine old train shed. Without delaying any trains, his workmen took down tons of wrought iron and glass. They would assemble the debris on a trestle by day and lower it onto waiting work trains at night. The tenements that then lined Lexington Avenue disappeared, and the blasting began. It was a monumental task; at one point the granite cropped up forty feet above street level forcing the old tracks to curve around the obstacle. Geologists were called in to lay out the drilling lines before the blasting. For ten years an average of four hundred carloads of dirt and granite left the excavation every day. In the end, a million cubic yards of earth and two million cubic yards of granite were hauled away, leaving a pit forty feet deep, 770 feet wide, and half a mile long.

The new station began to take shape. Whitney Warren, a partner in the architectural firm of Warren & Wetmore and a close friend of William K. Vander-

Ignoring an antediluvian candy machine, a woman waits patiently for the train at Ware, Massachusetts. She may board the Boston & Albany or the Boston & Maine; both lines serviced Ware.

bilt, wormed his way into the operation and must be given credit for the final form of Grand Central. It was a handsome, classical building bearing the imprint of the Beaux-Arts education then sought by American architects. The building was topped with a statue of Mercury surrounded by somewhat obscure allegorical figures. Inside there were great, cavernous rooms with marble wainscoting, and a huge Grand Concourse. Paul Helleu, a popular French artist of the day, was commissioned to paint a mural for the curved ceiling of the concourse, and he came up with a page from a medieval manuscript on astronomy that showed, in blue and gold, the zodiac and the middle region of the sky. Using this as a plan, he painted some twenty-five hundred stars in gold leaf on a field of cerulean blue.

Opening day was the second of February, 1913. Crowds came to marvel, and all agreed that the ceiling was a wonder. Gaggles of school children were brought in to study this edifying spectacle of the heavens, until someone pointed out that the whole thing was done in reverse—the stars were put on backward, with the west and east transposed. There was a surprising amount of fuss about this, with the New York Central publicity department commenting testily that "The ceiling is purely decorative, it was never intended that a mariner should set his course by the stars at Grand Central."

That minor peccadillo aside, the completed Grand Central was and is one of the most successful stations ever built. The multiple levels handle the complicated circulation superbly. One hundred and twenty-three tracks, sixty-six on the upper level and fifty-seven on the lower, feed forty-eight public platforms. And, beyond all that fine functionalism, the station is beautiful.

Today, like so many of the great stations, Grand Central is threatened. It has lost most of its long-distance trains, and it shuts down in the small hours of night. The feeling of elegance and excitement has vanished. Upkeep has fallen off, and a drift of trashy advertising pavilions clutter the great spaces. The red carpet of the *Twentieth Century Limited* has long been folded away. The lower level has a desolate atmosphere about it, and predators are nosing about with plans to tumble the station down and replace it with some glass-walled nonentity of a building. If they are successful—and, as this is written, it appears that they may well be—the country will have lost something precious and irreplaceable, our greatest monument to what has been called the age of heroic materialism.

But the vast urban terminals are only a part of the story. Whether the trains were pulling out of Grand Central Station, or Michigan Central Station in Detroit, or the Union Station in Indianapolis, they were heading out toward the country. There was more of it then, before the automobile and the airplane took the romance out of distance. On their way, the trains passed through thousands of tank towns and somnolent little villages, where the station was more apt to be called the depot.

The depot is perhaps the most eminently recognizable of all American buildings. Even when the tracks have disappeared from its neighborhood, and there is nothing at all to suggest that the train once came that way, one can immediately identify the building by its broad overhanging eaves and bay window through which the vanished stationmaster could keep an eye on the tracks. Of course, it was a rare builder of depots who would confine his creation to these bare essentials. The buildings had to be suitably embellished, and therein lies most of their considerable charm. Carpenters armed with jig saws constructed fanciful Gothic ornamentation; arched windows, for instance, or scrolled supports for the eaves. Sometimes the depot would be designed by a sophisticated hand, but more often it was the product of someone striving for a high effect with little knowledge or money. Nevertheless,

(Continued on page 220)

The station loafers below take a moment to peer at the photographer as the train pulls into West Penn Junction, a crossing situated outside of Pittsburgh on the Pennsylvania Railroad.

E. P. ALEXANDER

Lake George, New York, branch line terminal of the Delaware & Hudson

Tucker's Station, St. Louis, Missouri, on the old Iron Mountain line

Norfolk, Connecticut, on the Central New England

Trenton Junction, New Jersey, on the Reading

The Country Depot

This gathering of depots shows something of the wonderful diversity of this most American architectural form. The pleasant little building at the lower right enjoyed the peculiar distinction of serving the shortest railroad in the United States. It was less than two miles long, and ran from the Cheney Silk Mills in South Manchester, Connecticut, to North Manchester. The terrifying Tucker's Station, clinging to a cliff on the Mississippi, was built for commuters and is now part of the Missouri Pacific. Trenton Junction, with its unusual clock tower, was hurried to completion in 1876 to serve a line built to bring visitors from New York to the Philadelphia Centennial Exhibition. A peripatetic depot, the Ladson station was constructed miles away and moved to Ladson on flatcars.

Ladson, South Carolina, on the South Carolina Railway

White Plains, New York, on the New York Central

Gravers Lane, Pennsylvania, on the Reading system

Fredonia, Kansas, a Santa Fe depot on the St. Louis-San Francisco run

North Conway, New Hampshire, built for the Great Falls & Conway

Cambridge, New York, on the Delaware & Hudson

Cheneyville, Connecticut, on the South Manchester

A fine day at the depot at Edwardsburg, Michigan. Edwardsburg is 144 miles from Chicago, just over four hours on the Grand Trunk. It is 1908, the train is in, and all's right with the world.

the attempt had to be made, for the building was no mere store or stable; it was a very important proposition.

For a century and a quarter the depot was the very hub and heart of the town it served. News, mail, Sears Roebuck catalogues, sewing machines, strangers, relatives, new schoolteachers, scandal, delight, the circus—all came into town on the train. Here the stationmaster ruled, and he was a formidable figure. He found things out first. He could understand the messages which men up the line were sending in on the wire. He sold tickets, manhandled freight on and off the cars and into the freight house, and mastered the intricacies of brass baggage checks and waybills. To his domain came the town loafers to tell lies and speculate about goings-on, drummers to pass along their racy stories and complaints, and hordes of small boys to watch. For these last, the train was the most marvellous thing in the world.

The predominance of the depot in village life has gone forever, although many of the structures themselves remain. Some few are converted into homes or restaurants; most disintegrate slowly until a spark from the road sets them on fire, or until they are bulldozed under to make way for a shopping center. Urban renewal has also taken its toll of them, as have yahoo city governments which nurse the curious delusion that the proper kind of depot is a plastic rain shed five miles out of town.

220

But the transient buildings are revered in memory. Virtually everyone over forty who was born in a small town has something to say about the depot. Stewart Holbrook, for instance, vividly recalled the one at Columbia Bridge, on the Maine Central Railroad in northern New Hampshire:

"At Columbia Bridge as many as five persons might get off, but seldom more than two. Now and again a trunk came out of the mysterious recesses of the baggage car. Meanwhile, we boys gaped up at the lighted windows, seemingly a full mile of lighted windows, strange heads and faces at each window—men, women, girls, babies, all strangers, all going somewhere, all impatient to get going again, some looking doubtless with amusement or condescension at the bucolics beside the track, quaint natives who still thought a train of steamcars a sight worth walking three miles to behold, even on a night dark and biting with cold.

"They were right, those amused or condescending passengers, those travelers who never knew Columbia Bridge except as a hick depot in the wilderness, a picture suddenly framed by a car window, and just as suddenly dissipated by night as the train resumed its way. They were right, at least as far as I am concerned. Seeing a train of cars pass Columbia Bridge at night remains one of the greatest sights I ever saw. To watch a Constellation take off or land is nothing in comparison."

A Portfolio

11. Great Days for the Passenger Element

"A passenger train," Jim Hill once remarked, "is like the male teat—neither useful nor ornamental." And, indeed, not long ago a modern railroad official dismissed rail travellers with bland contempt as "the passenger element." The unctuous phrase is, of course, full of connotations: like the criminal element, the passenger element was to be discouraged. This the railroads did very well, and a whole generation grew up knowing train travel with a few exceptions as an uncomfortable, overheated, and unpredictable ride in a muggy day coach, its floors thick with paper cups, cigarette butts, and caked grime. So Jim Hill's view was turned into policy, although things were not that way when he made his sour comment. By the 1880's the first-class passenger, if not the lowly coach patron, could ride trains in wonderful luxury. He might, for instance, find himself in a superb parlor car like the one at right, which was built at the cost of more than $38,000, and, having been christened the "Santa Maria," was exhibited at the World's Columbian Exposition of 1893. It was built by the Pullman Palace Car Company. George Mortimer Pullman did not invent sleeping cars, but he made them better than anybody else. This autocratic man backed up his belief in the virtue of monopoly by buying up his rivals or driving them out of business. Ironically, Webster Wagner, his chief rival, burned to death in one of his own cars. Finally Pullman emerged pre-eminent in his field; his job was to supply the railroads with comfortable rolling stock, and this he did magnificently.

Pullman's name became synonymous with luxury, in America and in Europe, and railroads using his cars made the most of it. The name was featured prominently, for instance, on the brochure of the Boston & Mt. Desert Limited *(below)*, which made the run between Boston and the fashionable resort town of Bar Harbor, Maine, in nine hours. The Limited *made its first run in June of 1887, its five seventy-foot cars leaving, according to a newspaper account, "All in one piece, a long-drawn serpentine creation, having, to be sure, joints to insure flexibility." The "joints"—vestibules—are also described at enormous length in the brochure, and they were indeed a noteworthy innovation. The first ones were narrow, but vestibules were later extended to the full width of the car, with drop plates over the steps. Prior to their coming, passengers risked their lives as they passed from one lurching, windy, open platform to another. It was a superintendent of the Pullman plant, Henry H. Sessions, who patented the friction plates that connected the cars. They came in in 1887, and Sessions had not yet secured* his patent for them when they were adopted by the Boston & Mt. Desert. *In a few years they were standard on all Pullman cars, and soon trains became, in effect, one long car rather than a series of cars coupled together. In spite of this innovation, and its elegant cars and flower-bedecked stations, the* Boston & Mt. Desert Limited—*which parsimonious Yankees christened the "Dude Line"—lasted only three seasons. Other limiteds (that is, trains limited as to accommodations and class) fared better. The starched and composed ladies at the far right are enjoying the first electrically lit train to cross the Northwest—the Northern Pacific's* North Coast Limited. *Also an all-Pullman train, that long-time favorite made its first run between St. Paul and Seattle on April 29, 1900. According to a brochure, passengers had the run of "two smoking and card rooms each with six wicker chairs; buffet; barber shop . . . a library of 140 volumes . . . and* North Coast Limited *stationery free." At right, a carefully arranged group makes its farewells on another great train, the Santa Fe's* California Limited.

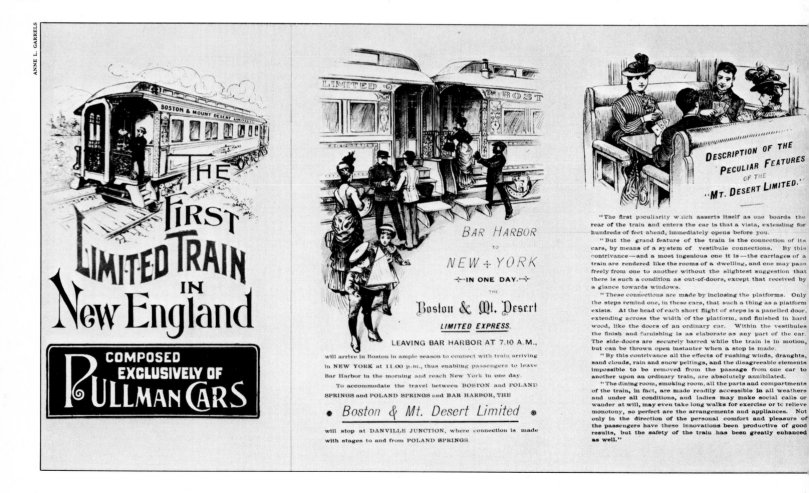

DINING CARS.

Another very important feature of this train is the Dining Car Service, the cars for which have been especially constructed for this Line by the Pullman Palace Car Co., and have been added to obviate the necessity of stopping for meals at dining stations. These cars will accompany the train through between Boston and Bar Harbor (Mt. Desert Ferry). Meals will be served at any time during the trip from a menu comprising the best which the season affords.

EXTRA FARE TICKETS,
INCLUDING SEAT IN DRAWING-ROOM CAR.

Between	and Portland.	and Danville Junction.	and Mt. Desert Ferry.
BOSTON	$1.50	$2.50	$3.50
EXETER			3.00

This extra fare will be charged in addition to the first-class passenger rate, and includes the usual charge for seats in Pullman Cars.

A COMPLETE DESCRIPTION OF THE ROUTE OF THIS TRAIN WILL BE FOUND IN

DOWN EAST LATCH STRINGS;
—OR,—

SEASHORE, LAKES AND MOUNTAINS
BY THE

BOSTON & MAINE RAILROAD,

Describing a trip through the tourist region of Northern New England, Lake Winnipesaukee, Mt. Desert, Moosehead and Rangeley Lakes, the White Mountains and the famous beaches along the coast. Beautifully and most profusely illustrated.

Sent, on receipt of 15 cents in stamps, by Passenger Department, Boston & Maine Railroad, Boston, Mass.

In the early days of railroading, the steamcars became the focus of much disapproval from clergymen, who felt that the iron horse should not profane the Lord's Day with its smoke and noise, let alone its labors. But Sunday was a profitable day for the railroads, and they ran despite some spirited opposition. Church and State compromised in Vermont in the 1850's when the legislature ruled that the trains could run on Sunday, but only if the conductors passed through the cars reading the Scriptures to the riders. Clerical disapproval dwindled when many roads made it their policy to give passes to clergymen. As trains became more luxurious, Sunday services got quite formal. At left we see hymn singing on the Pacific Railroad in 1876. Railroads provoked instant friendships, diversions, and romances. Tunnels had their uses, and hazards, a point belabored in the old Currier and Ives wheeze below. The fellow to watch out for, of course, was the ilk of Canada Bill Jones. Jones was so successful a confidence man that he is said to have offered the Missouri, Kansas & Texas Railway $25,000 a year to leave him alone, and promised to confine his activities to clergymen. He is shown at right approaching a mark. Railroad gamblers were a real problem; for a while the Pullman Company supplied its conductors with printed slips that read, "It is dangerous to play cards with strangers." These were passed unobtrusively.

Mischievous Conductor.-"Dark Tunnel, through in half an hour"!   Scene,- When the Train struck the light in just 3 minutes.

A KISS IN THE DARK.

Canada Bill Jones was not likely to break into the sedate card game shown above. These visions of serenity and comfort were photographed by George R. Lawrence in 1905 to publicize the Santa Fe's California Limited, which can be seen about to depart from Chicago on page 225. "Flashlight" Lawrence, one of the world's best-known photographers at the turn of the century, invented the blinding flash powder which made indoor shots possible and which remained in use until the development of the flashbulb. The passengers here appear undisturbed by the white explosions of his apparatus. The California Limited carried three Pullman palace sleeping cars, a dining car, a buffet-smoking car, and, the Santa Fe promised, "Persons you'd like to meet—successful men of affairs, authors, musicians, journalists, 'globe trotters,' pretty and witty women and happy children. . . ." The porter, who is displaying guarded amusement at the newlywed husband's obliviousness to his reading matter, is a highly trained, hard-working man. The Pullman Company not only both built

and operated railroad cars, it also supplied the personnel that went with them. Porters learned their trade from old hands in Pullman's own school, and preference in hiring was usually shown to the sons of men who were themselves porters. The porter learned a scrupulous routine—towels and linen, for example, once unfolded, were dirty and had to go back to the laundry whether they had been used or not—and the unflagging politeness that would keep him smiling even when somebody handed him a 3¢ tip. At about the time the above picture was taken, the porter's base pay was $20 a month. The rest came in tips, and it is hard to determine how the tips ran, since no porter was likely to boast about his take for fear of being bumped off a profitable run by a senior porter. Tips varied widely, but porters tended to agree that foreigners were terrible tippers, the worst being the English. New Englanders were poor, and show people good. Women were unpredictable, but Calvin Coolidge could be relied upon to give the same tip to one and all—15¢.

This wonderful picture of painstaking craftsmanship was taken in Pullman's first manufacturing plant in Detroit. So great was the demand for his cars that, prior to 1881, he was forced to purchase 283 cars from other car builders. They were all finished under Pullman Company supervision, but it rankled Pullman enough so that he finally built his huge works in Chicago. After that, Pullman acquired outside cars only when he absorbed rival companies. The care evident in the painter's crisp striping was echoed in every aspect of Pullman construction. In the Pullman Marquetry Room a score of Black Forest craftsmen turned and polished woods from all over the world. This extraordinarily varied panelling and inlay always bore the stamp of the individual artisan. Many other companies offered elegant railroad accessories. The examples shown here are taken from the immense 1,421-page Adlake catalogue of 1911. The curiously modern-sounding name is a contraction of the Adams and Westlake Company of Chicago. The rectangular object above is an engraved strip of sash glass. As the ornate, reiterative brass plaques on the opposite page suggest, Adlake gave its customer every opportunity to indulge his esthetic sense in outfitting his railroad.

At the World's Columbian Exposition—better remembered under the handier vernacular title of the Chicago World's Fair —hundreds of thousands of people peered into Edison Kinetoscopes, milled about the Midway Plaisance where Little Egypt was attracting the attention of Police Gazette artists, and witnessed the art of railroad-coach building brought to its rococo peak. At left is the observation car "Isabella," part of a showpiece five-car private train built by Pullman for exhibition at the fair. "This car," said a company brochure, "is seventy feet long; is heated with steam and lighted with electricity, with beautiful fixtures; . . . The section part of the car is finished in vermilion wood, and the observation room in mahogany, elaborately designed and carved." The "Marchena," with its Kochs patent barber's chair and stained glass Moorish dome, was another item from the same train. The bridal suite next to it was from the car "Republic." In the 1890's such private varnish was sold to the rich, or rented to them for about $50 a day; the New York Central ran a special siding underneath the present Waldorf Astoria Hotel to accommodate them. Eventually, however, a great many of these dazzling vehicles entered general service. William Dean Howells was no doubt thinking of this kind of plush and marquetry when he wrote of a transcontinental journey: "They reclined in luxury upon the easy-cushioned, revolving chairs; they surveyed with infinite satisfaction the elegance of the flying-parlor in which they sat. . . . They said that none but Americans or enchanted princes in the Arabian Nights ever travelled in such state. . . . But the general appearance of the passengers hardly suggested greater wealth than elsewhere; and they were plainly in that car because they were of the American race, which finds nothing too good for it that its money can buy."

The masculine place on the facing page is one of the Burlington's club cars. There is a brass spittoon on the floor, and plenty of hard liquor visible toward the rear. Women were not permitted in the club car, nor, in that simple time, did they wish to go there. A cheaper and grimmer type of masculine travel is shown on this page. Over the years an aura of glamor has grown up around the tramp; the shaggy bindle stiff who rode the rods, cooked mulligan stew in a tin can, and spoke his own, picturesque language has become something of an American folk hero. In fact, he led a violent, dangerous, desperate life. The dangers are obvious; William Davis, an Englishman bumming around North America at the turn of the century, told of trying to hop aboard a freight. "My foot came short of the step, and I fell, and, still clinging to the handle-bar, was dragged several yards before I relinquished my hold. And there I lay for several minutes, feeling a little shaken, whilst the train passed swiftly on into the darkness. . . ." At length Davis attempted to climb to his feet, and only then did he discover that his right foot had been cut off just above the ankle. The tramp was always at war with the railroad bull, a man hired by the railroads to keep him from stealing and destroying property. One effective bull gave this bleak remedy to the problem: "The best way to keep tramps off trains or other railroad property is to beat up any unauthorized person you find in the yards. . . . On the trains, I might talk a while with tramps riding the boxcars, and . . . then force them to jump, or push them off. . . ." False romance or not, the tramp certainly was a more attractive figure than the railroad bull. What the bull could never accomplish, the superhighway has. Today the tramp has almost disappeared, done in—like so many things connected with the railroad—by the automobile. His modern equivalent, the hitchhiker, is a very unsatisfying source of legend indeed.

235

Wagner Palace Car Company
Dining Car Service.
Dinner.

SOUP.
PUREE OF TOMATO.

FISH.
BOILED CALIFORNIA SALMON, ANCHOVY SAUCE.

BOILED.
JOWL AND SPINACH.

ROAST.
YOUNG TURKEY, CRANBERRY SAUCE.   SIRLOIN OF BEEF.
SHORT RIBS OF BEEF, WITH BROWNED POTATOES.

GAME.
ROAST MALLARD DUCK, CURRANT JELLY.

ENTREES.
RAGOUT OF MUTTON, GREEN PEAS.   CHICKEN CROQUETTES.
PEACH FRITTERS, WINE SAUCE.

SALAD.
CHICKEN.   LETTUCE.

RELISHES.
OLIVES.   GHERKINS.   CHOW-CHOW.   CELERY.

VEGETABLES.
MASHED POTATOES.   BAKED SWEET POTATOES.
STRING BEANS.   CORN.

PASTRY.
COCOANUT PUDDING, CREAM SAUCE.
SQUASH PIE.   MINCE PIE.

DESSERT.
PINEAPPLE ICE CREAM.   ASSORTED CAKE.
GRAPES.   MIXED NUTS.   FIGS.   ORANGES.   APPLES
PEARS.   RAISINS.   BENT'S WATER CRACKERS.
EDAM, ROQUEFORT, AND FROMAGE DE MENAUTA.
FRENCH COFFEE.

MEALS ONE DOLLAR.

SEE NEXT PAGE FOR WINE LIST.

Even with a library and a bathtub aboard, there was relatively little to do on a train, and it is not surprising that a meal in the dining car was usually the most diverting part of the trip. There was talk of eating aboard as early as 1838, but the first real diner was not put into service until 1867 when George Pullman installed his first "hotel car" on the Great Western Railway of Canada. Pullman offered that amenity for a number of years, but always at a loss. Finally he withdrew, leaving the operation to the railroads; they usually lost money too, but they knew a first-class diner was essential to attract passengers. So the railroads spent money, and all the best trains included a superb car like the B&O's turn-of-the-century diner at right. A large part of the credit for bringing decent food to the railroads must go to Frederick Henry Harvey, who in the 1870's approached the superintendent of the Santa Fe Railroad with a suggestion for a new type of railroad restaurant. At that time the depot restaurant was a nightmare place where customers had greasy food flung before them with only a few minutes to choke it down before the train pulled out. Harvey changed all that. He opened a restaurant in the Topeka, Kansas, station that served good food, and it was such a success that he went on to set up a truly great restaurant in the tiny railroad town of Florence, Kansas. The food was served by "young women of good character, attractive and intelligent," whom Harvey advertised for in newspapers. The Harvey Girls lived in dormitories under the iron rule of Harvey matrons, who saw to it that their charges obeyed the ten o'clock curfew. Some of the girls, looking wholesome if not ravishing, appear at left. Harvey served the best food in the West, and by the time of his death in 1901 he and the Santa Fe owned and operated fifteen hotels, forty-seven restaurants, and thirty dining cars. The kitchens on these last were ingeniously organized to make maximum use of restricted space. The kitchen area of any diner was rarely greater than thirty square feet, but as this menu suggests, meals of extraordinary variety emerged from the tiny galley. For years the traditional price was $1.00.

Santa Fe de-Luxe

..to Chicago
Kansas City
and a quick
way to
New York

..tuesdays

Limited
to sixty
people
extra fare
twenty-five
dollars

The haughty butler of the travel poster at the left suggests the direct, indeed crass, appeal of the Santa Fe de-Luxe, whose riders, claimed the railroad, liked "to be a bit exclusive. Thus, the 'Extra Fast—Extra Fine—Extra Fare' train has been evolved." Pullman built all-steel cars for its inaugural Chicago–Los Angeles run in 1911, and for a little while this white-tie limited was a truly splendid train. But World War I put the squeeze on that kind of travel, and the de-Luxe was an early casualty. The California Limited, however, survived; so heavy was its passenger traffic that it sometimes ran in several sections—each really a separate train—that pulled out of the station one after the other. Below are seven sections about to leave Los Angeles in the early 1920's. The snappily uniformed men above, guarding their gate with military punctilio, marked the Pennsylvania Railroad's Broadway Limited as another crack train. When it appeared in 1887 in its earliest form, as the Pennsylvania Limited, the Chicago Times intoned: "The railway as an agent of civilization is not inferior to the art of printing." The train made its first run as the Broadway Limited in 1902, when it and the Twentieth Century Limited began their famous rivalry. The Broadway Limited still survives, but in name only.

The most famous limited of them all was the New York Central's Twentieth Century. *Like the* Broadway Limited, *it ran between New York and Chicago, and both trains had the finest equipment of their day. Nevertheless, the* Broadway Limited *was always overshadowed. First of all, there was the genius of the* Century's *name; in 1902, when it made its first run, Americans were proud of this new century which was certainly going to belong to them. The train and its name were the inspiration of George H. Daniels, the wonderful showman (he learned his*

trade flogging patent medicines) who once succeeded in getting a New York Central train on a U.S. postage stamp. Another Century *advantage was the smooth "water-level route" up the Hudson and along the shore of Lake Erie. The* Century *was a success from the start, and became a bit of folklore even while it was still in service. The flappers above are soon to leave Grand Central, in 1925; the famous* Century *carpet is visible. The* Century *expired in 1967, deserted not by the New York Central, asserted President Alfred E. Perlman, but by the public.*

The first Twentieth Century Limited *along the shore of Lake Erie*

A couple of decades later, the train is powered by a big Hudson.

Leaving Chicago in 1938 (above), and running along the Hudson in 1962 (below)

12. They Went Everywhere

12. They Went Everywhere

In the days when nobody travelled light, brass tags, stamped with every known route and destination, were used to aid baggage handlers. These are a few of hundreds dug out of the site of the long-vanished Lyme, Connecticut, station by an enthusiast, Harold Fratus, then repolished and given to the author. Trains no longer stop at Lyme.

PRECEDING PAGES: *Looking mighty pleased with itself, this sporty group has just arrived on the Florida East Coast Railway for a stay at Palm Beach in the new Royal Poinciana Hotel, built by Henry Flagler in 1894. He had a special spur constructed to serve his huge hostelry, as well as service tracks for parking private rail cars.*

For every *Twentieth Century* in the great days of railroading, there were hundreds upon hundreds of limiteds, flyers, and expresses pressing their princely services on the gentry. And for every *Overland Limited* or *Bar Harbor Express* there were a score of more proletarian locals, not to mention branches, connecting trains, accommodations, railroad-owned steamboats, funiculars, cog railways, rural trolleys, and interurbans. Only those readers who are rather long in the tooth can remember that in the halcyon years, from the Gilded Age up into the twenties, you could go anywhere by rail. Or almost anywhere. Sometimes, to be sure, it was an elaborate journey, with many changes, but you got there. It was not just to the nearest big city terminal, one must understand, like the airports or railroad stations today. The tracks often went right to the mountaintop, or the hotel, as they did to the Royal Poinciana on the preceding pages, or the Redondo Hotel in California (pages 248–249), or to the great hostelries at Saratoga or White Sulphur Springs. If water got in the way, the railroad company's steamboats took you to an island, like Martha's Vineyard or Nantucket, where, like as not, a local narrow gauge would carry you the rest of the way. Sometimes it would ferry your sleeping cars, and in an extreme case, the tracks themselves went out to sea, when Henry M. Flagler pushed his Florida East Coast out 97 miles from the mainland across bridges, embankments, and intervening islands to Key West. This great feat of engineering, completed in 1908 when Flagler was eighty-two, was wiped out by a hurricane in 1935, and rebuilt as a highway. The vacationer and the tourist belonged to the railroads as they now belong to Detroit, and forests must have fallen to provide the paper for the extensive travel literature put out by the big companies. They ran trips and side trips, at all levels of expense, to all the resort areas, and made special pitches to that nervous traveller of earlier days, the rich invalid seeking a more salubrious climate—the White Mountains, the Adirondacks, the Thousand Islands.

Besides going everywhere, you could, within reason, go at any time. Without timetable or reservation, the traveller could find trains leaving, generally frequently, for almost any place. One can get a sad pleasure out of studying old copies of the *Official Guide of the Railways*. Look for a moment to New England. Its railroad map today, though depleted, looks busy enough, unless you know that many of the lines that still appear are rusting away in the sumac, either semi-abandoned or visited so rarely by a train that the occasional wayfreight stirs up a cloud of wildlife along the weedy tracks. Yet as recently as 1946, the *Guide* published sixteen pages of closely packed type listing the services provided by the Boston & Maine, and twenty pages of timetables for trains on the New York, New Haven & Hartford. Even the Rutland Railroad, which later closed down entirely, took three pages for its two main

The Active, *sole locomotive of the Martha's Vineyard Railroad, takes on passengers at Oak Bluffs for the trip to Edgartown and Katama.*

By the 1880's, railroads were advertising the scenic beauties of their rights of way in extravagant terms. The Ulster & Delaware, chartered in 1866, opened up the Catskills to large numbers of tourists and sparked a building of hotels and houses there that continued for years. The Old Colony Railroad served Cape Cod and New Bedford and was running as early as 1845; the White Mountains line advertised "Safety and power . . . at the expense of speed, which is not sought."

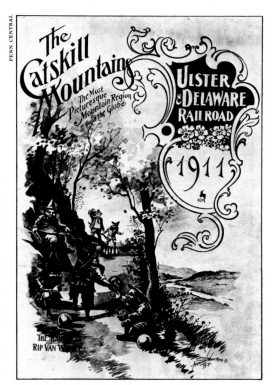

lines (Bennington–Rutland–Rouses Point and Bellows Falls–Rutland) and its branches to Chatham, Larrabee's Point, and Ogdensburg (which had two passenger trains a day each). Through service ran daily on "name trains" like the *Alburgh Express*, the *Mount Royal*, the *Cheshire*, and the *Green Mountain Flyer*. Similar things could be said of other big lines, like the Boston & Albany, with eleven trains a day each way between those two cities, and of little independents like the Narragansett Pier, the Belfast & Moosehead Lake, the St. Johnsbury & Lake Champlain. Even so, all these were a poor shadow of what once had been, in the days of the American railroads' greatest extent, back in 1916 when they had an all-time high of 254,037 miles of track and 98 percent of all intercity passenger travel.

Look now to the *Guide* for June, 1914, and revel in it for a minute. Want to go north from Manchester, Vermont, to Rutland? Four trains a day. South? Six trains. Down from Bennington to Chatham? Two trains, and there are other routes to New York as well. Move down to Massachusetts and study a few branches. For instance, Pittsfield to North Adams, a bridge line from New York to the north: eight trains a day, four through from New York via Chatham on the New York Central, others down the New Haven line along the Housatonic Valley. There are hundreds of lines like this, not counting electric interurbans. The Athol Branch, now lifted, runs three trains a day each way, covering forty-eight miles in two hours. The Ware River Branch loafs along from Palmer to Winchendon; three trains a day each way. Down in Connecticut for one minute more in dreamland, via the Central New England Railroad, a totally vanished pike from Hartford via Winsted, Norfolk, Canaan, and Poughkeepsie to the west: Six westbound trains a day, including expresses with diners and ornate parlor cars. But the brown pages of the 1914 *Guide* crumble away as you turn them, and the rug must be vacuumed after every consultation.

On the little fellows there existed another quaint and appealing world of travel of which almost no vestige remains, although they once had their moments of pride and glory. Then there was, for example, the little Narragansett Pier Railroad, which ran an entire eight and one-half miles from a junction with the New Haven at Kingston, Rhode Island, to that once mildly fashionable resort. In its heyday the big trains from other railroads would come down the line with their own Pullmans and parlor cars, taking the bankers back to work after the weekend. The family-owned railroad was otherwise a simple and unprofitable little affair which employed only the ricketiest of engines and rolling stock once the summer people were gone, but it had its pride. Its Homer, James N. J. Henwood, in his *A Short Haul to the Bay*, makes that clear enough. When the giant Pennsylvania Railroad, in an acquisitive moment, sent a telegram to Narragansett president John N. Hazard asking how much he wanted for the railroad, he sent back this impudent message: MINE NOT FOR SALE. HOW MUCH FOR YOURS?

The Narragansett Pier still carries a little freight, but the Martha's Vineyard Railroad, which we show on the preceding page, expired in 1896. (Nantucket's lasted until 1910.) There was a time when the *Active*, the solitary overworked locomotive, pulled such distinguished guests as General Grant and his retinue. To have eminent visitors, however, was not always helpful to little railroads, in those days of free passes. The General thought nothing of taking along as many as eighteen friends on his pass. This was also a common practice of Commodore Vanderbilt, on his trips to the White Mountains; one conductor remembered the Commodore genially walking him through the cars pointing out the twenty guests who were deadheading with him.

Independent railroads had easier, friendlier ways. The engineer might well be the president of the company and the brakeman his brother. On this kind of railroad one tended to find an older, more leisurely approach to life. The cars—or sometimes *the* car—were apt to be antiquated castoffs, or occasionally the original one purchased by the thrifty company during the Civil War, heated if at all by a coal stove, open to the breezes and smells of the countryside. On more informal runs, especially on the mixed trains which were never in a hurry, the engineer might stop at any time for a good shot at a rabbit, or possibly to show some agreeable passenger the local sights, from a waterfall to a prairie-dog town.

The hazards too of short-line railroading were different. Some of the little two-foot gauge lines of western Maine suffered from beavers and their energetic way of chewing away the pilings under bridges and embankments. On the other hand, small railroads like that could be built or fixed for very modest sums, especially when local people were willing, now and then, to come "give a day's work" to a well-liked project. Short lines were uneven, and tended less than big ones to alter God's own landscape; they simply followed it.

Nothing was certain on short lines, and sometimes, whether from modesty or indifference, they hid themselves from their public. The long-defunct Grasse River Railroad in the Adirondacks, once visited by the author, posted no signs and listed no telephone number. One simply appeared, hoping to ride behind their steam engine in an ancient coach with black leather seats and beautiful, if cracked, woodwork. Unless a crowd turned out, however, the Grasse River contented itself, if it liked your looks, with taking you on its rail bus, which, with an astonishingly large crew of three men in lumber jackets, carried you fifteen miles across country from Childwold to Cranberry Lake. There it left off a small mail pouch and a few express packages, cooled

(Continued on page 250)

The two nymphs above are dreaming of the sublime comforts afforded them on their crack train between New York and Buffalo. Reality, however, might take the form of the mixed train, like the one below creeping along on its daily run for the Wrightsville & Tennille in Georgia. Mixed trains were just that—baggage, freight, and a passenger car or two. They often ran on flexible schedules, stopping to pick up and discharge freight while weary drummers in the coach kept warm by the stove and peered out at the rubes.

The narrow-gauge Boston, Revere Beach & Lynn Railroad opened in 1875.

The first passenger train of the Seward Peninsula Railway crosses the Nome

Whole trains were often ferried from one track to another.

A magnificent display of motive power at Durand, Michigan, where the Ann

The Mount Washington cog railway strains up Jacob's Ladder in New Hampshire.

A Santa Fe passenger train stops in front of the large Redondo Hotel and bath

River Bridge in Nome, Alaska, in July of 1906.

The first run across the seemingly endless Long Key Viaduct, Florida, 1908

Arbor and Grand Trunk lines crossed.

The Pike's Peak railway runs up gradients as steep as one in four.

house at Redondo Beach in California.

Small horsecars like this took passengers from train to hotel in Florida.

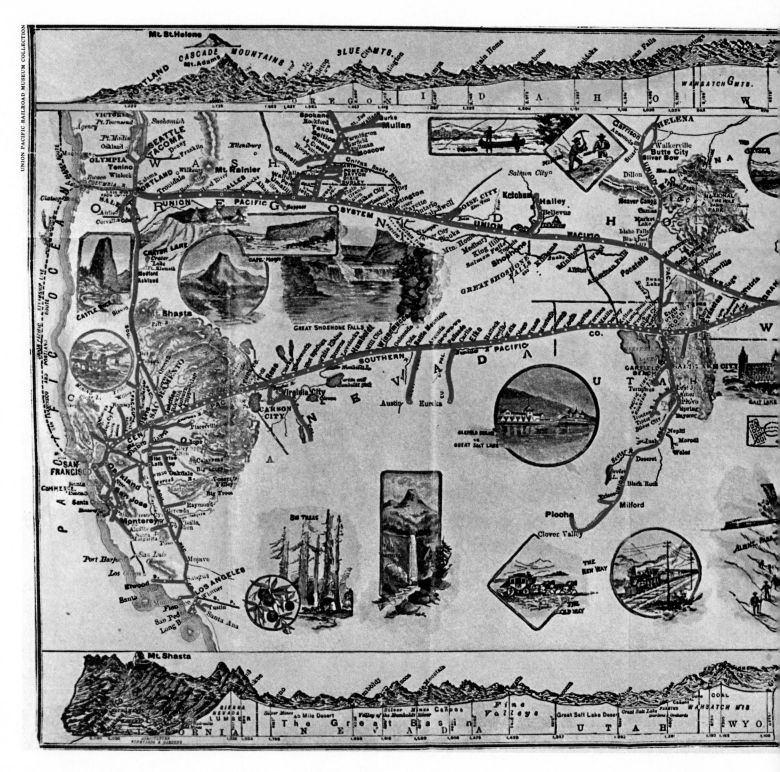

This colorful, highly distorted map is an 1893 bid by the Union Pacific for passenger trade. The year 1893 was a wild one for the Union Pacific— the company went broke and E. H. Harriman was replacing Jay Gould as the boss—but there is little sign of that in the authoritative red lines that show the various routes sightseers could choose. All the major attractions are shown in

off for a moment, and then heaved and bumped home, passengers being permitted to throw a few switches, look at the beaver dam, and inspect a long disused and decaying Wagner palace parlor car, sitting for some unaccountable reason on a siding in the wilderness.

Had it not been for the express, now mostly trucked, and for the mail, since taken away by the all-wise government in Washington, most of these short lines would have expired long before. Most of them, indeed, fought a long, losing struggle against the sheriff. The West River Railroad in Vermont, running north from Brattleboro to South Londonderry, was such a bad case that its chronicler, Victor Morse, simply called his work *Thirty-six Miles of Trouble*. It was the kind of line on which when it rained you opened your umbrella inside the car. The company could confidently expect to be wiped out from time to time either by snow or flood or attachments by the sheriff. Its emergency relief engine, patched together from old bits and pieces, had a

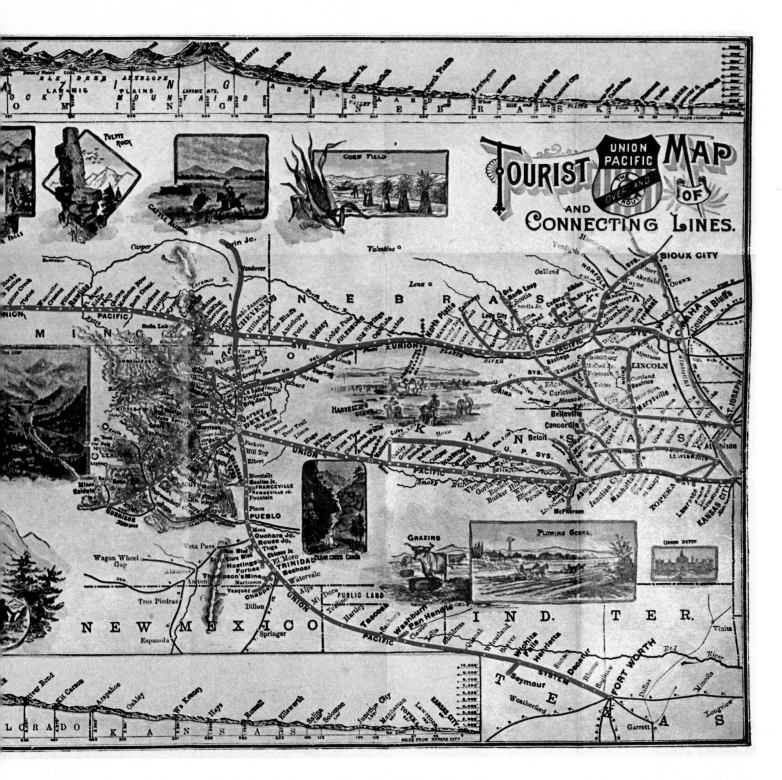

name that very aptly characterized the whole operation: the "Scrap Heap."

Many of the great railroads of America had romantic, often poetic, names, like Chicago, Milwaukee, St. Paul & Pacific, but the late Lucius Beebe was particularly taken with the names of the short ones. In his collection one can only sigh for the Andalusia, Florida & Gulf, the North Star & Mifflin, the Pittsburgh & Moon Run, the Marshall, Elysian Fields & Southwestern, or the Ultimate Thule, Arkadelphia & Mississippi. Their whistles blow no more. One might add to this ghostly parade the Tallulah Falls, the Brimstone, the Smoky Mountain, the Aberdeen & Rockfish, and a hundred more, but there is no room here and we must turn lovers of short lines over to Beebe's many books or the delights of Archie Robertson's *Slow Train to Yesterday*. All but a minute handful of these passenger trains have made their graveyard runs. The book is closed on a world which is quite invisible from the windows of Amtrak or automobiles hurtling down the interstates.

romantic insets. There is no indication of the thousands of short-line railroads that branched out from the main roads all across the West and, in fairness to the Union Pacific, there is not room enough to show them. However, it was simply good advertising for the company to leave out the lines of its major competitors, though it has been charitable about showing eastern connections.

This summery lady cradling her open-bench trolley car appears on a 1905 brochure that unfolds to reveal a map of the line. For a small fare people could ride up the Connecticut River Valley from Hartford via Springfield to Greenfield, Massachusetts. The Connecticut Valley Electric Transit route was an amalgam of interconnecting local street railways.

Under the Singing Wires

First there was the hissing sound along the copper wire, then a warning blast of the air horn, and the big interurban trolley bore down upon you, its powerful arc headlight giving added warning. From its wooden cowcatcher to its high, rounded "railroad" roof, with little ventilator windows in the clerestory, it was an impressive sight, strong and somewhat overbearing compared to a humble city trolley. Sometimes you would find these wooden behemoths swaying along the track by the side of the road, but almost as often on their own private rights of way, just like the steam road's although much less substantial. The interurbans operated on the same principle as the city streetcars, and usually made their way through the cities on their tracks. These intercity cars were logical extensions of the great new network of electric street railroads which sprang up in America almost overnight in the 1890's; they were the first real competitors of the railroads. Cheap to build, cheap to operate, cheaper than the steam roads to ride in, dusting along without soot or smoke through meadows and by country lanes, stopping almost anywhere, interurbans were the common people's new transportation.

Experiments with the use of dynamos or motor generators for electric propulsion go far back into the history of railroads, but the first truly successful street railway of any consequence, which overcame the problems of both operation and power distribution, was the one set up in Richmond, Virginia, in 1888 by Frank J. Sprague. Thereafter the urban scene was transformed as horses gave way to the new prime mover—although many street railroads also experimented with cables, battery cars, and even steam dummies to pull their equipment. One can argue about which was the first real interurban in America, whether the Newark & Granville Street Railway of 1889 in Ohio or other lines in the states of Washington or Minnesota. But it was an obvious development as street railways pushed into the outskirts of cities. Indeed it is a fact that the electric trolley played a large role in inventing the suburbs. For the first time it made possible local travel faster than the pace of a horse. By 1917, the peak year, there were eighteen thousand miles of interurbans operating in the United States, as part of a grand total of electric trolley systems of some forty-five thousand miles.

They had mostly been built in several bursts between 1900 and 1910. By that time, Connecticut, for example, had about a thousand miles of trolley lines, which was more than it has of railroads today. Interurbans mushroomed all over the United States and Canada, but especially in New England and the middle-western states. Although they were regarded by many railroads with great anxiety, because local steam railroad passenger traffic was often cut to a small fraction by the electric lines, they were often blessings in disguise. In general, most railroads lost money on their local service, which ran only from depot to depot and was much less flexible. Managements usually learned that two systems could work very well together interchanging passengers. And at night, when the passenger service ended, the interurban lines could haul freight cars directly to factories and carry mail and express to rural destinations. Sometimes, trolley wire was strung over steam railroad tracks as an inexpensive way of extending interurban service.

The interurbans were ambitious and some of their systems briefly imperial. A few of them had their own palace cars, one of which, Charles Mellen's *No. 500*, still survives at the Branford Electric Railway in East Haven, Connecticut, complete with wicker furniture, carpets, bar, convenience, and stained-glass windows. There were observation platforms, dining cars, and even sleeping cars on a few long runs. Such interurbans ran between St. Louis and Springfield, Illinois, and in Oregon on a six-hour ride of 143 miles between Portland and Eugene. The late and much lamented high-speed North Shore out

(Continued on page 256)

An "Indiana Limited" (70 miles an hour), Indianapolis, Ind.

TRACTION TERMINAL, INDIANAPOLIS, IND.

Indianapolis was one of the hubs of many interurban rail lines. Seven million passengers passed through the Traction Terminal in 1914.

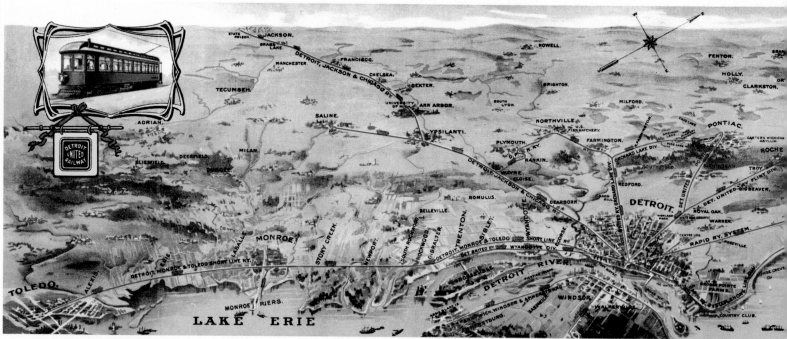

THE NIAGARA BELT LINE—AROUND AND THROUGH THE NIAGARA GORGE

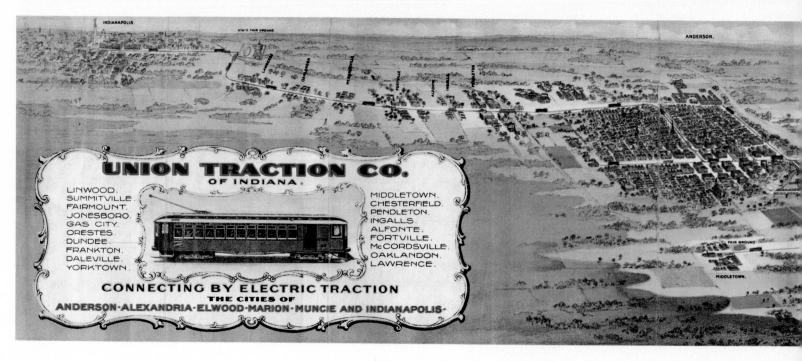

UNION TRACTION CO.
OF INDIANA.

LINWOOD.
SUMMITVILLE.
FAIRMOUNT.
JONESBORO.
GAS CITY.
ORESTES.
DUNDEE.
FRANKTON.
DALEVILLE.
YORKTOWN.

MIDDLETOWN.
CHESTERFIELD.
PENDLETON.
INGALLS.
ALFONTE.
FORTVILLE.
McCORDSVILLE.
OAKLANDON.
LAWRENCE.

CONNECTING BY ELECTRIC TRACTION
THE CITIES OF
ANDERSON · ALEXANDRIA · ELWOOD · MARION · MUNCIE AND INDIANAPOLIS·

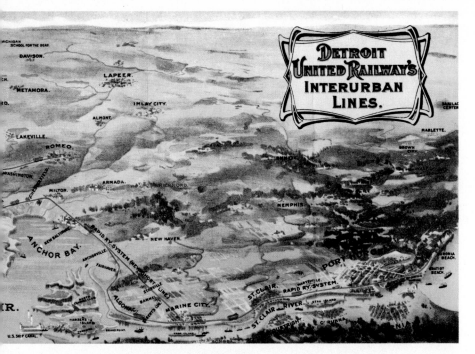

Trolley Exploring.

These vivid maps were issued by three of the scores of lines that made up the vigorous if short-lived interurban industry. The Detroit United Railway cars carried people to Toledo for a mere 80¢. Because of its location, this solid, well-built interurban was an early victim of the automobile. The Niagara Belt Line around and through Niagara Gorge was a popular ride for forty years. Cars left every fifteen minutes for the twenty-two mile trip, which cost $1.00. The first and largest of the great Indiana interurbans, the Union Traction Company, which began operations in 1898, grew to link Indianapolis with twenty-four other towns, and carried people over 163 miles of road for a penny a mile. The 1903 pamphlet above advertised the joys of trolley travel and somewhat ingenuously invited the populace to visit Cedar Grove in Flushing, Long Island, "the largest, most modern and best kept of any rural cemetery." And that reminds us that one could take a last ride in a trolley hearse.

255

LACKAWANNA
and WYOMING
VALLEY
RAILROAD
COMPANY
Industrial
Edition

SEPTEMBER, 1914

TROLLEYTALK
OFFICIAL TIME TABLES

Empire United Railways
Rochester-Syracuse Division
Syracuse-Oswego Division
Auburn-Port Byron Division

Buffalo, Lockport
& Rochester Railway

Auburn & Syracuse
Electric Railroad

Syracuse & South Bay
Electric R. R. and the

Syracuse, Watertown &
St. Lawrence River R. R.

Newark & Marion Railway

On the Way to Rubio Canyon, Pasadena in the distance.

2/20/07
Papa

"The age of steam like all other ages has had its reign," begins the jaunty Lackawanna & Wyoming Valley promotion pamphlet. The "Industrial Edition" spoke of the rich natural resources of Pennsylvania's industrial areas and, now that the "age of electricity" was upon us, suggested that the Laurel Line was the best way to get to them. The line ran from Nanticoke through Wilkes-Barre to Scranton and Carbondale. "Trolley Talk" not only contained the official 1914 timetable for eight upstate New York trolley lines, but a great many execrable jokes as well. Above at right an open car teeters out on a trestle on the north slope of the San Gabriel Valley in California. Who was "Papa"? No one will ever know.

of Chicago to Milwaukee provided full meals in dining cars as late as 1949.

The most ambitious of all interurbans, at least on paper, the once widely touted Chicago–New York Electric Air Line Railroad, proposed to run at an average speed of seventy-five miles an hour—a ten-hour trip of 742 miles for exactly $10. It would have been, if it had ever gotten off the ground, 150 miles shorter than any existing railroad.

What you could actually do by trolley and interurban was exciting enough. You could travel from Boston to New York, for example, for about $2.40; it was somewhere between eighteen and twenty hours of gruelling riding, the time depending upon whether you made good connections at the ends of about a dozen lines. A party of street railway officials is said to have done it in the best time in March, 1912, in the private car *Huguenot* of the Worcester Consolidated Street Railway, running from Park Square in Boston via

Worcester, Springfield, Hartford, New Britain, New Haven, and then down along the shore to Westchester and New York. There was another route, the last days of parts of it glimpsed by the author as a child: While most of southern New England's "interurbans" were really simply extensions of city trolley lines, a true interurban was built eastward along Long Island Sound from New Haven to Old Saybrook and New London, called the Shoreline Electric Railway, with later extensions to Westerly and the resort of Watch Hill, Rhode Island. The author remembers big lumbering interurban cars, interspersed with brigades of open-benched trolleys full of men in hard straw hats, climbing a long hill out of New London, motors grinding furiously, and then heading onto a rural track which ran on and off the highway twelve miles north to Norwich. From there the through line moved northwest toward a little hamlet called Elmville, whose few citizens enjoyed but usually ignored the unusual privilege of two routes to Boston. One ran north, including a fast twenty-five-mile stretch under wire strung along the steam road to Putnam and Worcester. The other struck east to Killingly, where one might catch the Providence car shown on pages 258–259.

For those with truly herculean stamina it was possible, by trolley and interurban, to go all the way from Maine to Boston to Chicago via Springfield, Illinois—if you did not mind two twenty-mile breaks in upstate New York where you had to resort to the steam railroad, or shanks' mare. If you were still breathing, you could push on to Sheboygan, Wisconsin. Excursions of this kind were basically stunts, but trolley men did affect the ceremonious ways of steam railroading, along with rosewood paneling, handsome inlaid wood, and genuine gold leaf lettering. When the first Boston–New York route was completed at Wallingford, Connecticut, in 1904, it pleased management to drive a golden spike.

There is also an echo of steam railroad experience in the disastrous financial history of the interurbans. Often they were launched by local interests, like the Bamberger lines in Utah; Simon Bamberger of Salt Lake City was a coal mine operator. The Kankakee & Urbana line was organized by C. L. Van Doren, an Urbana doctor. H. J. Heinz, the pickle king of Pittsburgh, helped build the Winona Traction Company of Indiana, to carry the faithful to hear Billy Sunday at his "Assembly" on Winona Lake. A good third of the interurban trackage remained in independent hands, but much of the industry was taken over by large systems like the Cincinnati & Lake Erie or the Connecticut Company, or by power companies or steam railroads. Of course, many interurbans were simply parts of city trolley systems.

Manipulators also appeared early. Their great instrument in the 1920's was the holding company, and the kind of pyramiding that helped bring on the great crash of 1929. Holding companies in the electric power field, like Electric Bond & Share and United Corporation, swept a great many interurbans into their bags of utilities. The most famous of the holding companies was developed by Samuel Insull, who controlled in various intricate ways at least twenty-five or thirty interurban companies in the Middle West, including three notable Chicago lines—the North Shore, the South Shore, and the Chicago, Aurora & Elgin. Insull kept his great complex going through the stock market crash only to witness its spectacular collapse in 1932. The South Shore is one of two interurbans that still exist, the other survivor working out of Philadelphia.

By the twenties, the interurban industry was already in trouble. In their best years few of the overbuilt and overcapitalized companies had done very well financially; the average rate of return, as far back as 1909, was only 3 percent. Many had been poorly built and carelessly operated. The Shoreline Electric of Connecticut, an unlikely speculation, did not put together its en-

Great but unfulfilled expectations, 1907

De luxe trolley parlor car on the Berkshire line, 1903

Off-hours freight movement in Norwich, Connecticut, 1909

The Chicago–New York Electric Air Line Railroad set out to build nothing less than a double-track electric railroad that would run in a straight line between the two cities in a mere ten hours. The line opened its first three-mile spur between La Porte and South La Porte, Indiana, with two standard wooden cars that had "New York" lettered on the front and "Chicago" on the rear. The company went bankrupt in 1915, but the Berkshire line shown below it did very well until it was bought up and debauched by the New Haven. Three lines radiated out of Franklin Square in Norwich, Connecticut (bottom), but in this picture they are empty save for an old work trolley hauling a load of freight.

257

With no competitive traffic in sight, an interurban sings along a Massachusetts road.

tire route until 1913; yet it did not last long enough for all the cars it had acquired by purchase and merger to be painted in the company's standard green livery. Of the few passengers it could coax into its cars, it managed to kill nineteen and wound thirty-five when two wooden Jewett interurbans met head-on in North Branford, Connecticut, in 1917. A strike in 1919 shut the company down for four years. In 1923 a new company tried to operate parts of the underpopulated line, but switched to buses within six years.

The automobile doomed the interurban, whose private, tax-paying tracks could never compete with the highways that a generous government provided the motorist. This dose of socialism, although very few people would have thought of it in that light, was aided and abetted by the active role played by General Motors and the automobile industry in buying up and junking electric trolley systems, then setting up new transit systems which could be sold expensive and much less durable buses. Their biggest victim was the Pacific Electric, the thousand-mile city and suburban railway of Los Angeles. Letting it happen was a folly for which that freeway-ridden, smog-filled city is still paying. More of that story is told on page 291.

Here and there, those with sharp eyes can spot the telltale relics of the interurbans. A narrow embankment will cut inexplicably away from the road, or a vine-grown, concrete bridge abutment will seem to lead nowhere. Along the side of an old blacktop road a corduroy effect will show where the macadam, poured over rotting crossties, has sunk a little between them. Most of the eighty thousand streetcars which ran in the 1920's have long since been scrapped. A few, like once good women, were sold to South America.

In Richmond, Virginia, that birthplace of the trolley, the abandoned cars, rolled ignominiously on their sides, were being burned out for the junkmen in 1949. As the flames roared through the very last car, however, a strange thing happened—agonizedly and slowly it turned right side up, as though it were trying to say something to forgetful Richmond and ungrateful America, a message about a day when cities that destroyed their railway systems would painfully have to rebuild them.

258

Looking like a city streetcar gone astray, a Providence

car pulls up to a country station in Connecticut, at one point a pause on a two-day Boston–New York interurban route.

13. Days of the Dinosaur

13. Days of the Dinosaur

Despite its summery, rather flimsy appearance, this is not a trolley car; it is an "electric motor car" on the Nantasket Beach line of the New York, New Haven & Hartford, where third-rail electrification was first used in this country in 1895. The third rail is clearly visible, running along Lionel fashion in the middle of the track.
COLLECTION OF AMOS HEWITT

PRECEDING PAGES: *The superb railroad photographer Richard Steinheimer waded through snowdrifts on a -28 degree morning to record this glimpse of a 2-10-2 making its way upgrade in Utah.*
RICHARD STEINHEIMER; DEGOLYER LIBRARY, S.M.U.

The wonderful scene on the preceding pages was photographed on a subzero December morning outside of Thistle, Utah, along the right-of-way of the Denver & Rio Grande Western. The big Santa Fe-type 2-10-2 is blasting up the west slope of the Soldier Summit grade with a drag of empty coal cars heading for the mines of Carbon County, and the locomotive looks as eternal and indestructible as the mountains beyond it. But that is all an illusion, for it is 1951, the steam engine is on the verge of becoming an anachronism, and in a few years it will be impossible to behold such a sight anywhere in the United States. Like the dinosaur, the steam locomotive is gone except as a museum piece, and like the dinosaur, it reached impossible dimensions of size and weight before it vanished.

At the turn of the century there were some 193,000 miles of main-line track in America. Forty thousand steam locomotives ran over that track, and they were not enough. More new locomotives were ordered in 1902 than in any preceding year, and the peak came three years later, when 6,300 new locomotives were ordered by the railroads. Traffic was increasing everywhere; the country that the railroads had done so much to build was making unprecedented demands on them. There was a universal need for more powerful engines, and in response to this, the steam locomotive was about to go through its last great period of development.

Before this could happen, though, certain innovations were necessary. For years locomotive builders had been experimenting with cast steel, which was infinitely stronger and more tensile than cast iron; once it was generally adopted, engines could grow larger. The larger the locomotive, however, the more difficult it was to fire, for no fireman could stoke a huge firebox by muscle and shovel alone. This problem was solved by the development of the mechanical stoker, which fed fuel from the tender directly into the firebox. Despite these and other innovations, however, there was still an inherent limitation on engine size. Anything larger than a Decapod—a locomotive with ten driving wheels, five on a side—was simply too long to negotiate a sharp curve in the tracks. But this obstacle was also overcome.

The century was only half a year old when eight individual locomotive factories merged to become the mammoth American Locomotive Company. An enormous staff of skilled personnel had been brought together under one management (American Locomotive's only large competitor at the time was the Baldwin Locomotive Works, which had been doing well at the game since 1831), and some of the designers looked to Europe, where a Swiss engineer named Anatole Mallet was building articulated compound locomotives. A compound locomotive uses steam more than once to drive it; that is, instead of escaping after it has passed through the cylinder, the steam is fed

into another cylinder and thereby provides an extra push. It was a good idea, and compound engines were in service in America, but they cost too much to build and maintain. An articulated engine has more than one pair of cylinders and driving wheels, and is really two or more engines under one boiler, suspended so that they can turn separately on curves. One had been built in this country as early as 1832, but never in combination with a compound. When in 1904 American Locomotive began building its first Mallet—an 0-6-6-0 for the Baltimore & Ohio—it was therefore pioneering a new kind of locomotive in this country. The engine was finished in time to go on display at the St. Louis World's Fair, and then entered service pulling freight over the heavy grades of western Pennsylvania. This giant was a success from the start; "Old Maud," as she was christened by the men who drove her, surpassed all expectations and touched off a lengthy vogue for articulated compounds.

Although smaller ones were still built for various purposes, road engines quickly got huge; in 1911 the Santa Fe's Topeka shops and Baldwin turned out a 2-10-10-2, whose twenty driving wheels exerted the then unheard-of tractive force of 111,600 pounds. Thirty years later the extravagant machines reached their zenith with twenty-five 4-8-8-4's built by American Locomotive for the Union Pacific. These were the "Big Boys," 132-foot-long monsters that weighed over six hundred tons, carried twenty-eight tons of coal and twenty-five thousand gallons of water, and produced upwards of seventy-five hundred horsepower. Nobody would ever build a steam locomotive larger than the Big Boy, and in fact, in less than a decade no American shop would build a steam locomotive.

It would have taken a very prescient witness indeed to read an augury of this in the ugly, boxy little switch engine that began doodling around in the *(Continued on page 268)*

This busy scene was photographed in the Baltimore yards of the Pennsylvania Railroad in 1902. The astonishing marshalling of motive power says much about the state of railroading at the turn of the century; there are upwards of fifty locomotives visible in the picture, more than could possibly be seen—or needed—in a modern yard.

The beautiful locomotive above is the New York Central & Hudson's famous No. 999, whose huge, spidery driving wheels enabled her to set the onetime world's speed record of 112.5 miles per hour near Batavia, New York, in 1893. According to the Whyte system of locomotive classification (top right), she was a 4-4-0. The Whyte system is sim-

plicity itself; while a railroad may assign any "class" designation it chooses to a locomotive, the "type" always depends on the wheel arrangement. As big road locomotives grew larger, they needed bigger fireboxes, and these, in turn, needed extra support. So the Atlantic type (4-4-2) evolved from the American type, the Pacific from the ten-wheeler,

the Prairie from the Mogul, and the Mikado from the Consolidation. In general, the swift, large-wheeled locomotives such as the Niagara, the Pacific, and the Hudson types were used in passenger service, and the locomotives with smaller drivers—the Consolidation, the Mikado, the Texas—pulled freight drags. As weight increased, more and more

TYPES OF STEAM LOCOMOTIVES

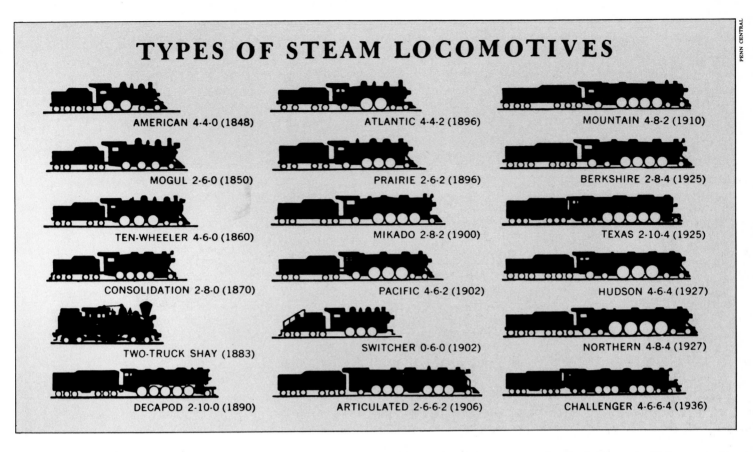

AMERICAN 4-4-0 (1848)

MOGUL 2-6-0 (1850)

TEN-WHEELER 4-6-0 (1860)

CONSOLIDATION 2-8-0 (1870)

TWO-TRUCK SHAY (1883)

DECAPOD 2-10-0 (1890)

ATLANTIC 4-4-2 (1896)

PRAIRIE 2-6-2 (1896)

MIKADO 2-8-2 (1900)

PACIFIC 4-6-2 (1902)

SWITCHER 0-6-0 (1902)

ARTICULATED 2-6-6-2 (1906)

MOUNTAIN 4-8-2 (1910)

BERKSHIRE 2-8-4 (1925)

TEXAS 2-10-4 (1925)

HUDSON 4-6-4 (1927)

NORTHERN 4-8-4 (1927)

CHALLENGER 4-6-6-4 (1936)

driving wheels were added, until the industry was turning out such monsters as the mammoth 2-10-10-2 shown below. This Mallet articulated compound locomotive was built by the giant American Locomotive Works. As the century progressed, the big locomotives became increasingly efficient and speedy. After 1910 the superheater boosted power by nearly 25 percent, and 1926 witnessed the introduction of the one-piece cast steel frame, replacing the eight hundred parts in a fabricated frame with a single unit. By the 1930's, grease had replaced oil as a chief lubricant, and locomotive efficiency had doubled since 1900. There were road engines capable of pulling 160-car trains, and locomotives often ran a hundred thousand miles a year. But these fast, powerful machines were frequently squandered by the railroads. The Big Boy, for instance, which reached its proper running speed at about forty miles per hour, often crept along with slow trains. This sort of misuse is one of the reasons the diesel was able to kill steam so quickly.

Steam power was still unchallenged at the Polson Logging Company when this picture was taken in 1940 by Darius Kinsey, famous for his western logging photos. The Polson Company was founded in 1895, and grew to have eighty-five miles of track. The West was veined with steam logging railroads; the first of them was founded in 1868 to supply timber to the Union Pacific. In time there were three thousand such railroads, many of them rough, rickety operations.

I T T RAYONIER

CHARLES B. GUNN

The three streamlined locomotives below look speedy but also faintly ridiculous, for all that has been achieved is a cosmetic effect. The hood merely covered the blunt, familiar outline of a steam locomotive, made its working parts difficult to reach, and affected its performance not a whit. From top to bottom: a publicity shot of a Pacific from the New York Central; the Pennsylvania Railroad's high speed, high horsepower 6-4-4-6, the largest passenger locomotive ever built, and a perpetual maintenance problem; sleek Dreyfuss-styled Hudsons that pulled the Twentieth Century Limited. *The photograph at right highlights a dramatic nighttime meeting between the two warring forms of motive power.*

COURTESY OF ED NOWAK

PENN CENTRAL

COURTESY OF ED NOWAK

yards of the Central Railroad of New Jersey in 1925, but that was the first diesel put into service in this country, and in a generation it would emerge pre-eminent. At that time it seemed more likely that, if there was to be an inheritor, it would be the electric locomotive. The railroads had already been hurt, or thought they had, by the interurbans. Once central-station electric power had been developed to a degree where a current could be transmitted along the right-of-way by third rail or overhead wire, the electric railroad became feasible. The New Haven's Nantasket Beach branch was the first standard railroad line to be converted to electric operation, and the same year —1895—the Baltimore & Ohio began to use heavy-duty electrification in its 7,200-foot tunnel beneath the city of Baltimore, where its smokeless operation was essential. Electric power made quick acceleration possible, and hence was very popular on suburban lines. It spread widely (and is still growing in Europe), only to diminish in recent years; hard-pressed railroads faced with heavy repairs to the overhead found a quick way out with diesels, and never mind the long term. Yet even in the diesel, the oil-burning engine turns a generator to make electric power which in turn drives the motor that makes the wheels revolve. At first this power was used entirely in switching operations, for which the diesel was ideally suited; it developed maximum power in starting and at low speeds, and it did not have to waste time taking on huge amounts of water. When new, it spent less time than its steam counterpart undergoing repairs. One did not start a little fire and build it into a big one; one pushed a self-starter. The tin horse was indeed convenient, but it wore out much faster than the iron one.

If one were to put a definite date on the passing of the age of steam in America, he could do worse than pick the opening day of the second year of the 1933 Century of Progress Exposition in Chicago, for it was there that the gleaming, stainless steel *Pioneer Zephyr*, euphoniously named after the Greek personification of the West Wind by the president of the Burlington Route, made its first public appearance. The *Zephyr* was diesel powered, and it was very fast indeed. The train was an instant success, and millions of people had already walked through it when it began regular service that November.

The first practical road freight diesel, the Electro-Motive FT, appeared five years later. Though it was first thought of as a supplement to the steam locomotive, it turned out to be tough, handy, and, after a stiff initial purchase price, it seemed cheaper to maintain. Steam might have been able to hold out

The lightweight train, it had long been believed, would be the future of passenger travel. The first of these gleaming, streamlined, diesel-hauled trains made its widely heralded appearance in 1934. It was the Burlington's Pioneer Zephyr, running between Lincoln, Nebraska, and Kansas City. The many Zephyrs (directly below) were successful, although General Motors' Aerotrain (center) was not. The electric Metroliners' popularity has not been equalled so far by the gas-turbine-powered TurboTrains (bottom), built by United Aircraft but somewhat over-engineered and vulnerable to the less than perfect roadbeds they use. New turbos are now being built to French designs, giving a quieter and smoother ride.

against the diesel incursion, but as Bill Withun points out in a well-reasoned essay in *Trains* magazine about that sad conflict, "In its fight for survival during the 1940's, the steam locomotive lost by default."

As we have seen, the steam railroading community was hidebound and myopic. Designers often worked their way up from the shops, and they tended to be traditionalists. The best talent went elsewhere. Walter Chrysler, for instance, who had started out as a boomer riding freight trains between western engine shops, turned his back on a $12,000 job at American Locomotive to take one that paid exactly half that but struck him as more exciting. It was at General Motors. The designers who remained felt that they had made innovations enough during the last few decades, and they did not want a lot of fresh graduates of M.I.T. telling them how to build a locomotive. Many of their modernization attempts were foolish or feeble, such as those strangely demeaning hoods they placed over locomotives to "streamline" them.

And the steam establishment was up against some very canny professionals. General Motors had bought Electro-Motive in 1930, and General Motors knew how to force a product. Against a shrewd assault of full-page color advertisements, the locomotive companies marshalled amateurish and ineffective rebuttals. Then came World War II, and for four years the shops were too busy building standard locomotives to do much steam research. (Oddly enough, many diesel locomotive engines were commandeered to drive anti-submarine naval vessels.) When the war was over, it was too late. American Locomotive and Baldwin had all but conceded defeat and were building diesels. Only the Lima Locomotive Works remained committed to steam, and tried to make up for lost time with a dismal succession of costly and futile experiments. Finally, in 1947, Lima merged with the Hamilton diesel-electric works, and that was that. The last commercially produced steam locomotive was built in 1949.

The electric engine may some day disturb the dominance of the diesel, but those who dream of a comeback for steam in America are usually waved aside with a tolerant smile. Yet the cry of its whistle can be heard increasingly these days in oil-short lands like South Africa, Thailand, and India, where steam engines are actually being retained and rebuilt. Like *Smoky Mary*, which ran one hundred years in Louisiana, they tend to be modest affairs of quaint and ancient cut, graying at the temples but full of the same magic that has spellbound the world ever since George Stephenson ran his first train a century and a half ago.

A Portfolio

14. The Long Haul

For over a century the main business of American railroads, the commerce that kept them alive, has been carried in freight cars. Despite the unhappy state of the bankrupt lines of the Northeast, a good many railroads are still doing very well in hauling heavy and bulky goods. In 1973, for instance, freight revenue increased to a record $12.8 billion, 10 percent over the previous high. In that year 1,610 million tons of freight rolled over American iron. The reason for this is simple enough; the great freight-hauling lines have, with a good deal of imagination and foresight, kept up with technological advances, as illustrated on the following pages.

The innovation of one generation can, of course, become the financial albatross of another. Consider, for example, the locomotives at right. They are two of the Milwaukee Road's 5,500-horsepower "Little Joes" (nicknamed for Joseph Stalin, who ordered them in 1946 but never got them), hauling tonnage up the Continental Divide in Montana. The Milwaukee Road had more than six hundred miles of track under wire, and its huge electric locomotives have become something of a legend. In 1913 it was a brave decision to make this first big electric installation, but the Milwaukee's steep grades and long tunnels made it imperative. The electrification was a great success, partly because of the ingenious system of regenerative braking in which a train going downgrade generated power to help out one that was climbing. Yet upkeep and the rising cost of power eventually doomed the electrics; the line went diesel in 1973.

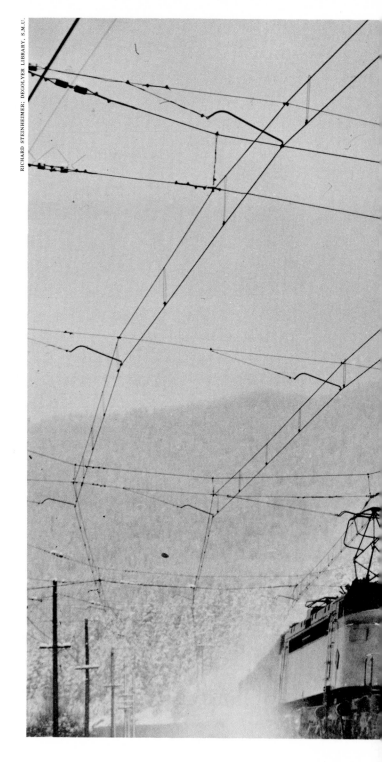

No railroad can operate without yards where incoming trains are broken down and the cars are classified, separated, and fed into a maze of tracks where they are either unloaded, forwarded to connecting lines, or held awaiting shippers' instructions. Often this is done by switch engines, but many of the major switchyards do the bulk of the job by gravity; cars are pushed up to the top of an artificial hill, and then let go, singly or in small groups, to roll through branching tracks until they arrive at their proper place. This complicated "hump switching" is automatically controlled from a central tower. The aerial view above shows the newly built part of the De Coursey automated classification yard, which opened in 1964. (The old section, a modest affair by comparison, can be seen at the top center of the pho-

tograph.) The yard, which is not far from Cincinnati on the Louisville & Nashville, can classify forty-five hundred cars in a twenty-four-hour period. But even in the most modern classification yard, switching is a time-consuming business, and cars often stand idle. One solution to this is the unit train, a modern version of the earlier single-cargo freights, for example the World War II coal train at lower right.

Unit trains carry single bulk products between two points, and since they are permanently made up, they spend no time at all being broken down, classified, and reassembled. At the top, two of the Santa Fe's unit sulphur trains pass each other at Buenos, Texas. The train on the left is coming home empty, while the one on the right is taking some six thousand tons of liquid sulphur to the port of Galveston.

In the peak year of 1916 the railroads carried 77 percent of intercity freight traffic. That figure has now declined to about 40 percent but, nevertheless, railroads are moving more freight today than they ever did before. Revenue ton-miles (the product of the weight of the freight and the distance it is carried) have soared from 447 million in 1929 to 852 million in 1973, despite the fact that there are only half as many cars in service today as there were then. Modern freight cars are larger than those of fifty years ago, but the main reason for this improved performance is the increased efficiency of road operation. Some of this hauling, to be sure, gives aid and comfort to the enemy, as in the trilevel car for piggy-backing automobiles shown at the left. The car was built by Pullman Standard to expedite factory-to-dealer shipments on the Frisco Railroad. The crane below it is at the Santa Fe's Houston, Texas, freight terminal, and is capable of lifting a forty-ton load on or off a flatcar in two minutes. Freight haulage accounts for more than 95 percent of the Santa Fe's total revenue; at right its unit train of intermodal containers snakes along near Kansas City on its way east. A relatively recent innovation, the intermodal container can be carried by train, truck, or ship, and need not be opened as it is transshipped. As for the moody silhouette below, it is a Great Northern freight rolling along west of Havre, Montana.

© DAVID PLOWDEN 1975

Four Santa Fe diesels haul large sections of concrete pipe around Sullivan's Curve in Cajon Pass. The pipe is destined to be part of the California Aqueduct near Summit. The picture demonstrates one of the reasons why diesel power so quickly replaced steam; a five-thousand-horsepower steam locomotive remains just that whether the drag it is pulling has three cars or thirty. Diesels, on the other hand, can be paired, tripled, or quadrupled together or used singly as the freight loads require. The three electric trains of the Kennecott Copper Corporation, opposite, are negotiating the steep, snow-dusted sides of the world's second largest copper mine, at Bingham Canyon, Utah. They are part of a fleet of sixty-two locomotives powered by the company's own 175,000-kilowatt plant. The trains carry 108,000 tons of ore a day, making the Kennecott the busiest railroad per ton-mile in the country. Since the mine's opening in 1906, its railroad has hauled 1.3 billion tons of ore.

A mixed freight rumbles over the high girders of the Penn Central's Poughkeepsie Bridge, above. The venerable bridge, which was first opened in 1889, suffered fire damage in 1974 and is now closed to traffic. This was convenient enough for the Penn Central, which was thereby able to reroute its trains circuitously and save itself a good deal of money on repair and track maintenance. Although there are new plans to reopen the damaged bridge, they are being pursued with a monumental amount of foot-dragging. But at least the bridge still stands; the yards opposite have disappeared. This lonely scene was photographed *looking away from the Jersey City passenger terminal of the Central Railroad of New Jersey. These yards were once crowded with trains of the B & O and the Reading, as well as the Jersey Central. The terminal was fed by a ferry operation from New York and when, in the unceasing war against the passenger, the ferry was abandoned in 1967, the Jersey City terminal quickly followed suit. Jersey riders now have to make out as best they can with an awkward, complicated, and unsatisfactory connection with other lines in Newark. The elegant pattern of interconnecting tracks has vanished without a trace.*

15. Days of Reckoning

15. Days of Reckoning

The New York Times

Slow freight: On the verge of bankruptcy, the Chicago, Rock Island & Pacific's crooked road-bed in Joliet, Illinois, suggests the sorry state of all too many American railroads in mid-1975, not to mention why in 1973 there were, on all the railroads across the country, 7,389 recorded de-railments, up 133 percent in a decade. As this is written the government has refused to rescue the 122-year-old Rock Island, whose seventy-five hundred miles of track reach fourteen states.

PRECEDING PAGES: *The railroad yard is battered and deserted but the highway and the oil tank, shown in the background, flourish like the green bay tree, epitomizing our national malaise.*
© DAVID PLOWDEN 1975

The old railroad yard is a tangle of weeds, twisted track, and seemingly derelict cars, an eyesore in a landscape dominated by crowded, en-circling highways. The depot, even in many big cities, has been demolished, or it is a lonely echoing chamber where only one or two lights burn, a place to make the occasional visitor feel like a trespasser into the past. Along the empty platform trash blows back and forth; graffiti mark the walls. Once a day, perhaps, there limps in a collection of patched-up cars decked out in garish reds and purples, like an old woman with too much lipstick, but the Amtrak train is more likely to stop by some little prefabricated hut on the outskirts of town. Everything about Amtrak—from its collegiate banners to its movie-usher uniforms and the soap-flake name—is ticky-tacky mod-ern, but the stations cannot be held against it. The cheap shelters may be inconvenient but the taxes are lower, and the railroads that own the tracks and stations are paying them. Amtrak is only a boarder. Watching the loose, untended rail joints move perilously up and down as each wheel passes over them, it is hard to remember the day when the vanished section gangs would line up by a beautifully ballasted trackside pulling at their caps as a Leland Stanford or an E. H. Harriman rolled by in his private car. But there is a generation now that has never ridden a train.

Only in the Northeast Corridor from Boston to Washington, around Chicago, and in the handful of cities that still provide a much-diminished service for that hardy breed, the commuter, does more than an occasional lonely train survive out of the once dense traffic of American passenger trains —twenty thousand a day in 1929. Even the rail passenger capital, New York City, has lost whole lines and complete companies—the West Shore, the Sus-quehanna, the Putnam Division of the New York Central, the New York, Westchester & Boston (for which Morgan and Mellen once paid so much), the New York, Ontario & Western (a major road torn up entirely), the Balti-more & Ohio service to Philadelphia and Washington, the Lehigh Valley, and more besides. Not a single one of the many Hudson River ferries still carries the train riders between Manhattan and the Jersey shore. Except for a few strong freight haulers, American railroads are in crisis, especially in the Northeast, their conquest by the automobile, the truck, and the airplane very nearly complete. Yet it is only a little over a century since a whole nation waited breathlessly for the sound of the spike being driven at Promontory, not quite sixty years since 1916, when the railroads, at their greatest extent, ruled American transportation, and only thirty since 1945 when, as the Sec-ond World War ended, they carried more people and more freight than ever before in their history. What brought the railroads so low?

To find prime rather than surface reasons one must go back very far indeed, to the legacy of dislike created by the robber barons, to the rates set only by what the traffic would bear, to the pools and the rebates, and to the imperious ways of the likes of Collis P. Huntington, E. H. Harriman, and J. P. Morgan. Central casting could have provided no better figures for villains to the earnest reformers of the Progressive and Wilsonian eras. Real teeth went into the thitherto harmless jaws of the Interstate Commerce Commission. Because the famous Sherman Anti-Trust Act of 1890 had proved so ineffective, there was great agitation to strengthen it, culminating in the passage of the Clayton Act of 1914, which was intended to bring an end to the interlocking directorates through which the financiers ruled. Observing the tumult, that habitual dissenter, Justice Oliver Wendell Holmes, uttered in 1910 a mild word of warning:

"I don't disguise my belief that the Sherman Act is a humbug based on economic ignorance and incompetence, and my disbelief that the Interstate Commerce Commission is a body fit to be entrusted with rate making. . . . The Commission naturally is always trying to extend its power. . . . However, I am so skeptical as to our knowledge of the goodness or badness of laws that I have no practical criticism except what the crowd wants. Personally, I bet that the crowd, if it knew more, wouldn't want what it wants."

The crowd likes to see someone humbled, and always has since the days of the Roman triumph when defeated kings and generals were paraded in chains behind the chariot of the victor. But in hanging their chains on the hated railroads, the victorious reformers and commissioners, congratulating themselves on a great victory for the people, had gotten their targets mixed. The financiers and their fortunes remained untouched. The Clayton Act proved so ineffective that in the twenties and early thirties, the era of holding companies, the interlocking directorates only multiplied. As the Pecora hearings of 1935 brought out, for example, Percy Rockefeller, son of the William who had joined the Morgan manipulations of the New Haven, took his place on sixty-eight boards; Samuel Insull, the interurban king, sat on eighty. J. P. Morgan, Jr., a chip off the old block right down to his steam yacht *Corsair*, helped finance another quick-rising, quick-falling empire, the jerry-built structure of borrowings and cross-ownerships erected by two brothers, the oddly named Mantis J. and Oris P. Van Sweringen. They had been minor real estate operators in Shaker Heights, near Cleveland, Ohio, who had parlayed their control of the Nickel Plate Road into an empire briefly composed of the Chesapeake & Ohio, the Kansas City Southern, the Erie, and enough other lines to make a system of twenty-one thousand miles—the same amount as that today held by the bankrupt Penn Central.

That the reformers never really mastered the manipulators has been evident over the years. Through elaborate stratagems, the late Robert R. Young took over the New York Central in 1954. The battered New Haven Railroad, bankrupt in 1935 but recovering in the late 1940's, was plundered again during the Dumaine and McGinnis regimes. For another and tremendous example, one can look to the giant merger of the Pennsylvania and New York Central, a company which went from supposed profit to bankruptcy almost overnight. It is still possible to show false profits by deferring vital maintenance, to shuffle assets between real and dummy corporations, to play all manner of tricks with nonrail properties, to make a killing for the insiders.

All these stories are too familiar to rehearse here; the important point, suspected at the time by only a few people like Holmes but now very obvious, was that the reformers themselves had started the trains along a track leading to destruction. The chosen instrument was the power to set "just and reasonable" rates. Nothing could seem more fair than that until, of course, one attempted to define "just and reasonable." Before the war, for example, at a

"I just never imagined they wouldn't finally come up with some form of government aid."

Sad passengers: Despite the millions wasted on commissions and "studies" and the sympathetic clucking of one governor and mayor after another, commuter service has only declined, with each new low sardonically hailed by The New Yorker. *This cartoon is by James Stevenson, from 1965. The commuter, to be sure, expects a little much: a special reduced rate and a service he ignores except at peak hours—yet a few well-operated lines are successful, like the Chicago & North Western's and the superb new electric Lindenwold line, running east from Philadelphia.*

That skulduggery on the railroads is not dead this stretch of torn-up first-class line bears eloquent witness. It was part of a twelve-mile run of the old Boston & Albany main passenger line between Schodack and Rensselaer, New York. The tracks were pulled up hastily by Penn Central in 1973 after some quiet arrangement with Roger Lewis, then head of Amtrak, and a complaisant ICC moving with unaccustomed speed. The PC, which runs its freight over another route which by-passes Albany, was eager to get rid of the passenger line and raise cash from the scrap. Moving fast would forestall any restoration of a train which had been abandoned with the coming of Amtrak. It ripped up the rails in spite of an informal agreement not to pending the outcome of a suit in Federal Court. So says Mrs. Lettie Gay Carson, of Millerton, New York, head of the Northeast Transportation Coalition, a group fighting to restore freight and passenger trains. Yet as this is written Amtrak is seeking to restore the Boston–Albany–Cleveland service. It must get around the vital gap in the line by a circuitous route—starting over the PC freight tracks, then stopping in the middle of a high bridge over the Hudson and backing down a spur onto the Hudson Division, adding at least forty-five minutes to the trip. That the track might simply be relaid, as Mrs. Carson urges, seems to be an idea whose time has not and may never come to the Penn Central, despite countless outlays of funds by the government.

time when prices and wages were moving suddenly upward, the ICC, mistaking the public clamor for the public interest, simply held down the rates. Shipping became cheaper, fares lower. Hallelujah!

Was such regulation "reasonable"? Railroads had the responsibility to move the business of America, but the authority and the resources with which to do it were slowly taken from them. The government, for example, ordered the railroads to install the eight-hour day; this was no doubt a noble idea, but not when at the same time the employers were not permitted to adjust their rates accordingly. A pattern was being set. In effect, the ICC denied the railroads, alone among the businesses of the era, the right to earn enough to accumulate or attract capital. Without sufficient capital investment, as every businessman knows, it is impossible to keep healthy and competitive in the long run. Instead of outlawing in some fashion highflying financial maneuverings, the government had struck a mortal blow at railroad operation itself, and thus at the future needs of the people themselves. Looking back with all the objectivity one can summon, the mistake lay not so much in regulation per se, but in singling out for it the rails alone, and then basing the rules on political pressures rather than on economic realities.

For a time the meaning of what had happened was masked by the coming of the First World War. Even before America entered it in April, 1917, an immense and unusual traffic in supplies and war material moved into the Atlantic ports. By February, 1917, the yards were clogged with 145,000 freight cars, some awaiting unloading, but many of them empty. Since it is the deepest conviction of railroad management that cars should not move anywhere empty, they stayed. Out west, shippers called in vain for a way to move their goods. With war actually declared, the industry itself set up with loud flourishes a Railroad War Board, which was supposed to get the trains moving and provide a priority system. Because the association was entirely voluntary, however, its achievements were scarcely impressive. The members of the board could not forbear shipping by their own railroads, however roundabout, and the favors were handed out so prodigally that a preposterous 85 percent of all shipments moved under a "top" priority. It is scarcely surprising that by November, 1917, the number of cars choking operations in the eastern yards had swollen to two hundred thousand. One result, in a very cold winter, was a coal famine. The companies were short of help; their wages, which for many decades had been higher than those of most other industries, were suddenly much lower.

At the end of December, 1917, President Wilson took possession of the nation's railroads, and installed William Gibbs McAdoo, the Secretary of the Treasury, as their director general. For a period of twenty-six months, from January 1, 1918, to March 1, 1920, the companies were thus nationalized, with their tracks, rolling stock, ships, grain elevators, and everything they possessed. After a time, McAdoo put in his own operating chiefs too. The argument over whether these drastic moves were necessary or too costly has never been settled, depending, as it does, so heavily on the interpretation of confusing statistics and one's outlook. It still gives railroad men bad dreams.

A federalized system had indeed many advantages from an operating point of view. The ports were made to function; men and materials got to where they were supposed to go. All tracks were used as a single system. To get the men to work for the railways the government in two stages raised wages by some 50 percent. What the private companies could not obtain from the baleful regulators—a compensating rise in the freight rates and passenger fares—the government simply decreed: 28 percent for the former, 18 percent for the latter. Like that. No tiresome hearings, no arguments, no waiting. A federalized system no longer had to worry as had the private companies about the

(Continued on page 289)

The smell of death suffuses the closed Jersey City terminal of the Jersey Central, whence vanished ferries carried passengers on to New York.

The Pennsylvania Railroad station at Cambridge City, Indiana

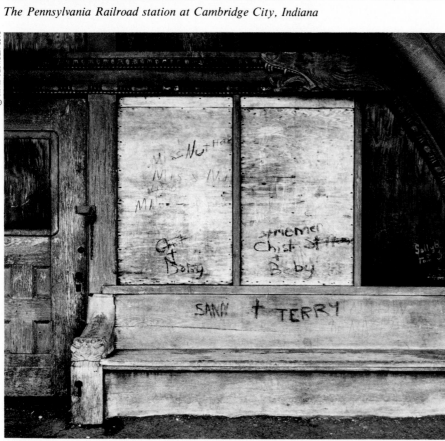

The Old Colony Station at North Easton, Massachusetts, pre-restoration

At Canaan, Connecticut, the disused Pittsfield line

The poignance of abandoned depots, where once all was life and bustle, has been captured eloquently in the photographs in this section (pages 285–288) by David Plowden. The bay window at Cambridge City, where the telegrapher kept his watch, is deserted. One passenger train still passes through each day, without stopping, which is better than at totally desolate Canaan. The North Easton station, designed by H. H. Richardson and landscaped by Frederick Law Olmsted, was a gift to the town in 1881 from the Ames family, the shovel kings encountered earlier in this book in their less benevolent connection with the Crédit Mobilier. It is years since a passenger alighted here, but the Easton Historical Society has since restored the place as a community center and museum.

of the New Haven crosses a stub of the long-dead Central New England, ending in the woods at rear. The handsome old building survives.

© DAVID PLOWDEN 1971

A graceful staircase in the abandoned Jersey Central station at Wilkes-Barre, Pennsylvania; the Queen of the Valley *calls here no more.*

myriad rules and regulations imposed on railroads by the separate states, a situation which any railroad president would envy. It was hardly a true preview of socialism, however, since by the terms of the takeover the government guaranteed the bond interest of the companies and saw to it that the stock paid dividends up to 8.5 percent. When the railroads were returned to their owners in 1920, there was a great uproar. Managements complained about the new wage rates they had been saddled with, and they protested that their lines and equipment had been left in sorry condition, making a claim for more than a billion dollars or more in damages. The claims were later settled for about $48,000,000; many roads which had demanded recompense were instead compelled to pay the government for heavy improvements.

Realization that a day of reckoning was surely coming was disguised again by the boom in the twenties, and by the fact that the railroads during the thirties only shared in the general woes of the Great Depression—a third of them at one time were in bankruptcy and two-thirds of the trackage in the

country was not earning its fixed charges. Many branch lines and much passenger service disappeared, together with most of the interurban network and a large portion of the nation's electric streetcar system, a great deal of which would be invaluable today had it not been heedlessly destroyed. But World War II, in its ironic way, came to the rescue of the railroads, just as it solved the problem of American unemployment.

This time there was no nationalization. Eager to avoid the mistakes of World War I, the industry outdid itself in cooperative effort, aided by the government's wartime Office of Defense Transportation. Although they were working with fewer miles of line, 25 percent fewer freight cars, 30 percent fewer passenger cars, and 32 percent fewer locomotives, the railroads were nonetheless able, through greater efficiency, to carry, in 1944 for example, 82 percent more freight than in the busiest year of World War I. During the Second War, with its rationed gasoline and halt in automobile production, passenger traffic reached all-time highs, more than double the numbers of 1918. Paramount, perhaps, for the last time, the railroads carried 90 percent of the freight and 97 percent of all the armed forces.

In the sunshine of peace, the prosperity of the war years melted away like the snow after one of those strange heavy storms of late spring. America resumed its reckless love affair with the internal combustion engine, a romance enthusiastically encouraged by a generous uncle in Washington, a profligate old fellow who scarred the land with new highways and "interstates" and airports as though there were no tomorrow and no end to the world's supplies of energy. Trucks, airlines, buses, even the long-forgotten canals and waterways benefited from government largesse, and only the railroad remained regulated, unsubsidized, and fully taxed—indeed, sometimes taxed at three

In many cities big stations have mouldered away slowly, prey to vandals and derelicts; very recently, active preservation groups, towns, and Amtrak itself have begun rescue work even in the face of the most determined "urban renewal" speculators and their friends in city halls. But what happened to the landmark station in careless Portland, Maine, in 1961, is shown in these photographs. A swinging steel ball toppled the clock tower in one great crash, dislodging the last tenant, a seagull. Though crossed by Canadian trains, Maine no longer has passenger service to the United States, but Portland has a jim-dandy shopping center where the historic depot stood.

and four times the rates of others. The ICC would in many cases not even let it underprice its competitors.

In a last bid for the long-distance passenger, the big railroads placed large orders for new, lightweight equipment. To replace the heavy, old-fashioned steel cars came a procession of reclining-seat coaches, diners, lounge cars, and sleepers that ended the days of the "section," with its upper and lower berths behind the swinging green curtains. During the late forties, they made up the de luxe air-conditioned service that still thrived on trains like the *Century*, the *Broadway*, and the *Chief* and *Super Chief*. But the growth of airlines, not only faster but competitive in price because of many subsidies, cut into business heavily after the early fifties. Indeed no new de luxe cars were built thereafter, so that Amtrak is still using what good cars the roads did not sell abroad or to that one profitable new long-distance passenger operation, Autotrain, which carries passengers and their cars from Washington to Florida, and from Louisville to Florida.

Perhaps the railroads downgraded and cut back their passenger service faster than was necessary, but they could read the handwriting on the wall. By the 1970's, as one famous fixture of American life after another disappeared—the *Phoebe Snow*, the *Nellie Bly*, the San Francisco *Zephyr*, even the famous *Century*—it seemed that the passenger train would soon be one with Nineveh and Tyre. That the newly devised Amtrak might only be a propaganda façade, behind which the remaining service could be liquidated, seemed entirely possible when Louis Menk, chairman of the Burlington Northern, was appointed an Amtrak director. He told the press that the passenger train was as outdated as the stagecoach and that "it's time to let it die an honorable death."

But as has so often happened to the best laid plans, not only of mice and men but of the Nixon Administration, something went wrong with the scenario. Friends of all varieties, expected and unexpected, began to gather at the bedside. The patient, although still very ill, showed signs of a faint rally.

The scrap pile of Pacific Electric rapid transit cars above and the yard full of now vanished steam locomotives below are signs of our "throw-away" society; we forebear to include an auto graveyard where our short-lived motorcars end their days. The steamers might have been stockpiled against emergency; the electric cars should never have perished at all, as the sad but instructive story on the opposite page makes clear.

A Tale of Two Cities

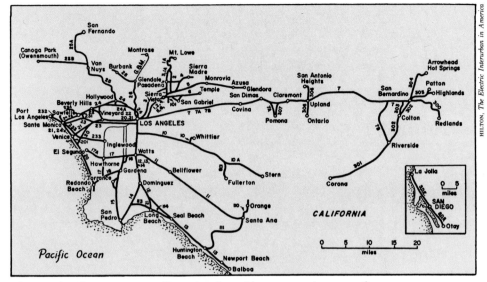

The Pacific Electric system of Los Angeles, with route numbers, as of 1930

Our auto-choked big cities are building or planning billion-dollar rail transport systems (like San Francisco's BART) to replace long-vanished electric city and interurban railways like Pacific Electric. Did the original systems simply fall apart and fade away, or were they pushed? In statements before the Senate Subcommittee on Antitrust and Monopoly in 1974, two California mayors strongly took the latter view.

First Mayor Thomas Bradley of Los Angeles:

"Thirty-five years ago Los Angeles was served by the world's largest interurban electric railway system. The Pacific Electric System branched out from Los Angeles for more than 75 miles, reaching north to San Fernando, east to San Bernardino and south to Santa Ana. The 'big red cars,' so-called to distinguish them from the narrow-gauge street railway, ran literally all over the Los Angeles area. At its point of greatest extension, it operated 1,164 miles of track in fifty-odd communities, which pretty well defines Los Angeles as it is today....

"In 1938, General Motors and Standard Oil of California organized Pacific City Lines (PCL) as an affiliate to the National City Lines (NCL, a national firm) to 'motorize' West Coast electric railways. The following year PCL acquired and substituted bus lines for three northern California electric rail systems in Fresno, San Jose, and Stockton. In 1940, GM, Standard Oil, and Firestone took the reins of management of Pacific City Lines, in order to supervise its California operations more directly. That same year, PCL began to acquire and 'scrap' portions of the $100 million Pacific Electric System including rail lines from Los Angeles to Burbank, Glendale, Pasadena, and San Bernardino. Subsequently, in December, 1944, another NCL affiliate —American City Lines—was financed by GM and Standard Oil to 'motorize downtown Los Angeles.' At the time, the Pacific Electric shared downtown Los Angeles trackage with a local electric streetcar company, the Los Angeles Railway. American City Lines purchased the local system, scrapped its electric cars, tore down its power transmission lines, uprooted the tracks, and placed GM diesel buses fueled by Standard Oil on Los Angeles city streets. By this time, Los Angeles' . . . quiet, pollution-free, electric train system was totally destroyed. With the destruction of the Pacific Electric System, one historian has stated, Los Angeles may have lost its best hope for mass rapid transit. . . . The substitution of GM diesel buses, which were put on the streets, apparently benefited GM, Standard Oil, and Firestone considerably more than the riding public. The Pacific Electric System, with its extensive private rights of way, provided a more efficient system than buses on crowded streets.

"By 1949, General Motors had been involved in the replacement of more than 100 electric transit systems with GM buses in 45 cities including New York, Chicago, Philadelphia, Detroit, St. Louis, and Baltimore, besides Los Angeles. In April of that year, a Chicago federal jury convicted GM of having criminally conspired with Standard Oil of California, Firestone Tire, and others to replace electric transportation with gas- or diesel-powered buses, to monopolize the sale of buses and related products to local transportation companies throughout the country. The court imposed a sanction of $5,000 on GM. In addition, the jury convicted H. C. Grossman, who was the treasurer of General Motors. Grossman had played a key role in the 'motorization' campaign and had served as a director of the Pacific City Lines when the company undertook the dismantlement of the $100 million Pacific Electric System. The court fined Grossman the sum of one dollar."

And now Mayor Joseph L. Alioto of San Francisco:

"A demonstration of the terrifying power of the automobile monopoly occurred in the demise of the Key System that once linked San Francisco to Oakland and other communities of the east bay region. Key operated 180 electric streetcars and 50 sleek, fumeless, electric passenger trains across a right of way on the lower deck of the San Francisco–Oakland Bay Bridge. . . .

"In 1946, National City Lines, a holding company organized and financed by General Motors, acquired the controlling interest in Key's parent company. A scant two days later, GM's newly acquired transit company announced that streetcars would be replaced by buses. The buses, a fleet of 200 vehicles, were purchased during the next two years from GM.

"In 1954, Key announced its intention to replace its bridge trains with buses. The announcement came amid reports that the once sleek and comfortable trains had been allowed to deteriorate and that Key already had been running parallel buses on the transbay span.

"In early 1958, Key began demolishing its track system so that the bridge deck would be paved and readied for additional auto traffic. This occurred at a time when the embryonic BART Commission was making first plans for a transbay mass transit system and could have used the Key System bridge right of way. Ultimately, BART was forced to spend $180 million to make a transbay tube connection. . . ."

In a heated defense against these and many other charges of monopolistic practices, General Motors stated that the violation for which it was convicted was "a close point of law" and said "not one word" about eliminating street railway systems. Many of the lines had been abandoned before GM appeared on the scene. The company's lawyers argued that it had motorized service that was no longer "practicable," that the rail lines were worn out and could not show a profit. "Profitability" seems to be GM's only criterion, but it was long America's too. Mr. Grossman's fine of one whole dollar speaks volumes on that subject.

Constant Riders

It was not until some years after the decline of railroad passenger traffic set in, and track began to dwindle all over the country, that the companies themselves took notice of a strange and unexpected source of good will, the private enthusiast, who was known, somewhat demeaningly, as a "rail fan." At first, it must be admitted, management sneered at him. This devotee was a lost-cause man, a crank at best, and at worst a thorn in the side of the company lawyers when he turned up at public utility commission hearings to protest the abandonment of this or that branch line.

You could make a monkey out of him in a minute, the attorneys discovered. Get him on the stand and it would turn out that his best argument for keeping on the old, unprofitable local to the junction was that he liked to hear the whistle blow. And you could demolish his case by proving that most of the protest delegation had come to the hearing not by rail but by automobile. In the ensuing laughter, of course, the commissioners overlooked the fact that the company, seeking to make the service as unpopular as possible, ran the only train on the line between five and six in the morning, or on odd Thursdays, and at about eight miles an hour, treating its very existence like a military secret. Still, the train fanciers only multiplied. The automobile was losing its former quality of excitement. As the makes grew more alike and the thrill wore off, the old, neglected train seemed, by constrast, to recapture a lot of its former power and charm. It had the dignity and exquisite melancholy of age, and its huge, snorting bulk exerted a kind of magic. The man at the hearing could not put it into words, but that was why he had come.

After a while the railroad public relations men gave the enthusiast a tentative welcome. They let him into the roundhouse, but they never glimpsed his soul. They offered him a "fan trip" on the main line when he preferred the weed-grown branch. Finally, when they capitulated to this whim and produced a diesel engine and streamlined car for the ride, they were astonished all over again when he begged instead for steam. Could he ride, please, in the locomotive cab? To the astonishment of the working crew, he wondered if it would be all right for him to help shovel coal. That he would do until he dropped. Simple rewards, like being allowed once or twice to pull the whistle cord, were accepted with gratitude, while the firemen sat back in unaccustomed leisure.

Through a kind of underground, the rail enthusiasts learn when *Old 77* is going to make her last run, or when the branch is to be closed; they turn out by the thousands ready to swap endless pictures, old timetables, tickets, post cards, even rusty spikes. They jabber away happily in railroad jargon, sometimes going further than the railroad men themselves: Every engineer is a "hogger," the passenger train always "varnish," each rusty rail line a "pike." It is usually necessary to break out anything that will move to carry the hordes on the "last ride," and sometimes a few more rides after that. Through the cars pass other enthusiasts hawking souvenirs of all sorts, buttons with anti-diesel slogans, authentic denim caps, badges with heralds of famous railroads, tie pins, enthusiast publications, recordings of railroad sounds, even notices of other planned wakes of the same kind. The hobby attracts men from all walks of life and levels of society. King George VI and the late Vincent Astor were enthusiasts, and William Gillette, the actor who so long played Sherlock Holmes, built a little railroad which circled its way up to his strange hilltop castle overlooking the Connecticut River at Hadlyme, Connecticut. The fan publications are numerous both in America and abroad. The most sizeable is *Trains* magazine, astutely edited by David P. Morgan for a circulation of some 64,000. Its parent company, A. C. Kalmbach of Milwaukee, Wisconsin, publishes an extensive library of specialized

What is an enthusiast without a camera? Eighty or ninety years but little else separate the dignified couple above, waiting for a train on the old Naugatuck Railroad in Connecticut, and the busy young man below, snapping "the action" on a rail fan special along the route of the vanished Berkshire Express. *He had got there just before the axe fell. The more extreme fans wear their hearts not only on their sleeves, but on every possible bare spot on their railroading costumes.*

Train buffs greet a giant Canadian 4-8-4 locomotive pulling a special excursion in Vermont.

and handsome picture books and histories (as does Howell-North of Berkeley, California). Another famous and beloved publication is *Railroad* magazine, edited by Freeman Hubbard and Gorton Wilbur in a little rabbit warren of railroad pictures and memorabilia adjoining Grand Central Terminal. These are only the most notable of many fugitive sheets, some of them ephemeral and many of them devoted to the most specialized interests, like, for example, the collectors of streetcar transfers. The classified advertising gives some indication of the enthusiasm of the addicts, like this item offering pictures of the Western Pacific Railroad:

> The Take Off! Wide open (running late), drivers spinning, hogger reefs her to the pin, down in the corner! . . . One of the most dynamic starts in steam I have ever lensed. Sound! L.I. L 3/4 complete, every train with desert background—clouds.

Like every other group in American life, the enthusiasts have formed their organizations, the earliest and in many ways most distinguished being the Railway and Locomotive Historical Society, organized in Boston in 1921 by the late Charles E. Fisher; the R & LHS *Bulletins* over the years are a valuable collection of railway history. There are many others, to be sure, like the National Railway Historical Society, the Railroad Enthusiasts, and the Electric Railroaders Association. Every religion, of course, has denominational problems. There are, for example, the model makers, whose great layouts in various scales often put major railroads to shame—men who will go to the trouble of building not only a railroad but a landscape around it and carry realism to the extent of painting false rust on the side of the track. There are the collectors of iron and tin toys, once discarded but now enormously valuable. And there are the trolley lovers, known as "juice fans," whose love object in its pristine form has almost disappeared from the scene.

The enthusiasts have their bards and their prophets, like the late Lucius Beebe, author of many railroad books and owner (with his partner Charles Clegg) of an operating private car. They also include the late Archie Robertson, who wrote delightfully of branch lines and mixed trains; Elliot Donnelley of the noted Chicago printing company, proprietor of several small private lines and organizer of week-long special steam excursions through the West; Everett DeGolyer of Dallas, Texas, collector par excellence of railroad books and pictures; John H. White, Jr., of the Smithsonian, locomotive expert and current editor at the R & LHS; Rogers E.M. Whitaker, the most constant rider of all, who in covering some two and one-half million miles to date has made his way along almost every piece of track in the Americas, Europe, Africa, India, and the Levant. His goal, which he will probably realize, is imperial: the rest of the world.

What organized enthusiasm can do is exemplified in the story of the narrow-gauge Silverton passenger service of the Denver & Rio Grande, which we have mentioned earlier in this book. In the mid-fifties this lonely survivor had dwindled to a twice-weekly mixed train, hauling a little freight and a single passenger car along the edge of the magnificent canyon of the Rio de las Animas Perditas. Application was made for abandonment, at which, sniffing death, the steam admirers took notice. Suddenly the car was full on every trip and it was necessary to add another car, and another, and more trips, until now, throughout the summer tourist months, the railroad is running long tourist trains with every available car and steam locomotive.

A few big railroads like the Southern and the Canadian National understand the enthusiasts and run steam excursions for them, but in the last few years, with nothing much left in the passenger line except Amtrak, they have usually had to shift for themselves. The astonishing result has been the sudden mushrooming all over the United States and Canada (and Great Britain, too)

On opening day, 1971, the restored all-steam Valley

Railroad of Essex, Connecticut, brings the first passengers in thirty-eight years into nearby Deep River, to be met by fifes, drums, and citizenry.

An ancient miniature steam engine from the Bridgton & Harrison, late of Maine but now installed on the seven-mile Edaville Railroad at South Carver, Massachusetts, drags its venerable varnish through the snow. The uneven places in the two-foot-gauge track are exaggerated by a telescopic lens. Edaville, which has a museum and much other historic equipment, is named from the initials of its late founder, E. D. Atwood, the cranberry king, and does a big year-round business.

of restored short railroads. The 1974 *Steam Passenger Service Directory,* which also includes restored trolley operations, lists over 110 operating lines, not counting other more static museums of the iron horse. Generally the enthusiasts have laid hands in some way on an old short line as it gave up the ghost, a section of country trolley, or a branch that no one wanted. About one jump ahead of the scrap dealer, they have acquired old locomotives and cars, restored them to life, and started running trains, at first mostly for themselves, but later, it turned out, for millions of unsuspected well-wishers among the general public. The little roads can be found all over the continent, from the beautifully restored four-and-one-half-mile Strasburg Railroad, with its period nineteenth-century equipment, near Lancaster, Pennsylvania, to the "Super Skunk" steam line through the redwoods, run by the California Western Railroad at Fort Bragg on the Pacific Coast. Pennsylvania, for example, has twelve restored railroad museums, as well as country trolleys and a narrow-gauge line, the East Broad Top of Orbisonia. A list of some of these operations can be found on page 315.

Sometimes the enthusiasts take on too much and fail financially. But they can also succeed famously, as in the case of the late Ellis D. Atwood, owner of an extensive cranberry operation in South Carver, Massachusetts, who vastly admired the old two-foot-gauge railroads of Maine. When the Bridgton

& Harrison Railroad stopped running with World War II, it was more than he could stand. He bought the railroad—tracks, switches, equipment (and a diminutive private car from the adjoining Sandy River and Rangeley Lakes Railroad)—and brought the whole business to South Carver. Eventually the old Down East lines were reborn among the bogs.

A group at Essex, Connecticut, has reconstructed an abandoned steam railroad along the beautiful lower valley of the Connecticut River. The enthusiasts in this case, among whom the author is one, not only have restored 1910–20 vintage trains, slowly clearing mile after mile of jungle growth from the old tracks, but have established daily connections with excursion boats on the river. The Valley Railroad's train, which is illustrated on page 295 reaching Deep River on its opening day, in July, 1971, carried fifteen thousand people in that season, and as the word spread, forty-five thousand, sixty thousand, and over seventy thousand in the next three years, at the same time steadily repairing more track and cars each year. Who are all these people streaming to Strasburg, to South Carver, to Silverton, to Essex? Many have never ridden on a train before. Few of them are "enthusiasts." They are everyman, answering the call of the bell and the whistle, proving once again that the passenger train, despite management's scorn and government's inattention, strikes some deep chord of affection within the American soul.

Making smoke for the photographers, a big Reading locomotive, long used to haul trainloads of rail fans, pauses during a main-line excursion organized by the High Iron Company. This enterprise was set up by New York commodity broker Ross Rowland, who also launched the Golden Spike Centennial steam train of 1969 and the American Freedom Train, now traversing all the continental states with a lively Bicentennial show on American history, and pulled by steam.

The Highway of the Future

What are we going to do about the troubled railroads of America? The conventional wisdom in Washington seems to be that we will do as little as possible to disturb the powerful highway trust and just enough to mollify the shippers, the "eco-freaks," and the tiresome constituents who insist on riding trains. The Nixon Administration scenario for passengers was Amtrak, whose barebones original map appears on the facing page. It is hard to escape the conclusion, simply by studying Amtrak's first directors and management and ridiculous underfinancing—way below the cost of a single "freeway"—that it was a kind of flimflam, designed to waste away faster than a new Chevvie and prove that no one really wanted trains outside of, perhaps, the Boston–Washington corridor. Yet, strangely enough, under improving management, it has grown steadily in ridership.

The game plan for freight, which was more important and necessary to big shippers, has struck a good number of observers as a kind of bail-out for the many interests caught in the bankruptcy of the huge Penn Central, together with such lesser red-ink roads as the Lehigh Valley, Ann Arbor, Jersey Central, Reading, and Lehigh & Hudson. The United States Railway Association, a government corporation, was created to devise a plan to solve the problems of all these weak Northeast railroads; it came up in February of 1975 with a two-volume book, the size of a big-city telephone directory, proposing to create still another merger. To be called ConRail, from Consolidated Rail Corporation, the giant combination of bankrupts would utilize fifteen thousand miles of track in a great quadrilateral area drawn roughly between Chicago and St. Louis and Boston and Norfolk. As much as seven to ten billion dollars in federal funds might be expended by the government in repairing the bad roadbeds and re-equipping the new company. Such a funding comes to less than half the average annual outlay for the interstate highway system alone, to be sure, but it is quite impressive compared with the original grant for setting up Amtrak; that was $40,000,000, with another hundred in government-backed borrowing powers.

Due attention was paid to shibboleths. There would be "competition," because two profitable eastern railroads, the Norfolk & Western and the Chessie (the combination of the Chesapeake & Ohio and the Baltimore & Ohio), would be invited to pick up some pieces of bankrupt lines as well—from the Erie-Lackawanna and the Reading—to provide alternative services in some part of the area. And there would be "profits," as much as $161,000,000 a year by 1980 and more later, predicted the USRA chief, Arthur D. Lewis, a former airline executive and investment banker, if . . . and the line of ifs was long and optimistic, not the least of them requiring inflation to be cut in half. The Norfolk & Western soon announced that it viewed the plan, and the lines to be bestowed on it, with intense skepticism. In the back accounting office of one bankrupt line, the Reading, someone carefully applied the proposed ConRail accounting methods and assumptions to Reading figures. Without changing the cash position at all, they converted a real $1,100,000 loss into a profit of $5,700,000.

That Congress might not allow ConRail to come to actual life was a possibility at this writing. One big hitch in the proposal was that it provided for simply abandoning 6,200 miles of unprofitable, deteriorated track, a goal which the bankrupts had been trying to achieve for years. Many cities and towns and factories, studying the detailed plans, saw themselves cut off from rail service, and the political uproar was predictable and intense. The USRA plan did propose a system of temporary subsidies to keep any of the so-called "light-density" lines going for two years if the states or localities were willing to meet 30 percent of the losses. Governors and mayors, however, are long on

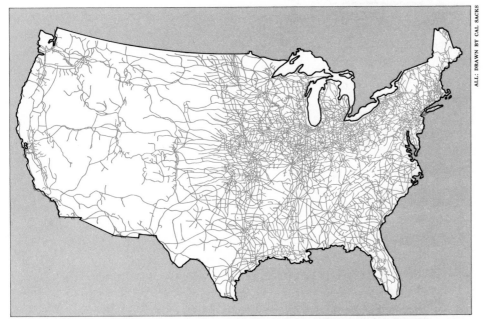

ALL: DRAWN BY CAL. SACKS

1950 map shows all 226,296 miles of railroad; of this, 147,511 miles carried passengers.

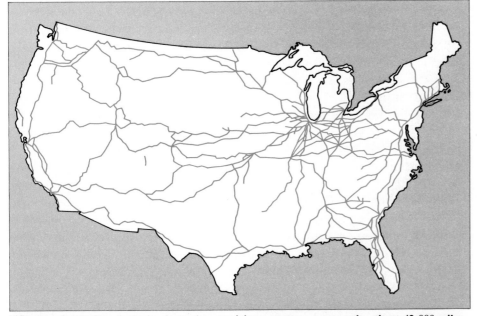

1971 map, just before Amtrak, shows then-surviving passenger routes only, about 42,000 miles.

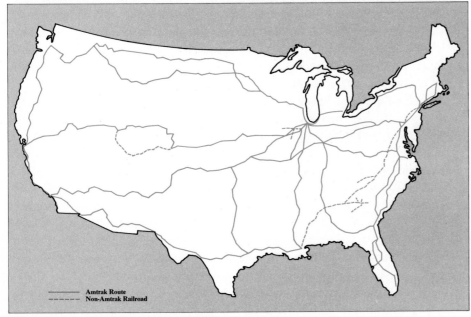

Amtrak Route
Non-Amtrak Railroad

1971 map shows first Amtrak system (21,000 miles), plus non-Amtrak passenger routes.

How passenger service declined within the last twenty-five years is demonstrated by these maps, although we caution readers that the one at top shows all major *railroads, freight and passenger, while the bottom two indicate only passenger lines, before and after Amtrak appeared on May 1, 1971. The total of all railroad route mileage in this country is still a little over two hundred thousand. Amtrak, whose formal name is the National Railroad Passenger Corporation, was set up by Congress in 1970 to relieve the railroads of the burden of their ailing passenger service. Thirteen companies paid the required lump sums to enter the new quasi-government corporation, but three decided to stay out and run their own skeletized services: the Southern, the Denver & Rio Grande Western, and the Rock Island. Commuter services and Autotrain were not involved. Under the Nixon Department of Transportation, Amtrak not only relied heavily on airline executives and their methods with everything from timetables to hostesses, and looked to the ideas of aerospace technology, but it aimed to show a profit. That the last goal, at least, was impractical soon became apparent. With a low volume, equipment at first totally and still mainly veteran, and with little control over the tracks or operating staff (who were still railroad employees with often low morale), costs skyrocketed so that Amtrak still loses 4.6¢ on every passenger mile. Trains were late, even though their schedules were frequently officially slower than those of five, ten, or twenty years before. Service was poor and sometimes rude. "Go take a bus!" shouted a ticket seller to his grumbling long line of would-be buyers, in the hearing of an official of NARP, the National Association of Railroad Passengers, the nonprofit gadfly organization which struggles to keep the roads up to the mark. Yet Amtrak, for all its fainthearted top management, which travelled by air itself, had a dedicated staff. And since March of 1975, it has a first-class authentic railroad man in charge, Paul H. Reistrup. New lines have been added already, and more will come. New engines are on the line in many places, and new cars on order. More of the staff now works for Amtrak, and business, all early predictions to the contrary, has grown. It is still only a toy train compared to European railroads, and funded on that basis, but the new management is at least trying to succeed.*

The coming of Amtrak on May 1, 1971, with passenger service cut in more than half, was a sad day for the working men, like the one above during the last days of the San Francisco Chief. It was bleak in Chattanooga's Union Station, whose bulletin board had already shrouded some trains, although with preposterous optimism it painted "On Time" after them all. The Dixie Flyer was gone, and the Georgian of April 30 was the last train from the once busy hub. Soon after, the depot, a "protected" landmark (1859), was razed.

outrage but short with ready cash. What was less noticed was that the abandonments proposed would fragment many hitherto continuous lines; for example, in Connecticut, five out of six lines heading north into Massachusetts would be cut at one point or more, leaving no alternative routes for trains in time of trouble or disaster and frustrating any future restoration of passenger routes when the energy shortage—as it will—grows worse. True foresight, history reminds us, is the rarest of all commodities, especially in political life. Such lightly used lines should at least be "banked" for the future.

If one views ConRail as Congress and the Administration require, as a regular, for-profit, tax-paying corporation, which should try to stand on its own eventually unsubsidized feet in the present American transportation system, it is hard to fault USRA. Anything that loses money, or has no reasonable potential for turning a profit, must go. The same kind of thinking applies, at least in theory, to Amtrak, which is supposed to operate for profit, to concentrate on winning lines and dispose of losers.

That thinking, however, is sheer fantasy; it verges on madness. The railroad is the only single segment of our chaotic transportation system which has been expected to behave like a private business, to build and maintain its own routes, supply all its own equipment, do its own signalling, and pay its full quota of taxes—indeed, much more than full. New Jersey, for one of many examples, for years taxed railroad property at 100 percent of valuation, three times the rate on other businesses. In the ten-year period of the 1950's, the Lackawanna paid New Jersey $32,000,000 in taxes, the exact amount of its collective loss on its passenger service. The railroads provide their own terminals, taxed of course. The tax on Washington, D.C.'s, Union Station in 1961, for another example, exactly equalled the deficit the government picked up that year on Washington's National Airport. Airports, air traffic controls, weather assistance, even outright subsidies have been provided airlines. For the trucker, the bus operator, and the automobilist everything has been provided by a bountiful government; related "user charges," only a modest portion of the outlay, all went to the highway trust fund for more highways. Even the rivers and canals have been dredged and improved out of the bottomless congressional pork barrel, until the waterway has become again an important competitor of the railroads, a ghost returned from the past.

Robert R. Young, then head of the New York Central, put the situation into a few pungent words: "There isn't any business man who could long survive if the Government went into competition with you and didn't have to pay the taxes you did. That is the problem we are facing."

Behind the fantasy and foolishness that brought the railroads low and created the present mess, there is a simple enough explanation. It is the idea, widely held in America, the land of "go-ahead," that almost any change is Progress, and with a capital P. The fact that in an even race, without favoring any contestant, the railroad is by far the most efficient method of ground transportation ever conceived was not even considered. Until the reawakening of recent years, newspapers were wont to treat the departure from town of the last passenger train as a purely nostalgic event, as if the railroad were like the stagecoach or the clipper ship, quaint, no doubt, but out of date. Something new was *ipso facto* something better. Speed was the measure of enjoyment, size the indicator of temporal success. If America, with only 5.7 percent of the world's population, had more than half its automobiles and most of its big highways—yes, and consumed 30 percent of its crude oil—then the good old U.S.A. was that much ahead of a pokey and backward world. Even railroad men seemed to share in that myth of Progress, and were fertile with ideas for discouraging passengers and getting rid of service; trains ran almost empty while ticket offices gravely informed would-be riders that they were sold out. The poor results would then be reported and accepted with a straight face at ICC abandonment hearings—although nothing will match the reason a New Haven Railroad executive once gave for discontinuing a heavily patronized weekend train: "It was so popular we couldn't handle it."

That something was wrong with this kind of thinking, that the conventional wisdom was in fact folly, we now realize. Cars have choked our cities until it often takes longer to get to the suburbs than it does for an astronaut to circle the earth. What was once a pleasure called "motoring" is all too often a nightmare of speed and danger, with the private driver fighting for his life against the traffic and careening trailer trucks. The death rate per annum in 1974 exceeded forty-six thousand—and it was more than nine thousand under the usual figure because of lower speeds during the fuel shortage. The total of the injured and maimed was 1,800,000, with incalculable social costs.

Carving up and defacing the landscape, the automobile destroyed the place it got one to, the once peaceful glade or quiet village. National parks like Yellowstone eventually had to shut the cars out. The internal combustion engine polluted the air with 80 percent of the carbon monoxide, not to mention the hydrocarbons and the lead. Its emissions were at best imperfectly controlled, and even then with such howls of anguish from Detroit that standards were lowered and rules postponed. Its fumes mixed with the atmosphere and bestowed upon us "smog" which killed the trees and even ate away the stone and steel of buildings, not to mention its effect on the human lung. Six million tons of rock salt, spread on the highways, were soon poisoning wells, waterways, wildlife, and even the general water table along the verges. The machines themselves were so hard to get rid of in most cities that as much as half of downtown needed to be turned over to parking or servicing them; in death their unsightly remains littered the landscape. Their waste oil fouled the sewers and rivers, the giant oil tankers that supplied them poisoned the seas themselves.

All this public policy created, and private citizens until recently accepted. The robber barons gave way to the rubber barons of Detroit, a three-part automobile monopoly so great as to make a Morgan or a Harriman look at his

Reduced to a lone coach, with that most hunger-deadening of all American eating facilities, a "snack bar," Penn Central's remnant of its great Boston to Chicago sleeping-car train, the New England States, *rolls past cut-up ties on the old Boston & Albany main line, a few days before Amtrak wiped that last Albany service from its card. This is the route which Amtrak has announced it will revive and which Penn Central tried to finish off by lifting twelve miles of track at Rensselaer, New York, as noted on page 284.*

In *The Freeway Failure*, a report prepared for the Third National Conference on the Transportation Crisis, 1972, Dr. George W. Brown, a researcher and consultant in the field, summed up from the public record what the trucking subsidy means:

"One example of special interest money which is illuminating is the record of trucking subsidy obtained from Federal Bureau of Public Roads and Commerce Department reports. During the years of 1968 and 1969, 12.3 billion dollars per year were collected in road use taxes and fees. Of this amount, 11.7 billion dollars were paid by automobile, bus, and small truck operators. Six hundred and eleven million dollars were contributed by interstate trucking operations. According to a study sponsored by the U.S. Bureau of Public Roads, one 72,000 lb. interstate truck causes as much damage to high grade pavements as 6000 passenger automobiles. Therefore, adjusting for deterioration of pavements per mile traveled, the tax structure should have been inverted, with the heavy interstate trucks contributing 12.1 billion dollars in road use taxes, and the other highway users 211 million dollars. *The motoring public was subsidizing heavy truck interstate freight shipments to the tune of 4.6¢ per ton per mile. If rail freight shipments had been subsidized at the same rate as truck freight during 1969, we would have paid the railroads a 35.6 billion dollar subsidy!*"

On to the horizon, mile after mile, go the glistening rails, the greatest highway of them all. This happens to be the main line of the Great Northern, old Jim Hill's arrow-straight railroad, near Doran, Minnesota, but it could be anywhere.

shoes in shame. The revenues of General Motors alone exceeded those of all the governments in this hemisphere save that of the United States. The discovery of the principle of built-in obsolescence only increased the sales and income. With its near monopoly in bus and diesel locomotive manufacture, General Motors succeeded in dieselizing electric railroads that should not have been altered. By calculated maneuvers for which it was fined, it destroyed invaluable urban transit systems. The public subsidized the automobile and gave the highway lobby a kind of added gift, a forty-one-thousand-mile system of interstates costing some $75 billion, which was like building a largely free new railroad system for the truckers. The lobby's naked power in Washington, transcending that of any mere political party, simply kept the juggernaut rolling ever faster—although it must be added in fairness that the oil and auto trust did all this with a generally good conscience, as had Morgan or Rockefeller in their time. Everyone, after all, had a lobby. They saw no sin in subsidies or oil depletion allowances, in destroying railroads and transit systems; they waved aside the rising concern for the environment. What was good for General Motors was good for America. Were they not providing employment, carrying the people and business of America, and laying their tribute at the altar of Progress?

It has taken a series of blows—recession, the inability to move in cities, most of all the energy crisis—to shake our faith in total reliance on the automobile and the airplane, and to make us question our submission to their insatiable demands and worry about our lack of alternative modes of travel. Stockpiled railroad cars, for troop movements, were quietly scrapped. What would we do, some have wondered, in another war? In the course of that reexamination it has become clear that half a century ago we took the wrong fork in the road, that we wrote off the railroad too soon. Whether we look to the successful state-supported railroad systems of Europe or just to the idea of balanced transportation, it is obvious that we have misinterpreted the meaning of "progress." It is not simply change, or bigness, or even speed, it is the application of common sense to human needs. Not the least of these, as the Founding Fathers put it so well, is "the pursuit of happiness," of which there is a simple corollary, that it should not be pursued at the expense of someone else's. The airliner of a progressive society would sacrifice some size and speed, of which it has aplenty, in order not to brutalize vast settled areas around the airports. The automobile roads of such a society would neither overwhelm nor deafen its cities and towns, and would respect its wildernesses

and quiet places; largely excluded from the central cities, they would serve their original rural or small-town purposes, going where public transportation did not. The cars themselves would be modest in size, economical of fuel, perhaps powered more by electricity or alcohol, inexpensive because not perpetually "restyled" by hustling manufacturers. Un-American as the idea sounds, they might have durable, old-fashioned workmanship. The big truck, so arrogant that it constantly transgresses the speed limit, would give way to containers or trailers moved by rail, taking the roads only for short delivery distances. It should no more terrorize the highways of a well-designed society than a fast freight train should roar at full speed down Main Street, because there is a better means available: the private right of way of the railroad.

What can the railroad do? One track can carry forty to sixty thousand people an hour in comfort, as against a six-lane highway, which can handle only nine thousand in the same time, each driver fighting all the way. In fuel expended per passenger mile the railroad is twelve times more efficient than the automobile, and fifteen times more than the airplane. It is more efficient than the bus, which is less comfortable and suffers from the same traffic paralysis as the private car. In consequence even diesel trains pollute the air less, and electric ones least of all. On a per-mile-travelled basis, the railroad is two and a half times safer than a plane, and twenty-three times as safe as the automobile. It was once, and can be again, the most delightful way to go.

None of this is new, but now we are going to have to do some thinking of the unthinkable. The government will probably have to go back to first principles, perhaps owning and maintaining the railroad network as it does the highways, and allowing private companies to operate the trains. Such a program has growing support, and many believe that, on a basis of fair competition, the profit motive could again provide first-class service for both freight and passengers. Healthy railroads will require extensive electrification, more hydroelectric power, more of everything. Only competition between manufacturers, such as exists in most Western countries, can spur the development of new ideas, keep down prices, and give every mode of transportation a chance to develop, but it is not likely to appear so long as one giant corporation dominates the scene. Our transportation system needs surgery, not Band-Aids. Whether this will come to pass depends of course on whether we have the common sense to bring it about. Common sense has as yet a very small lobby, yet it seems to say, unmistakably, that the flanged wheel on the long steel rail is the true highway of the future.

16. Epilogue: Two Railroads

RICHARD STEINHEIMER, FROM THE DEGOLYER LIBRARY, S.M.U.: STEAM AT GLENDALE, CALIFORNIA, 1948

There are always two railroads; they run side by side yet in spirit thousands of miles apart. One is the railroad of top officials and bottom lines, whether red or black; the railroad so beset by regulators that accountants must keep 258 separate sets of records just for the ICC; the railroad of space-age technologists busily designing Buck Rogers equipment for Casey Jones tracks; the railroad of featherbedders, snappish ticket agents, and service homogenized at the plebeian level; the railroad of the bankruptcy courts, a corpse feasted on by regiments of lawyers; that is, the railroad of polemics.

The other railroad is better sought on the plains or in mountain valleys, or best of all down by the depot at night, when darkness casts it charitable shadows and where fathers and sons of a certain turn of mind are apt on occasion to visit. This other railroad is our most ancient show of "sound and light," with its mysterious and compelling pantings, clankings, hissings, and authoritative voices in dimly lit places; with its thundering procession of giant cars gathering speed until it is harder and harder to make out the romantic names and heraldry—whereupon, in an instant, the roar ends and nothing remains but twin red lights disappearing into the night. At home in bed the generations of such fathers and sons have listened to the steam whistle or the air horn blowing in the distance, the magic voice that still speaks of strange cargoes, far places, and unrealized dreams. This is the railroad of memory, but also, for all its anguish, the railroad of today, which somehow keeps going; the railroad they believe in their hearts will never cease to run.

Bibliography

Abdill, George B., *Civil War Railroads*, New York, Bonanza (1961)
    Rails West, Seattle, Superior Publishing Co. (1960)
Adams, Charles F., Jr., and Henry, *Chapters of Erie and other essays* (1871)
Adams, Kramer A., *Logging Railroads of the West*, New York, Bonanza (1961)
*Adlake Trimmings for Railway Cars and Steamships, Catalogue No. 127, Chicago (1911)
Alexander, Edwin P., *Down at the Depot*, New York, Clarkson N. Potter (1970)
    The Pennsylvania Railroad, New York, W.W. Norton & Co., Inc. (1947)
Allen, Frederick Lewis, *The Great Pierpont Morgan*, New York, Harper (1949)
Association of American Railroads, *Railroad Transportation, A Statistical Record 1911–1951*, Washington, D.C. (March, 1953)
Athearn, Robert G., *Rebel of the Rockies, The Denver & Rio Grande Western Railroad*, New Haven, Yale University Press (1962)
Baker, George Pierce, *The Formation of the New England Railroad Systems*, Cambridge, Harvard University Press (1937)
Beebe, Lucius, *Highball*, New York, D. Appleton-Century Co. (1945)
    Mansions on Rails, Berkeley, Howell-North Books (1975)
    Mixed Train Daily, Berkeley, Howell-North Books (1975)
Beebe, Lucius and Clegg, Charles, *Hear the Train Blow*, New York, E. P. Dutton & Co. (1952)
Best, Gerald M., *Iron Horses to Promontory*, San Marino, Golden West Books (1969)
Binzen, Peter and Daughen, Joseph R., *The Wreck of the Penn Central*, New York, New American Library (1971)
Bishop, Morris, "Selections from the Journeys of Samuel J. Parker," No. 4, *The Cornell Library Journal* (Autumn, 1969)
Botkin, B. A. and Harlow, Alvin G., eds., *A Treasury of Railroad Folklore*, New York, Bonanza (1953)
**Brown, William H., *The History of the First Locomotives in America*, New York, D. Appleton & Co. (1871)
Bruce, Alfred W., *The Steam Locomotive in America, Its Development in the Twentieth Century*, New York, W.W. Norton & Co. (1952)
Bruce, Robert V., *1877: Year of Violence*, Indianapolis, Bobbs-Merrill (1959)
**Clarke, Thomas C., *The American Railway*, New York, Charles Scribner's Sons (1889)
Cochran, Thomas C., *Railroad Leaders 1845–1890*, New York, Russell & Russell (1965)
Combs, Barry B., *Westward to Promontory*, Palo Alto, American West Publishing Co. (1969)
Daggett, Stuart, *Railroad Reorganization*, New York, Houghton Mifflin (1908)
Dodge, Grenville M., *How We Built the Union Pacific Railway*, Ann Arbor (1910). Reprint University Microfilms (1966)
Droege, John A., *Passenger Terminals and Trains* (1916). Reprint Milwaukee, Kalmbach Books (1969)
Dubin, Arthur D., *Some Classic Trains*, Milwaukee, Kalmbach Books (1964)
    More Classic Trains, Milwaukee, Kalmbach Books (1974)
Edmonson, Harold A., ed., *Journey to Amtrak*, Milwaukee, Kalmbach Books (1972)
Educational Facilities Laboratories, Inc., *Reusing Railroad Stations*, New York (1974)
Fishlow, Albert, *American Railroads and the Transformation of the Antebellum Economy*, Cambridge, Harvard University Press (1965)
Fogel, Robert William, *Railroads and American Economic Growth; Essays in Econometric History*, Baltimore, Johns Hopkins University Press (1964)
Griswold, Wesley S., *Train Wreck!*, Brattleboro, The Stephen Greene Press (1969)
    A Work of Giants: Building the First Transcontinental Railroad, New York, McGraw-Hill (1962)
Hamblen, Herbert Elliot, *The General Manager's Story*, New York, The Macmillan Co. (1898)
Handy Railroad Atlas of the United States, Chicago, Rand McNally & Co. (1973)
Harlow, Alvin F., *The Road of the Century*, New York, Creative Age Press (1947)
    Steelways of New England, New York, Creative Age Press (1946)
Henry, Robert S., "The Railroad Land Grants Legend in American History Tests," *Mississippi Valley Historical Review*, Vol. XXXII, No. 2 (1945)
    This Fascinating Railroad Business, Indianapolis, Bobbs-Merrill (1942)
Henwood, James N. J., *A Short Haul to the Bay*, Brattleboro, The Stephen Greene Press (1969)
Hilton, George W. and Due, John F., *The Electric Interurban Railways in America*, Stanford, Stanford University Press (1960)
Holbrook, Stewart H., *The Age of the Moguls*, Garden City, Doubleday & Co., Inc. (1956)
    The Story of American Railroads, New York, Crown Publishers (1947)
Howard, Robert West, *The Great Iron Trail*, New York, Putnam (1962)
Hubbard, Freeman H., *Railroad Avenue*, New York, McGraw-Hill (1945)
Hungerford, Edward, *Men & Iron*, New York, Thomas Y. Crowell Co. (1938)
    Men of Erie, New York, Random House (1946)
    The Story of the Baltimore & Ohio Railroad 1827–1927, New York, Putnam (1928)
Huntington, C. P., "California, Her Past, Present and Future," a speech given at the Annual Dinner, Southern Pacific Co., San Francisco (1900)
Interstate Commerce Commission, *Railway Statistics Before 1890*, Washington, D.C. (1932)
    Statistics of Railways in the United States, Washington D.C. (1901)
Johnson, Robert Underwood and Buel, Clarence Clough, eds., *Battles and Leaders of the Civil War*, New York, The Century Co. (4 vols., 1884–1887)
Kennan, George, *E. H. Harriman*, Boston, Houghton Mifflin (2 vols., 1922)

Kindig, R. H., Haley, E. J., and Poor, M. C., *Pictorial Supplement to Denver South Park & Pacific*, Denver, Rocky Mountain Railroad Club (1959)
Kraus, George, *High Road to Promontory*, Palo Alto, American West Publishing Co. (1969)
Laut, Agnes C., *The Romance of the Rails*, New York, R. M. McBride (1929)
Lewis, Edward A., *New England Country Depots*, Arcade, New York, The Baggage Car (1973)
Lewis, Oscar, *The Big Four*, New York, Alfred A. Knopf (1946)
Lindsey, Almont, *The Pullman Strike*, Chicago, Chicago University Press (1964)
Lyon, Peter, *To Hell in a Day Coach: An Exasperated Look at American Railroads*, Philadelphia, Lippincott (1968)
McAdoo, William G., *Crowded Years*, Boston, Houghton Mifflin (1931)
Marshall, David, *Grand Central*, New York, McGraw-Hill (1946)
Martin, Albro, *Enterprise Denied, Origins of the Decline of the American Railroads 1897–1917*, New York, Columbia University Press (1971)
Mason, Alpheus Thomas, *Brandeis, A Free Man's Life*, New York, Viking (1968)
Mead, Edgar T., Jr., *"Busted and Still Running,"* Brattleboro, The Stephen Greene Press (1968)
Meeks, Carroll L. V., *The Railway Station*, New Haven, Yale University Press (1956)
Mencken, August, *The Railroad Passenger Car*, Baltimore, The Johns Hopkins Press (1957)
Middleton, P. Harvey, *Railways and Organized Labor*, Chicago, Railway Business Association (1941)
Middleton, William D., *The Interurban Era*, Milwaukee, Kalmbach Books (1961)
    The Time of the Trolley, Milwaukee, Kalmbach Books (1967)
Mohr, Nicolaus, *Excursion Through America*, Chicago, The Lakeside Press (1973)
Moody, John, *The Railroad Builders*, New Haven, Yale University Press (1920)
Morse, Victor, *Thirty-six Miles of Trouble*, Brattleboro, The Stephen Greene Press (1973)
**Mott, Edward Harold, *Between the Ocean and the Lakes*, New York, John S. Collins (1899)
National Safety Council, *Accident Facts, 1975 Edition*, Chicago (1975)
O'Connor, Richard, *Iron Wheels and Broken Men*, New York, Putnam (1973)
The Official Guide of the Railways, New York, National Railway Publication Co., (1868–1975)
Parks, Pat, *The Railroad that Died at Sea*, Brattleboro, The Stephen Greene Press (1968)
Perlman, Selig, *A History of Trade Unionism in the United States*, New York, The Macmillan Co. (1922)
Plowden, David, *Farewell to Steam*, Brattleboro, The Stephen Greene Press (1966)
    The Hand of Man on America, Washington, D.C., The Smithsonian Institution Press (1971)
Poor, M. C., *Denver South Park & Pacific*, Denver, Rocky Mountain Railroad Club (1949)
Reed, Robert C., *Train Wrecks*, New York, Bonanza (1968)
Reinhardt, Richard, *Out West on the Overland Train*, Palo Alto, American West Publishing Co. (1967)
    Workin' on the Railroad, Palo Alto, American West Publishing Co. (1970)
Ripley, William Z., *Railroads: Rates and Regulation*, New York, Longmans, Green (1927)
Robertson, Archie, *Slow Train to Yesterday*, Boston, Houghton Mifflin (1945)
Rolt, L.T.C., *The Railway Revolution: George and Robert Stephenson*, New York, St. Martin's Press (1960)
Russell, Charles Edward, *Stories of the Great Railroads*, Chicago, Charles H. Kerr & Co. (1912)
**Smiles, Samuel, *Lives of the Engineers; George and Robert Stephenson*, London, John Murray (1879)
**Smith, E. Boyd, *The Railroad Book*, Boston, Houghton Mifflin (1913)
Southerland, Thomas C., Jr., and McCleery, William, *The Way to Go*, New York, Simon & Schuster (1973)
Stover, John F., *American Railroads*, Chicago, University of Chicago Press (1961)
Tarbell, Ida M., *The History of the Standard Oil Company* (1902). Reprint New York, Peter Smith (1950)
Thomas, Lately, *Delmonico's*, Boston, Houghton Mifflin (1967)
U.S. Department of Transportation, Federal Railroad Administration, Office of Safety, *Accident Bulletin*, Washington, D.C. (1973)
U.S. Railway Association, *Preliminary System Plan for Restructuring Railroads in the Northeast and Midwest Region pursuant to the Regional Rail Reorganization Act of 1973*, Washington, D.C. (Feb. 26, 1975)
U.S. Senate, Subcommittee on Antitrust and Monopoly of the Committee on the Judiciary, *The Industrial Reorganization Act*, Hearings, 93rd Cong., 2d sess., on S. 1167, Parts 3 and 4A, Washington, D.C. (1974)
Weber, Thomas, *The Northern Railroads of the Civil War 1861–1865*, New York, Columbia University, Kings Crown Press (1952)
Weissenborn, G., *American Locomotive Engineering*, New York (1871)
Weller, John L., *The New Haven Railroad*, New York, Hastings House (1969)
Whitaker, Rogers E. M. and Hiss, Anthony, *All Aboard with E. M. Frimbo*, New York, Grossman (1974)
White, John H., Jr., *American Locomotives, An Engineering History 1830–1880*, Baltimore, The Johns Hopkins Press (1968)
    ed., *Early American Locomotives*, New York, Dover (1972)

*Author's collection volume, illustrations from which are reproduced in these pages.

Operating Railroad Museums

For those wishing to ride some of the restored steam railways and trolley lines mentioned on pages 293–297, we include this list of some of the more interesting operations. It is taken with kind permission from the Steam Passenger Service Directory, published every June on behalf of the Empire State Railway Museum Inc., Marvin H. Cohen, Editor. The directory itself is illustrated and gives complete information on every line; it may be obtained for $2.50 by writing to the Empire State Railway Museum, P.O. Box 666, Middletown, New York, 10940. Since we cannot be responsible for the possibility that some line may not be operating, or may have given up the ghost, we recommend a telephone call first. The numbers are included. All are steam operated save the trolley lines. Steam is indicated by S, trolleys by T. NG stands for narrow gauge.

California: Bay Area Electric Railroad Association, T, Rio Vista Junction, (707) 374-2978. California Western Railroad, S, Fort Bragg, (707) 964-3798. Orange Empire Trolley Museum, T, Perris, (714) 657-2605. Roaring Camp & Big Trees Railroad, NG-S, Felton, (408) 335-4484. Sierra Railroad, S, Jamestown, (209) 532-6835 or (209) 984-5388. Yosemite Mountain-Sugar Pine Railroad, NG-S, Fish Camp, (209) 683-7273
Colorado: Colorado Central Railway, NG-S, Central City, (303) 279-9670. Cripple Creek & Victor Railroad, NG-S, Cripple Creek, (303) 689-2640. Denver & Rio Grande Western Railroad, NG-S, Durango, (303) 247-2733. Georgetown Loop Railroad, NG-S, Silver Plume, (303) 279-9670
Connecticut: Branford Electric Railway, T, East Haven, (203) 469-9627. Connecticut Electric Railway Association, T, Warehouse Point, (203) 623-7417. Valley Railroad, S (connects with riverboat excursions), Essex, (203) 767-0103
Delaware: Wilmington & Western Railroad, S, Greenbank, (302) 998-1930
Florida: Gold Coast Railroad, S, Fort Lauderdale, (305) 522-2937
Georgia: Southern Railway System, S (occasional special trips on various lines), Atlanta, (404) 522-6414. Stone Mountain Scenic Railroad, S, Stone Mountain, (404) 469-9841
Hawaii: Lahaina, Kaanapali & Pacific Railroad, NG-S, Lahaina (Maui), (808) 661-0089
Illinois: Crab Orchard & Egyptian Railroad, S, Marion, (618) 993-5769. The Fox River Line, T, South Elgin, P.O. Box 752. Illinois Railway Museum, S, T, Union, (815) 923-7488. Monticello & Sangamon Valley Railway, S, Monticello, (217) 382-1481 or (217) 762-9201
Maine: Seashore Trolley Museum, T, Kennebunkport, (207) 967-2712
Maryland: Baltimore Streetcar Museum, T, Baltimore, (301) 727-9053. National Capital Trolley Museum, T, Wheaton, (301) 384-9797
Massachusetts: Edaville Railroad, (2-foot) NG-S, South Carver, (617) 866-4451
New Hampshire: Conway Scenic Railroad, S, North Conway, (603) 447-5832. Mount Washington Cog Railway, S, Mount Washington, (603) 846-5404. Wolfeboro Rail Road, S, Wolfeboro, (603) 569-4884
New Jersey: Black River & Western Railroad, S, Ringoes-Flemington, (201) 782-6622. Morris County Central Railroad, S, Newfoundland, (201) 697-8446. Pine Creek Railroad (N.J. Museum of Transportation), NG-S, Allaire State Park, 07727
New Mexico: Cumbres & Toltec Scenic Railroad, NG-S (65 miles), Chama-Antonito, Colorado, (505) 756-2151
New York: Arcade & Attica Railroad, S, Arcade, (716) 496-9877. Cooperstown & Charlotte Valley Railway, S, Cooperstown, (607) 547-2555. Livonia, Avon & Lakeville Railroad, S, Livonia, (716) 346-3559
Ohio: Hocking Valley Scenic Railway, S, Nelsonville, (614) 451-7863. Ohio Railway Museum, S, T, Worthington (near Columbus), (614) 885-7345
Oregon: Oregon Electric Railway Historical Society, T, Glenwood, (503) 357-3574. Oregon Pacific & Eastern Railway, S, Cottage Grove, (503) 942-3368
Pennsylvania: East Broad Top Railroad, NG-S, Orbisonia, (814) 447-3011. New Hope & Ivyland Railroad, S, New Hope, (215) 862-5206. Shade Gap Electric Railway, T, Orbisonia, (814) 447-9576 (weekends only). Strasburg Rail Road, S (with Pennsylvania State Railway Museum adjoining), (717) 687-7522
South Dakota: Black Hills Central Railroad, S, Hill City–Custer, (605) 574-2222
Tennessee: Clinchfield Railroad, S (irregular), Erwin, (615) 743-9161. Tennessee Valley Railroad Museum, S, Chattanooga, (615) 622-5908 or (615) 265-8861
Utah: Wasatch Mountain Railway, S, Heber City, (801) 654-2621
Vermont: Steamtown Foundation (large museum), S, Bellows Falls, (802) 463-3937
Washington: Lake Whatcom Railway, S, Wickersham, (206) 595-8858
West Virginia: Cass Scenic Railroad, S, Cass, (304) 456-4300
Wisconsin: Kettle Moraine Railway, S, North Lake, (414) 782-8074. Laona/Northern Railway, S, Laona, (715) 674-2391. Mid-Continent Railway Museum, S, North Freedom, (608) 522-8805. National Railroad Museum, S, Green Bay, (414) 437-9775

Canada
British Columbia: British Columbia Forest Museum: Cowichan Valley Railway, NG-S, Duncan, (604) 748-9389. British Columbia Railway, S, North Vancouver, (604) 987- 5211
Manitoba: Prairie Dog Central, S, Winnipeg, (204) 452-7024
Nova Scotia: Cape Breton Steam Railway, S, Glace Bay, (902) 562-6876
Ontario: Canadian National Railways, S (irregular), Toronto, (416) 367-4300. Halton County Radial Railway, T, Rockwood, P.O. Box 121, Scarborough, Ont. Ontario Rail Association, S (irregular), Toronto, (416) 451-9523

Permissions

Grateful acknowledgment is made for permission to reprint material from the following works:

Autobiography by Andrew Carnegie. Copyright renewed 1948 by Margaret Carnegie Miller. Reprinted by permission of Houghton Mifflin Company, Boston and New York.
The Complete Poems of Emily Dickinson edited by Thomas H. Johnson. Published by Little, Brown and Company, Boston.
The Electric Interurban Railways in America by George W. Hilton and John F. Due. Copyright © 1960 by the Board of Trustees of the Leland Stanford Junior University. Reprinted by permission of Stanford University Press.
To Hell in a Day Coach by Peter Lyon. Copyright © 1967 by Peter Lyon. Reprinted by permission of J. B. Lippincott Company, Philadelphia and New York.
Internal Revenue by Christopher Morley. Copyright © renewed 1961 by Helen F. Morley. Reprinted by permission of J. B. Lippincott Company, Philadelphia and New York.
"Journeys of Samuel Parker" edited by Morris Bishop, from *Cornell Library Journal*, Autumn, 1969.
Sixes and Sevens by O. Henry. Reprinted by permission of Doubleday & Co. Inc.

Acknowledgments

The author and the staff wish to express their deep appreciation to the following individuals and institutions who kindly gave them special help in obtaining illustrations and information for this book, as well as advice and research assistance.

Edwin P. Alexander, Yardley, Pennsylvania
Albany Institute of History and Art: Norman S. Rice, Director
Railway Employees Department, AFL-CIO: Robert Ostrowitz
Association of American Railroads: Anne Bennof, Peggy Burns, Frank Danahay, Kenneth Hurdle
John W. Barriger, Washington, D.C.
Jacques Barzun, New York City
Blair & Ketchum's Country Journal, Brattleboro, Vermont: Richard M. Ketchum, Editor
Stephen Bogen, New York City
Brotherhood of Locomotive Engineers, Cleveland
James Burchard, New Haven
Burlington Northern Railroad: Patrick Stafford
Bruce Catton, New York City
Chicago Historical Society: Mary Frances Rhymer, John Tris
Church of Jesus Christ of Latter-Day Saints: K. Habron Adams

Colorado State Historical Society, Denver
DeGolyer Library, Southern Methodist University, Dallas: Everett L. DeGolyer, Sue Herzog Johnson
Denver Public Library, Western History Department
Denver, Rio Grande & Western Railroad Company
Educational Facilities Laboratories, Inc., New York
The Family Lines, Louisville: Edison Thomas
Henry Morrison Flagler Museum, Palm Beach
Charles Barney Harding, New York City
Herbert G. Harnish, Fort Wayne
Herbert H. Harwood, Jr., Assistant Editor of *Railroad History* Magazine, Baltimore
Mrs. Jack E. Haynes, Bozeman, Montana
Amos Hewitt, North Stonington, Connecticut
ITT Rayonier: Roy Peacher
Library of Congress: Jerry Kearns
Richard F. Lind, Cedar Glen, California
Stephen D. Maguire, Belmar, New Jersey
David McLane, Brewster, New York
Edgar T. Mead, Hanover, New Hampshire
National Archives
National Association of Railroad Passengers: Orren Beaty, Anthony Haswell, Charles W. Schoeneman
National Safety Council, Chicago: Robert J. Peszek
Northeast Transportation Coalition: Mrs. Lettie Gay Carson

Oakland Museum, California
Andrew Pavlucik, Milford, Connecticut
Penn Central Railroad: Robert Benish, Charles Dunlap, Cecil Muldoon, Ed Nowak
David Plowden, Sea Cliff, New York
Railroad Magazine, New York City: Freeman Hubbard, Editor; Gorton T. H. Wilbur, Associate Editor
Railway & Locomotive Historical Society, William Wait
Cal Sacks, New York City
Santa Fe Railroad: Bill Burk, Jerry Curto, Robert Gehrt
Allen A. Sharp, Groton, Connecticut
Sheet Metal Workers International Association: J. W. O'Brien, Vice-President
National Museum of History and Technology, The Smithsonian Institution, Washington, D.C.: John H. White, Jr., Curator of Transportation
Southern Pacific Railroad: George Kraus, William Robertson
Southern Railway System: James Bistline, Vice-President
Richard Steinheimer, Cedar Glen, California
Union Pacific Railroad: Barry B. Combs, Valerie Young
United Transportation Union
Valley Railroad Company, Essex, Connecticut
Robert Wayner, New York City
Rogers E. M. Whitaker, New York City

Index

Page numbers in **boldface** *refer to illustrations.*

A

Accidents/disasters/wrecks, 25, 27, 53, 138, 145, 174, 176–88, **176–87**, 199, 213, **282**; boiler explosions, 178, **184**, **185**, 187; brakes and brake failures, 182, 184, **185**, 188, 189, **189**; "cornfield meets," 179; federal investigation of, 186; and fire, 22, 25, 178, **179**, 182, **182**, 183, 188; floods, 39, **106**, **107**, 138, **184**, 188; in popular literature and press, **170**, 178, **179**, **182**; in popular song, **174**, 178; staged, **186–87**; "telescoping," **185**, 188; and train crews, 178, 186, **188**, **189**, 194, 196, 198, 199, 201; *see also* Safety measures
Active, **245**, 246
Adams, Charles Francis, Jr., **52**, 53, 92, 108, 117–18, 186
Adams, John Quincy, 186
Adams Express, 65
Atkins, T. L.: engraving by, **13**
Adlake (Adams and Westlake) Company, 230
Adonis, 46
Advertising: by engine builders, **44**, 45, **45**; by interurbans, **252**, **254–55**, **256**; on railroad cars, **167**; by railroads, **168**, **169**, **224–25**, **228**, **229**, **238**, **246**, **247**, **250–51**
Aerotrain, 269
Air brakes, 144, 182, 188, 189, **189**, 199
Airlines, 300; vs. railroads, 282, 290, 299, 302, 303
Ajax, 46
Alaska-Yukon-Pacific Exposition (1909; Seattle), 117
Albany & Susquehanna Railroad, 142
Alburgh Express, 246
Aldrich, Nelson, 153, 155
Alioto, Joseph L., 291
Allegheny Portage Railroad, 38–39
Allen, Horatio, 20, 26, **26**, 27, 45
Allen, William Frederick, 144
America, 49
American City Lines, 291
American Federation of Labor, 160
American Freedom Train, 297
American Locomotive Company, 49, 262, 263, 265, 269
American Railway Union, 159
American Telephone & Telegraph, 152
Ames, Oakes, **89**, 91, 92, 93, 94
Ames, Oliver, 91
Ames family, 286
Ammonoosuc, 46
Amoskeag Manufacturing Company, **46–47**
Amtrak (National Railroad Passenger Corporation), 7, 36, 84, 240, 282, 284, 289, 290, 294, 298, 300, 301; 1971 route map, **299**
Andalusia, Florida & Gulf Railroad, 251
Andrews, James J., and Andrews Raid, 71, **74**, 74–77
"Angola Horror," 182, **182**
Ann Arbor line, **248–49**, 298
Appleton's Railway & Steam Navigation Guide: illustration from, **145**
Argent lumber railroad, **306–07**
Armstrong, George B., 199
Arthur, Chester A., 110
Ashtabula (Ohio) wreck, 182, 182–83, 186
Astor, Vincent, 293
Atalanta, 46
Atchison & Topeka Railroad, 111
Atchison, Topeka & Santa Fe Railway, 111, 113, 149, **219**, 236, **248–49**; *California Limited,* **225**, **228**, **229**, 238; freight, **273**, **274**, **275**, **277**; Royal Gorge and Raton Pass, 111, **112**, 113; *Santa Fe de-Luxe,* **238**
Atlanta: Civil War and railroads, 58–81 *passim,* **58–77** *passim*
Atlanta & West Point Railroad, 60
Attila, 46
Atwood, Ellis D., 296–97
Austin, Henry, 206–07
Automotive industry, 153, 160, 300–01, 302, 303; vs. interurbans, 255, 258, 291; vs. railroads, 8, 235, 282, 293, 302, 303; *see also* Highways and turnpikes
Autotrain, 290, 299

B

Baird, Matthew, 49
Baker, George F., 152, 153
Baldwin, Matthias William, **48**, 49
Baldwin Locomotive Works, 45, 48–49, 152, 262, 263, 269
Baltimore: interurban, 291; Mount Royal Station, **204–05**
Baltimore & Ohio Museum, 307
Baltimore & Ohio Railroad, 20, 22, 28, 29, **32**, 35, 156, 158, 184, 236, **237**, 268, 278, 282; Chesapeake & Ohio merger (Chessie), 298; John Brown's raid and Civil War, 63, 65, 70, 81, 158; stations, **204–05**, 206
Bamberger, Simon, 257
Bamberger lines, 257
Bangor Express, 53
Bar Harbor (Me.): limited to, **224–25**
Beame, Abraham, 84
Beebe, Lucius, 251, 294
Belfast & Mooshead Lake Railroad, 246
Benham's City Directory and Annual Advertiser: on New Haven Station, 206–07
Bensinger, William, 77
Benton, Thomas Hart, 97
Berkshire Express, 293
Berkshire line (trolley), **257**
Bernard, George, 139, 141
Best Friend of Charleston, 26, 27, **27**, 45
Big Shanty Museum (Kennesaw, Ga.), 77
Billard, John L., 153, 155
"Black Friday," 141, 142
Blaine, James G., 91
Blenkinsop, John, 14–15
Blucher, 15
Boston: railroads and stations, **34**, 35, 56, 206
Boston & Albany Railroad, 216, 246, 284, 301
Boston & Lowell Railroad, **34**; Charles Dickens on, 50–51
Boston & Maine Railroad, **34**, 35, 52, 53, 150, 153, 155, 178, 216, 244; *Boston & Mt. Desert Limited,* **224–25**
Boston & Mt. Desert Limited, **224–25**
Boston & Providence Railroad, **34**
Boston & Worcester Railroad, 32, **34**
Boston Herald, 28–29
Boston, Revere Beach & Lynn Railroad, **248**
Boyd, J. J., 24
Bradford, 46
Bradley, Thomas, 291
Brady, James B. (Diamond Jim), 152, 153
Bragg, Braxton, 66
Braithwaite, John, 16
Brakemen, 156, 160, **188**, **189**, 194; *see also* Railroad workers
Brakes and brake failures, 182, **184–85**, 188, **189**; *see also* Air brakes
Brandeis, Louis D., 152
Branford Electric Railway, 252
Brooks, James (locomotive builder), 49
Brooks, Representative James, 92, 93
Brooks, John W., 56
Brotherhood of Locomotive Engineers, 160
Brotherhood of Locomotive Firemen, 159, 160
Brotherhood of Railroad Trainmen, 161
Brown, George W.: *The Freeway Failure,* 302
Brown, John, 60, **60**, 63
Brown, William H.: "The First Locomotives in America," 25; silhouette by, **24**
Bryan, William Jennings, 186
Bryce, James, 110, 133, **133**; *American Commonwealth,* 133, 136
Buchanan, James, 85
Buffalo, 97, 111, 123, 124, **124–25**
Building News, 206
Burlington Northern Railroad, 290
Burlington Railroad *see* Chicago, Burlington & Quincy Railroad
Burnham, D. H., 207

C

Caboose, **198**
California Limited, **225**, **228**, **229**, **238–39**
California Western Railroad, 296
Cambridge (N.Y.) station, 219
Cambridge City (Ind.) station, **286**
Camden & Amboy Railroad, 20, **20–21**, 25, 39, 186
Camden & Atlantic Railroad, 192
Campbell, Henry R., 47–48
Camp Hill disaster, 180, 182
Canaan (Conn.) station, **286–87**
Canada: railroads and rail links with, 35–36, 119, 236, 289, 294; Mennonites, 119; short-line railroads, 294, 296
Canadian National Railway, 294
Canals and waterways, 15, 20, 22, 25, 26, 32, 34, 56; Delaware & Hudson Canal Company, 20, 26; Erie Canal, 20, 22, 25, 28, 32, 35, 36; *see also* Steamboats and ferries
Carbaugh, Henry, **53**
Carnegie, Andrew: *Autobiography,* 202
Carrabassett, 46
Carroll, Charles, 28
Carrollton Viaduct (Relay, Md.), 28, **28**
Carson, Mrs. Lettie Gay, 284
Casement, Dan, 97
Casement, Jack, 93, 97, 98
Casey, "Bat," **195**
Cassidy, "Butch," 128, 129
Cavanagh, Tom, 203
Central New England Railroad, **150**, **218**, 246, **286–87**
Central Pacific Railroad, 84–88 *passim,* **86–87**, 88, **90**, 91, 98, 99–100, 106, **153**, 175; Chinese construction crews, 84, **97**, 98, 99, 100; and finance, 85, 87, 88, 104, 149; *see also* Pacific Railroad; Southern Pacific Railroad
Central Railroad (of Georgia), 149
Central Railroad of New Jersey, 263, 268, 298; stations, 207, **279**, **285**, 288
Century of Progress Exposition (1933; Chicago), 268
Chapin, Chester W., 56
Charleston Courier, 26, 27
Chattanooga: Union Station, **300**
Chattanooga National Cemetery, 77, **77**
Cheneyville (Conn.) station, 219
Chesapeake & Ohio Railroad, 28, 148, 283; Baltimore & Ohio merger (Chessie), 298
Cheshire, 246
Chessie (Baltimore & Ohio Railroad and Chesapeake & Ohio Railroad), 298
Chicago: Century of Progress Exposition, 268; interurbans, 252, 256, 257, 291; railroads and stations, 54, 56, **56–57**, 63, **206**, **209**; World's Columbian Exposition, 77, 222–23, 233
Chicago & North Western Railroad, 54, 209, 283
Chicago, Aurora & Elgin (interurban), 257
Chicago, Burlington & Quincy Railroad, 56, 105, 149, **234**; *Pioneer Zephyr,* 268, **269**
Chicago, Milwaukee, St. Paul & Pacific Railroad, 251, **270–71**
Chicago-New York Electric Air Line Railroad, 256, **257**
Chicago, Rock Island & Pacific Railroad, 56, **123**, 152, **158–59**, 282, 299; special emigrant ticket, **131**
Chicago Times, 238
Chief see San Francisco Chief
Chinese construction crews, 84, **97**, 98, 99, 100, 108, 130, 131
Chrysler, Walter, 269
Cincinnati & Lake Erie Railroad, 257
Circus trains, **166–67**, **184**
Civil War and railroads, 48, 56, 57, **58–59**, 60, **61–74**, 63, 65, 66, 70–72, 74–78, 81; Andrews Raid, 71, **74**, 74–77, **77**
Clark, Horace, 143
Clark, John T., 25
Clayton Act (1914), 283
Clegg, Charles, 294
Cleveland, Grover, 147, 159
Cleveland & Toledo Railroad: "Angola Horror," 182, **182**
Clinton, DeWitt, 25
Coal, 20, 26, 35, 45, 144, 169, 194, 195, 203, 262, 263, **273**, 284; in England, 12, 13, 14, 15, 17, 28
Cobden, Richard, 54

Cody, William F. ("Buffalo Bill"), 111
Coffin, Lorenzo, 188, **189**
Cog railways, 244, **248**; early experiments, 14, 15
Colfax, Schuyler, 91, **98**, 99
Collins, Charles, 186
Colorado: narrow-gauge railroads, 113, 116–17, 294; route map, **110**
Colorado & Southern Railway, 113, **308–09**
Colorado Midland Railroad, **109**
Columbus, Hocking Valley & Toledo Railroad, **187**
Commodore, **62**
Conductors, **24**, 35, 50, 131, 156, 160, 192, **193**, 194, 195, **227**; *see also* Railroad workers
Connecticut Company (trolleys), 257
Connecticut Valley Electric Transit, advertisement for, **252**
ConRail (Consolidated Rail Corporation): proposal for, 298, 300
Construction crews, 40, **62–63**, 84, **102–03**, 108, **116**; Chinese, 94, **97**, 98, 99, 100, 108, 130, **131**; Irish, 40, 84, **97**, 98, 99, 108; Mormons, 104, 108; sleeping accommodations, 97, **116**; *see also* Railroad workers
Cooke, Jay, **105**, 107–08, 111
Cooke & Company, Jay, 105, 107–08
Coolidge, Calvin, 228
Cooper, Peter, 26, 28–29, **29**, 45, 142
Corbin, Abel, 141
Cornell, Ezra, 52, **52**
Cornell University, 52
Corning, Erastus, **24**, 25, 36, 139
Corsair (steam yachts), 147, 148, 283
Coupling, automatic, 144, **188**, 189, 199
Crazy Horse, 124
Crédit Mobilier, 89, 91–92, 94, 95, 98, 104, 286; stock certificate, **94**
Cripple Creek line, 117
Crocker, Charles, 87, 88, **88**, 98, 99, 100, 104
Crockett, Davy, 26
Crush, William G., 187
Cuban Special, **200–01**
Cugnot, Nicolas, 13, 14
Cullom, Shelby M., 156
Cumberland Valley Railroad: stations, **208**
Currier and Ives: "The Great Race for the Western Stakes, 1870," **136**; "A Kiss in the Dark," **227**
Custer, George Armstrong, 72
Custer, Ted, 195
Cyclone, 46

D

Daggett, Stuart: *Railroad Reorganization,* 117
Dakotas: immigrants and homesteaders, **120–21**, 123, 124
Danforth, Cooke & Co., 53
Daniels, George H., 240
Davis, Gussie L.: "In the Baggage-Coach Ahead," **174**
Davis, Jefferson, 85
Davis, William, 235
Davy, Sir Humphry, 13
Debs, Eugene Victor, 159, **159**
DeGolyer, Everett, 294
Delaware & Hudson Canal Company, 20, 26
Delaware & Hudson Railroad: stations, 218, **219**
Delaware, Lackawanna & Western Railroad, 40, 158, 162, **162–63**, 300; "Phoebe Snow," **169**; *see also* Erie-Lackawanna Railroad
Denver & Rio Grande Railroad/Denver & Rio Grande Western Railroad, 105, **113**, 117, 199, **260–61**, 299; Durango-Silverton line, 116, 117, 294; narrow-gauge lines, 113, 116, 117, 294; Royal Gorge and Raton Pass, 108, 111, **112**, 113, 117
Denver Pacific Railroad, 105
Denver-Pueblo-Cañon City lines, 113
Denver, South Park & Pacific Railroad, **106**, 117–18, 160
Depew, Chauncey, **143**, 148
Depots *see* Stations/depots/terminals
Detroit United Railway: route map, **254–55**
DeWitt Clinton, **24**, 25, 36
Dey, Peter A., 91, 93
Dickens, Charles, **51**; *American Notes,* 50–51
Dickinson, Emily, **50**; poem by, 50
Diesel locomotives *see* Locomotives, diesel
Dillon, Sidney, 91, **95**

Dining and dining cars, 117, **172**, **225**, **236**, **237**, 246, 290; on interurbans, 252, 256; "snack bars," **301**; station facilities, 131, **236**
Disasters *see* Accidents/disasters/wrecks
Dispatchers, 198, **202**; *see also* Railroad workers
Dix, John A., 88
Dixie Flyer, 300
Dobbin, John: sketch by, **18–19**
Dodge, Grenville Mellen, 72, **85**, 93, **94–95**, 96–97, 98, 100, **101**
Donnelley, Elliot, 294
Dorsey, Daniel, **77**
Douglas, Stephen A., 54
Drew, Daniel, 136–37, 138; "Erie Ring" and Vanderbilt, 136–42 *passim*, **140**
Drew (side-wheeler), 137
Dreyfuss, Henry, 268
Dripps, Isaac, 20
Duff, John, **95**
Dumaine, Frederick C., 283
Dunn, Tom, 198
Durango-Silverton line *see* Denver & Rio Grande Railroad
Durant, Thomas C., 88, 91, **94–95**, 96, 98, 99, 100

E

East Broad Top line, 296
Eastern Railroad of Massachusetts, **34**, 53
Eckert, T. T., 70
Edaville Railroad, 296–97, **296–97**
Edwardsburg (Mich.) station, **220–21**
Eidlitz, C. L. W., 206
Einstein, Albert, 13
Electric Bond & Share, 257
Electric lighting, 188, 224
Electric Railroaders Association, 294
Electric railroads and engines, **204–05**, 256, **257**, 268, 269, 270, **270–71**, **276**, 302, 303; *see also* Interurbans and street railways
Electro-Motive Corporation, 268–69
Elkins Act (1903), 156
Emerson, Ralph Waldo, 56, 63
Emigrants *see* Immigrants
Empire State Express, 139
Engineering, 25, 26, 28, 39, 40, **40**, 85, 105, 111, 116, 118; Florida East Coast Railway, 244; Georgetown Loop, **114–15**, 117; Horseshoe Curve, **38–39**, 39; Northern Pacific, **102–03**, 108; Pacific Railroad, **82–83**, 84–100 *passim*, **86–87**, **90**, **92–93**, 93, **96**, **97**, **99**, **100**; Royal Gorge, **108**, 111, **112**, 113, 117; *see also* Bridges/viaducts/trestles; Civil War; Tunnels
Engineers ("hoggers"), **24**, **26–27**, 27, 45, 156, 160, 192, 194, **194**, **195**, 195–96, 198, **199**, 293; Brotherhood of Locomotive Engineers, 160; *see also* Railroad workers
England: bridges, 17, **17**, **18–19**; collieries and coal transport, 12, 13, 14, 15, 17, 28; emigrants, 122; narrow-gauge lines, 116; railroads, 12–17, **14–19**, 20, 22, **23**, 26–27, 28, 46, 48, 49; short-line railroads, 294, 296; stagecoaches, 15; stations, 206, 207
English Electric Company, 17
Ericsson, John, 16
Erie Canal, 20, 22, 25, 28, 32, 35, 36
Erie-Lackawanna Railroad, **169**, 298
Erie Railroad, 26, 32, 39–40, **40**, **41**, 52–53, 65, 72, 179, **196**, 283; broad gauge, 39, 40, **53**, **54**, 116; and finance, 136, 137, **137**, 138–39, **140**, 141, 142, 148, 149, 186; and Vanderbilt, rivalry, **134–35**, **136**, 137, 138–39, **140**, 141, 147; wages and strikes, 138, **155**, 156, 158, wrecks, 138, 186–87; *see also* Erie-Lackawanna Railroad
Europe: railroads, 268, 269, **299**, 302; *see also* England
Evans, Oliver, 13–14, 26
Evarts, William Marcy, 110, 111

F

Fall River Line (steamboats), 141–42, 153, **246**; route map, **151**
Fast Mail (of Lake Shore & Michigan Southern), **164**
Fast Mail (of Southern Railway), 174, 183
Federal Express, **185**, 188
Ferries *see* Steamboats and ferries
Field, David Dudley, 136
Fillmore, Millard, 40
Finance, 25, 32, 39, 40, 54, 105, 107, 111, 124, 270, 282–84, 289, 298, 300, 304; Amtrak, 298; "Black Friday," 141, 142; Central Pacific, 85, 87, 88, 104, 149; Chicago, Rock Island & Pacific, **282**; Clayton Act, 283; ConRail, 298, 300; Jay Cooke & Company, 105, 107–08; Crédit Mobilier, 89, 91–92, 94, 95, 98, 104, 286; Denver, South Park & Pacific, 117, 118; Erie, **136**, 137, 138–39, **140**, 141, 142, 148, 149, 186; Great Northern, 118, 119; holding companies and interlocking directorates, 257, 283; Illinois Central, 148, 149; interurbans, 257–58; Kansas Pacific, **111**; Money Trust, 152, 160; New York Central, 147, 148, 149, 283; New York, New Haven & Hartford, 152, 153, 155, 160, 283; Northern Pacific, 105, 107–08, 110, 111, 148; Pacific Railroad, 88, 91, 92, 149; Panic of 1837, 32, 35, 54; Panic of 1873, 108, 118, 123; Panic of 1893, 148; Panic of 1907, 147, 155; Penn Central, 283, 284, 298; Pennsylvania Railroad, 147, 148; rates, 144, 152, 155–56, 283–84, 289, 290; robber barons and stock manipulation, 39, 40, 63, **134–37**, 136–60, **140–44**, **146**, **148–51**, **153**, 282–83; Sherman Anti-Trust Act, 283; short-line railroads, 246, 250; Southern Pacific, 149; taxation, 7, 289–90, 300; Union Pacific, 88, 91–92, 93, 94, 104, 105, 117, 148–49; Henry Villard, 108, 110, 111, **133**
Firemen, **26–27**, 27, 156, 160, 194–95, **195**, 203, 262; Brotherhood of Locomotive Firemen, 159, 160; *see also* Railroad workers
Firestone Tire and Rubber Company, 291
Fisher, Charles E., 294
Fisk, James, 137–38, **140**, **141**, 142; "Erie Ring" and Vanderbilt, 136, **136**, 137, 138–39, **140**, 141, 142, 147; Fall River Line, 141, 142
Fitchburg Railroad, **34**, **35**; Thoreau on, **50**; *see also* Boston & Maine Railroad
Flagler, Henry M., 144, 244
Floods (and railroads), 39, **106**, 107, 138, **184**, 188
Florida East Coast Railway, **242–43**, 244
Flying Dutchman, 26
Flying Express, **178**
Folklore and legend: railroad men, 187, 192; in song, 126, **174**, **175**, **183**, 201
Forbes, John Murray, **55**, 56, 105
Ford, Henry, 160
Franklin, Benjamin, 13
Fratus, Harold, 244
Fredonia (Kans.) station, **219**
Freight/freight trains, 20, 25, 26, 32, 34, 35–36, 48, **48–49**, 49, 54, 63, 104, 119, 144–45, 152, **166–67**, **173**, 188, 189, 194, 264, 268–69, 270, **270–75**, 282, 284, 289, 298; advertising on cars, **167**; fast-freight, 144; federal government, 54, 65, 119 (*see also* Civil War; Mail, transport of; World War I; World War II); intermodal containers, **275**; on interurbans, 153, 252, **257**; mixed trains, 247, **247**, **278**; piggy-backing, **274**; rates, 144, 152, 155–56, 284; revenue ton-miles, 274; tramps, **235**; unit trains, **273**
French, Harry, 199
"Frisco Railroad" (St. Louis-San Francisco Railway), 274
Frugality, 46
Fuller, Annie Laurie, 74
Fuller, W. A., 74, 75, 76
Fulton, Robert, 13

G

Galena & Chicago Union Railroad, 54
Garfield, James A., 91, 186
Garrett, John W., 63, 158
Gauge *see* Tracks, gauge
General, 74, **74**, 75, 77, **77**
General Motors Corporation, 258, 269, 291, 301; *Aerotrain*, 269
George VI, King, 293
George, Dave: "The Wreck of the Old 97," 174, **183**
Georgetown, Breckinridge & Leadville Railroad, **114–15**
Georgetown Loop, **114–15**, 117
George Washington, 49
Georgian, 300
Georgia Railroad, 39, 60
Georgia State Railroad *see* Andrews, James J., and Andrews Raid
Germans: construction crews, 40; immigrants, 34–35, **120–21**
Germany, West: transportation, 7
Giant, 46
Gibson, Charles Dana: *Love's Express*, **170**
Gillette, William, 293
Gladstone, William Ewart, 54
Gold and Gold Rush, 35, 85, 123; "Black Friday," 141, 142; J. P. Morgan and Panic of 1907, 147
Golden Spike Centennial (train), 297
Goliath, 45
Gould, George, 149
Gould, Jay, 104, **105**, 108, 113, 117, **134–35**, 136, 156, 160, 250; "Erie Ring" and Vanderbilt, 136, 137, 138–39, **140**, 141, 142; and Russell Sage, 136, 142, 148
Government: Elkins Act, 156; freight 54, 65, 119 (*see also* Civil War; Mail, transport; World War I; World War II); Hepburn Act, 156; Interstate Commerce Act, 186; land grants, 54, 65, 85, 88, 91, 106–07, **118–19**, 124; Pacific Railroad Acts, 87–88, 91, 96, 98, 105, 106; railroad charters, 85, 87, 105, 106; Railroad Safety Appliance Act, 188, 189, 199; and railroads today, 302, 303 (*see also* Amtrak; ConRail; Penn Central); railroad strikes, 158, **158–59**; railroad surveys, 85, 105; transportation and subsidies, 289, 300 (*see also* Airlines; Automotive industry; Canals and waterways; Highways and turnpikes); United States Railway Association, 298, 300; *see also* Interstate Commerce Commission; Supreme Court
Gowan & Marx, 49
Grand Trunk line, **248–49**
Grangers and Granger laws, 152, **152**, 153, 156
Grant, Donald, **116**
Grant, Ulysses S., 71, 72, **94**, 96, 98, 110, 111, **141**, 246
Grasse River Railroad, 247, 250
Gravers Lane (Pa.) station, **219**
Great Falls & Conway Railroad, **219**
Great Northern Railroad, 105, 116, 118, 119, 122, 159, **274–75**, **302–03**; route map, **110**
Great Western Railway of Canada, 36, 236
Greeley, Horace, 104, 108
Green, Henry, 186
Green Mountain Flyer, 246
Griswold, Wesley: *Train Wreck*, 183
Grossman, H. C., 291

H

Hackworth, Timothy, 16
Halleck, Henry W., 70
Hamblen, Herbert E.: *The General Manager's Story*, 194, 195–96
Haney, Henry, **77**
Hannibal, 46
Hannibal & St. Joseph Railroad, 199
Hanover Branch Railroad, 78
Hanover Junction (Pa.) station, 78, **78–79**
Harding, Warren G., 141
Harlem Railroad (New York & Harlem Railroad), 40, 138–39, **143**, 208, **310**, **311**; *see also* New York Central Railroad (and system)
Harney, William A., **95**
Harper's Weekly: illustrations, **35**, **145**, **179**
Harriman, Edward Henry, 148, 149, **149**, 152, 153, 250, 282
Harrisburg (Pa.) station, **208**
Harrison, Joseph, Jr., 48, 49
Harte, Bret, 100
Harvey, Frederick Henry, 236
Haupt, Herman, 66, **66–67**, 71, 72, 78
Haynes, F. Jay: photograph by, **107**
Hazard, John N., 246
Hedley, William, 15
Heinz, H. J., 257
Helleu, Paul, 216
Hemingway, James S., 155
Henry, Edward Lamson: paintings by, **20–21**, **24**, 25, **42–43**
Henry, O. (William Sidney Porter), 126; train robbery story, 126–29
Henry, Robert Selph, 118
Henwood, James N. J.: *A Short Haul to the Bay*, 246
Hepburn Act (1906), 156
Hercules, 46
Hiawatha, 46
Hicks, Thomas, 179
High Iron Company, 297
Highways and turnpikes, 8, 25, 28, 32, 34, 148, 153, 258, **280–81**, 289, 298, 300, 302–03; *see also* Automotive industry; Stagecoaches
Hill, James Jerome, **117**, 118–19, 122, 124, 160, 169; 222; Great Northern, 105, 116, 119, 122, 159, **302–03**; Northern Pacific, 148, 149
Hinckley Locomotive Works, **45**
Hoar, George, 84–85
Holbrook, Stewart, 144, 174, 221; *The Story of American Railroads*, maps from, **118**, **119**
Holliday, Cyrus K., 111
Holly, Henry Hudson, 207
Holmes, Dr. Oliver Wendell, 179
Holmes, Justice Oliver Wendell, 283
Hood, John B., 71–72, 77
Hooker, Joseph ("Fighting Joe"), 70
Hopkins, Mark, 87, 88, **88**, 104
Hoppel, Alfred F., 180, 182
Horses, 13–17 *passim*, 20, 26, 28, 29, **249**; *see also* Stagecoaches
Horseshoe Curve, **38–39**, 39
Howe, William, 186
Howell-North Press, 294
Howells, William Dean, 233
Hubbard, Freeman, 294
Hudson River Bridge, **143**
Hudson River Railroad (New York Central & Hudson River Railroad), 80, **136**, 142, **143**, 147, **195**, 207–08, **264**; *see also* New York Central Railroad (and system)
Hungerford, Edward, 63
Hunt, Richard Morris, 139
Huntington, Collis P., 87, 88, **88**, 91–92, 100, 104, 113, 149, 153, 156, 160, 283
Huntington, Henry, 153
Huntington Library, 153
Huskisson, William, 17

I

Illinois Central Railroad, 54, 56, 65, 119, 148, 149, 174
Immigrants, 34–35, 40, 54, **118–23**, 119, 122–23, 124; emigrant trains, **123**, **130**, 130–31, **169**, 178; *see also* Construction crews; Land grants
Indianapolis: interurbans and station, **253**, **254–55**
Indians, 52, 88, 96–97, 98, 106–07, 123–24, 131
Inness, George: *Lackawanna Valley*, **162–63**
Inebriate's Express, **170–71**
Insull, Samuel, 257, 283
International Harvester Company, 148
Interstate Commerce Act (1887), 186
Interstate Commerce Commission, 284, 301, 304; establishment of, 156; investigations by, 148, 149, 155, 160; regulation and rates, 7, 283, 284, 290
Interurbans and street railways, 105, 136, 153, 246, 252, **252–59**, 256–58, **262**, 268, **283**, 289, **290**, 291, 294, 296; vs. automotive industry, 255, 258, 291; freight and mail carried by, 153, 252, **257**; parlor/palace cars, 252, **257**; railroad-owned, **150–51**, 153, 155, 244, 257, **257**, **262**, 268
Irish: construction crews, 40, 84, **97**, 98, 99, 108; immigrants, 35
Iron: cast, for locomotives, 262; cast, for rails, 13–17 *passim*; cast, for stations, 208; cast or wrought, for boilers and engine parts, 13; freight, 35, 144; for rails, 13, 16–17, 65, 97, 144, 178, 187; strap, for rails, 22, **24**, 28, 36, 65
Iron Mountain line, **218**

J

Jackson, Thomas Jonathan ("Stonewall"), 63, 66, 156
Jackson, William H.: photographs by, **108**, **114–15**, **186–87**

James, Frank, 126
James, Jesse, 126
James, Thomas L., 201
Janney, Eli H., 188
Jason, 46
J. C. Ayers, 46
Jersey Central *see* Central Railroad of New Jersey
Jersey City (N.J.) station, 207, 278, **285**
Jervis, John B., 25, 26, 47
John Bull, 20
Johnstown flood, 38, 188
Jones, "Canada Bill," **227**
Jones, John Luther ("Casey"), 174, 187, 195
Joseph, Chief, 124
Judah, Theodore Dehone, **84**, 85–88, 100
Judd, Jasper B., 187
Jupiter, **100**

K

Kalmbach, A. C., 293–94
Kankakee & Urbana (interurban), 257
Kansas: immigrants and homesteaders, **119**, **122–23**, 123
Kansas City Southern Railroad, 283
Kansas Pacific Railroad, 105, 111, **124–25**
Kemble, Fanny, **16**
Kennecott Copper Corporation: railroad, **276**
Killingworth (Eng.) Colliery, 13, 15, 17
King, William R., 119
Kinsey, Darius: photograph by, **266–67**
Kittson, Norman W., 118
Knight, Jonathan, 28
Knight, William, 75, **77**
Knott, James Proctor, 132, **132**
Kuhn, Loeb & Company, 149, 152
Kurtz, Wilbur G., Sr.: painting by, **74**

L

Lackawanna Railroad *see* Delaware, Lackawanna & Western Railroad; Erie-Lackawanna Railroad
Lackawanna & Wyoming Valley Railroad Company (interurban), 256
Ladson (S.C.) station, **218**
Lake George (N.Y.) station, **218**
Lake Shore & Michigan Southern Railroad, 143; *Fast Mail*, **164**; wrecks, **182**, 182–83, 186; *see also* New York Central Railroad (and system)
Land grants, 54, 65, 85, 88, 91, 106–07, **118–19**, 124
Latrobe, Benjamin H., 28
Laurel Line (interurban): advertisement for, **256**
Lawrence, George R.: photographs by, **228**, **229**
Lawrence, Sir Thomas: portrait by, **16**
Lawrence Machine Shop: advertisement for, **44**
Ledyard, Lewis Cass, 153
Lee, Robert E., 63, 66, 70, 71, 72
Lee, William, 180
Lehigh & Hudson Railroad, 298
Lehigh Valley Railroad, 148, 158, 282, 292
Leslie's Illustrated, **154**; illustration from, **182**
Levy, Lester, 174
Lewis, Arthur D., 298
Lewis, Isaac, 52
Lewis, Roger, 284
Lightning, 46
Lima Locomotive Works, 269
Limited Trains, 139, 217, **224**, **238–39**, **240–41**, 244, **268**, 290
Lincoln, Abraham, 54, 56, 104, 108; Civil War, 65, 70, 71, 72, 78; funeral train, **80–81**, 81; Pacific Railroad, 87, 88, 91, 93, 96, 100, 106
Lincoln, Willie, 81
Lindbergh, Charles A., Sr., 152
Link, Theodore C., 207
Literature: popular, 126, 162, 170–71, 172–73, 178, 179, 182; for railroad fans, 293–94
"Little Joes," **270–71**
Liverpool & Manchester Railway, **13**, 17; Rainhill Trials, **16**, 17, 20, **26–27**
Livingston, Chancellor Robert R., 25
Locomotion No. 1, **15**, 16, 17, **18–19**
Locomotives: cabs, **195**; "camelback," 28; cowcatchers, 20; diesel, 263, 265, 268–69, **269**, 270, **277**, 302, 303, 312; electric, **204–05**, 268, 269, 270, **270–71**, **276**, 302, 303; gas-turbine, 269;

horse-drawn, 26; repair and maintenance, **200**; steam, **26**, **27**, **44**, **45**, 45–49, **100**, **107**, **164**, **165**, **260–61**, 262–63, **264–69**, 268–69, 277, **290**, **292**, 293, 294, **296–97**; steam—types: American, **44**, **45**, **46–47**, 47–49, 74, **74**, **264**, **265**, articulated, 253, **265**, Atlantic, **265**, Berkshire, **265**, Big Boy, 263, **265**, Challenger, **265**, Consolidation, **265**, Hudson, **265**, **268**, Mallet articulated compound, 262–63, **264–65**, Mikado, **265**, Mogul, **48–49**, **265**, Mountain, **265**, Niagara, **265**, Northern, **265**, **292**, Pacific, **265**, Prairie, **265**, Santa Fe, **261–62**, 262, Shay, **265**, switcher, **107**, **265**, ten-wheeler, **265**, Texas, **265**; steam—woodburners, **24**, 25, 45–49, **46–47**, 194
Loder, Benjamin, 40, 52
London & Birmingham Railway, 17
Long, Stephen H., 28
Long Island Railroad, 84
Long Key Viaduct (Fla.), **249**
Longstreet, James, 66
Lord, Eleazar, 40, **40**
Los Angeles: Pacific Electric Railway System, 153, 258, **290**, 291; route map, **291**
Louisville & Nashville Railroad, 65, 71, 77, **176–77**, **272–73**
Lowden, Frank O., 158
Lyon, Peter: *To Hell in a Day Coach*, 149

M

McAdoo, William Gibbs, 284
McCallum, Daniel C., 52–53, **65**, 68, 72
McClellan, George Brinton, 54, 56, 68
McGaffey, Elmer E., 167
McGinnis, Patrick B., 283
McKay, William, 60
McKim, Mead & White, 210–11
McKinley, William, 167
McMurtie, J. A., 113
Mail, transport of: interurbans, 252; railroads, 54, 63, **164**, **165**, 199, 201, 250; stagecoach, 32
Mail clerks, 183, **198**, 199, 201; *see also* Railroad workers
Maine Central Railroad, 150, 155
Mallet, Anatole, 263–64, 265
Mammoth Hot Springs Hotel, 168
Mansfield, Helen Josephine ("Josie"), **140**, 142
Marshall, Elysian Fields & Southwestern Railroad, 251
Martha's Vineyard: Railroad, 244, **245**, 246; steamboats, **151**, 244
Massachusetts: railroads, 32, 35, 36, 53, 56, 153, 206, 246, 300; stations, **34**
Masterson, "Bat," 113
Matthew, David, **24**, 25
Meade, George Gordon, 70, 78
Meeks, Carroll L. V., 215
Mellen, Charles S., **148**, 150–51, 152–53, 155, 156, 160, 256, 282
Memphis & Charleston Railroad, 27
Mennonites, **118–19**
Menk, Louis, 290
"Merriwell, Frank," **170**
Metroliner, 269
Mexican National Railway, 111
Michigan Central Railroad, 56, 158, 178
Michigan Southern railroad, 53, 178
Miller, G. MacCulloch, 153
Miller, John, 24
Miller, J. S., **195**
Mills, Darius Ogden, 124
Milwaukee Road *see* Chicago, Milwaukee, St. Paul & Pacific Railroad
Mining (and railroads), 85, 87, 98, 113, 116, 117, 123, 124; *see also* Coal; Gold and Gold Rush
Minot, Charles, 40, **52**, 52–53, 179
Missouri, Kansas & Texas Railway ("Katy"), 122, 187, 227
Missouri Pacific Railroad, 105, 218
Mitchell, O. M., 74, 75, 76
Mixed trains, 247, **247**
Mobile & Ohio Railroad, 72
Mohawk, 188
Mohawk & Hudson Railroad, **24**, 25, 36
Mohr, Nicolaus, 110
"Money Trust," 152, 160
Montague, Samuel, 100, **101**
Morgan, David P., 293
Morgan, J. Pierpont, **146**, 147, 149, 302; and

railroads, 147, 148, 149, 150, 152–53, 155, 160, 282, 283
Morgan, J. Pierpont, Jr., 283
Morgan & Co., J. P., 152
Morley, Christopher: *Internal Revenue*, "On Time," 202–03
Mormons, 124; construction crews, 104, 108
Morris & Essex Railroad, **42–43**
Morse, Victor: *Thirty-six Miles of Trouble*, 250
Morton, Levi P., 91
Morton Salt Company, **167**
Mott, Edward Harold: *Between the Ocean and the Lakes; the Story of Erie*, 52
Mount Royal, 246
Mount Washington (N.H.) cog railway, **248**
Mumford, Lewis, 8
Murdock, William, 14
Murphy, Anthony, 75, 76, **77**
Murray, Marion E., 169
Murray, Matthew, 14, 15
Museums, 25, 77, 104, 296, **296–97**; operating, list of, 315
Music: railroading songs, 126, **174**, **175**, 178, **183**, 201

N

Nantasket Beach line, **262**, 268
Nantucket: railroad and steamboats, **151**, 244, 246
Narragansett Pier Railroad, 246
Narrow gauge *see* Tracks, gauge
Nashville & Chattanooga Railroad, 71
Nast, Thomas: drawing by, **145**
National Association of Railroad Passengers, 299
National Car Builder, The, 117
National City Lines, 291
National Police Gazette, The, 126, 232
National Railway Historical Society, 294
Naugatuck Railroad, **293**
Nellie Bly, **290**
Newark & Granville Street Railway, 252
New Bedford: railroads and steamboats, 151, 153, 246
Newcomen, Thomas, 12
New Englander (magazine), 25
New England States, **301**
New Haven Railroad *see* New York, New Haven & Hartford Railroad
New Haven (Conn.) station, 206–07
New York & Erie Railroad *see* Erie Railroad
New York & Erie Telegraph Company, 52
New York & Harlem Railroad *see* Harlem Railroad
New York & New England Railroad, 150
New York & Western Union Telegraph, 52
New York Central Railroad (and system), 36, **36**, 39, 56, 116, **136**, 139, 142, 143, 147, 157, 158, **200**, **201**, 213, **219**, 233, 246, 268, 283; and finance, 147, 148, 149, 283; Grand Central Station, 207–08, **212**, **213**, 213–17, **214–15**; and Harlem Railroad (Harlem Division), 40, 138–39, **143**, 208, **310**, **311**; and Hudson River Railroad (Hudson Division), 81, **136**, 142, **143**, 147, **195**, 207–08, **264**; and Pennsylvania Railroad merger *see* Penn Central; Putnam Division, 282; *Twentieth Century Limited*, 139, 217, 238, **240–41**, 244, 268, 290; *see also* Lake Shore & Michigan Southern Railroad; Vanderbilt, Cornelius
New York City: Delmonico's Restaurant, 136, 137, **137**; Grand Central Station, 207–08, **212**, **213**, 213–17, **214–15**; interurbans, 105, 136, 291; Pennsylvania Station, **210–11**; railroads, 35, 63, 138, 139, 141, 282; Tammany, 138, 139, 141
New Yorker, The: cartoon from, **283**
New York, New Haven & Hartford Railroad, 148, 150–51, 152, 153, 155, 160, 188, 208, 213, 244, 246, 283, **286–87**, 301; and finance, 152, 153, 155, 160, 283; interurbans and steamboats owned by, 150–51, 153, 155, **257**, **262**, 268; route map, **150–51**
New York, Ontario & Western Railroad, 150, 153, 282
New York Sun, 95
New York Times, The, 7, 211, 298
New York, Westchester & Boston Railroad, 148, 155, 282

New York, West Shore & Buffalo Railroad, 147, 148; *see also* West Shore Railroad
New York World, 105
Niagara Belt Line (electric), **254–55**
Niagara Falls Suspension Bridge, 36, **36–37**, **143**
Nickel Plate Road (New York, Chicago & St. Louis Railroad), 283
Nome River Bridge, **248–49**
Norfolk (Conn.) station, 218
Norfolk & Western Railroad, 148, 298
Norris, William, 49
North Coast Limited, **225**
North Conway (N.H.) station, **219**
Northeast Corridor, 35, 282
Northeast Transportation Coalition, 284
North Easton (Mass.) station, **286**
Northern Central Railroad, 78, 208
Northern Pacific Railroad, **102–03**, 105, **106**, 107–08, 110–11, 119, 133, 148, 149; advertisement for, **168**; and finance, 105, 107–08, 110, 111, 148; *North Coast Limited*, **225**
Northern Securities Company, 149
North Pennsylvania Railroad, 180, 182
North Shore (Chicago interurban), 252, 256, 257
North Star & Mifflin Railroad, 251
Northumbrian, 16, 17
Norwich & Worcester Railroad, 22, 35
Novelty, **16**, 26, 45

O

Official Guide of the Railways and Steam Navigation Lines, 144, 244, 246
Ogden, William B., 54
Oil, 124, 265, 268, 300; oil trust, 144, 302 (*see also* Standard Oil)
Old Colony Railroad, **34**, 150, **190–91**, **286**; advertisement for, **246**
Old Ironsides, **48**
"Old Maud," 263
Olmsted, Frederick Law, 139, 286
O'Neill, William G., 28
Orange & Alexandria Railroad, **66–67**
Oregon & California Railroad, 108, **195**
Oregon Railway and Navigation Company, 108
Oruktor Amphibolus, 14, **14**
Overland Limited, 244

P

Pacific City Lines, 291
Pacific Electric Railway System, 153, 258, **290**, 291; route map, **291**
Pacific Express: wreck, **182**, 182–83
Pacific Railroad, 40, 84–88 *passim*, 91, 93, 96, 104, 149, **226**; and finance, 88, 91, 92, 149; meeting point at Promontory, Utah, 91, 97, 98–100, **100**, **101**, 104, 145, 282; *see also* Central Pacific Railroad; Union Pacific Railroad
Pacific Railroad Acts (1862, 1864), 87–88, 91, 96, 98, 105, 106
Palace cars *see* Parlor/palace cars
Palm Beach: Royal Poinciana Hotel, **242–43**, 244
Palmer, William Jackson, 111, **111**, 113, 116
Parker, Samuel J., 22, 25
Parlor/palace cars, 22, 45, **226**, **234**, 246; on interurbans, 252, **257**; Pullman Company, 117, 147, 158–59, 175, **200–01**, **222–23**, **224–25**, 227, **228–33**, 236, 238; Wagner Palace Car Company, 143, 147, 236; Woodruff Sleeping and Palace Car Company, 175
Parrott, Jacob, 77
Passenger travel (by airplane), 282, 290, **299**, 300, 302, 303
Passenger travel (by automobile) *see* Automotive industry
Passenger travel (by railroad), 7, 172, 222, **222–41**, 264, 268, 269, 278, 282, 283, 285, 289, 290, 293, 294, 296, 297, 298, 299, 300–01, 302, 303; Amtrak, 7, 36, 84, 240, 282, 284, 289, 290, 294, 298, 299, 300, **301**; baggage tags, **244**; cartoon, **283**; connecting vestibules for cars, 224; early trains, 17, 20, 22, **23**, **24**, 25, **26–27**, 33, 34, 48, 50; emigrant trains, **123**, **130**, 130–31, **131**, 169, 178; limited trains, 139, 217, **224**, **238**, **239**, **240–41**, 244, **268**, 290; mixed trains, 247, **247**; passes, free, 152, 156, 227, 246; resorts, sightseeing, and advertisements, 153, **168**, **169**, **224–25**,

238, **242–43**, 244, **245**, 246, **246**, **248–49**, **250–51**, 257, wooden cars and fire danger, 22, 25, 178, **179**, 182, **182**, 183, 188; *see also* Dining and dining cars; Interurbans and street railways; Parlor/palace cars; Private cars and trains; Sleeping cars and accommodations; Stations/depots/terminals
Passenger travel (by stagecoach), 15, 20, 25, 32, **32**
Passenger travel (by boat) *see* Canals and waterways; Steamboats and ferries
Passes, free, 152, 156, 227, 246
Patrons of Husbandry, 152
Peale, Franklin, 48
Pease, Edward, 16
Penn Central (Pennsylvania New York Central Transportation Company), 151, **278**, 283, 284, 298, **301**, **310**, **311**
Pennsylvania: railroads, 36, 38–39, **39**, 65, 116
Pennsylvania Limited see *Broadway Limited*
Pennsylvania Railroad, 20, 39, **44**, 144, 145, 149, 156, 158, 178, 188, **201**, 202, 246, **263**, **268**; *Broadway Limited*, **239**, 240, 290; and finance, 147, 148; Horseshoe Curve, **38–39**, 39; and New York Central merger *see* Penn Central; stations, **208**, **210–11**, **217**, **286**
Pennsylvania Society for Internal Improvements, 20
Pennsylvania Turnpike, 148
Perham, Josiah, 106, 107
Perkins, Charles Elliott, 105
Phelps, A. J., 60
Phelps, George D., 162
Philadelphia: interurbans, 257, **283**, 291
Philadelphia & Reading Railroad, 49, 148, 278, 298; stations, **208**, **218**, **219**
Philadelphia, Germantown & Norristown Railroad, 48
Phillips, Charlie, 198
Phillips, Wendell, 53, 54
Phoebe Snow, 290
Phoenix, 27
Pierce, Franklin, 178
Pierson, H. F.: photograph by, **187**
Pike's Peak railway, **249**
Pinchot, Gifford, 139
Pinkerton's National Detective Agency, **128**
Pioneer Zephyr, 268, **269**
Pittenger, William: on Andrews Raid, 74–77
Pittsburgh: railroad strike (1877), 156, 157, 158
Pittsburgh & Moon Run Railroad, 251
Pittsfield line, **286–87**
Planet, 17
Plowden, David: photographs by, **104**, **285–88**
Polson Logging Company: railroad, **266–67**
Poor, M. C.: *Denver South Park & Pacific* and *Pictorial Supplement*, 118
Pope, John Russell, **208**
Porter, John R., **77**
Porters, **200–01**, **228**; *see also* Railroad workers
Portland (Me.) station, **289**
Poughkeepsie Bridge, **278**
Prescott, Jeremiah, 53
Private cars and trains, 117, **222–23**, **232**, **233**, 244, 294, **296–97**
Promontory (Utah): meeting point of Pacific Railroad, **91**, 97, 98–100, **100**, **101**, 104, 145, 282
Providence (steamboat), 141
Providence & Stonington Railroad, 138
Puck: "Let Them Have It All, And Be Done With It," **134–35**
Puffing Billy, 15
Pullman, George Mortimer, 147, **158**, 159, 160, 222, 224, 230
Pullman Company (Pullman Palace Car Company/Pullman Standard), 117, 147, 159, 175, **200–01**, **224**, **225**, **228–33**, 236, 238, 274; private train for World's Columbian Exposition (1893), 222, 233; strike (1894), **158–59**, 159

Q

Queen of the Valley, 288

R

Racer, 46
Railroad (magazine), 294
Railroad Book, The: illustrations from, **172–73**
Railroad Enthusiasts (organization), 294
Railroad fans and enthusiasts, 77, 117, **292–97**, 293–94, 296–97, 304, **306**
Railroad land grants *see* Land grants
Railroad Safety Appliance Act (1893), 188, 189, 199
Railroad workers, **35**, 45, **190–202**, 192, 194–96, 198–99, 201–03, 299; accidents and safety measures, 25, 27, 178, 186, **188**, **189**, 194, 196, 198, 199, 201; strikes, 138, **154–59**, 158, 159; unions and brotherhoods, 159, 160, **161**; wages, 156, **201**, 284, 289; *see also* Brakemen; Conductors; Construction crews; Dispatchers; Engineers; Firemen; Mail clerks; Porters; Section gangs; Stationmasters; Switchmen; Telegraphers
Railroad yards, 235, **263**, **272–73**, **279**, **280–81**, **312**; *see also* Signal and control systems
Railway and Locomotive Historical Society, 294
Railway Mail Service (Postal Transportation Service), 199
Rainhill Trials, **16**, 17, 20, 26–27
Rates *see* Finance, rates
Raton Pass, 111, 113
Ravensworth, Lord (Sir Thomas Liddell), 13, 15
Reading Railroad *see* Philadelphia & Reading Railroad
Redfield, William C., 40
Redondo Beach (Calif.): Redondo Hotel, **248–49**
Reed, Robert C., 178
Reed, Samuel, 87
Reed & Stem, 214–17
Reinhardt, Richard: *Workin' on the Railroad*, 192
Reistrup, Paul H., 9, 299
Reno boys, 126
Resorts and sightseeing, 151, 153, **168**, **224–25**, **242–43**, 244, **245**, 246, **246**, **248–49**, **250–51**, 257
Revere (Mass.) wreck, 53, 180
Richards, Grover Cleveland, 155
Richardson, H. H., 207, 286
Richmond (Va.): Broad Street Station, **209**; trolley, 252, 258
Richmond & York River Railroad, **68–69**
Richmond, Fredericksburg & Potomac Railroad, **71**
Right Arm, 46
Ringling Brothers and Barnum and Bailey Circus train, **166–67**
Rio Grande Railroad *see* Denver & Rio Grande Railroad/Denver & Rio Grande Western Railroad
Rio Grande Southern line, 117
Roberts, George, 148
Robertson, Archie, 294; *Slow Train to Yesterday*, 251
Robinson, Albert, 111, 113
Robinson, Lucius, 158
Rochester & Utica Railroad, 25
Rockefeller, John D., **144**, 160, 302
Rockefeller, Percy, 283
Rockefeller, William, 152, 153, 283
Rocket, **15**, 16, 17, 26–27, 46
Rock Island Railroad *see* Chicago, Rock Island & Pacific Railroad
Roebling, John Augustus, 36
Rogers, Thomas, 49
Rogers, W. A.: cartoon by, **179**
Rogers, Ketchum & Grosvenor, 74
Rolt, L. T. C., 14
Roosevelt, Theodore, 149, 156
Rosecrans, William S., 66
Route mileage, 7; (1865), 144; (1870's–1880's), 144; (1890), **110**; (1900), 262; (1916), 110, 246; (1950), **299**; (1971), **299**
Rowland, Ross, 297
Royal Gorge, **108**, 111, **112**, 113, 117
Russell, Andrew J.: photographs by, **82–83**, **96**, 99, **99**, **100**
Russell, Charles Edward, 153
Rutland Railroad, 244, 246

S

Safety measures, 178–79, 188; air brakes, 144, 182, 188, **189**, 199; automatic coupling, 144, **188**, 189, 199; Railroad Safety Appliance Act, 188, 189, 199; telegraph, use of, 52, 53, 178, 179–80, 188, 195, **196**, 198, 202, **202**; and train crews, 25, 27, 178, 186, **188**, **189**, 194, 196, 198, 199, 201; *see also* Accidents/disasters/wrecks; Signal and control systems
Sage, Russell, 104, **134–35**, 142, 148
Sail cars, 26, **27**
St. Croix & Lake Superior Railroad, proposal for, 132
St. Johnsbury & Lake Champlain Railroad, 246
St. Louis: interurban, 291; stations, **207**, **218**; World's Fair, 263
St. Louis-San Francisco Railway *see* "Frisco Railroad"
St. Louis Southwestern Railroad, 105
St. Paul & Pacific Railroad, 118–19
St. Paul, Minneapolis & Manitoba Railroad, **116**
Samson, 46
Sandy River and Rangeley Lakes Railroad, 297
San Francisco: BART, 291; earthquake and fire, 153; Key System, 291
San Francisco Chief, 113, 290, 300
San Francisco *Examiner*: cartoon from, **153**
San Francisco-Oakland Bay Bridge, 291
San Juan, 117
Sans Pareil, 16
Santa Fe Railway *see* Atchison, Topeka & Santa Fe Railway
Santa Fe de-Luxe: advertisement for, **238**
Sargent, Aaron, 88
Saunders, Wallace, 174
Savery, Thomas, 12
Schenectady (N.Y.) station, 206
Schiff, Jacob H., 149
Schmidt, C. B., 118
Schurz, Carl, 110
Scott, Thomas A., 147, 148, 202
Seattle: Alaska-Yukon-Pacific Exposition (1909), 117
Section gangs, **199**, 282; *see also* Railroad workers
Senecawanna, 46
Sessions, Henry H., 224
Seward Peninsula Railway, **248–49**
Shelley, Kate, 187
Sheppard, Hayward, 60, 63
Sherman, William Tecumseh, 60, 70, 71–72, **94–95**, 96, 97, 106
Sherman Anti-Trust Act (1890), 283
Shoreline Electric Railway, 257–58
Short-line railroads, 244, 246–47, 250–51, 294, 296, 315; Canada, 294, 296, 315
Sickles, Daniel, 142
Signal and control systems, 144, 188; and accidents, 178, 180, 182, 188; dispatchers, 198, **202**; hand signals, **192**; "hump switching," **272**; switchmen, **188**, **196–97**, 198–99; *see also* Telegraph, railroads' use of
Sill, J. W., 74
Simmons, W. H.: engraving by, **23**
Sitting Bull, 110, 124
Sleeping cars and accommodations, 22, **35**, 290; for construction crews, 97, **116**; for emigrants, 130; on interurbans, 252; Pullman, 117, 147, **228**, **229**; Wagner, **143**, 147; Woodruff, **175**
Smeed, E. C., 72
Smiles, Samuel, 14, 15
Smith, Donald A., 118
Smith, E. Boyd: *The Railroad Book*, **172–73**
Smith, William Prescott, 60, 63
Smoky Mary, 269
Socrates, 183
South Carolina Canal and Rail-Road Company, 27
South Carolina Railway, **218**
South Carver (Mass.): Bridgton & Harrison Railroad moved to, 296–97, **296–97**
Southern Pacific Railroad, 87, 104, 105, **106**, 111, 113, 118, 153, **198**; and finance, 149; *see also* Central Pacific Railroad
Southern Railway, 27, 148, 294, 299; *Fast Mail*, wreck, 174, **183**
South Manchester Railroad, **219**
South Pennsylvania Railroad, 148
South Shore (Chicago interurban), 257
Southwestern Limited, 188
Sprague, Frank J., 252
Stagecoaches, 15, 20, 25, 32, **32**
Stalin, Joseph, 270
Stampede, 46
Standard gauge *see* Tracks, gauge
Standard Oil Company, 144, 152, 156
Standard Oil of California, 291
Stanford, Leland, 87, 88, **88**, 98, 100, 104
Stanford University, 153
Stanton, Edwin M., 53, 64, 66, 70, 72, 77
Stark, Otto: drawing by, **178**
Stationmasters, 220; *see also* Railroad workers
Stations/depots/terminals, **42–43**, 45, 56, **56–57**, 63, **78–79**, **122–23**, **173**, **204–21**, 206–21, 278, 282, **285–89**, 300; eating facilities, 131, **236**; England, 206, 207
Steam locomotives *see* Locomotives, steam
Steamboats and ferries, 13, 20, 21, 32, 35, 36, 63, 97, 151, 153, 244, **245**, **248**, 278, 282, **285**; Fall River Line, 141–42, 151, 153, **246**; *see also* Canals and waterways
Steam Passenger Service Directory, 296
Steel: cast, for locomotives, 262, **265**; freight, 144; passenger cars, 188; rails, 104, 144, 188
Steichen, Edward, 147
Steinheimer, Richard: photograph by, **260–61**
Stephen, George (Lord Mount Stephen), 118, 148
Stephenson, George, 12–17 *passim*, **13**, 26, 28; *Blucher*, 15; Killingworth locomotive, 13, **15**; *Locomotion No. 1*, **15**, 16, 17, **18–19**; *Rocket*, **15**, **16**, 17, 26–27
Stephenson, George Robert, 17
Stephenson, Robert, 13, 16, 17, 20; *Locomotion No. 1*, **15**, 16, 17, **18–19**; *Northumbrian*, 16, 17; *Planet*, 17; *Rocket*, **15**, **16**, 17, 26–27, 46
Stephenson, Robert ("Old Bob"), 12
Stephenson Locomotive Works, 16, 17, 26
Stetson, Francis Lynde, 148
Stevens, Edwin A., 20
Stevens, John, 20, 21, 25, 26
Stevens, Robert Livingston, 20, 21
Stevens Institute (Hoboken), 20
Stevenson, James: cartoon by, **283**
Stevenson, Robert Louis, 122; *Across the Plains*, 130–31
Stewart, W. H., 52
Stockton & Darlington Railway, **15**, 16–17, **18–19**
Stokes, Edward S., **140**, 142
Stone, Amasa, 186
Stourbridge Lion, 26
Stover, John F., 144, 152
Stowe, Harriet Beecher, 54
Strasburg Railroad, 296
Street railways *see* Interurbans and street railways
Strickland, William, 20
Strikes, 138, **154–59**, 158, 159
Strong, Daniel, 85
Strong, George Templeton, 187
Strong, William Barstow, 111, **111**, 113
Suez Canal, 104
Sullivan, Louis, 207
Sunday, Billy, 257
Super Chief, 290
Supreme Court: Granger laws upheld, 152, 156; and Interstate Commerce Commission, 156; Northern Securities Company outlawed, 149
Susquehanna Railroad (New York, Susquehanna & Western Railroad), 282
Sweeney, Peter B., 141
Swedes: construction crews, 108; immigrants, 122
Swinnerton, James: cartoon by, **153**
Switchmen, **188**, **196–97**, 198–99; *see also* Railroad workers

T

Tapy, A.: "The Neigh of an Iron Horse," **10–11**
Telegraph, 52, 105; at Promontory ceremony, 99, 100; railroads' use of, 52, 53, 178, 179–80, 188, 195, **196**, 198, 202
Telegraphers, 195, **196**, 198, 202, **202**; *see also* Railroad workers
Texas, **74**, 77
Texas & Pacific Railroad, 105, 113
Thomas, Evan, 28
Thomas, Lately, 136
Thomas, Philip, 28
Thomson, John Edgar, 39, 111
Thoreau, Henry David, **50**; quoted, 50
Tiger, **44**

Time: standardization of zones, 144, **145**
Toledo, Peoria & Western Railroad, 188
Tom Thumb, 29, **29**, 45
Torrance, Daniel, **143**
Toucey, J. M., **143**
Tracks, 25, 47; cogged, 14, 15, 244, **248**; destruction of, during Civil War, **70**, 72, **72–73**, 75, 76; "compromise" cars, 182; gauge, broad, 40, **53**, 116, 144; gauge, narrow, 110, 116–17, 244, 247, 294, 296, **296–97**, **306–07**; gauge, standard, 17, 54, 113, 116, 144, **145**, 182; iron, 13, 16–17, 65, 97, 144, 178, 187; iron, cast, 13–17 *passim*; iron, strap, 22, **24**, 28, 36, 65; laying of, 97–98 (*see also* Construction crews); repair and maintenance by section gangs, **199**, 282; roadbed, 28, 178, 182, 269, 282; steel, 104, 144, 188; ties, stone block, **24**, 28; ties, wood, 20, 65, 71; wood, 13; wood, with strap iron, 36, 65; *see also* Route mileage
Train, George Francis, 91
Train robbers, 123, **126–27**, **128**, **129**; O. Henry story, 126–29
Trains (magazine), 269, 293
Tramps, **235**
A Treasury of Railroad Folklore, 122
Tredegar Iron Works, 65
Trenton Junction (N.J.), **218**
Trevithick, Richard, 14, 15, 17
Trolleys *see* Interurbans and street railways
Trustee, 46
Tully, George, 203
Tunnels, 39, 98, 108, **109**, 206, 227
TurboTrains, **269**
Turnpikes *see* Highways and turnpikes
Tweed, William Marcy, 139
Twentieth Century Limited, 139, 217, 238, **240–41**, 244, 268, 290; Christopher Morley on, 202–03

U

Ulster & Delaware Railroad: advertisement for, **246**
Ultimate Thule, Arkadelphia & Mississippi Railroad, 251
Uncas, 46
Union Pacific Railroad, 72, **82–83**, 84, **87**, 87–88, 91–101, **93**, **96**, **97**, **99**, **100**, **101**, 104, 105, 106, 117, 130, **130**, 142, 160, 263, 267, **312**; Crédit Mobilier, 89, 91–92, 94, 95, 98, 104, 286; and finance, 88, 91–92, 93, 94–95, 104,

105, 117, 148–49; route map (1869), **91**; route map (1893), **250–51**; *see also* Denver, South Park & Pacific Railroad; Pacific Railroad
Unions, 159, **159**, 160; *see also* Strikes
Union Traction Company, **253**, 255
United Aircraft Corporation: *Turbo Train*, **269**
United Corporation, 257
United States Express Company, 142
United States Military Railroads (Civil War), 53, **61**, **64**, 65, 66, 67, **68–69**, 70–71, **71**, 72
United States Railway Association, 298, 300
United States Steel Company, 148, 152
United Transportation Union, AFL-CIO, 160
Unit trains, **273**
Utica & Schenectady Railroad, 25, 36

V

Valley Railroad, **294–95**, 297, **306**
Vanderbilt, Cornelius, 25, 45, 137, **140**, 142, **143**, 186, 189, 246; Civil War, 64; Grand Central Station, 207–08, **212**, 213, **213**; Lake Shore & Michigan Southern Railroad, **164**, **182**, 182–83; New York Central, 56, 138, 139, 142, **143**, 207–08; New York Central and Erie Railroad, **136**, 137, 138–39, 141, 142
Vanderbilt, Cornelius, II, 138, 139, **143**
Vanderbilt, Frederick William, 139
Vanderbilt, George Washington, II, 139
Vanderbilt, William Henry, **134–35**, 138, 142, **142**, **143**, 156, 158, 165
Vanderbilt, William K., 138, 139, 147, 148, 215–16
Vanderbilt, William K., Jr., 138
Vanderbilt (locomotive), **143**
Vanderbilt (side-wheeler), 137
Vanderbilt family, 138, 139, **143**, 149
Van Doren, C. A., 257
Van Sweringen, Mantis J., 283
Van Sweringen, Oris P., 283
Vanstavoren, William, 180, 182
Velocity, 46
Viaducts *see* Bridges/viaducts/trestles
Villard, Henry (Ferdinand Heinrich Gustav Hilgard), 108, 110, 111, **133**

W

Wabash Railroad, **206**
Wagner, Webster, **143**, 222
Wagner Palace Car Company, 143, 147; dinner menu, **236**

Wannalancet, 46
War of 1812, 35
Ware (Mass.) station, **216**
Ware River Branch, 246
Warren, Whitney, 215–16
Washington, D.C.: Baltimore & Ohio station, 206; Union Station, 184, **185**, 188, 300
Waterways *see* Canals and waterways
Watt, James, 12, 13
Wawayanda, 46
Webb, Sim, 187
Webster, Daniel, 40
Weed, Thurlow, **24**
Weissenborn, G.: *American Locomotive Engineering*, illustration from, **48–49**
Weller, John L., 153
Wellington, Duke of, 15, 17
Western & Atlantic Railroad, 27, 71, 72; Andrews Raid, 71, **74**, 74–77
Western Pacific Railroad, 294
Western Railroad of Massachusetts, 35, 36, 56
Western Union, 52, 105
Westinghouse, George, 182, **189**; *see also* Air brakes
West Penn Junction station, **217**
West Point, **26–27**, 27
West Point Foundry, 25, 26, 27
West River Railroad, 250–51
West Shore Railroad, 282
Whistler, George Washington, 28
Whitaker, Rogers E. M. ("Mr. Frimbo"), 178, 294
White, John H., Jr., 9, 47, 187, 294
White, Stanford, 207, 214
White Mountains and White Mountain line, 244, 246; advertisement for, **246**
White Plains (N.Y.) station, **219**
Whitney, Asa, 85
Whitney, Josiah, 88
Whyte, Frederic M., 47; system of locomotive classification, 47, **265**
Wilbur, Gorton, 294
Wilgus, William J., 213–14, 215
Wilkes-Barre (Pa.) station, **288**
William Mason, **306**
William R. Smith, 77
Wilmington & Weldon Railroad, 65
Wilson, Henry, 91
Wilson, Woodrow, 283, 284
Winans, Ross, 22, 28, 29
Winona Traction Company, 257
Withun, Bill, 269

Wood: in construction (bridges, stations, houses), 71, **71**, 72, 120, 122, 206; as fuel, **24**, 25, 45–49, **46–47**, 194; logging railroads, 124, 266–67, **306–07**; for railroad cars, 178, **179**, 182, **182**, 183, 188; in railroad construction, 13, 20, 36, 65, 71, 97, 111; timber, sale of, and freight, 85, 105, 107, 119, 124, 144, 149; *see also* Bridges/viaducts/trestles
Woodruff, Jonah, **175**
Woodruff Sleeping and Palace Car Company, 175
Worcester Consolidated Street Railway, 256–57
Worcester Salt Company: special train, **167**
World's Columbian Exposition (1893, Chicago), 77, 222, 232
World War I (and railroads), 238, 284; Railway War Board, 284, 289
World War II (and railroads), 104, 269, **273**, 282, 289, 302
Wrecks *see* Accidents/disasters/wrecks
Wrightsville & Tennille Railroad, **247**
Wylam (Eng.) Colliery, 12, 15, 17

Y

Yellowstone National Park, 301; advertisement for, **168**
Yonah, 75, 77
Young, Brigham, 91
Young, Robert R., 283, 300
"Younger boys," 126

Z

Zephyrs, 268, **269**, 290
Zogbaum, Rufus: sketch by, **130**

Library of Congress Cataloging in Publication Data

Jensen, Oliver Ormerod, 1914–
   The American heritage history of railroads in America.
   Bibliography: p.
   Includes index.
   1. Railroads—United States—History. I. American heritage. II. Title.
HE2751.J38   385'.0973   75-19438
ISBN 0-07-032526-X (McGraw-Hill)
ISBN 0-07-032527-8 de luxe